Late 19th and Early 20th Century Decorative Arts

Late 19th and Early 20th Century Decorative Arts

The Sydney and Frances Lewis Collection
in the Virginia Museum of Fine Arts

by
Frederick R. Brandt

Virginia Museum of Fine Arts
Richmond, Virginia

Distributed by the University of Washington Press,
Seattle and London

Publication of this catalogue was made possible in part by a research and editorial grant from the Andrew W. Mellon Foundation.

Library of Congress, Cataloging-in-Publication Data

Brandt, Frederick R., 1936—
    Late 19th and early 20th century decorative arts.

    Bibliography: p. 278.
    Includes index.
    1. Decorative Arts—History—19th century—Catalogs. 2. Decoration and ornament—Art nouveau—Catalogs. 3. Decorative arts—History—20th century—Catalogs. 4. Art deco—Catalogs. 5. Lewis, Sydney—Art collections—Catalogs. 6. Lewis, Frances—Art collections—Catalogs. 7. Decorative arts—Private collections—Virginia—Richmond—Catalogs. 8. Virginia Museum of Fine Arts—Catalogs. I. Virginia Museum of Fine Arts. II. Title. III. Title: Late nineteenth and early twentieth century decorative arts.

NK775.5.A7B73 1985   745′.09′034   85-22499
ISBN 0-917046-17-X
ISBN 0-917046-16-1 (pbk.)

Color Photography by Katherine Wetzel, Richmond, Virginia

Cover: detail of a stained-glass window, 1901-02, Georges de Feure (catalogue number 31).

Contents

Foreword

The ebb and flow of taste have seldom been demonstrated more forcefully than by the change that has occurred in our perception of Art Nouveau and Art Deco during the last twenty-five to thirty years. These two styles—intimately woven into the cultural ethos of the half-century extending from the 1880s to the 1930s—were not so long ago either ignored or violently rejected. The one, as it were, banished the other, and in the period immediately following World War II, both practically vanished from our consciousness. It was in the early '50s that the eyes of a few connoisseurs, the daring of a few dealers, and the vision of a few museum curators restored to Art Nouveau a sense of respectability. Renewed interest in Art Deco did not surface until some fifteen years later, in the wake of a 1966 exhibition in Paris, *Les Années "25"*.

It is difficult to explain today how it could be that the dashing, lyrical curves of a sculpture of Loïe Fuller; the brilliantly evocative colors of a Tiffany Wisteria lamp, flowering above its carefully wrought base; the elegant handling of form and texture of a Ruhlmann desk; or the handsome lines of a Goulden clock/sculpture could have been considered anything but praiseworthy, indeed, admirable.

The objects represented in these pages testify to the magnitude of that recent myopia, and are a vindication of the significance of these two interconnected movements, the complexity and richness of which are the source of endless enjoyment and engrossing study. These works, in the mysterious evolution of their forms, most surely reflect the complex interactions that occurred in Western society, as emerging new economic, political, and intercultural relationships fundamentally altered the world's order and our perception of it.

This collection, so carefully documented here by Frederick Brandt, is undoubtedly the largest in scope and the highest in quality to come on public view in any institution. That it was assembled by two collectors, and in less than two decades, is evidence of extraordinary determination and surprisingly unerring judgment. As it grew from their acquisitive passion, it became central to their everyday experience. These were not objects placed in a cabinet or loaned to a museum; they became part of their daily lives, the very tools of their household.

Now these objects have acquired another significance beyond their evidence of human creativity at critical junctions of world history: they testify to civic generosity. By this gift, Sydney and Frances Lewis have brought a new dimension to the Virginia Museum of Fine Arts: henceforward, it must be reckoned as a major center for the study, understanding, and enjoyment of two movements whose creativity, though ignored in the recent past, permanently affected our concepts of function and design, and whose influence will undoubtedly continue to be felt as new styles emerge.

The brilliant introduction of Denys Sutton evokes admirably the extraordinary richness of this period and helps us realize that, no matter how beautiful or how intriguing are the objects themselves, they must be seen in the broader context of cultural development to be truly understood. If we look at them thus, they become a synthesis of their times and permit us to appreciate perhaps more fully the subtleties of their counterparts in music, literature, and philosophy. And is not that the prime function of museums and the very source of their importance for the well-being of this and future societies?

Paul N. Perrot
Director
Virginia Museum of Fine Arts

Preface

Sometime during the years 1970 and 1971, Richmond art collectors Sydney and Frances Lewis applied intelligence, love, patience, confidence, and a discerning intellect, as they began to assemble what has been called one of this nation's greatest collections of decorative arts of the Art Nouveau and Art Deco periods.

The Lewises acquired their first Art Nouveau objects once their interest in that era was kindled through their friendship with the artist Theodore Stamos, an enthusiastic collector of Art Nouveau, particularly Tiffany glass. They quickly familiarized themselves with the various auction houses that had begun to offer such objects for sale and with a few select dealers who specialized in this once-forgotten field. Within two years, the Lewises' collection had grown to include later works, of the Style 1925, and now—less than two decades later—presents itself as the remarkable collection that is documented here.

Because so much of this collection is now available to the public, it is the purpose of this book to enhance understanding and appreciation among all who see it.

The essays that follow place this collection in a broad historical context comprising the five decades, from 1885 to 1935, during which these works were created. This period spans a half-century of innovation and experimentation—not only in style and technique, but also in attitude—brought about by highly creative artist-designers who broke with convention to set the pace of what we now think of as the Modern Age.

Although the terms Art Nouveau and Art Deco are used throughout the text, it should be noted that they are not accurately applicable to all decorative arts created within the fertile years spanning the two styles. A great variety of styles existed within—or without—each of these two rather vague classifications. In fact, it might even be more correct to refer to them as "Style 1900" and "Style 1925," for these two dates mark the two great Paris expositions that became the cornerstones of this era of rich design. And yet, although 1900 and 1925 are the high points of this period of the

decorative arts, it should not be assumed that monumental works were not produced before, between, and after these dates. For reasons of familiarity and convenience, then, the terms Art Nouveau and Art Deco are used throughout this book, but it should be remembered that they refer generally to the periods they represent and are neither limiting nor all-encompassing descriptions.

The emphasis of the Lewis Decorative Arts Collection is predominantly French, simply because so many great works were produced by French artists, in both the 1900 and the 1925 styles. This phenomenon is partly due to the artistic climate of that country, the social and economic factors affecting it, and its centuries-old tradition of fine craftsmanship.

These works reflect the personal tastes of those who assembled it in the first place—two highly intelligent, intuitive, and discerning individuals, Sydney and Frances Lewis. Thus, as with any private collection, certain omissions may become apparent.

The 100 objects illustrated in color in this book are presented more or less chronologically, as they are in the galleries. And although neither this book nor the collection is meant to represent an encyclopedia of every major artist working in the period, both reflect some of the rarest examples known by major Western designers, craftsmen, and artists of this era. These works were selected not only to represent the best of the collection, but also to mirror the various cultural and national tendencies, the artists themselves, the diverse range of media they mastered, and the many types of objects they created.

Although the entire collection is too large to be fully documented in this inaugural publication of the collection, it is intended that future publications will do so. In the meantime, the checklist of almost 600 objects at the end of the book serves to reflect the overall scope of the Lewis Decorative Arts Collection.

While most of the objects on display are from the Lewises' personal collection and the Sydney and Frances Lewis Foundation Collection, some very important objects—such as the Tiffany punch bowl (cat. no. 17) and the Guimard cabinet (cat. no. 15)—were purchased by the Virginia Museum with funds donated by the Lewises for such acquisitions. Other objects of the period have been generously donated by other friends and benefactors.

From the time of their original acquisition until their presentation and eventual display in the Virginia Museum, the objects in the Lewises' personal collection were kept in their own home for daily use and frequent admiration—just as the original designers had intended. For years, the Lewises' home was a mecca for those interested in seeing the finest objects of this period, and they always welcomed scholars and interested amateurs alike to share their appreciation and enjoyment of these beautiful works.

Now that this collection is at the Virginia Museum for all visitors to enjoy, we hope that this catalogue will make possible a deeper understanding and appreciation of the art of this period, through a collection built with intelligence and love.

Frederick R. Brandt
Curator of Twentieth-Century Art
Virginia Museum of Fine Arts

Acknowledgments

Many individuals and organizations have aided in the research and development of this book; to each of them a great debt of gratitude is owed. During the course of the development of the collection over the past fifteen years, a number of people have willingly shared their knowledge and given their advice and helped locate objects that would eventually play an important role in the formation of the Lewis Collection. Of special importance among them are Alastair Duncan, Consultant to the Department of Nineteenth- and Twentieth-Century Decorative Arts at Christie, Manson & Woods International, Inc., New York; Philippe Garner, Expert, Department of Decorative Arts & Photographic Material, Sotheby Parke Bernet & Company, London; and Félix Marcilhac, Decorative Arts Expert, Paris.

Many other scholars, collectors, friends, and colleagues have shared their knowledge of this innovative period of the decorative arts and helped in other ways to produce this catalogue. My deep appreciation must be expressed to Jay Barrows, Richmond, Virginia; Marc Bascou, Conservateur, Musée d'Orsay, Paris; Roger Billcliffe, The Fine Art Society Ltd, Glasgow; W. Scott Braznell, New Haven, Connecticut; Robert K. Brown, New York; Yvonne Brunhammer, Conservateur, Musée des Arts Décoratifs, Paris; Beth Cathers, Jordan-Volpe Gallery, New York; David Cathers, New York; Dr. Robert Judson Clark, Princeton, New Jersey; Prunella Clough, London; Georges de Bartha, Christie's International S.A., Geneva; Madame Marie deBeyrie, Paris; Barbara E. Deisroth, Vice President, Sotheby Parke Bernet, Inc., New York; Paul Doros, Christie, Manson & Woods International, Inc., New York; Robert Edwards, The Artsman, Bryn Mawr, Pennsylvania; Scott C. Elliott, Kelmscott Gallery, Chicago; Mrs. Elisabeth Eskes-Rietveld, Amsterdam; Audrey Friedman, Primavera Gallery, New York; Barry Friedman, Barry Friedman Ltd., New York; Stuart Friedman, Barry Friedman Ltd., New York; Dennis Gallion, San Francisco; Oscar Ghez, Le Président-Fondateur, Petit Palais Musée, Geneva; Knut Günther, Frankfurt-am-Main, West Germany; David Hanks, David Hanks and Associates, New York; Sarah F. Hill, Assistant Vice-President, Sotheby Parke Bernet, Inc., New York; Steven B. Holcomb, Richmond, Virginia; Dr. Hans-Jorjen Houser, Hamburg, West Germany; Penelope Hunter-Stiebel, New York; John Jesse, London; J. Stewart Johnson, Curator of Design, The Museum of Modern Art, New York; Patricia E. Kane, Curator of American Decorative Arts, Yale University Art Gallery, New Haven, Connecticut; Ivan Karp, O.K. Harris Works of Art, New York; Dr. Robert and Mrs. Gladys Koch, Stamford, Connecticut; Erik Lassen, Museum of Decorative Art, Copenhagen; Alain Lesieutre, Paris; Dr. Glenn D. Lowry, Curator, Islamic Art, Freer Gallery of Art, Washington, D.C.; Lloyd and Barbara Macklowe, Macklowe Gallery, Ltd., New York; Alastair B. Martin, Katonah, New York; Pierre Matisse, Pierre Matisse Gallery Corp., New York; Larry Matlick, Macklowe Gallery, Ltd., New York; Nancy A. McClelland, Expert, Department of Art Nouveau & Art Deco, Christie, Manson & Woods International, Inc., New York; David Revere McFadden, Curator of Decorative Arts, Cooper-Hewitt Museum, New York; C. James Meyer, Assistant Professor, Metalsmithing and Jewelry, Department of Crafts, Virginia Commonwealth University, Richmond; Ian Millman, Paris; Lillian Nassau, Lillian Nassau Ltd., New York; William B. O'Neil, Charlottesville, Virginia; Derek E. Ostergard, New York; Michel Perinet, Paris; Sumpter Priddy III, Richmond, Virginia; Nicola Redway, Expert, Decorative Arts & Photographic Material, Sotheby Parke Bernet & Company, London; Dr. Joseph Sataloff, Philadelphia; Theodore Stamos, New York; Lynne Thornton, Paris; J. J. Vogels, Curator, Stedelijke Musea Gouda, Gouda, The Netherlands; Todd M. Volpe, Jordan-Volpe Gallery, New York; Johanna and Robert Walker, London; Gabriel Weisberg, Assistant Director for Museum Programs, National Endowment for the Humanities, Washington, D.C.; Mr. and Mrs. L. Wittamer-de Camps, Brussels; and Charles L. Wyrick, Jr.,

Director, The Gibbes Art Gallery, Charleston, South Carolina.

In addition, those who have made gifts of objects to the collection are acknowledged in the preface to the "Checklist of the Collection," at the back of this book. Through their gifts, they have helped to formulate this collection of decorative arts, and we are truly grateful to them for their kindness and philanthropy.

Many members of the staff of the Virginia Museum of Fine Arts have contributed to the preparation of the manuscript for this publication. Paul N. Perrot, Director, lent encouragement and confidence in his support of the project; Pinkney Near, Chief Curator, played an active and important role in acquiring objects through The Sydney and Frances Lewis Art Nouveau Fund; Patricia Bayer, Assistant Manager of Art Services, researched the black-and-white photographs and offered many helpful suggestions in preparing the manuscript; Mary Ann Kearns, Curatorial Intern, spent countless hours doing preliminary research, alphabetizing lists, searching for photographs, and accomplishing many other assignments connected with this project; Chief Photographer Ronald Jennings and Photographic Services Coordinator Mary Moore Jacoby, together with the help of photographers Lorna Clark and Katherine Harbury, lent their invaluable skills in providing photographs; and Museum Librarian Betty A. Stacy and her assistant Margaret Burcham provided immeasurable aid in locating rare books, magazines, and other important reference materials.

In the production of this book, George A. Cruger, Chief Editor and Publications Manager, ably guided the editorial and production teams from conception to completion; Monica M. Hamm, Senior Editor and Publications Coordinator, edited the text and supervised its publication through the various stages of production; Raymond Geary, Chief Graphic Designer, expertly formulated the book's design; Katherine Wetzel was responsible for the color photography; Lisa Hummel, Registrar; Bruce Young, Associate Registrar; and Diane Hart and Kathleen Morris, Assistant Registrars, together with Art Handlers Frank Milik, Jim Attkisson, Roy Thompson, and Andrew Kovach, all ably and cheerfully helped prepare the objects for documentation; and finally Polly Bozorth, Secretary of the Collections Division, and Carolyn Maxey, Secretary of the Publications Office, patiently and efficiently brought the manuscript to its accurate completion.

I also want to thank my wife Carol for her thoughtful reading of the manuscript and for her always helpful comments and suggestions.

Finally, my thanks are extended, however insufficient, to Sydney and Frances Lewis, for it is their foresight, generosity, intelligence, and munificence that have made this project possible. Their friendship, compassion, thoughtfulness, and sincerity have made working with them one of the greatest pleasures of my life. It is with great humility that I dedicate this catalogue to these two fine people.—F.B.

The Fin de Siècle and Its Aftermath

by Denys Sutton

For many years the history of nineteenth-century art was presented with banner headlines, from the Romantics through the Realists and the Impressionists to the Post-Impressionists. This schematic way of treating events, however convenient, was not in any real sense historically valid. It meant that too much was left out and that the emphasis was apt to be misplaced. To take one instance, in considering French painting can we neglect J. L. Gérôme? Without a knowledge of his work, it is difficult to understand the style of that highly individual American artist, Thomas Eakins, who even sent a watercolour of one of his most famous paintings to his former teacher in Paris.

Moreover, this approach has led to a considerable over-simplification of the artistic climate of the fin de siècle, and especially of the range and variety of Art Nouveau which almost dropped out of sight until the revival of interest in it some two decades ago. That this was so was due, in no small degree, to the general critical concentration on one particular genre, French landscape painting, which became a major industry in the nineteenth century, as is attested to by the number of painters who exhibited works of this type in the Paris Salon. Corot and the Barbizon masters had popularized the beauties of the French countryside; however the darkish tones used by Théodore Rousseau and even by Diaz and Troyon evoke a melancholy spirit. The School of 1830 and the Impressionists were different in mood as well as in technique. In fact, a study of French art in the middle of the century soon underlines its intellectual range, yet it is dangerous to adopt too cerebral an approach in judging artists and their works; thus to claim, as is sometimes done, that J.-F. Millet's choice of peasant themes necessarily reveals a sympathy for the Left is to forget that the agrarian tradition was also revered by many on the Right.

Paradoxically, the Second Empire is generally considered to have been an epoch of political reaction. Victor Hugo, a fierce opponent of Napoleon III, remained firmly entrenched as an exile in Guernsey but, in addition to the gracious portraits of Winterhalter and many pleasing decorative schemes in private houses, this period witnessed the birth of a revolutionary movement, Impressionism. This style corresponded to the reputation of Paris as the pleasure capital of the world, one adored by Americans, British, Russians, and South Americans.

The essence of Impressionism lies in its technical freedom and its presentation of the modern world—the train puffing smoke in the Gare Saint-Lazare, the yachts at Argenteuil, a luncheon party at Chaton, or a Paris street in the sun; the pictures of Manet, Monet, and Renoir, to name three of the major artists, express pleasure in the good things of life. Their political views, whatever they were, are irrelevant. However surprising it might seem that many such pictures were painted shortly after the Franco-Prussian War and the Commune, the memory of which haunted more than one generation, we should recall that in a similar fashion the Jazz Age succeeded the horrors of the First World War.

By its very nature Impressionism is not a profound style, although Degas, who is loosely affiliated to the movement, can make us reflect on life, the psychology of his sitters, the drab existence of washerwomen, and the fate of the denizens of the brothels. He has the power to do this but, in the end, the magic of his colour, the strength of his drawing, and the sureness of his composition rather than his subject matter retain their hold on the imagination. Art was a compensation for his withdrawn and secretive nature.

The visual arts do not lend themselves to the portrayal of human problems in the same way as do fiction and verse. Yet literary and moralistic painting enjoyed considerable support in the nineteenth century, and is closely associated with the Victorian masters who have now returned to favour. That painting of this sort was popular is understandable in a flourishing age for the long narrative novel, such as *War and Peace*, *La Cousine Bette*, *David Copperfield*, and the Barchester Series. These offer a broad and detailed survey of life and often contain searching reflections on society and human nature. When Edmond de Goncourt writes about prostitutes in *La Fille Elisa* or Tolstoy does the same in *Resurrection*, the psychology of such women is presented in a way that is impossible in a painting even if Degas's drawings of Elisa reveal insight and Toulouse Lautrec's images of the brothels are brilliant. Yet a comparison of Lautrec's paintings with photographs of "real" life shows that the painter's approach was essentially decorative.

The examination of art thematically can prove rewarding. One major feature of nineteenth-century fiction was an interest in crime: Balzac, Dickens, Dostoevsky, Poe, Zola and many others, including Conan Doyle with Sherlock Holmes, are among those writers attracted by murder and mystery. This taste is reflected in art, with Fuseli, Degas, Cézanne, Munch, Manet, Corinth, and Klinger. These artists depict violent action, but one painter, Whistler, created the setting in which crime might be expected to take place—those foggy scenes that suggest a love of the amorphous which emerged in the fin de siècle, and which partly accounts for the stylistic characteristics of Art Nouveau.

As the range of nineteenth-century art starts to be more closely assessed, numerous points await clarification. Just as it is now realised that in the seventeenth century local schools existed in France, such as those at Toulouse and Nancy, or in the eighteenth century at Bordeaux, the same is seen to be true in nineteenth-century France: Lyons possessed its group of indigenous landscape and flower painters and Nancy was a stronghold of Art Nouveau.

The role of individual cities as "art centres" is a pertinent one, and the social historian will require to determine the circumstances that led Brussels, with the architecture of Victor Horta, or Barcelona, with that of Antoni Gaudí, to become two of the most active. Then, too, we must attempt to explain that the Belgian railway king, Adolphe Stoclet, both commissioned the Viennese architect Josef Hoffmann to build the Palais Stoclet at Brussels and collected superb gold-ground Italian paintings. The Palais, with its decorations by Gustav Klimt, is a masterpiece of the late phase of the Art Nouveau movement.

Impressionist landscape painting has become so popular that it has occasioned some neglect of the powerful current of religious art that existed in the nineteenth century, starting with Delacroix and Ingres and including Gauguin, Paul Sérusier, Puvis de Chavannes, Maurice Denis, and Georges Desvallières. At this period in France the battle between the anti-clericals and the supporters of religion was intense.

The recent revival of interest in baroque art, in the history-painting of the eighteenth century, and in Neo-Classicism has afforded an impetus to the search for the existence of parallel styles in the middle and later years of the nineteenth century. The eclecticism of the period is illustrated by the extent to which classical and Japanese art could be combined, as happens in the paintings of Whistler. The Antique constituted a strong element in erotic art, another feature of the 1890s; for instance Beardsley's debt in this respect to Greek vase painting is evident. The evocation of the mysterious sensual atmosphere in the Villa Stuck, the home of the painter Franz von Stuck, is largely due to the antique echoes found in its decoration. For many a nineteenth-century artist and designer the satyr, as it had been for Rubens, was a symbol of male sexual appetite.

The discovery of Japanese art is an oft-told tale, and it is significant of the affinity between Art Nouveau and Japanese art that S. Bing, one of the most successful art dealers of the period, should have dealt in both. Although the Japanese influence on the West is apt to be exaggerated, it certainly occurs in Art Nouveau, notably with furniture and ceramics. Art Deco boxes are close to Japanese lacquer, and Netsuke are important for Fabergé's objects, which are also in line of descent from the enamelled gold boxes of the eighteenth century. The relationship between Chinese jades of the Ming and Ching dynasties and Art Nouveau ceramics and glass has yet to be fully explored.

The expansion of the population and the development of economic power meant that an increasing number of people enjoyed a higher standard of living and could spend more money on the embellishment of their homes: the building of great apartment blocks and spacious villas in Paris, Berlin, and Vienna provided opportunities for the decorator. A knowledge of earlier art was felt to contribute to the improvement of the quality of design and manufactured goods. This belief is a key to an understanding of the historicist character of design in these years, especially in England, where it was considered that the British lagged behind their foreign competitors; it provided one of the main motives for the staging of the celebrated international Great Exhibition of 1851 in London, and for the foundation of the Museum of Ornamental Art at Marlborough House, the precursor of the Victoria and Albert Museum. Men such as Sir Henry Cole, Sir A.W. Franks, and Sir J.C. Robinson took the lead in England, with the result that Italian Renaissance sculpture—often of the highest quality—maiolica, and decorative pieces of all types entered the museum, and the Italianate influence is particularly evident in ceramics. During the years leading up to 1914, in addition to the Victoria and Albert Museum, the museums at Berlin, Boston, Hamburg, and the Metropolitan Museum, New York, enriched their collections of decorative arts. Moreover, increasing attention was paid to Islamic art, which fascinated such turn-of-the-century fashion designers as Paul Poiret and the painter Henri Matisse, and even Bernard Berenson collected Islamic miniatures.

The relationship between the fine arts and art promotion is a challenging topic. Already in the eighteenth century a critic such as the Rev. Sir Henry Bate Dudley supported his friend Thomas Gainsborough in the pages of the *Morning Post*, while Diderot championed Greuze in his reports on the Salons which, however, were for private circulation. During the nineteenth century, when artists often fell afoul of the juries of the Salon, those who had been rejected found champions to support them in the press, and Théodore Duret, Thoré-Burger, Octave Mirbeau, and Armand Silvestre were among those who fought for their heroes. The role of the critic is dealt with by Balzac with considerable insight in his novel *Illusions Perdues*: the passage in which Lousteau tells the young poet Lucien de Rubempré how to destroy a fellow writer's book is a *tour de force*, as relevant now as it was then. The part played by advertising in shaping not only the promotion of art but also in explaining certain forms of art is considerable. Balzac's novel contains a fascinating description of the posters that used to be seen in Paris; he refers, though not by name, to those of Rouchon, examples of which are in the Bibliothèque Nationale, Paris. The subsequent development of the poster was furthered by the Beggarstaff Brothers, Bonnard, Chéret, Grasset, Toulouse-Lautrec, Mucha, various members of the Berlin and Viennese Secessions, and later by men such as Capiello; all turned walls into radiant shop-windows of art. Modern art was radically changed by the existence of the poster, which brought about simplified and direct means of artistic expression.

The skill of an entrepreneur such as Bing lay in his use of the term "art nouveau" to designate his shop in Paris, thus underlining the difference between ancient and modern art and thus proposing a style that could correspond more closely with contemporary needs. He was not the only person to ram this message home—the Belgians Octave Maus and Oliver Picard also expressed their belief in *art moderne*. This faith has been strongly supported ever since and helps to explain the rapid way in which one form of "new" art succeeds another, never more so than at present.

Art Nouveau, the movement that sprang up in the 1880s, was an individual style, as individual as Mannerism or Baroque, and just as international as these. If certain iconographical elements remain more or less constant, each country contributed its own component to the whole. The stylistic roots of Art Nouveau were varied; William Blake's watercolours and Celtic motifs, for example, helped in its formation. As far as concerns France, the relationship with the craftsmanship of the mid-century is possibly closer than is sometimes suspected. It is shown in the remarkable *Coupe de Vendange* by F.D. Froment-Michel of 1844 (now in the Louvre), which was made for the Duc de Montpensier, the son of Louis-Philippe.

Considerable differences exist between the plain, rather utilitarian style created in England, which became widely admired on the Continent, and those in France, Italy, and Central Europe. The austere furniture designed by Edward William Godwin, the first husband of Whistler's wife, accorded with Japanese taste: the emphasis was less on the curvilinear than was the case in France. English Art Nouveau, including the style created by Charles Rennie Mackintosh, is barely tinged with decadence, Aubrey Beardsley being the main exception. To claim that this was a consequence of the strict morality of the Victorians is tempting, but we must not forget that whatever the public image might appear, English life in the major cities was savage and sordid, as was realised by several French writers and artists (Gustave Doré among them); it was a period of child prostitution, alcoholism, and the abuse of laudanum.

The English Arts and Crafts movement with its relationship to Ruskin was essentially a call to order; it suggested an attempt to create an oasis in a world of increasing materialism. This rear-guard action was later reflected in the foundation of the National Trust in Britain in 1895 and by the desire to preserve the past in the face of marauding property developers. So often the fin de siècle is interpreted in terms of decadence, but it had another dimension — the idealism that accompanied the rise of Liberalism, which had offspring in William Morris, Bernard Shaw, and the advocates of Fabian Socialism. This current in English life has only now more or less vanished with the onslaught of inflation.

The swooning women who appear in the works of Whistler and, above all, in those of D.G. Rossetti, are typical of Art Nouveau. Mario Praz's celebrated book, *The Romantic Agony*, relates the extent to which Woman interpreted as a Medusa figure haunted the imagination of musicians, painters, and poets. Oscar Wilde's *Salome* and Richard Strauss's opera based on this libretto reflect the morbid sexual dreams of the fin de siècle. That woman should have been a dominating force, and even seen as evil, as a *femme fatale*, may have been due to the fear of catching venereal disease. Many writers, including Baudelaire, were victims. The thrills of illicit sex are continually alluded to in French fiction, especially that of the afternoon rendezvous, "from five to seven" (*de cinq à sept*), favoured by the leisured classes, familiar to us in books by Paul Bourget and Guy de Maupassant. Yet such escapades were not confined to France. The Countess of Cardigan and Lancastre in her delightful *My Recollections* (1909) recounts the story of the Parrot Club which existed in London in the 1850s, where three ladies, Mrs. D- W-, Lady P-, and Lady K- would receive their lovers, Lord Strathmore, Captain Vivian, and one other, whose name is not recorded, in a house in Seymour Street, Portman Square. The brothel was sometimes treated as if it were a club, and as such it appears in Alexander Kuprin's novel *Yama* (English translation, *The Pit*) of 1915, which is set in Odessa.

The cult of Woman found one of its most brilliant exponents in Rodin, a famous satyr who had an ability to capture sensuality or sensibility, as the case may be: the fluid, melting forms of his sculpture are characteristic of

Art Nouveau, and his love of floating hair was shared by Rossetti and Mucha, as well as by Debussy in his opera *Pelléas and Mélisande*.

Art Nouveau jewellery is evocative of the era when great cocottes such as Cora Pearl and Germaine Paillet held sway in Paris and often "ate" the fortunes of their lovers. The bed designed by Louis Majorelle in the Lewis Collection is reputed to have been made for Germaine Paillet, the mistress of the Crown Prince, son of Kaiser Wilhelm II. The rings, bracelets and chains designed by Lalique and Vever conjure up images of those svelte and alluring women depicted by Boldini or Helleu. Proust's famous novel *A la recherche du temps perdu* might even be considered as a major expression of the spirit of Art Nouveau. By coincidence, Marie Nordlinger, who assisted the novelist with his translations from Ruskin, was employed in Bing's shop and was a close friend of Charles Lang Freer, the celebrated collector of Far Eastern art and patron of Whistler.

Proust admired Gallé, whose astonishing glass pieces were often inspired by literature, an example of the concept of the "correspondance" between the arts advocated by Baudelaire. This craftsman designed a commode, *Hortensia*, for his friend, that almost professional aesthete, Comte Robert de Montesquiou. Various references to Gallé occur in Proust's novel. Thus in *A l'ombre des jeunes filles en fleur*, he conveys the sense of sea spume by a reference to this artist's work; in *Le Côté de Guermantes*, he writes of winter with, at the corner of the window, "comme sur un verre de Gallé, une veine de neige durcie." One of the favourite and most original motifs used in Art Nouveau, the whiplash, is not incompatible with the sexual practices favoured by Baron de Charlus; the concept, too, of Albertine as a "prisoner" suggests confinement to those claustrophobic rooms designed by several French Art Nouveau designers.

The use of enclosed space and the fear of emptiness that typify Art Nouveau are paralleled in the introspective society portrayed by Henrik Ibsen, perhaps the leading playwright of the age, in *Hedda Gabler* or *The Wild Duck*, with the drama of emotional conflicts waged behind four walls: outside, the presence of mountains and fjords can be sensed, symbols of eternity.

Art Nouveau contains a strong strain of mysticism. The effects on a sensitive soul of a world moving from a primarily agrarian society to an industrial one must have been as appalling then as are the destruction of inner cities and intense noise today. The longing for escape may help to explain the popularity of spiritualism, the revival of interest in Blake, and the extensive range of dream-painting that occurred in the late nineteenth century, Odilon Redon and L. Lucien-Dhurmer being among its main exponents.

Electricity is such a part of modern life that it requires an effort of the imagination to recognize the effect that its novelty exerted on artists and craftsmen; not surprisingly, one of the most original minor art forms of the time was the lampshade. Louis Comfort Tiffany designed multi-coloured glass lampshades with flower motifs that introduce an exotic note into the gloomiest interior. Degas's pastels of dancers would probably have been less vivid without the effects of electricity.

That the cult of the flower is no new thing is shown by the tulip-mania that raged in seventeenth-century Holland, by the number of flower pictures executed then and in the eighteenth century, and by Josephine's patronage of Redouté. The symbolism of flowers—lily for a young girl—is important. The synonym used by Swann for making love to Odette was the type of orchid known as cattleya. Plant forms and exotic flowers were constantly drawn on by Art Nouveau artists and designers: some of Fabergé's more effective pieces are of single flowers.

Various French painters delighted in painting flowers in the latter part of the nineteenth century, Fantin-Latour among them, but one artist in particular, Monet, revealed an almost obsessional passion for the lilies in his garden at Giverny. The floating amorphous forms of such pictures and the changing moods of his paintings of haystacks and cathedral façades reveal a relationship between Symbolism, late Impressionism, and Art Nouveau. May we also see in his attempts to capture Time an echo of Bergson's philosophy?

Many of the most original creations of Art Nouveau designers were in ceramics and glass where the curving, gnarled forms or tenderly coloured surfaces possess considerable quality. They also reflect the influence of classical, Far Eastern, Islamic, and Byzantine shapes and colours as befitted an eclectic and historicist age. The undulating forms of flowers corresponded to those of feminine fashion, emphasizing that relations between art and costume provide considerable information about the cross-fertilization of culture. Whistler, for instance, was keen on arranging the clothes as well as the settings for portraits of such sitters as Mrs. Leyland, the wife of a Liverpool ship-owner and one of his chief patrons, and Cicely Alexander.

The precious quality of the objects produced by Art Nouveau craftsmen and their generally eclectic character were in tune with the cult of the Aestheticism characteristic of the 1890s when an international leisure class, of varying degrees of wealth, took an interest in the arts and enthused about Venice, Bruges, and Bayreuth. The connections between Aestheticism, Symbolism, and Art Nouveau are complex, but the fin de siècle was innovative and deeply artistic. A typical English aesthete and a leader of the Arts and Crafts style of typography was Herbert Horne. He edited *The Hobby Horse*, was the author of a *magnum opus* on Botticelli—a painter admired by Proust—and was a man of practical business, selling early Italian pictures to J.G. Johnson of Philadelphia. Yet the mood of the fin de siècle was aptly captured by Hugo von Hofmannsthal with the words:

"today two things seem modern: the analysis of life and flight from life."

That the need for a new universal conception of art was considered vital is clear from the Belgian designer Henry van de Velde, who declared: "Everything, absolutely everything which constitutes modern life, ought to be determined by the new rhythms, by the new harmonies. The new rhythm determines the position of man who in a salon crosses his arms lower and wears more open waistcoats, just as it determines the attitude of women who expose more of their bosom and wear lower cut dresses, thus displaying the accents of their silhouette."

The importance of stage design for the diffusion of a new mood is not always appreciated, but the sets of the Swiss Adolphe Appia, who meant much for Edward Gordon Craig, possess a dreamy nebulous quality that accords with the amorphous spirit of Art Nouveau.

It was significant of the new "world" that an American dancer, Loïe Fuller, whose memory was commemorated in a comprehensive exhibition at the Virginia Museum of Fine Arts, Richmond should have invented a fresh way of presenting her dances by means of changing lights: her movements appealed to artists such as her compatriot, the poster designer W.H. Bradley and Toulouse-Lautrec, as well as to Pierre Roche, whose bronze of her with flowing robes is the quintessence of Art Nouveau.

The lure of the total work of art—the *Gesamtkunstwerk* desired by Wagner—found its most attractive visual expression in the Russian ballet, to which character and coherence was given by Sergei Diaghilev. It was an emanation of the "World of Art" movement in St. Petersburg; the designs of Leon Bakst and Alexander Benois combine exoticism and a love of the eighteenth century. In the same way Stravinsky moved from composing the music for *The Rite of Spring* to that for *Pulcinella*, with its debt to Pergolesi. In his ballets, Diaghilev drew on the best of the arts—the new men as well as those of an older generation—and provided a bridge between the pre- and post-1914 World War, stimulating artists especially in France and England. Today, Russian design of the 1920s seems to possess something of a similar spell for the young.

The eighteenth century exerted a powerful influence not only on the work of some of the prime designers for the Russian ballet, but also on architecture and interior design in general. This is understandable. Of all periods, the eighteenth century—the age of the *Ancien Régime*—was considered to be the one in which art and luxury were most closely entwined. Balzac in *La Cousine Bette* makes Crevel clamour for a setting *à la Régence* in which to establish his mistress.

At one stage it used to be believed that French eighteenth-century style was not revived until the 1880s or so, and that it could not resist the conquest of Neo-Classicism and the Empire, but this is now realised to be untrue and that the continuity remained strong. Thus it comes as no surprise to discover such a substantial connection between the Rocaille, the Rococo, and Art Nouveau, as well as later on with Louis XV. Moreover, the taste for Japonism, which was appreciated by several Art Nouveau artists, Hector Guimard especially, corresponds to that for Chinoiserie in the eighteenth century. To some extent an eighteenth-century influence was also evident in Germany where, to take one example, the façade of the Elvira studio in Munich echoed the decorations of the Bavarian Baroque and Rococo.

During the second part of the century, the world-wide development of international finance brought about the emergence of a class of new rich bankers, financiers, and industrialists, many of whom felt that they could achieve social legitimacy by living in houses decorated in the eighteenth-century French taste. Nevertheless, a banker such as R.H. Benson of Robert Fleming's, who was responsible for arranging much of the finance for the development of railways in the United States, was a passionate devotee of early Italian art, acquiring several of the masterpieces by Duccio and others that now hang in the National Gallery of Art, Washington, D.C.

Until the end of the nineteenth century much art took its tone from the Court. This was decreasingly the case in France, for instance, where Napoleon III's fall from power spelled the end of the Empire, and at Berlin, to take one leading centre, where Kaiser Wilhelm II was hostile to advanced modern art. The main exception to this was the Grand Duke Ernst Ludwig of Hesse (1868-1937), who established an artists' colony at Darmstadt in 1899. This existed until the outbreak of the 1914 War. The result was that this small city, with little more than 70,000 inhabitants, bacame one of the main centres of the movement; the Austrians Joseph Maria Olbrich and Peter Behrens were among those who went there. The exhibition held in Dusseldorf in 1901 was a major event; according to the publisher Anton Kippenberg, "this was the decisive act in which twenty or thirty years of German artistic development had their roots."

The Grand Duke, who was a son of Queen Victoria's daughter Princess Alice, had arranged for Baillie Scott and C.R. Ashbee to decorate rooms in the Neues Palais in Darmstadt. That the British influence was strong was hardly surprising in view of the fact that the country was the heart of a great Empire and that English nannies often brought up the children of the Continental upper-classes. The drawings of Randolph Caldecott and other draughtsmen who went in for children's books influenced Gauguin.

Olbrich, who worked for the Grand Duke, came from Vienna, the last main European city to succumb to the love of Art Nouveau, which produced one of its most appealing artists, Gustav Klimt. He painted three symbolic decorations for the assembly room of the University of Vienna, which created an immense scandal in this conservative capital. Klimt's pictures use geometric shapes, rich, almost Byzantine colours in which gold is abundantly employed; he was at his best in portraits of rather neurotic women who could appear in the plays of Schnitzler or seek advice from Dr. Freud. Hitherto no examination in depth has been devoted to the patrons of Art Nouveau, who presumably differed in Paris, Berlin, London, New York, and Vienna. Yet as far as can be ascertained they were sophisticated, not unlike the group who appreciated Boucher, and Fragonard, and belonged to a cosmopolitan world that typified the swan song of the Old Europe and the declining civilization that haunted Otto Spengler and which Thomas Mann captured in his enigmatic novel *The Magic Mountain* (1924).

Despite considerable optimism, many adopted a pessimistic attitude, of which Schopenhauer was one of the principal exponents. The idea of decadence was vented by numerous commentators—the emphasis on eroticism, on neurosis, and on the macabre constituted one side of the art of the fin de siècle—one strictly contrary to the love of Nature found with the Impressionists. That much of the work produced at this period was considered to be decadent was the view of Max Nordau (born Südfeld) in his once famous book *Entartung* (*Degeneration*) of 1892. What is striking about European life in the 1900s was the pace of events; the rise of the radical Left, the Russian revolution of 1905, the emergence of the Suffragettes, the development of nationalism in Central Europe, the Irish problem, the power hunger of Germany with its fight for world markets, and the spread of colonialism in Africa. Certainties that had existed now started to vanish as Europe marched towards the 1914 War.

Nevertheless, as the old order collapsed, a new one emerged. The extent to which the character of the style of interior decoration changed between 1914 and 1920 is difficult to determine, but it altered in the same way as did the novels of Paul Bourget and Edith Wharton, whose first publication was devoted to interior decoration: both admirably capture the mood of their period. Yet misinterpretations can, and do, occur. It would be easy to believe that a playwright such as Franz Wedekind expressed a post-war mood, but his most famous play, *Spring's Awakening*, was written in 1891.

The collapse of society and of various monarchies in Central Europe did not entail complete lack of support for the arts. The art magazines of the early 1930s show the intense activity that existed on the art market in Berlin, the new Sodom and Gomorrah. This is the society reflected in the art of George Grosz and in Neue Sachlichkeit, which has recently returned to favour; the hard quality of the paint reflected the hard quality of life. Although minor craftsmen such as Ferdinand Preiss and Bruno Zach produced small objects in line with Art Deco—in one by the latter artist a woman is shown brandishing a whip—the severe and business-like style of the moment was that associated with the Bauhaus. A fresh factor, the rise of the masses, was recorded by Munch and by Otto Griebel in his powerful painting L'*Internationale* (1931) in the Museum of German History, Berlin.

The difference between Berlin on the one hand and Paris and London on the other was striking. Fundamentally modern Central European art, whether it be that of Alban Berg and Kurt Weill in music or Max Beckmann and Otto Dix in painting, was opposed to the amiability of French Art. Nevertheless, the Cologne firm of Rath and Bilbach designed delightful neo-Sheraton or Louis Seize rooms, sometimes with Chinoiserie motifs.

That French interior decoration retained considerable allure despite the difficulties of the time was confirmed at the Exposition des Arts Décoratifs et Industriels held at the Grand Palais in 1925 and designed to honour France's allies during the 1914 War; Soviet Russia, though not diplomatically represented in Paris, was also invited to collaborate in the affair.

The opening gala was an astonishing event and reveals something of the nature of the *années folles*: turns were given by Loïe Fuller and

Mistinguette, the Hoffman girls from the Moulin Rouge, and the Tiller girls from the Folies Bergère. Sixty of the best known actresses, accompanied by actors in white tie, modelled clothes by the main Paris couturiers. In addition, a performance was staged by members of all the corps de ballet then performing in Paris.

The conviction that wealthy individuals would continue to exist (as fortunately they did then and as they still do) was implicit in the design for the "Hôtel d'un Riche Collectionneur" designed by Pierre Patout for Emile-Jacques Ruhlmann. That the love of the eighteenth century persisted is clear from the distinguished furniture made by André Groult, Paul Iribe, Armand-Albert Rateau, Ruhlmann, and Süe et Mare.

The relations between Art Deco, which found some of its finest expression in theatre and cinema decoration and the Ecole de Paris have not yet been precisely established. Should we consider, as do some authorities, that the main Art Deco painters are Tamara de Lempicka—who favored "butch" type women—and André Lhôte, or cast the net wider and include Dufy and Van Dongen, even Matisse and, in certain pictures, Bonnard? One question concerns the connection of the Neo-Classicism of Picasso and Derain to the modern style: can we claim (as perhaps we should) that the delight in the Commedia dell'Arte shared by Derain, Picasso, and Severini was a late echo of Mannerism rather than the portent of a new world? Has that renewal only taken place with the brutalism of Expressionism? Possibly there is an analogy here between the death of Mannerism in the late sixteenth century and the emergence of the Caravaggesque realism that is now so popular.

The division of art, at any one time, into separate categories is a complex matter. However, it is now clear that links connect the sculpture of Brancusi, Lipchitz, Modigliani, and Elie Nadelman. A different view of the originality of their contribution may be taken when it is related to that of such little-known Art Deco sculptors as Chauvin, Alexandre Kelety, and Jean Lambert-Rucki.

For many, life in Paris in the 1920s was delightful—art was charming, a shade effete no doubt, but possessed the lightness of touch that is reflected in Marie Laurençin's designs for the ballet Les Biches with music by Poulenc, or in the syncopation of Jazz which had its visual equivalent in the designs of Jean Dunand and its high priestess in the singer Josephine Baker. The city offered varied artistic experiences: Coptic, Negro, and Islamic art were favoured by the elite. Paris was one of the most artistically stimulating and entertaining cities in the world, much appreciated by those Americans, English, and Scandinavians who thronged the cafés of Montparnasse. Here, as the English art critic Clive Bell used to say, "one was in the movement." Little was then known about modern German art and about Russian constructivism, though refugees from Bolshevism abounded in Paris: Paris's hegemony over the arts was consecrated in the exhibition of 1937.

The history of patronage in the twentieth century remains to be written and when it is, due attention should be given to fashion designers such as Jacques Doucet and Paul Poiret, or actresses such as Jane Renouardt. A chapter deserves to be devoted to that exercised by the major shipping companies and grand hotels. The decoration for one of the most splendid ocean-going liners, the Normandie, launched in 1935, epitomizes the final flowering of Art Deco or, more correctly, the French decorative tradition. This was carried out by a team of varied talents—lacquer work by Dunand, mirrors by Dupas, bas-reliefs by Jeanniot, ceiling decorations by Picard le Doux and D'Espagnat, metal work by Subes, paintings by Gernez, Lévy, Bouchard, Méheut, and Ducos de la Haillé (all forgotten men), and furniture by Süe, Montagnac, Leleu, and Ruhlmann.

Art Deco was in many ways the product of a dream world, in which the man about town and the elegant hostess moved in a perfumed and enchanting society, one which is reflected in George Gershwin's *An American in Paris*. Luncheon at the Ritz or dinner in the Bois, a visit to select a tie at Charvet's immortalized by Proust, a look at the jewels at Cartier or Boucheron, a glance at an art show at Bernheim-Jeune, and an evening at the Casino de Paris, or perhaps that attractive Russian nightclub, *Schéhérazade*. Such is the background against which Art Deco must be viewed in France, while in Britain we may think of the plays of Noël Coward and Somerset Maugham, whose wife, Syrie Maugham, was especially keen on white interiors.

One feature of Art Deco was the use its designers made of Egyptian motifs which became *à la mode* after the sensational discoveries at the tomb of Tutankhamen made by the Earl of Carnarvon and Howard Carter. Perhaps it is symbolical that this should be so. These relics from a past age, that of the XVIIIth Dynasty, possess an elegance and luxury that are related to the finest objects made in the two decades on either side of the First World War. Now that the world of Art Nouveau and Art Deco is fast vanishing—only a few restaurants with Art Nouveau decorations survive from the 300 or so that once existed in Paris—these echoes of a passing phase in Western civilization can cast a spell on those nostalgic for the past, or, at any rate, those aspects of it which excite their imagination.

Style for a New Century
The Sydney and Frances Lewis Decorative Arts Collection

by FREDERICK R. BRANDT

I. A New Age of Design for the Machine Age

The period from about 1885 to the mid 1930s saw an unprecedented development in the world of design. It was a fertile era in the arts, founded not on fashion and historicism, but on the singular creativity of highly skilled, uniquely talented, and, above all, innovative artists and craftsmen. Just as this period marks the beginnings of the Modern School of painting and sculpture, so too does it mark the birth of an exciting new age of design, encompassing what we today call Art Nouveau, Art Deco, Modernism, Functionalism, and a host of other styles.

During this period, designers in all countries freed themselves from the bonds of copying the past and instead created new forms based not on historical precedents but instead on their own surroundings and experiences. In many cases their new forms were the outgrowth of new materials. In addition, these designers rebelled against the dull tastes that had characterized the products of the Industrial Revolution and all its failings to return to the concepts of hand craftsmanship. Artist-designers who sought to free the decorative arts from their role of "minor arts," and to elevate them to the "fine arts" of painting and sculpture, now proudly signed their works.

II. Pioneers of the New Design

Much of the early development in the movement to elevate crafts to the aesthetic consciousness of the fine arts can be credited to two English philosopher-artists who firmly believed that art should serve man and should be widely available, regardless of social background or financial status. These two Englishmen—John Ruskin and the designer William Morris—laid the foundation for what would result in a deluge of activity in these fields by individuals seeking to express their own personalities, not to reflect past masters or civilizations in their work.

The second half of the nineteenth century found the typical middle-class home decorated in what one author called "dead monotony, ugliness, and a good deal of sham." Walls hung with festooned draperies were often dark and dreary. Furniture was based on earlier prototypes, veneered in cheap materials and painted in garish colors. The fine art of handcrafted furniture was no longer a priority; speed of production and cheapness of materials led the way. The standards of quality were lost and the object was made for sale rather than for practical and lasting use. Machine-turned legs, butted joints, and cheap finishes made inexpensive but tawdry furniture available to the general public. There was no concern to establish a style for its own time, but only to rely on styles that had gone before. Some reformers who abhorred these shabby products could only recommend a return to the Queen Anne or some other historic style rather than demand honesty to the period and freshness of vision.

The ideas of Ruskin and Morris partially grew from the turbulent changes occurring throughout Europe and America during this period. It was a time of violent upheaval in world politics, resulting in the Russo-Japanese War, the Boer War, the Paris commune, and, eventually, World War I. It was also a time of significant social changes brought about by continuing class struggles. Many of these events contributed to the formulation of the Socialistic writings of the various Arts and Crafts philosopher-artists of the last decades of the century.

The period was marked by tremendous technological developments that were intended to help free workers from the burdens of poverty, disease, and early death. At the same time, Morris and his followers realized that these industrial advances were not all to the benefit of the worker, but instead contributed to his substandard of living. The rural peasants who had been freed from servitude to the soil now faced a new, more monotonous, and even deadlier form of slavery. Their new masters

11

were the great "Satanic mills" referred to by William Blake, along with the other new industries that attracted more people to the cities than could be gainfully employed. Housing was inadequate to the demand, and the workers toiled at the whim of their employers, who unilaterally set hours and wages. Disease, crime, and poverty were rampant, and the need for social reform grew.

John Ruskin (fig. 1) tried to use his own power as an art critic and writer, as well as his elevated social status, to foster what he felt was right in the arts, while vanquishing what he felt were its evils. Much of what he preached was predicated upon the belief that the Industrial Revolution had created certain evils that appeared in the arts. He believed that only by returning to the standards of the earlier Gothic period, and its accompanying hand craftsmanship, could the arts be redeemed and thus made one with nature again. Ruskin felt that certain standards of art must be met and kept or the producing country would suffer.

In a lecture he presented in January 1858 at the South Kensington Museum entitled "The Deteriorative Power of Conventional Art Over Nations," Ruskin wrote that "Art, so far as it was devoted to the record or the interpretation of nature, would be helpful and ennobling. . . ."[1] He was opposed to art for art's sake and wrote that "Wherever art is practised for its own sake, and the delight of the workman is in what he *does* and *produces*, instead of what he *interprets* and *exhibits*—there art has an influence of the most fatal kind on brain and heart, and issues, if long so pursued, in the *destruction both of intellectual power* and *moral principle*; whereas art, devoted humbly and self-forgetfully to the clear statement and record of the facts of

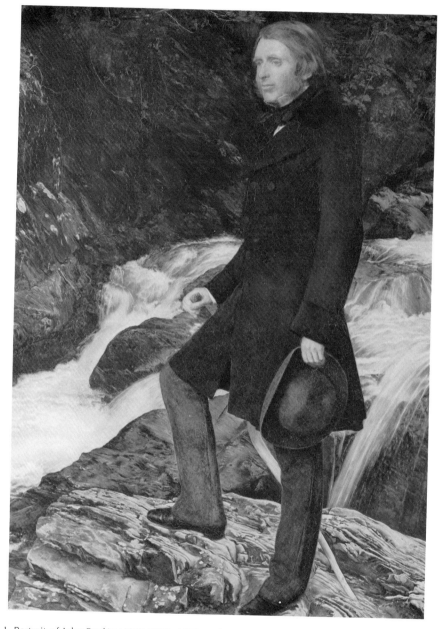

1. Portrait of John Ruskin (1819-1900), 1853-54, by John Everett Millais (1829-1896). Private collection, England. (Photograph courtesy of Royal Academy of Arts, London.)

1. John Ruskin, *The Two Paths: Being Lectures On Art, And Its Application To Manufacture, Delivered In 1858-9* (New York: John Wiley & Sons, 1885), p. 22.

2. Ruskin, pp. 22-23.

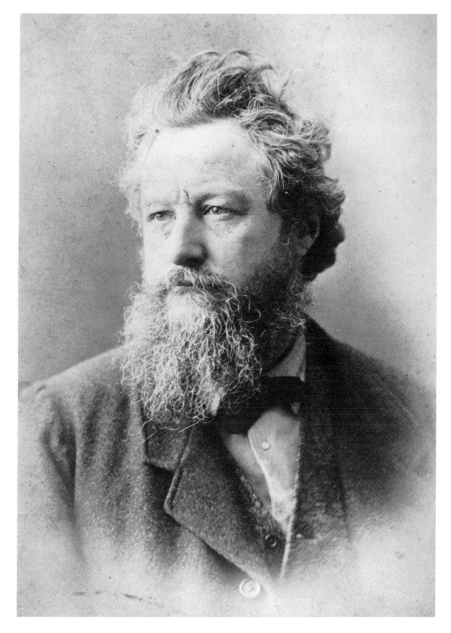

2. William Morris (1834-96), 1880, by an unknown photographer. (Photograph courtesy of William Morris Gallery, Walthamstow, London.)

the universe, is always helpful and beneficent to mankind, full of comfort, strength, and salvation."[2]

It is obvious that Ruskin believed that art could have strong curative or destructive powers on mankind. Of course, he felt that only art based on his strict guidelines would be effective.

In an address delivered at Manchester on March 14, 1859, he further commented that "Art may be healthily associated with manufacture, and probably in the future will always be so; but the student must be strenuously warned against supposing that they can ever be one and the same thing, that art can ever be followed on the principles of manufacture. Each must be followed separately . . . ."[3]

Ruskin felt that industrialism was here to stay but he also made it quite clear that art could never be produced by the machine, a tenet that was to be followed by William Morris (fig. 2) and others. "Fine art," Ruskin declared, "must always be produced by the subtlest of all machines, which is the human hand. No machine yet contrived, or hereafter contrivable, will ever equal the fine machinery of the human fingers."[4]

Some years later, Morris felt that he could make a more positive contribution to the concepts of hand production by denying machine production. Morris originally set out to be an architect but abandoned that goal to become a painter, designer, and decorator. He employed his friend, the English architect Philip Webb, to design his home, Red House, and furnished it with specially designed objects to complement his own decorative schemes. Realizing there were few furnishings and other accessories that met his own demanding taste, Morris eventually set up a

3. Ruskin, p. 53.
4. Ruskin, p.54.

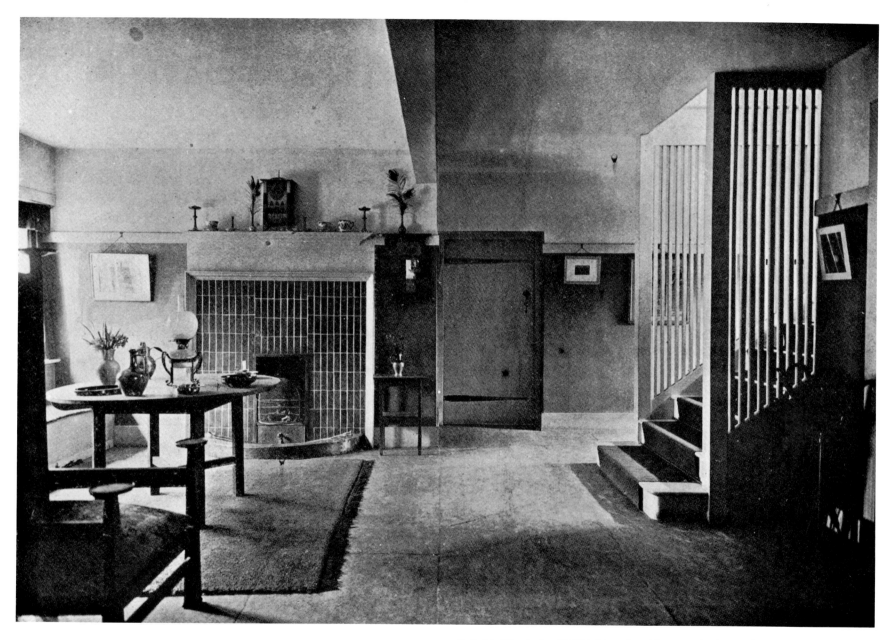

3. Hall in "The Orchard," C.F.A. Voysey's residence at Chorleywood, Hertfordshire, completed in 1900. Voysey designed most of the interior and furnishings, including the mantel clock, now in the Lewis Collection (cat. no. 2). (Photograph courtesy of Philippe Garner.)

firm in 1861, collaborating with some of England's finest artists, including not only Webb but also the painters and designers Dante Gabriel Rossetti, Edward Burne-Jones, W. A. Benson, William de Morgan, and Ford Madox Brown. He designed a wide variety of objects—including books, furniture, fabrics, and glass—with the idea that their elevated, moralizing designs would help to abolish the ugliness of the surroundings of the working class. In truth, however, the objects Morris produced were so expensive that only the wealthy could afford them. He could not produce such objects less expensively except by machine. Ideally, Morris and his followers wanted the houses of the workers to be beautiful in their own right and to be filled with fine objects the homeowners themselves had created. It was his belief that this endeavor would raise their spirits and strengthen their moral fiber.

In America, the writer-philosopher Elbert Hubbard established a movement called The Roycrofters in East Aurora, New York. His group, too, produced books, furniture, metalwork, and other objects based on the idealistic principles established by Morris (see cat. no. 50), of whom Hubbard wrote as though he were a savior:

> To the influence of William Morris does the civilized world owe its salvation from the mad rage and rush from the tawdry and cheap in home decoration. It will not do to say that if William Morris had not called a halt someone else would, nor to cavil by declaring that the inanities of the Plush-Covered-Age followed the Era of the Hair-Cloth-Sofa. These things are frankly admitted, but the refreshing fact remains that fully one-half the homes of England and America have been influenced by the good taste and vivid personality of one strong, earnest, courageous man.[5]

Such strong praise clearly shows how much influence Morris must have exerted on his fellow writers and craftsmen.

The major contribution Ruskin and Morris made to the design of this age consisted in raising the standards of design and making the public aware of them. In addition, Morris's philosophy of making art for the people was to form the basis for other, more successful theories expounded in the twentieth century. Without Morris, Ruskin, and the Arts and Crafts Movement, the design concepts of the following decades might well have been quite different.

The English architect-designer C.F.A. Voysey also echoed the ideals put forth by Ruskin and Morris, but Voysey carried them a step further. In so doing, his own work laid the foundation for a style that was growing at that time in other parts of Europe and would soon sweep the world: *Art Nouveau* (see fig. 3).

While Ruskin and Morris felt that artists could look back to the Middle Ages for inspiration, and considered the Gothic style perfectly acceptable, Voysey condemned such revivalism:

> And most important it is to avoid the lazy and contemptible practise of relying upon precedent for justification of what is done. The Revivalism of the present century, which is so analogous to this reliance on precedence, has done more to stamp out man's artistic common sense and understanding than any movement I know. The unintelligent, unappreciative use of the works of the past, which is the rule, has surrounded us at every turn with deadly dullness, that is dumb alike to the producer and to the public. This imitative, revivalistic temper has brought into our midst foreign styles of decoration totally out of harmony with our national character and climate. Also the cultivation of mechanical accuracy, by close attention to imitation, has so warped the mind and feelings until invention to many is well-nigh impossible.[6]

5. Elbert Hubbard, *This Then is a William Morris Book Being a Little Journey by Elbert Hubbard, & Some Letters, Heretofore Unpublished, Written to His Friend & Fellow Worker, Robert Thomson, All Throwing a Side-light, More or Less, on the Man and His Times* (East Aurora, New York: The Roycrofters, 1907), p. 34.

6. As quoted in "Some Recent Designs By Mr. Voysey," by E.B.S. in *The Studio* 7 (1896): 215.

III. L'Art Nouveau: International Design Dynamics

The style that dominated the history of design for approximately ten years before and after the turn of the century is today commonly known as "Style 1900," or Art Nouveau. It is a style that had roots in the teachings and philosophies of Morris and Ruskin, but it was also based on some of the design concepts of English architects such as Arthur Mackmurdo, and was influenced by the arts of Japan and Byzantium, the earlier Aesthetic Movement, and such diverse stylistic developments as Celtic illuminated manuscripts and the French Rococo style. Its greatest success occurred not in England but in France, Belgium, Austria, and Germany, eventually reaching out to all parts of the world, including the United States. As the critic André Hallays observed at the 1900 Paris Exposition, "The most original feature of this decorative parody is its universality. The Modern Style is European. Visit the exhibition of furniture. Everything is contorted, attenuated and unbalanced according to the new fashion."[7]

As common as the term Art Nouveau is today, it is still difficult to define precisely, because it represents so many stylistic variations. The name has been applied to work as flamboyant as Majorelle's furniture, decorated with waterlilies; as erotic as Carabin's sinuous figures; as classic and geometric as Mackintosh's spartan chairs; and as fresh and exuberant as Tiffany's jewel-like glass lamps. It is therefore ambiguous to include all these designers under the single term Art Nouveau. But because each designer exercised his unique vision during the same brief era, and each strove to achieve similar goals, perhaps it would be more accurate to identify their work as "Style 1900."

But where did this term "Art Nouveau" originate? It has long been believed that it is derived from the name of a shop Siegfried Bing opened at 22 Rue de Provence in Paris on December 26, 1895.[8] Bing, a German-born entrepreneur, called his shop *La Maison de l'Art Nouveau*. In 1902, he explained the concept of his shop in *The Architectural Record*: "L'Art Nouveau, at the time of its creation, did not aspire in any way to the honor of becoming a generic term. It was simply the name of an establishment opened as a meeting ground for all ardent young spirits anxious to manifest the modernness of their tendencies, and open also to all lovers of art who desire to see the working of the hitherto unrevealed forces of our day."[9] Lately, however, it is more generally agreed that although Bing capitalized on this term, he did not indeed invent it. In 1884 Octave Maus and Edmond Picard spoke out against the art of the past and said that they were "believers in Art Nouveau."[10] Regardless of its origin, it is the term widely used today to indicate the extravagant and extraordinary arts created around the turn of the century.

As this "New Art" movement swept across Europe, it took on other names. In Germany, for example, it was known as *Jugendstil*, for the name of the magazine *Jugend* (Youth), first published in Munich in 1896. The Italians referred to it as "Stile Liberty," after Arthur L. Liberty's shop in London, which offered items similar to those sold by Bing. The French called it the Modern Style, *Style Nouille* (Noodle Style), or *Style de Bouche de Métro*. The latter term refers to elegantly swirling ironwork on the Paris subway entrances designed by Hector Guimard around 1900. The Belgians applied the name of various avant-garde groups, such as *Le Style des Vingt* or *La Libre Esthétique*. The *Wiener Sezession*, the name of a group of Viennese artists who banded together in 1897, lent its name to *Sezessionstil*, the Austrian version of Art Nouveau.

Regardless of the name, the ideology was the same: in every country, artists tried to free their work from the shackles and restrictions forced upon them from the past. As with Morris and Ruskin, these artists hoped to bring the finely crafted object back into the home, where it would become part of an integrated design concept.

Although not strictly followed, functionalism also played an important role at this time. As Bing wrote in *The Architectural Record*, "Each article is to be strictly adapted to its proper purpose; harmony is to be sought for in lines and color."[11]

Some artists were derisive in their references to the current Victorian tastes in decorating and interior design. From the beginning of this century down to comparatively recent times, the housekeeping world seems to have been in thrall to six haircloth chairs, a slippery sofa to match, and a very cold, marble-top center table. In all the best homes there was also a marble mantel to match the center table; on one end of this mantel was a blue glass vase containing a bouquet of paper roses, and on the other a plaster-Paris [sic] cat. Above the mantel hung a wreath of wax flowers in a glass case. In such houses are usually to be seen gaudy-colored carpets, imitation lace curtains, and a what-not in the corner that seemed ready to go into dissolution through the laws of gravitation.[12]

In the same manner, Henry van de Velde, the great Belgian architect and designer, described Victorian-era interiors as ". . . the insane follies which the furniture makers of past centuries had piled up in bedrooms and drawing rooms . . . . Processions of fauns, menacing apocalyptic beasts, benevolently hilarious Cupids (bawdy in some cases and complaisantly anxious to please in others), and swollen-cheeked satyrs in charge of the winds."[13]

To some, Art Nouveau was a negative style. It did not seem to have a central focus but instead only denied what had preceded it rather than looking to the future to create a unique personality.[14] To others, it had a positive force. For although it protested against the works of the nineteenth century that copied the past, the new style was also a logical evolution of the exquisite forms of eighteenth-century France, the oft-acknowledged apogee of Gallic design. Some critics felt that the very historicism that Art Nouveau reacted against was negative, in that such revivalist tendencies did not bring the artist's originality and skill to the art.[15]

In any event, Art Nouveau was both revolution and evolution. No matter what variations of the style the artist created, certain characteristics seem to appear. For example, much of the subject matter of Art Nouveau derives from nature. In some cases, such as Tiffany lamps, it is broadly realistic; in others, as in the designs of Joseph Maria Olbrich, it is a more abstracted form (see cat. no. 48). It appears that nature and its plants, flowers, insects, animals, and birds were the prime inspiration for the Art Nouveau artist.

Another common element was that exquisite and beautiful materials were used by many artists, who resurrected and revived what had more or less been abandoned or had become secondary to more common materials.

Finally, and perhaps most importantly, each artist brought his or her own original concept to the design. With respect for the past, artists looked

7. André Hallays, a critic reviewing the Exposition Universelle 1900, as quoted in Philippe Jullian, *The Triumph of Art Nouveau: Paris Exhibition 1900* (New York: Larousse & Co., Inc., 1974), p. 99.

8. There has been continuous speculation as to what S. Bing's first name was. Through extensive research, Gabriel P. Weisberg has uncovered the fact that his first name was Siegfried. For detailed information concerning Bing's life and activities, see "L'Art Nouveau Bing," *Arts in Virginia* 20 (no. 1, Fall 1979): 2-15, especially footnote 1, which elaborates upon Weisberg's earlier research and resultant articles.

9. Siegfried Bing, "Art Nouveau," *The Architectural Record* (August 1902): 281.

10. Roger-Henri Guerrand, "Art Nouveau: The Birth of a Modern Style," in Philippe Garner, ed., *The Encyclopedia of Decorative Arts 1890-1940* (London: Quarto Publishing Limited, 1978), p. 17.

11. Bing, "Art Nouveau," p. 283.

12. Hubbard, *William Morris Book*, p. 32.

13. Henry van de Velde, *Les Formules d'une Esthétique Moderne*, quoted in Maurice Rheims, *The Flowering of Art Nouveau* (New York: Harry N. Abrams Inc., 1966), p. 223.

14. A.D.F. Hamlin, "L'Art Nouveau, Its Origin and Development," *The Craftsman* (December 1902): 129-43.

15. Jean Schopfer, "L'Art Nouveau: An Argument and Defence," *The Craftsman* (July, 1903), pp. 229-38.

to the present but applied their own stylistic trademark to their creations. Thus an artist's style throughout his or her body of work can be recognized in much the same manner that one might recognize the hand of the artist in a series of paintings.

IV. The Paris Exposition 1900: Zenith of Art Nouveau

It is generally acknowledged that the Paris World's Fair of 1900 (fig. 4) was the high point of the Style 1900.[16] Here artists from many countries showed their works in their respective national pavilions, many of which were avant-garde in style and design. Important designers from France, Germany, Austria, Holland, and even America were represented. Although the architecture of the pavilions was varied, it was basically exotic and in certain cases reflected the principles of the Style 1900.

One of the most outstanding displays at the Fair was the salon entitled "Art Nouveau Bing" (fig. 5). Here Siegfried Bing displayed six rooms—vestibule, dining room, drawing room, dressing room, bedroom, and boudoir—designed by Georges de Feure, Edward Colonna (fig. 6), and Eugène Gaillard. One rather over-enthusiastic reviewer, Gabriel Mourey, called this group "the triumphant result of the endeavour on the part of a little group of artists, to attain as nearly as may be the absolute of novel decoration."[17] Mourey further praised it as "one of the most perfect pieces of combined decorative art-work in the whole Exhibition. It does the

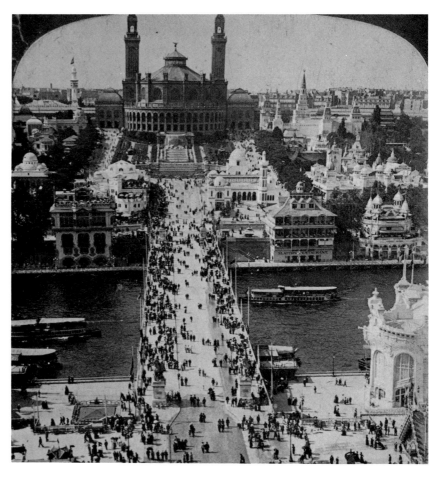

4. A view of the 1900 Paris Exposition from the Eiffel Tower, from a photograph by R. Y. Young for the American Stereoscopic Company, New York. (Photograph courtesy of the author.)

highest honour alike to the creative artist and to him [Bing] who inspired them."[18]

Bing was an exceptional entrepreneur who combined a brilliant sense of business with a connoisseur's eye. Well-established as an importer and dealer in Oriental art, particularly the art of Japan, Bing soon became more interested in the artists working in his own time, eventually commissioning

16. Victor Arwas, in *Art Deco* (New York: Harry N. Abrams, Inc., 1980) refutes this claim and says that the Exposition reflected more traditional and regional tastes, with only the School of Nancy being shown as a coherent group. Thus the Style 1900 was not represented cohesively enough to influence the public awareness of its new forms and philosophies.

17. Gabriel Mourey, "Round the Exhibition.–I. The House of the "Art Nouveau Bing'," *International Studio* (1900): 165.

18. Mourey, p. 180.

19. Philippe Jullian, *The Triumph of Art Nouveau: Paris Exhibition 1900* (New York: Larousse & Co., Inc., 1974), p. 21.

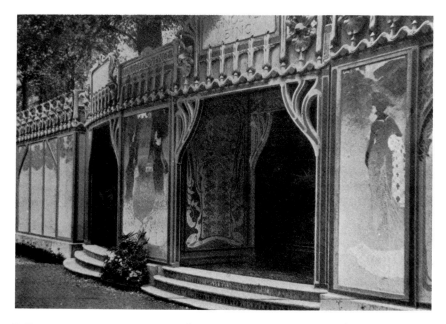

5. The entrance to Art Nouveau Bing at the 1900 Paris Exposition, featuring designs by Georges de Feure. (Photograph courtesy of Gabriel and Yvonne Weisberg.)

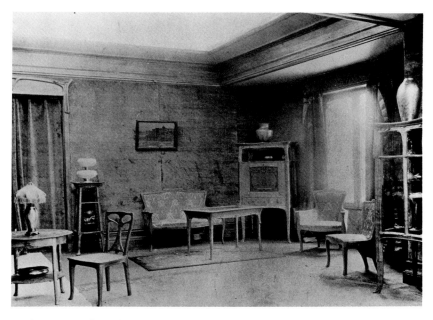

6. Salon in S. Bing's pavilion at the 1900 Paris Exposition, designed by Edward Colonna. The settee and chair in the background are similar, if not identical, to those in the Lewis Collection (cat. no. 20). (Photograph courtesy of the Art and Music Department, Newark Public Library, Newark, New Jersey.)

them to produce objects that were not only beautiful in concept but were also available at reasonable prices. Bing seemed determined to change the style of the French decorative arts and to make France again a leader in this field. He began by opening his shop in 1895 and culminated with his salon at the Paris Exposition of 1900.

Built at an estimated 100 million francs, the Exposition attracted visitors to Paris from around the world.[19] Planned over an eight-year period, it was to serve as a capstone for a century of progress of all human endeavor and as a gateway into a new century predicted to be one of vast technological and cultural accomplishments.

The buildings of the various countries were created in a multitude of architectural styles, many of them reflecting the national heritage of country they represented. Exceptional examples of architecture in the new style, Art Nouveau, did exist, however, and it is these for which the Exposition is best remembered. In addition, interiors such as Bing's and such cultural innovations as the sound-and-light dances of Loïe Fuller turned out to be artistic highlights of the Exposition. Undoubtedly such novelties helped to spread the style to those who saw or read about the them. Loïe Fuller, in fact, provided valuable visual inspiration for a number of important designers and artists of the turn of the century.

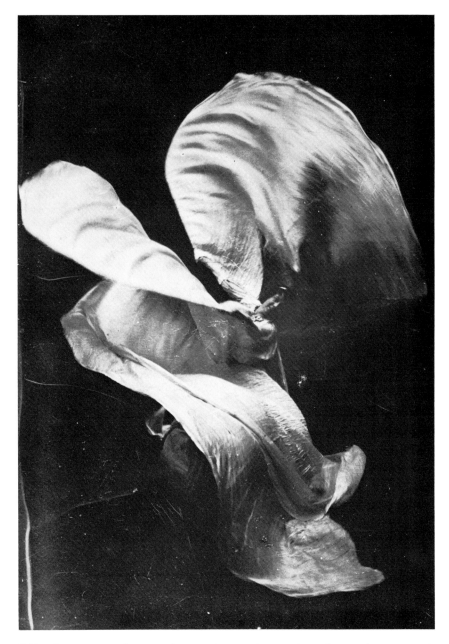

7. The dancer Loïe Fuller, 1896, by an unknown photographer. (Photograph courtesy of Margaret Haile Harris.)

Loïe Fuller (1862-1928) was an American dancer-choreographer who became the toast of France with her unusual and flamboyant performances (fig. 7). She was remarkably well-skilled in creating flowing movement and spectacular effects by incorporating yards and yards of diaphanous fabric into her costumes. As she swirled rapidly around the stage to the rhythm of music by her contemporaries, specially colored lights were shone onto the shimmering fabrics. Her performances were veritable spectacles, and today she is considered one of the pioneers of modern dance. With her sinuous, swirling movements, "La Loïe" became the favorite of Art Nouveau sculptors and painters; countless images of her were created by artists such as Pierre Roche, Henri de Toulouse-Lautrec, Rupert Carabin, and François-Raoul Larche.[20] Indeed, as an icon of the feminine, the elegant, the dynamic, and the sensuous, she came to personify the Style 1900 (see cat. no. 3).

Whether or not the Paris Exposition was the pinnacle of Art Nouveau, it is clear that after that date the style, although continuing to disseminate throughout the world, gradually became more commercial, eventually deteriorating in quality, and finally giving way to new thoughts and ideas of design.

V. The Modern Movement Emerges in Glasgow and Vienna

In the same year as the Paris Exposition, Charles Rennie Mackintosh and three of his colleagues, all members of the so-called "Glasgow Four," were invited to show their work in an exhibition in Vienna. These remarkable Scottish artists—Mackintosh, his partner Herbert MacNair, and the sisters Frances and Margaret Macdonald—individually and collectively created work that would not only influence the style of the Viennese but would also open the doors to the concepts of Modernism.

Although these four young Scots were each remarkable in their own way, the work of Mackintosh stands out above the others. Relatively unappreciated in his own time, he managed to create a body of work distinguished for its sophisticated simplicity, its extraordinary use of color and materials, and the total integration of the furniture and interior designs with the architecture. Considered one of the outstanding artists of this period and often categorized as an Art Nouveau artist, Mackintosh made little use of the sensuous "whiplash" line that his contemporaries did in other parts of Europe (see cat. nos. 44 and 61).

Using simple, geometric shapes with a singular sense of abstraction, Mackintosh created furniture that was not only modern in concept and design, but also beautiful and elegant when placed in his interiors (fig. 8). Mackintosh, perhaps more than any other artist of the time, was able to bring a fresh approach to design in the twentieth century, design completely free from any reflections of the past.

Although Mackintosh eventually dominated the Glasgow art scene, fine work was also produced there by MacNair and the Macdonald sisters. MacNair and Mackintosh were married to Frances and Margaret Macdonald, respectively, whom they had known since about 1893. Because of their close working relationships it is sometimes difficult to identify individual designs. The output of MacNair and the Macdonald sisters is fairly similar, particularly in graphic design (see cat. no. 56), but Mackintosh's work is usually distinguishable from the others.

Some writers have suggested that *The Studio* magazine may have been the source from which the Viennese Secessionists first knew about the work of the Glasgow Four.[21] In any case the Scottish artists were known in Austria and were appreciated enough to be invited to show their work in the 1900 Sezession Exhibition.

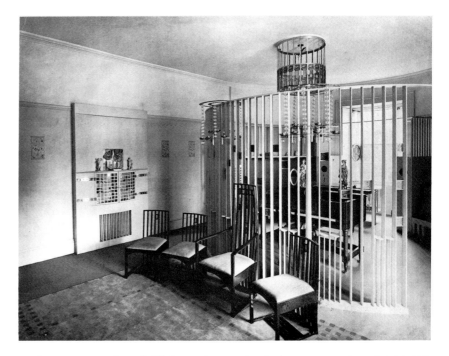

8. The Music Room, "Hous'hill," designed in 1904 by Charles Rennie Mackintosh in Nitshill, Glasgow, for Miss Cranston and her husband, Major Cochrane. The tall chair is now in the Lewis Collection (cat. no. 44). (Photograph by T. & R. Annan, Glasgow; courtesy of Philippe Garner.)

20. For a more complete documentation on Loïe Fuller and her influence on the artists of her time see the exhibition catalogue *Loïe Fuller: Magician of Light* (Richmond: Virginia Museum of Fine Arts, 1979).

21. Roger Billcliffe and Peter Vergo explain why they feel *Studio* rather than *Dekorative Kunst* influenced the Viennese in this area. See Billcliffe and Vergo, "Charles Rennie Mackintosh and the Austrian Art Revival," *The Burlington Magazine* 119 (November 1977): 739-44.

"There can be no doubt," say Roger Billcliffe and Peter Vergo, "that, at the time of the 1900 Exhibition, it was Mackintosh and the Scots who were the leaders, Hoffmann, Moser and the Viennese artists the admiring followers. Numerous influences can be traced back to the Scottish contribution to the eighth Sezession show, beginning with the layout of the Scottish Room itself, which was decorated very simply, being painted all white, and quite sparsely furnished."[22]

In 1900 the Viennese artists may indeed have been strongly influenced by the designs of the Glasgow Four, but it appears that the reverse would also occur, particularly in Mackintosh's later designs.[23]

VI. Innovation at Paris and Nancy

In France, the sensuous line continued to dominate all aspects of the work of the Style 1900 artist. In Paris, Hector Guimard completed remarkable buildings furnished with beautifully carved furniture as part of his total concept of interior design (see cat. nos. 15 and 55). Guimard had the ability to design an interior completely, to the smallest detail. These designs, plus those he did for the Paris Métro stations for the 1900 Exposition, made his name a household word. In fact, at times the entire stylistic movement of turn-of-the-century France was referred to as "Style Guimard."

Guimard literally carved his distinctive line into metal, wood, and stone to create buildings that have been referred to as Mannerist and Surrealist in concept, while remaining very modern in construction technique.[24]

---

22. Billcliffe and Vergo, p. 740.

23. Billcliffe and Vergo, pp. 743-44. The authors logically point out that the work of Otto Prutscher exerted a strong influence on Mackintosh's work of this period and later. In fact, they also imply that much of his later work was based on what he could extract from the periodical *Deutsche Kunst und Dekoration*.

Guimard's importance as a major architect of the period can be seen in the fact that he continued to design buildings in a revised Art Nouveau idiom well into the late 1920s, but the work he produced at the turn of the century stands out as the epitome of his style. In the Castel Béranger (begun 1894, completed 1898), for example, Guimard developed a complete architectural plan whereby he designed not only the structure of the building but also the furnishings, carpets, stained-glass windows, fireplaces, and other accessories and ornaments. Thus the building was a complete statement by the artist with no intrusion from outside creative sources. The concept of complete design was carried even further in the design of his own house in Paris in 1909. Here the style of the exterior strongly suggests that of the interior. Again, all embellishments—from the carpets and wall coverings to the lighting fixtures, furniture, and other accessories—were part of the total design.

Paris was also the center of some of France's greatest jewelry designers. Outstanding among them was René Lalique. Born in France, Lalique studied in Paris and in England, and became a free-lance designer before opening his own studio in 1885. Four years later he received recognition for his jewelry at the 1889 Exposition in Paris.

It was at the 1900 Exposition Universelle, however, that Lalique saw his greatest success in jewelry design. Here his work was shown in a pavilion he designed himself, and it was perhaps because of the success of this display that he received so many important commissions for the next ten years.

His highly imaginative jewelry designs continue to be recognized for their use of unusual materials in compositions based on the themes of nature (see cat. nos. 7 and 38). The ubiquitous fin-de-siècle female shares an important role in his oeuvre with creatures such as insects, dragonflies, flowers, seahorses, and peacocks. There is no doubt that he was the most

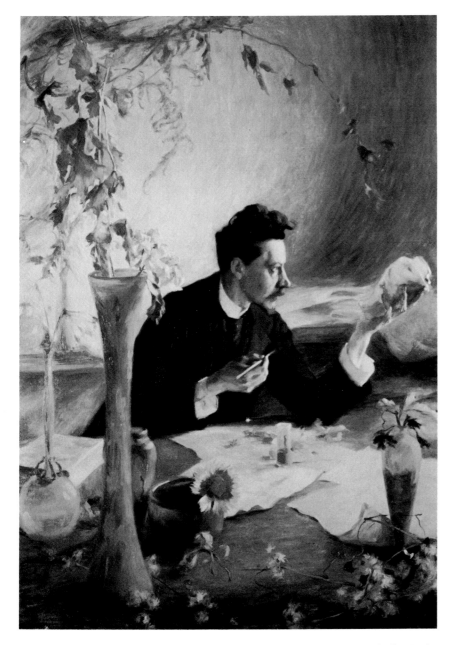

9. *Portrait of Emile Gallé*, 1892, by Victor Prouvé (1858-1943). Collection Musée de l'Ecole de Nancy. (Photograph courtesy of Philippe Garner and The Corning Museum of Glass.)

important Art Nouveau jeweler of his day. By 1910 Lalique more or less abandoned jewelry design to give his full attention to producing glass, for which he is now perhaps better known (see cat. no. 90).

Lalique's compatriot Georges Fouquet continued a jeweler's dynasty founded by his father Alphonse and later carried on by his son, Jean. Like Lalique, Fouquet was a Parisian jeweler (see cat. no. 49). Both had received important commissions from outstanding personalities of the day, such as Sarah Bernhardt. Perhaps most memorable was his collaboration with the Czechoslovakian painter-printmaker Alphonse Mucha. Around 1900 Fouquet and Mucha collaborated on the design of Fouquet's jewelry shop and in the actual design and fabrication of several very important pieces (see cat. no. 18). The two artists were seemingly a perfect match: Mucha's fantastic graphic and design skills complemented Fouquet's exquisite craftsmanship.

Outside Paris, the French Style 1900 was dominated by the artists working at Nancy. Located approximately 120 miles east of Paris in the province of Lorraine, Nancy had a history of glassmaking since the late sixteenth century. By the mid to late nineteenth century a number of glass factories still flourished there. One of these was owned by Charles Gallé, whose son Emile was to become the leader of the Ecole de Nancy and one of the most important French creative artists of this period.[25]

Gallé (fig. 9) was trained in botany and natural history as well as literature, all of which would later affect the development of his work. In addition, he studied glassmaking and later built a new factory at Nancy.

24. See James Grady, "Hector Guimard: An Overlooked Master of Art Nouveau," *Apollo* 89 (April, 1969): 284-95 for a general discussion of the relationship of Guimard's work to that of Mannerism and Surrealism.

25. For a complete study of the life and work of Emile Gallé see the definitive biography of the artist by Philippe Garner, *Emile Gallé* (New York: Rizzoli, 1976).

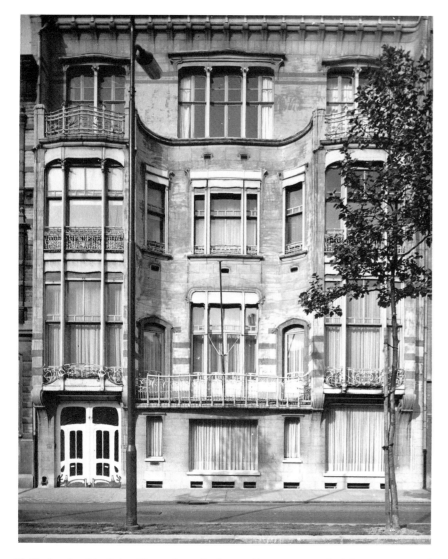

10. The façade of the Solvay House, Brussels, designed by Victor Horta; built between 1894 and 1903. (Photograph courtesy of Mr. and Mrs. L. Wittamer-de Camps, Brussels.)

Although much of Gallé's work was devoted to the production of art glass, he later concentrated on furniture design and manufacture.

The Ecole de Nancy was established as a formal group of artists, encouraged by Gallé to revitalize the artistic production of the province. The group was incorporated in 1901 with Gallé as president. Among its members were Louis Majorelle, the brothers Auguste and Antonin Daum, Jacques Gruber, Victor Prouvé, Eugène Vallin, and others who, although important designers, are not as well-known today (see cat. nos. 10, 11, 19, 23, 24, 39, and 57).

Nancy seems to have been unique in the development of such a closely knit group. Henri Frantz, writing in *The Studio* in 1903, summarized this small city's contribution to the art of the period:

> Of all the towns in France, Nancy is perhaps the only one which can pride herself on having, during the latter part of the 19th century, given birth to a group of decorative artists of distinct originality, and of having seen rise up in her midst a pleiad of painters, sculptors, and decorators, all imbued with a similar ideal, or working out principles of a similar kind, in forming what may really be justly called a school which, although each member is free to follow the dictates of its own individuality, cannot fail to strike even a superficial observer as a homogeneous whole, working harmoniously for the same aim. Of course, such a movement as this cannot be compared with the same kind of thing in a great city such as Paris, but the comparative unimportance of that in the ancient capital of Lorraine is made up for by the greater unity and cohesion of its component parts whilst the whole bearings of the case in point can be taken in at once.''[26]

VII. Two Belgian Architects: Horta and van de Velde

In Belgium, where carved plasticity characterized much new design, Victor Horta and Henry van de Velde were leading proponents of the style. In fact it is Horta's Tassel House, built in Brussels in 1892-93, which is often considered the first true example of Art Nouveau architecture.[27]

But it is Horta's Hôtel Solvay (fig. 10) that today gives us the best idea of the elegant environment he created for his houses. Built between 1894 and 1900, the house is a total statement of the Style 1900 as practiced by Belgian architects, particularly Horta. Nature is evident everywhere but is abstracted to a line that both defines and outlines as it encloses space. But to Horta decoration and design were not all-consuming. The Hôtel Solvay also demonstrates his ability to employ up-to-date technology in his architectural designs. Great masses of glass bring natural light into the building, and complex structural designs allow for a free circulation of fresh air. Thus not only nature's individual shapes, but also its total ambiance, pervade the interior of this remarkable building.

One of the great theoreticians and writers of the Style 1900 was Horta's compatriot Henry van de Velde. Originally trained as a painter, van de Velde became an architect and by 1896 had built his own house at Uccle, near Brussels (cat. no. 4). His work was admired by Bing, who invited him to show at his *Maison de l'Art Nouveau* in Paris. Similarly, in 1897, Julius Meier-Graefe invited van de Velde to design the interior of his new showroom, *La Maison Moderne*. Van de Velde's work there and the work he did later in Germany were so well received that the style was at the time referred to in Germany as *Veldesche* and *Belgische* in his honor. It was very much due to the influence of van de Velde that the style pervaded German design and eventually made Germany the leader in the decorative and applied arts throughout Europe.

VIII. The Youth Style Flourishes in Germany

In his landmark book *Sources of Art Nouveau*, Stephan Tschudi Madsen writes that the sudden deluge of new design activity in Germany was primarily due to three factors:

> In the first place Germany was permeated by a marked national consciousness and a desire for national assertion; secondly Germany possessed, thanks to her leading position in art research, a great many competent art historians and art critics who devoted themselves with great intensity to the problems of applied art; and finally there was the fact that Germany had a great deal of leeway to make up in the development in architecture and applied art, in order to keep abreast of the times.[28]

Although van de Velde's writings and his exhibition in Dresden in 1897 undoubtedly influenced German designers, there was already a firm basis for the new style's development in that country. In 1895 Julius Meier-Graefe had begun to publish the periodical *Pan* and this was soon followed by several other important periodicals; including *Jugend*, which lent its name to the *Jugendstil* (Youth Style) in Germany. In this milieu, two centers of activity arose at Munich and Darmstadt. The Munich group was led by the designers Otto Eckmann, Hermann Obrist, Bernhard Pankok, Richard Riemerschmid, August Endell, Bruno Paul, and Peter Behrens. But in 1899 Behrens (see cat. no. 34) was summoned to Darmstadt by the Grand-Duke of Hesse to form a creative arts center there with Joseph Maria Olbrich of Austria.

In general, the new style was short-lived among German designers, who gradually expanded their own design concepts, eventually breaking away from the *Jugendstil* and becoming more involved in designing furniture for industrial production. In this way the Germans brought the movement full circle: where William Morris wished to divorce completely the handcrafted product from the machine-made, German designers such as Riemerschmid sought to integrate the two concepts so that the highest

26. Henri Frantz, "Emile Gallé and the Decorative Artists of Nancy," *The Studio* 28 (March 16, 1903): 108-9.

27. Peter Selz and Mildred Constantine, eds., *Art and Design at the Turn of the Century* (New York: The Museum of Modern Art, 1959), p. 49.

28. Stephan Tschudi Madsen, *Sources of Art Nouveau* (New York: George Wittenborn, 1956), p. 412.

quality of industrial design might be produced in the most efficient manner. This concept was eventually to be a building block of the Bauhaus, the influential international design center, an outgrowth of the *Weimar Kunstgewerbeschule* that had been led for a time by van de Velde himself.

IX. The New Style in America: The Tiffany Empire

It was in the United States that the Style 1900 had the least effect. Perhaps this was due to Americans' general unwillingness to embrace new innovations in the arts, and their stylistic admiration for the past, having still a relatively new and unformulated design sense compared to that of the Europeans. The sense of "old" tended to make Americans regard earlier styles and objects with higher reverence than did Europeans. In some areas, however, great strides were made in innovative design. Dominating the decorative arts of the United States in the Style 1900 was the work of the studios of Louis Comfort Tiffany.

By the time of the Paris Exposition, Tiffany had become well established in the design and sale of lamps, stained-glass windows, decorative tiles, metalwork, jewelry, and to some extent furniture and other related accessories. Constantly experimenting, Tiffany developed glass that was outstanding not only for its color and luminosity but also for its unusual shapes and combination with other materials. His dramatic lamps graced the mansions of the wealthy and were never considered inexpensive, even in their own day.[29] Tiffany supervised a huge conglomerate of specialized workers who produced the many objects of high quality (see cat. nos. 17, 25, 26, 27, 51, and 52).

Tiffany's work triumphed at the Paris Exposition (fig. 11). His glass received no less than five gold medals and a Grand Prix. Singled out for particular attention by the critics was a fabulous punch bowl with ladles

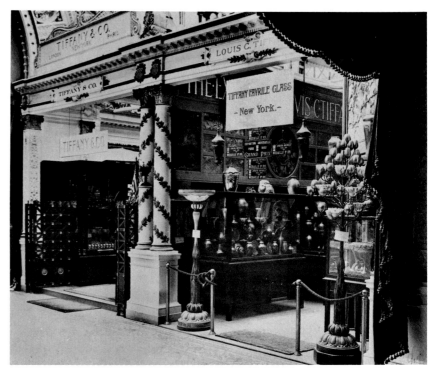

11. View of the Tiffany Favrile Glass display at the Paris Exposition 1900. The Tiffany Punch Bowl, now in the collection of the Virginia Museum, can be seen in the case at the right (cat. no. 17). (Photograph courtesy of Dr. Robert Koch.)

created especially for the Exposition (cat. no. 17), a piece that has been called "the weirdest, most exuberant, most Art Nouveau, most Expressionist object of its era ever produced in America."[30] Elsewhere in America the Style 1900 was most evident in the architecture of Louis Sullivan and his Chicago contemporaries.

X. Fathers of the Modern International Style

While the Style 1900 swept Europe and made its way into the decorative arts of the United States, certain artists were determined to stay away from the curves of the style and instead formulated a straightforward American style free of decoration that emphasized structure through simplicity of design, quality workmanship, and well-integrated construction.

One American practitioner-theoretician who was more successful than his European counterparts in fulfilling the dream of Morris and Ruskin to make finely crafted art for the people was Gustav Stickley. In the preface to his *Catalogue of Craftsman Furniture*, published in 1909, Stickley wrote:

Anybody who knows Craftsman furniture has no difficulty in realizing that the principles upon which it is based are honesty and simplicity. This is quite true, for when I first began to make it [in 1898] I did so because I felt that the badly-constructed, over-ornate, meaningless furniture that was turned out in such quantities by the factories was not only bad in itself, but that its presence in the homes of the people was an influence that led directly away from the sound qualities which make an honest man and a good citizen. There is more in the influence of inanimate things than we suspect and the home environment has an astonishing effect upon the development of character, especially in the case of children, whose earliest impressions are naturally gained from their home surroundings. It seemed to me that we were getting to be a thoughtless, extravagant people, fond of show and careless of real value, and that one way to counteract this national tendency was to bring about, if possible, a different standard of what was desirable in our homes.[31]

Here Stickley precisely summed up the thoughts of Ruskin and Morris, and in so doing he put into practice what he preached. His furniture, well-made and extremely durable, was affordable and thus not restricted to the wealthy. Its design was characterized by straight lines that emphasized structure. White oak, leather, and hand-wrought copper hardware were his primary materials; no ornament or decoration was applied. Each of the materials was selected to harmonize with the others to create a unified whole, a design integrity he envisioned as a truly American style (see cat. no. 40). Stickley's dream failed, however. People soon tired of the plain lines of his "American style" furniture, and sought instead Colonial reproductions and other styles of the past. Eventually his firm went bankrupt, and his spirit was disillusioned.

In the introduction to the same 1909 furniture catalogue, Stickley briefly outlined the philosophy he followed in the creation of his furniture, houses, metalwork, leatherwork, and textiles.

Therefore, when the idea came to me that the thing for me to do was to make better and simpler furniture, I naturally went at it in the most direct way. Having been for many years a furniture manufacturer, I was of course familiar with all the traditional styles, and in trying to make the kind of furniture which I thought was needed in our homes, I had no idea of attempting to create a new style, but merely tried to make furniture which would be simple, durable, comfortable and fitted for the place it was to occupy and the work it had to do. It seemed to me that the only way to do this was to cut loose from all tradition and to do away with all needless ornamentation, returning to plain principles of construction and applying them to the making of simple, strong, comfortable furniture, and I firmly believe that Craftsman furniture is the concrete expression of this idea.[32]

To accomplish these ends Stickley chose American white oak, for which he painstakingly perfected a finish in warm and mellow tones to complement other furniture. He added carefully selected leathers and metalwork to accent it (cat. no. 40). Believing that the environment shaped the lives of its inhabitants, Stickley designed the "Craftsman house," published *The Craftsman* magazine to give full expression to his ideas, and designed and manufactured various smaller objects that could blend into

---

29. For example, a catalogue issued by Tiffany around 1915 lists a library lamp in the Laburnum pattern for $300, a veritable fortune in terms of what the average worker was earning at that time.

30. Robert Koch, "The Tiffany Exhibition Punchbowl," *Arts in Virginia* 16 (1976): 32-39.

31. *Catalogue of Craftsman Furniture made by Gustav Stickley at the Craftsman Workshops*, 1909 (Watkins Glen, New York: The American Life Foundation, 1978), p. 3.

32. *Catalogue of Craftsman Furniture*, loc. cit.

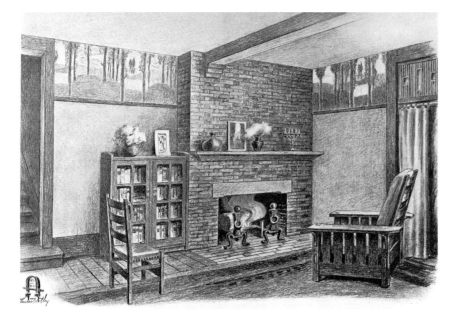

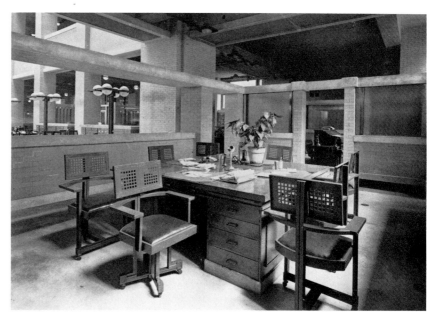

12. "A Friendly Living-Room with Craftsman Fireplace" as illustrated in Gustav Stickley's magazine, *The Craftsman*, July 1906, p. 524.

13. Executive section of the first floor of the Larkin Company Administrative Building, Buffalo, New York, designed by Frank Lloyd Wright in 1904. The armchairs, also designed by Wright, are of painted steel with oak seats. A similar chair and desk from the Larkin Building are now in the Lewis Collection. (Photograph courtesy of the Buffalo and Erie County Historical Society, Buffalo, New York.)

the interiors for a total of design (fig. 12). For approximately eighteen years Stickley tried to change the habits of his countrymen, finally giving in to failure in 1916.[33]

As Charles Rennie Mackintosh can be considered a pioneer of European Modernism, Frank Lloyd Wright must be considered the father of Modernism in the United States. The straight-line simplicity of Wright's furniture can be compared to that of Stickley. Wright's furniture, however, is better characterized in terms of its distinctive architectural motifs. His straightforward, rectilinear furniture was for the most part designed to fit within a specific architectural interior rather than to be incorporated into a room shaped by another artist's vision. Wright's "cube chair" of around 1895 is often considered the first piece of modern furniture designed in the United States.[34]

There is little wasted motion or surface in any of Wright's designs (see cat. nos. 42 and 47). In his designs for the Larkin Administration Building of 1904 in Buffalo, New York, Wright's geometric, no-nonsense, metal furniture exudes a power and dignity unrivaled in its day (fig. 13). It is interesting to note that both Wright and Stickley were producing their visionary modern furniture at the same time that French designers of the Style 1900 were creating equally interesting but contrastingly different, quasi-Baroque furniture in Paris and Nancy.

Austrian designers in Vienna, organized in 1897 as the Wiener Sezession by Josef Hoffmann, Koloman Moser, and Joseph Maria Olbrich, produced a geometric and rectilinear style of furnishings influenced by both Mackintosh and Wright. Six years later, in 1903, Hoffmann and Moser founded the remarkable *Wiener Werkstätte*. Joined by other leading Viennese architects, designers, and painters, they produced buildings, interiors, and accessories until 1932. It is their work, perhaps more than that of any other artists working in this period, that looked forward to the style that would dominate the 1920s, a style that would later be called Art Deco (see cat nos. 33, 43, 45, 46, and 48).

XI. L'Art Deco

Because of the geographic and stylistic diversity of the decorative art produced during the fin de siècle, the term Art Nouveau is actually a misnomer for many of these objects. In any event, the term Art Nouveau was used during the period but did not represent any distinct style; this was done by later historians. The same cannot be said of the term Art Deco, which has been applied to designs of the 1920s and '30s, particularly that period of design centered again in Paris, this time at the 1925 World's Fair.

Though many names were suggested for the stylistic phenomenon that grew during this period, none was applied or accepted universally. In 1966 the Musée des Arts Décoratifs in Paris produced an exhibition entitled Les Années 25. The subtitle of the catalogue was Art Deco. Two years later, Bevis Hillier applied the same term to the entire stylistic movement in his book Art Deco.[35] The phrase is simply an abbreviation for the official title of the 1925 fair, "Exposition Internationale des Arts Décoratifs et Industriels Modernes, Paris, 1925." Just as the Paris Exposition of 1900 is considered the apogee of the Art Nouveau style, there is no question that the 1925 fair was the triumph of Art Deco. Yet it is inaccurate to assume that no advances in the decorative arts were made between these two dates. For

although much arts activity was stifled by World War I, many stylistic changes were made that would eventually link the two styles. In fact, many of the designers featured in the 1925 Exposition had already made their mark in the earlier style. The new Art Deco style, in some cases, became a logical progression of their work. Others could not adapt their concepts to change and were soon completely overshadowed by the newer, more innovative artists and designers of the 1920s.

As noted earlier, the Art Nouveau style experienced a fairly rapid decline after 1900. Some architects continued to work in a modified Art Nouveau style into the next decade, but for the most part, interest in the style—both from the point of view of the public and that of the artists themselves—declined rapidly after the beginning of the new century. Bing's shop, which had been such a catalyst for change during the Art Nouveau era, closed in 1903, and Bing himself died in 1905.[36]

The demise of the Art Nouveau style came about through a gradual decline in production and changes in taste. Some of the leading artists continued to exhibit work in the Art Nouveau style. For example, those of the Ecole de Nancy continued to work and showed as a group in Paris in 1903. In addition, the Turin Exposition of 1902 is noteworthy as the last

---

33. For a complete history of the stylistic development of Stickley, see David M. Cathers, *Furniture of the American Arts and Crafts Movement* (New York: New American Library, 1981).

34. Philippe Garner, *20th Century Furniture* (New York: Van Nostrand Reinhold Company, 1980), p. 56.

35. Bevis Hillier, *Art Deco* (London: Studio Vista Limited, 1968).

36. See Weisberg, "L'Art Nouveau Bing," p. 15, for further information about the decline and eventual close of Bing's shop.

outpost of Art Nouveau as a current style, but it is probably more important as an exposition that reflected a complete break with the past to reveal new design and quality.

Of particular note at this Exposition was an interior design by Carlo Bugatti, whose work, although reflecting the exotic influence of the Near East, also exhibited a great degree of innovation and individualized expression (see fig. 14 and cat. no. 32).

Probably the most important design event in the first decade of the new century was the establishment of several arts organizations to emphasize the decorative arts and to give artist-members a chance to exhibit together. The Société des Artistes Décorateurs was founded in Paris in 1901, and two years later the Salon d'Automne was organized. As author Victor Arwas points out, "The decorative arts had, indeed, recently been admitted to the two annual Salons, but their selection and placing was kept under the control of the painters, keeping the decorators in a subordinate position. The new society and its Salons [were] to promote the supremacy of the decorators."[37] The Salon d'Automne was especially important in encouraging complete freedom of expression; no work was rejected for failure to adhere to specific rules, as the various other salons of painting and sculpture had always done. These two organizations were landmarks in the display and promotion of the decorative arts in France and elsewhere in Europe. Their creation actually anticipated the formulation of the principles behind the great Paris Exposition of 1925.

XII.   Influences from Other Areas

During this early period of Art Deco, designers incorporated many other significant influences into their work. In 1905, a group of painters nicknamed *Les Fauves* (the wild beasts) exhibited for the first time in Paris at

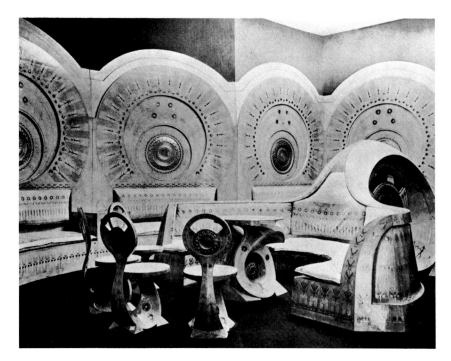

14. *Salle de Jeu et Conversation* at the 1902 Turin Exposition designed by Carlo Bugatti. One of the chairs from this "Snail Room" is in the Virginia Museum Collection (cat. no. 32). (Photograph courtesy of Stuart Friedman.)

the Salon d'Automne. Led by Henri Matisse, these artists displayed paintings in brilliant colors and executed in vibrant brushstrokes, much to the shock and consternation of the more conservative factions in the painting community. The Fauves' liberation of color is believed to have had significant impact on how decorative arts designers used color.

Another major factor in the development of this new design style was the Ballets Russes, brought to Paris in 1909 by Sergei Diaghilev. The Russian ballet's exotic themes were supported and complemented by the bold stage and costume designs of Alexandre Bénois and Léon Bakst.

Other exotica were also coming into the French capital and were disseminated from there to other parts of Europe. As early as 1905 African art and artifacts were being exhibited and recognized as a major art form by the collectors and museums of Europe. The African influence is readily apparent in the paintings of Picasso of this period, and its bold, simple forms were appreciated by the designers of the early part of the century.

Most of the stylistic influences and significant events mentioned thus far took place in France, and particularly Paris. France was obviously striving to lead in design, its only rival being Germany. Henry van de Velde had founded the Weimar School of Applied Art in 1906, and Herman Muthesius had begun the *Deutscher Werkbund* in Dresden the following year. Made up of some of the most influential and important designers in Germany, Belgium, and Austria, the Werkbund attempted to bring together designers and manufacturers in order to produce high quality, innovative furniture for the public market. The success of the Werkbund was reinforced when its artists were invited to show at the Salon d'Automne in 1910. Of course the French press, while recognizing some attributes of the German designers, for the most part tried to play down their contributions in favor of their own native designers. The rivalry between Germany and France continued until after the First World War, when France gained supremacy in the decorative arts.

XIII. Modernism and The Great War: Dada and De Stijl

America was aware of what was happening in Europe, not only in world affairs, but in the affairs of art as well. The Armory Show, presented in New York City in 1913, brought to the United States works by the leading proponents of Europe's new aesthetic. Although reviled by the press and received with disdain by the public, the exhibition had a very strong influence on the American painting community and tended to bolster the efforts of artists in this country who were interested in advanced concepts of design and composition.

That same year, 1913, another important event in the history of modern design occurred: the French furniture designer Emile-Jacques Ruhlmann showed his first works in Paris and was immediately recognized for his outstanding creative design and ability. From then until his death in 1933, Ruhlmann consistently displayed what could well be described as the highest taste in design—an aesthetic standard that many critics felt was the equivalent of the great eighteenth-century French cabinetmakers (see cat. nos. 60, 69, and 95).

Another important event that same year was the establishment of the Omega Workshops by the painter-designer Roger Fry in London. Fry brought together a group of fellow artists who worked on a wide variety of furniture, carpets, ceramics, and paintings. Some objects were designed, made, and decorated by the artists themselves, while others were mass-produced items the artists painted in a Post-Impressionist style. Just as had happened earlier during the Art Nouveau period, the major changes in design and decoration occurring on the Continent did not seem to influence the work of designer-craftsmen in Great Britain. Although the Omega Workshops' output was significant, it was still more closely related to the earlier Arts and Crafts Movement than to the modern aesthetic that was developing elsewhere.

The years 1914 to 1918 saw all Europe struggling through one of the most devastating wars known to mankind. The conflict took a heavy toll not only of human resources, but also of economic stability. In the horror of battle, the arts tended to fade in importance, but some new concepts did manage to surface during these terrible years. Dada, for example, was an anti-art movement that emerged in Zurich around 1916 to protest the

---

37. Arwas, *Art Deco*, p. 10.

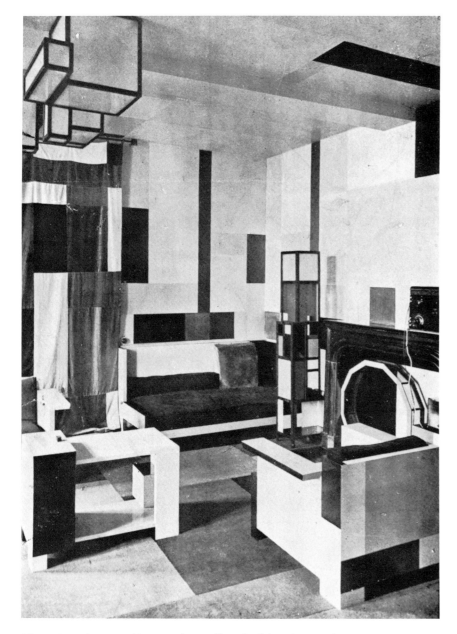

15. Interior with a suite of furniture designed by Félix del Marle for Madame B in 1926. All of the furniture shown here, including the two chandeliers, is now in the Lewis Collection (cat. no. 79). (Photograph courtesy of the Lewis Archives.)

destruction that had been inflicted upon Europe. In Holland, in the meantime, Theo Van Doesburg founded a magazine *De Stijl* in 1917 to voice the concepts of the so-called "Neo-Plasticism." In his monograph on the history of the De Stijl movement, Hans Jaffe explains this new aesthetic:

> De Stijl was founded during World War I. Though its origins were in a then neutral country |Holland|, it came out of a period of utter chaos, when harmony and balance were longed for by the majority of the Europeans. But it was clear that future harmony implied changes in the traditional ways of life. De Stijl artists discovered these changes everywhere in contemporary life: in industrial production, in the organization of politics and trade unions, in the growth of large cities . . . and in the execution of their conceptions, the De Stijl group was striving for precision such as that found in the products of the machine.[38]

Besides Van Doesburg, other artists involved in the De Stijl movement were the painters Bart van der Leck and Piet Mondrian, architect J.J. Oud, architect-furniture designer Gerrit Rietveld, and the French painter and furniture designer Félix Del Marle (fig. 15, cat. nos. 62 and 79).

XIV. The Structure of Modernism: The Bauhaus

With the end of the war, people tried to reconstruct their lives and their shattered surroundings. As the French and their allies won the war against Germany, they also fully established their dominance in Europe, if not in the world, in the field of decorative arts. Yet aspects of creative design in Germany and other countries had not altogether ceased. Walter Gropius speaks of his establishment of the Bauhaus at Weimar in 1919:

> When the Bauhaus was founded, I had already come to the conclusion that an autocratic, subjective, learning process choked off the innate, creative tendencies of talented students (when the teacher, even with the best of intentions, impressed on them his own thought and production results) . . . . I concluded that the teacher must beware of passing on his own formal

vocabulary to the students and that he must rather allow them to find *their own way*, even if they were detoured. Artists at the Bauhaus attempted to find an objective common denominator of form—in a way to develop a science of design . . . . The importance of the Bauhaus did not lie in a decree of a stylistic absolute, but in a new spiritual attitude intended to provide the art forms of our environment with an objective method of work and thought developed from elementary roots, whose spontaneous, artistic initiative was anchored in communal life to protect it from its own despotism."[39]

Gropius's key proclamation was "Art and technology—a new unity."

Others besides Gropius who worked at the Bauhaus were the artists Paul Klee, Gerhard Marcks, Lyonel Feininger, and Wassily Kandinsky. Later they were joined by the architect Marcel Breuer and the painter Josef Albers. These and other artists produced a remarkable body of work that would completely revolutionize the relationship between artist and manufacturer. Here, they developed such innovations as tubular steel furniture and stackable chairs, while they laid out theories of design and architecture that, in general, were the very foundation of International Modernism.

While all this was happening in Germany, even more important developments were taking place in France. As a result of its victory in the war, France not only wished to exert its political force as a world power but also wanted to reestablish its dominance and supremacy in the arts—particularly design and decoration—a position it had not held since the eighteenth century.

XV. L'Art Deco and the Design Renaissance

The French remembered the glory that was theirs during the reigns of Louis XV and Louis XVI, when such cabinetmakers as Jean-Henri Riesener and Jean-François Oeben created the sumptuous designs that we associate

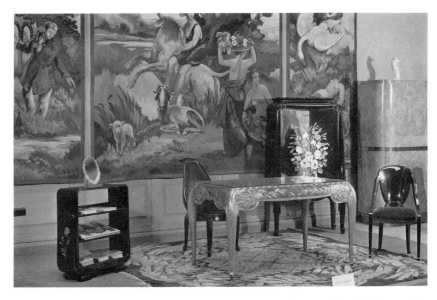

16. Exhibition of furniture by the firm of Süe et Mare as displayed in 1930. The tall cabinet, in the background to the right, is now in the Lewis Collection (cat. no. 83). (Photograph courtesy of the Lewis Archives.)

with the epitome of eighteenth-century taste. It had long been felt that France had lost its impetus as a world leader in the years following the French Revolution. With this in mind, an exposition devoted exclusively to design art was proposed as early as 1907. The world's leading artists and designers would be invited to match their skills against those of France. Due to internal squabbling and economics and eventually delayed further by World War I, the exposition was continually postponed until 1925.

From the end of World War I in 1918 until the 1925 Paris Exposition, French designers attempted to establish themselves as leaders both in their own country and on an international basis. In 1919, the architect and painter Louis Süe and the painter André Mare established the Compagnie des Arts Français, a firm that was to last for nearly a decade (fig. 16). Using

38. Hans L.C. Jaffe, *De Stijl 1917-1931: Visions of Utopia* (Minneapolis and New York: Walker Art Center and Abbeville Press, 1982), p. 12.

39. Walter Gropius in *Bauhaus and Bauhaus People* (New York: Van Nostrand Reinhold Company, 1970), pp. 19-20.

some of the rarest and most exotic materials, this remarkable team of painter and architect created memorable interiors that owed some allegiance to their eighteenth-century predecessors (see cat. no. 83).

Two of the major department stores in Paris, Galeries Lafayette and Au Bon Marché, established important interior design and decoration departments, headed by, respectively, Maurice Dufrêne, formerly a leading designer for Julius Meier-Graefe's *Maison Moderne* (specializing in Art Nouveau), and Paul Follot, also formerly noted as an Art Nouveau designer. Both of these very talented men were able to exert great influence on the public by creating *ensembles*, where they could gather together in their own studios what they felt were the best works being designed at that time. To this end, they exhibited not only their own work but also that of their fellow designers. In addition to public exposure in these ateliers, the superiority of French design was also spread throughout Europe by way of a great number of high-quality periodicals that fostered their work. Among these were *Art et Décoration, Art et Industrie, Arts de la Maison*, and *Echos des Industries d'Art*.

One more significant event occurred in 1922, an event that would strongly influence the Art Deco style. Designers and artists of this era had long been intrigued by exoticism. They had been captivated by rare materials and the bold forms of African art, particularly masks and sculpture.

In November of 1922, the archaeological team led by Howard Carter opened the sealed portal of Tutankhamen's royal tomb in Egypt's Valley of the Kings, in Thebes. The news of this discovery was immediately flashed around the world, and a vogue for things Egyptian soon followed. It was only natural that designers of the day would also be attracted by the new forms. One curious transformation was to make bronze ashtrays in the form of an Egyptian slave girl, based on the design of a wooden unguent spoon

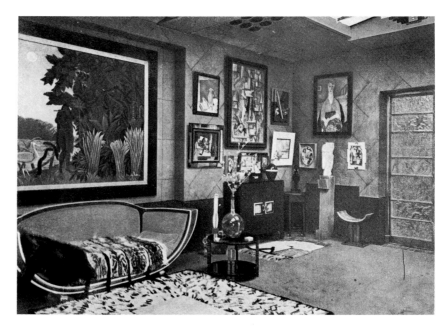

17. A section of the studio of Jacques Doucet showing the sofa by Marcel Coard now in the Lewis Collection (cat. no. 88); a sharkskin cabinet and a carpet both by Pierre Legrain; and a crystal door by Lalique. The paintings include works by the Henri Rousseau, Georges Braque, Amedeo Modigliani, and other masters of the early twentieth century. (Photograph reproduced from *l'Illustration*, May 3, 1930.)

from 14th-century B.C. Egypt.

Edgar Brandt, the highly skilled craftsman who worked primarily in iron, incorporated the cobra image into many of his designs; and Albert Cheuret created perhaps the most famous piece of all, a sterling silver mantel clock in the shape of a stylized Egyptian hairdo (see cat. no. 96). These designs reflected not only the designers' interest in exotic art—particularly that of Egypt—but also proved that the designers were responsive to new ideas and were not merely reworking the styles of their immediate predecessors.

XVI. Art Deco Patrons and Designers

In French society, the desire for showing the world that one was up-to-date and the belief in the work of these artists and designers led to an

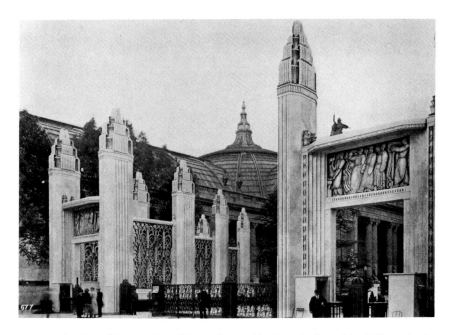

18. View of *La Porte d'Honneur* (*Gate of Honor*), designed by Henry Favier and André Ventre for the 1925 Paris Exposition. The fountain motif was used at the tops of the columns, as well as on the ironwork, designed by Edgar Brandt. The molded-glass reliefs are by Lalique. (Photograph reproduced from *International Studio*, November 1925.)

unparalleled patronage of the arts. Those who seemed most responsive to the new styles were the great French couturiers and other renowned public figures, such as leading actors and actresses, and top government and industry officials. Especially noteworthy are the design commissions completed for the fashion designers Coco Chanel, Jeanne Lanvin, and Jacques Doucet.

Born in 1853, Doucet had established himself as a important couturier by the 1920s. Prior to World War I he had assembled a magnificent collection of eighteenth-century painting, furniture, sculpture, and other objets d'art. In June of 1912, he sold at auction his entire eighteenth-century collection, including works by Boucher, Clodion, Houdon, Fragonard, and other masters of French painting and design. The sale of this magnificent collection was prompted by his desire to collect works by his contemporar-

ies. With this in mind, he hired the painter and designer Paul Iribe who, in turn, enlisted the aid of the designer and bookbinder Pierre Legrain to decorate and furnish Doucet's home. He acquired great paintings by Picasso (*Les Demoiselles d'Avignon*), Van Gogh (*Iris*), Matisse (*Les Poissons rouges*), and Henri Rousseau (*La Charmeuse des serpents*). In addition, between 1912 and his death in 1929, Doucet acquired furniture, carpets, sculpture, screens, glass, ceramics, and various accessories by Marcel Coard, Eileen Gray, Gustave Miklos, Jean Dunand, Rose Adler, and so many others whose names comprise an encyclopedia of the great designers of the period (see cat. nos. 80, 81, 82, 88, and 89).

Doucet's apartment at Neuilly (fig. 17) became a showcase for the art of the period and the epitome of good taste. It also presented a true picture of one of the great collectors and patrons of the time. Unfortunately, Doucet did not live very long to enjoy his new surroundings. His obituary in *The Art News* of November 23, 1929, said: "He accepted modern art fully and loved all its audacities . . . he continued to buy paintings, sculpture and books which appealed to him and to patronize assiduously artists of the advance guard."[40] Doucet was also noted for the generous gifts of his paintings to such institutions as the Louvre and for the establishment in Paris of what was called "one of the richest and most complete [art libraries] in the world."

XVII.   The Paris Expo 1925

And so it came about that in 1925, a quarter of a century after the great Paris Exposition that had introduced Art Nouveau to the West, the *Exposition Internationale des Arts Décoratifs et Industriels Modernes* brought together the designs and concepts of Art Deco from all parts of the world (fig. 18) to form

40. Paul Fierens, "Paris Letter," *The Art News* 28 (November 23, 1929): 15.

a new vision of luxury and elegance. By that time, the various elements mentioned previously had come together, and the design concepts established during the Art Nouveau period were continued. The result was a unity of design, through *ensembles*, by which all of the arts played an equal role, and the style was very much "au courant," as opposed to that of the past.

The military, economic, and aesthetic leadership of France and its allies in World War I made Paris the logical site for the exposition. Although France, like other countries, had serious economic problems, it was felt that the prestige from this world exposition would more than offset any economic losses that might be suffered. If France could prove to the world that it was supreme in taste, it could recoup its economic losses through the sale of its merchandise. Thus, in June 1925, the French opened the doors to the exposition to show to the world that their country was indeed the master of design and decoration.

With great confidence, France invited every major nation in the world, except Germany, to participate in the Exposition. (The war and its horrors were still too recent to allow any fraternization with France's former enemy.) Of the countries that were invited, all except China and the United States accepted the invitation.

The American public was not as willing to accept the new styles as were the people of Europe, particularly of France. Although many designers were producing exceptional objects and interiors in the United States, the vast majority of their American counterparts still were grounded in traditionalist concepts. In addition, the rapport that was developing between French designers and manufacturers barely existed in the United States.

As Arthur Pulos has noted, "American manufacturers of decorative periods . . . remained particularly insensitive to the growing influence of modernism. They were preoccupied with their adaptations of traditional styles, and unwilling to be diverted by threats of a new style—at least until it had become popular enough to make copying profitable."[41]

The Secretary of Commerce at the time, Herbert Hoover, consulted with other state officials and declined the French invitation to participate in the Exposition. Hoover and his advisors felt that the United States could not submit objects that would adhere to the guidelines that had been set up. That is, they did not feel "that we could contribute sufficiently varied design of unique character or of special expression in American artistry to warrant such a participation."[42] The decision outraged many of America's former allies, and to appease them, Hoover appointed a select committee to visit the exposition in order to advise how these new design innovations might affect comparable industries and trades in this country.

The Exposition had a remarkable unity of feeling, most likely because the organizers stipulated that the displays had to be innovative and new in design and quality without any references to historicism or the past. With that in mind, most countries created pavilions in the modern style, although with varying degrees of success. Laid out on a major axis from the Grand Palais to the Place des Invalides, and perpendicular to that axis along the banks of the Seine, the site was composed of almost 100 special pavilions showing the most current styles in both the decorative and industrial arts.

Because the most prominent locations were assigned to French designers and architects, their work dominated, a result that was both intentional and well-deserved. Looking at photographs in one of the catalogues of the Exposition, it is evident that the foreign pavilions, although somewhat innovative, still owed a great debt to their respective historic traditions. A few of them, such as the Russian pavilion, were truly extraordinary architectural designs. In contrast, the French buildings were remarkable for their brilliant use of new materials, their landscaping, and their total disregard for the designs of the past. In fact, in an article in the *Art Bulletin* of September 1925, Roger Gilman entitled his review "The Paris Exposition: A Glimpse into the Future." According to Gilman, "Modern construction and methods of erection tend to straight lines and flat surfaces, to be left in the plaster or finished with some sort of facing. From this come the rectangular shapes of walls, with recesses or projections to give solidity and movements . . . . The designers have logically discarded all cornice mouldings, as seeming to be part of the construction while purely an addition to it. The desire to avoid every hallmark of a worn tradition is apparent."[43] Gilman concluded with an appreciation of the forward look of the Exposition while noting America's absence, and challenged American designers to overcome "our conservatism in the arts" in order to create "our own version of the style."[44]

The 1925 Exposition became a compendium of outstanding French designers and their works. This is particularly evident in the special pavilion designed as a French embassy by the Société des Artistes Décorateurs. Here twenty-five rooms were furnished by such designers as Pierre Chareau, André Groult, Jean Dunand, Maurice Dufrêne, Rose Adler, Jean Puiforcat, Gérard Sandoz, Dominique, and many others.

Another outstanding design was the *Hôtel d'un Riche Collectionneur* built by architect Pierre Patout for designer Emile-Jacques Ruhlmann (fig. 19). In this small, lovely building, Ruhlmann completely furnished a grand salon, dining room, bedroom, bath, boudoir, and office for an imaginary, wealthy collector. Sparing no expense and using the most elaborate and exotic woods and materials, Ruhlmann created a tour de force of the ultimate in Art Deco taste and design.

Perhaps one reason for the outstanding success and sense of unity of the French pavilions and their contents was the establishment of a new category of exhibition specifically for the 1925 Exposition. "The general

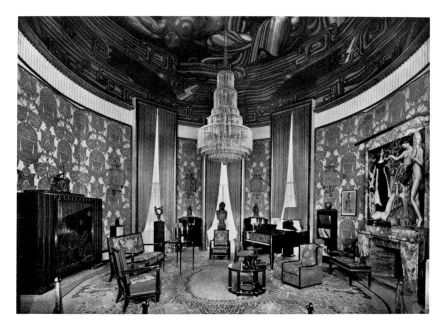

19. The Grand Salon of l'Hôtel d'un Riche Collectionneur, designed by Emile-Jacques Ruhlmann for the 1925 Paris Exposition. Ruhlmann, the *ensemblier*, enlisted the talents of numerous designers to create this pavilion. Among them were Jean Dunand, Jean Lambert-Rucki, and Jean Dupas. (Photograph courtesy of Patricia Bayer.)

classification of the Exposition of 1925 requires a class unknown in previous expositions: that of *ensembles de mobilier* . . . [which] reflect the spirit of today . . . ."[45]

With this new classification of exhibitor, the leading French designers could inspire other designers to create complete rooms, as various designers had already been doing in the French department stores. Thus a room by Domin and Genevrière (Dominique) might include objects

41. Arthur J. Pulos. *American Design Ethic* (Cambridge, Massachusetts: The M.I.T. Press, 1984), p. 300.

42. Pulos, *American Design Ethic*, p. 304.

43. Roger Gilman, "The Paris Exposition: A Glimpse into the Future," *The Art Bulletin* 8 (September 1925): 34.

44. Gilman, "Paris Exposition," p. 42.

45. *Encyclopédie des arts décoratifs et industriels modernes au XXème siècle* 4 (Paris: Impr. nationale, Office central d'éditions et de librairie, 1925): 9-10.

designed by Charles Hairon, Hélène Lantier, Mannati, Gaveau, Lalique, Buthaud, Pilorget, Lunot, and Buscaylet and Robin. The result would be a beautifully and comfortably furnished room allowing the viewers and future customers to envision these furnishings and accessories in their own homes and offices.

As Helen Appleton Read observed of the new designers, "The *ensemblier* is not the interior decorator, but an artist or designer who designs a room or an interior with material that he commands or else designs the textiles or furniture to suit his scheme. 'The Apartment of an Ambassador,' a problem given to the Artists Decorators of France, and shown under the patronage of the Ministir [sic] des Beaux Arts is an example of the art of the *ensemblier*. This apartment represents the best selected examples of the modern movement . . . ."[46]

Perhaps to make up for America's non-participation in the Exposition, and to allow Americans to see the new work emerging from Europe, New York's Metropolitan Museum of Art installed an exhibition of new designs from Paris in 1926. The following year, a similar exhibition, *Art In Trade*, was organized at Macy's department store. The Metropolitan continued its support of the new style: a special exhibition of American design, *The Architect and the Industrial Arts*, was shown in 1929.

XVIII. Design and the Great Depression

In October 1929, the failure of the American stock market signaled the beginning of the Great Depression. This economic catastrophe affected many patrons of the new style who had amassed paper riches but could now no longer afford to support their exorbitant tastes. Yet some historians propose that this economic cataclysm may have even advanced design in the United States. Arthur Pulos, again in *American Design Ethic*, writes: "As

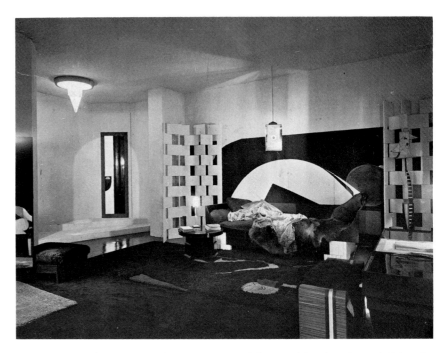

20. Eileen Gray's "bedroom-boudoir for Monte Carlo" was exhibited at the 14th Salon des Artistes Décorateurs, Paris, in 1923, prior to her membership in the Union des Artistes Modernes. The installation included the standing lamp at the far right, now in the Lewis Collection (cat. no. 65). (Photograph courtesy of the Lewis Archives.)

the United States plunged into the Depression, it became evident that the public could be stimulated to spend its hoarded and often limited money on a manufactured product only if it took on an entirely new appearance—one that was more than a simple shift in style and that promised better times ahead for those who had faith in America and American industry. This state of mind gave product design a sense of responsibility that helped to establish industrial design."[47]

In spite of the Depression, the 1930s witnessed more exhibitions of the decorative arts and design. The decade saw the demise of certain collective interior design firms, as well as the rise of new organizations, such as the Union des Artistes Modernes in Paris. This group—which included the Irish-born designer Eileen Gray—was formed in protest against the Salon des Artistes Décorateurs, which excluded certain forms of decoration in their displays. The new Union des Artistes Modernes, true to its name, looked forward to the concept of modernism (see fig. 20 and cat. no. 65).

Two important expositions were held in the United States during the 1930s: the Century of Progress in Chicago, celebrating the technological changes that had occurred in the 100 years since the Columbian Exposition in that same city, and the New York World's Fair of 1939. Although of considerable nostalgic interest to us today, both of these fairs were mere reflections of the great Paris Exposition of 1925. Originality was sparse, and the "The World of Tomorrow," the theme of the 1939 World's Fair, became merely a prelude to world disaster.

At the end of the 1930s, the enchantment of exotic and faraway places was replaced by the horrors of another devastating war that was tearing Europe apart. A world that had prided itself on good taste and fashion now found itself enmeshed in the machinery of war and destruction. The elegant and fashionable world of the twenties and thirties was lost forever, to be replaced by a technological sophistication that only a highly industrialized society can achieve.

46. Helen Appleton Read, "The Exposition in Paris: Part II," *International Studio* 82 (December 1925): 163.

47. Pulos, *American Design Ethic*, p. 333.

CATALOGUE

The 100 objects featured in this section are selections from the Lewis Decorative Arts Collection. They are listed chronologically by date of object. A checklist of the entire collection follows this section. All measurements are in centimeters and in inches; height precedes width.

Paul Ranson
French, 1864-1909
and
France Ranson
French, dates unknown

1   Folding Screen, ca. 1892

Mahogany, silk embroidery, dyed stencil designs
154.3 × 207 × 6.1 (60¾ × 81½ × 2⅜)
Unsigned
Virginia Museum of Fine Arts, Gift of Sydney and Frances Lewis,
85.92

Paul Ranson was a member of the group of painters known as the Nabis, which also included Maurice Denis, Paul Sérusier, Pierre Bonnard, H.-B. Ibels, René Piot, K.-X. Roussel, and Edouard Vuillard. Their theories were based on principles they formulated after studying Paul Gauguin's paintings from Pont-Aven.[1] The Nabis, a name derived from the Hebrew word for prophet, felt that their art should be a unique visual translation of a particular scene or event from nature, based on the artist's response to it. They felt strongly that art should be a form of communication.

Of all the Nabis, perhaps Ranson was most closely aligned with the Art Nouveau style, although many examples of the work of Bonnard and Denis show similarities to the typical sensuous line of Art Nouveau. Ranson was born in Limoges in 1864 and studied at the Académie Julian. His studio became a favorite meeting-place for the Nabis, where they were welcomed by Ranson and France, his wife and collaborator. Ranson founded the Académie Ranson in 1908 but died the following year. His wife continued the Académie with the help of their fellow artists.

This screen was probably made after 1892 as there is a preparatory design in distemper of that date in a private collection in Paris. There is also a pounced drawing at the Petit Palais de Genève.

As with certain other projects, Ranson designed the screen's central panel as cartoons on paper, which were then executed in embroidery by his wife. This design, typical of Ranson's work, features two female figures, a cat, and what appears to be a swan, all intertwined with various sensuous arabesque motifs in silk embroidery dyed through stencils in beige and light maroon. The two side panels are in beige silk with light maroon stripes, and all three panels are enclosed in a mahogany frame that has a stylized leaf motif in a frieze at the bottom of each panel.

There is a close relationship between the elements in this frieze and the designs of Dr. Christopher Dresser. In 1862, Dresser published his *Art of Decorative Design*, in which he delineated, in plate XXVI, a series of stylized plant forms to illustrate his chapter on "Principles Common to Ornament." Although not exactly the same as those used by Ranson almost thirty years later, these patterns bear a strong relationship to the later designs and could likely have served as prototypes.

PROVENANCE: France Ranson; Drouot-Rive Gauche, Paris, 1976.

PUBLISHED: "20th Century Works of Art Now on the Market," *Burlington Magazine* (April 1972), plate IV.

1. For a history and study of this group see Charles Chassé, *The Nabis and Their Period*, translated by Michael Bullock (New York: Frederick A. Praeger, 1969).

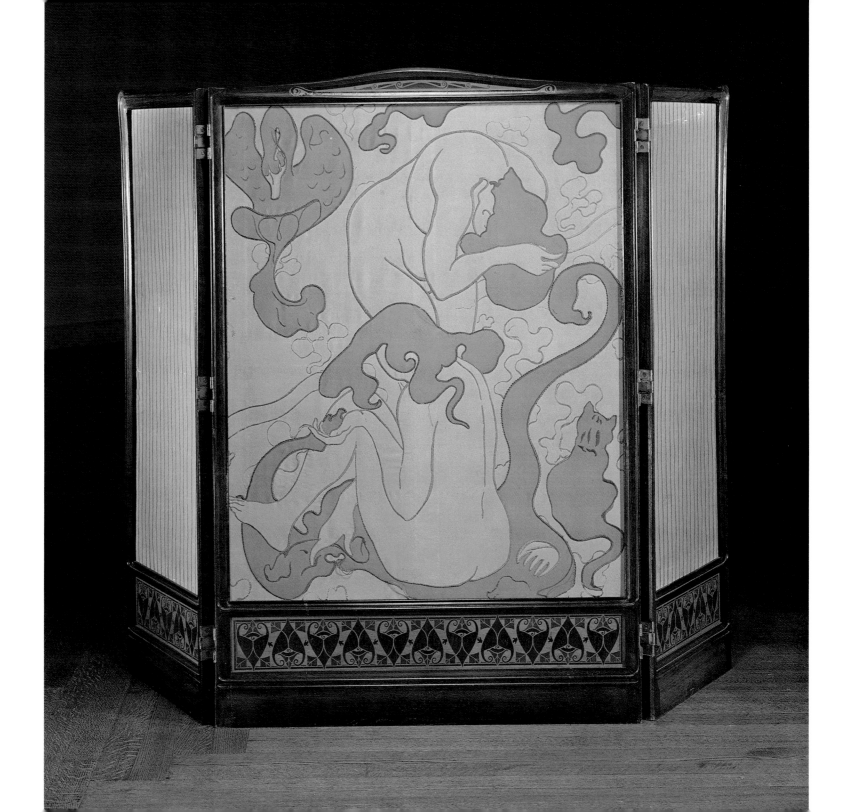

Charles Francis Annesley Voysey
English, 1857-1941

2 Mantel Clock, 1896

Painted wood, brass
50 × 27 × 17.8 (19¹¹/₁₆ × 10⅝ × 70)
Unsigned
Virginia Museum of Fine Arts, Gift of Sydney and Frances Lewis, 85.217

It is typical of the English Arts and Crafts Movement to include sayings as part of the decorative motif on furniture and other objects. Thus, "time & tide wait for no man" appears on the ribbon painted across the lower face of this wooden clock designed by C. F. A. Voysey.

Voysey, born at Hessle, England, studied at Dulwich College and with private master teachers. After being associated with J. P. Seddon, the Gothic-Revival designer and architect, he set up his own shop in 1881. He designed a wide range of materials during his long and fruitful career.

As with many of his contemporaries, Voysey designed not only buildings but also many of the furnishings for them. He designed this particular clock for his own house, "The Orchard" at Chorleywood, which was under construction in 1895.

A signed pencil drawing (78 by 55.5 cm., dated January 1895) in the collection of the Royal Institute of British Architects in London shows elevations, half-plan, and full-size details of the clock. The title is given as "Design for a Clockcase to be made in wood and painted in oil colour full size." The actual clock differs slightly from the watercolor in that the upper side panels, which are banded in solid color in the clock, were drawn with a floral vine motif. There are a few other insignificant changes.

The body of the clock, which was painted in bright colors by Voysey himself, features a landscape with three stylized trees before a floral field, on the bank of a river or lake with two sailboats. A banner unfurls across the trees with the previously noted motto. In place of numerals on the face there are stylized letters forming the Latin words *Tempus Fugit* (time flies). The clock is topped by a gilt finial, while a frieze of stylized birds dominates the uppermost band of the front of the clock. These are directly related to a wallpaper design called "Fairyland" that Voysey executed for Essex & Company. This bird motif appears in other instances and, interestingly

enough, it is very closely related to the design of the front of a cabinet designed by Joseph Maria Olbrich around 1899, which he called *Herbst* (Fall).[2]

The mechanism of the clock was made by a London clockmaker and an inscription appears in pencil on the inside of the back door, which reads "Mary, Countess of Loveless [illegible], Park."

This same clock design was also later created in aluminum by W.H. Tingey. The unpainted metal case was exhibited in *The Arts and Crafts Exhibition* in 1903.[3] In an 1896 issue of *The Studio*, in an article entitled "Some "Some Recent Designs by Mr. Voysey," the Lewis clock appears with a rather strange stuffed bird perched upon it. It also appears in an 1897 display of furniture and other objects by Voysey, and can be seen quite prominently in an 1899 photograph of the interior of the architect's house.[4]

PROVENANCE: Collection of the artist; Mary, Countess of Lovelace; John Jesse, London, 1976.

PUBLISHED: E.B.S., "Some Recent Designs by Mr. Voysey," *The Studio* (May 14, 1896), p. 216. Isabelle Anscombe and Charlotte Gere, *Arts and Crafts in Britain and America* (New York: Rizzoli International Publications, Inc., 1978), p. 132, plate 164. John Brandon-Jones and others, *C.F.A. Voysey: Architect and Designer 1857-1941* (London: Lund Humphries Publishers Ltd., 1978), p. C 6. Philippe Garner, *Twentieth Century Furniture* (New York: Van Nostrand Reinhold, 1980), illus. p. 55. Virginia Museum of Fine Arts, *La Bella Mano: Pre-Raphaelite Paintings and Decorative Arts* (Richmond: Virginia Museum of Fine Arts, 1982), cat. no. 103, illus. p. 24.

EXHIBITED: *La Bella Mano: Pre-Raphaelite Paintings and Decorative Arts*, Virginia Museum of Fine Arts, Richmond, September 14-October 24, 1982, cat.no. 103, illus. p. 24.

2. For an illustration of this cabinet, see sales catalogue of *The Modern Movement*, Christie, Manson & Woods Ltd., London, April 17, 1984, no. 525, illustrated p. 137.
3. John Brandon-Jones and others, *C.F.A. Voysey: Architect and Designer 1857-1941* (London: Lund Humphries, Ltd., 1978), p. 75. The drawing for this clock is also illustrated in this catalogue on p. 84 as entry C 31.
4. For illustrations of these two photographs see Mario Amaya, *Art Nouveau* (London: Studio Vista Limited, 1966), pp. 45 and 46.

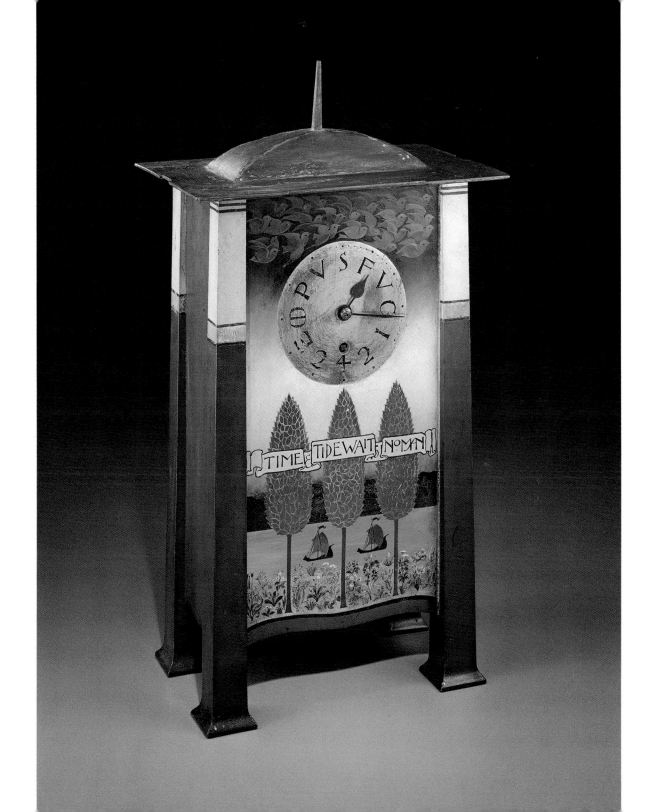

François-Raoul Larche
French, 1860-1912

3
Lamp, Loïe Fuller, ca. 1896

Gilt bronze
44.5 × 16.5 × 13.4 (17½ × 6½ × 5¼)
Signed in cast, proper right side: *RAOUL LARCHE*; numbered
proper left, rear: K474; impressed circular foundry stamp lower
edge, rear: S*iot-Decauville*
Virginia Museum of Fine Arts Purchase, The Sydney and Frances
Lewis Art Nouveau Fund, 79.72

Larche was born in St.-André-de-Cubzac, France. At the age of eighteen he went to Paris, where he studied at the Ecole des Beaux-Arts and later with Jean Alexandre Falguière, François Joffroy, and Eugène Delaplanche. His work encompassed a wide variety of subjects and media, including terra cotta, seashells, pewter, and bronze. He was awarded a gold medal for sculpture at the Paris Exposition Universelle in 1900.

Larche is today perhaps better known, and probably unfairly so, for the subjects he chose rather than for the sculpture itself. There are at least four variations of this figural lamp of Loïe Fuller, all cast in the late nineteenth century by the firm of Siot-Decauville. Two of these four lamps, the one illustrated here and another sold at auction at Christie's, New York, in 1979, are almost mirror images. In these two, as well as in a third, the dancer is depicted in a long vertical format supported by diaphanous veils that swirl up around her body, flow out through her hair, and travel over her head like a plume of smoke. In the fourth and most familiar image, she holds her arms outstretched as her veils whirl up around her body, suspended above her head to form a canopy in which a small, unobtrusive light bulb is hidden.

The sculptor has successfully combined several elements in this piece. Most notable are the swirling movement and excitement of Loïe Fuller's dance that also suggest the bustling ambiance of Paris, and the busy array of pavilions at the 1900 Paris Exposition. Also apparent is the sensuous undulation of her draperies, typical of the Art Nouveau line. She has become the ubiquitous fin-de-siècle femme fatale. Finally, Larche also ingeniously included the new scientific wonder of the late nineteenth century—electricity.

Larche was not the only artist to be enchanted by the vision of Loïe Fuller. She was the subject of countless posters by such noted lithographers as Jules Cheret and Henri de Toulouse-Lautrec; ceramics and bronzes by François Rupert Carabin; glass by François-Emile Décorchemont, Pierre Roche and Albert-Louis Dammouse, and Almaric-V. Walter; and innumerable bronzes by Louis Chalon, Théodore Louis-Auguste Rivière, and Pierre Roche.

PROVENANCE: Walter S. Bromley, Milford, Delaware, 1979.
PUBLISHED: Patricia Bayer, "Art Nouveau," *Antiques World* (October 1981), illus. p. 24.

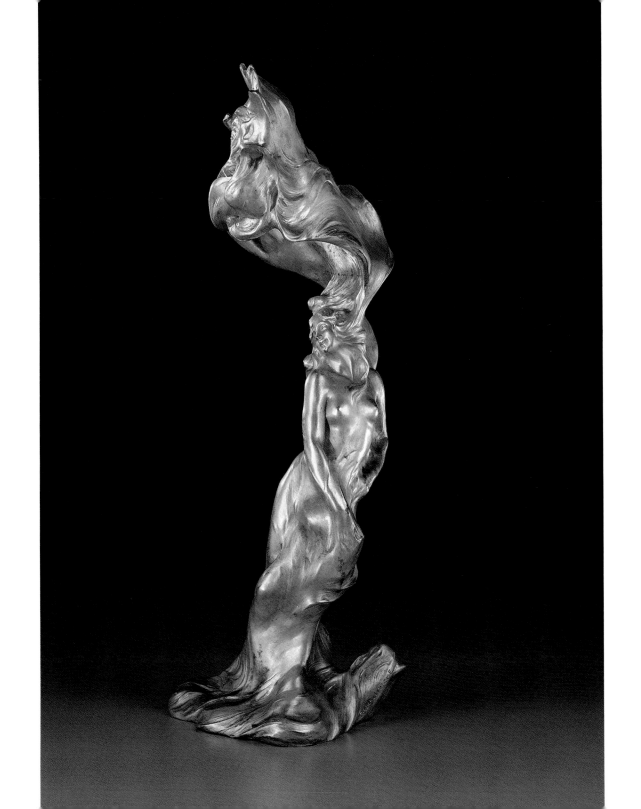

Henry van de Velde
Belgian, 1863-1957

4 Side Chair, designed ca. 1895, executed 1896-98

Padouk wood, rush
94 × 44.1 × 41.7 (37 × 17⅜ × 16)
ZOLL 1-10 printed in circle; painted inscription: *Brooklyn* TL1
980.102.151and 111.60 59 SC77; remnants of a paper
label printed *LE GARLE MEUBLE PUBLIC 18 RUE ST.
AUGUSTINE* 937
Virginia Museum of Fine Arts, Gift of Sydney and Frances Lewis,
85.82

In 1895 van de Velde designed and built his first major architectural work, his own house, "Bloemenwerf," in Uccle near Brussels. In addition, he designed all of the interior furnishings including this chair, which was part of a set for his dining room.

Although van de Velde is considered one of the great theoreticians of the modern style, this particular chair owes a greater debt to the earlier Arts and Crafts Movement in England and to the traditional art of his native Belgium.

The chair and other furnishings were probably designed about the same time as the house, that is, 1895, but are thought to have been executed in 1896-98. There is much in common between the concept of an architect designing the complete interior furnishings of the house and the aesthetic principles of Arts and Crafts proponent William Morris. It is apparent in much of van de Velde's work that he was very sympathetic to the writings of both Morris and John Ruskin. At times he carried this principle of unity to an extreme, such as designing his wife's dresses so that she, too, would be coordinated with his interiors.

In their book on Art Nouveau, authors Peter Selz and Mildred Constantine note van de Velde's innovative approach to design:

> The interiors created for Bloemenwerf are his first interiors which indicate the New Style. The chairs, for instance, are a characteristic example of the furnishings. Made entirely from individual staves with rush seats, their somewhat harsh form goes back to peasant prototypes; each line and joint exist because of structural necessity. These skeletal shapes already possess the characteristic springiness and energy of his later designs. In this chair the eye perceives the surrounding space of the complementary form, fusing the solid members and voids into a complex entity. The furniture is undecorated; its ornamental quality is inherent in the movement of the lines.[5]

Indeed the fairly straightforward, traditional lines of the chair's staves, with the slight curve of their opposing members, give only a hint of the dynamic swirling line that van de Velde would develop later.

It is interesting to note that it was van de Velde who designed the Belgian pavilion for the 1939 New York World's Fair. This building was later moved to Richmond, Virginia, as a gift from Belgium to Virginia Union University.

PROVENANCE: Richard Engelmann Residence; Weimar Kunstgewerbemuseum, Zurich, Acq. 1958; Museum of Modern Art, New York, 1960; Christie, Manson & Woods International Inc., New York, 1983.

PUBLISHED: Sigfried Giedion, *Space, Time and Architecture* (Cambridge: Harvard University Press; London: H. Milford, Oxford University Press, 1941), p. 292. Nikolaus Pevsner, *Pioneers of Modern Design* (New York: The Museum of Modern Art, 1949), p. 62. Stephan Tschudi Madsen, *Sources of Art Nouveau* (Oslo: H. Aschehoug, 1956), illus. p. 326. Peter Selz and Mildred Constantine, eds., *Art Nouveau* (New York: The Museum of Modern Art, 1960), illus. p. 94. Robert Schmutzler, *Art Nouveau* (New York: Harry N. Abrams, 1962), p. 141. Henry Clement van de Velde, *Geschichtes meines Lebens* (Munich: R. Piper Verlag, 1962), illus. p. 37. Abraham Marie Hammacher, *Le Monde de Henry van de Velde* (Paris: Anvers, 1967), p. 80, illus. 175. *Pionniers du XXème Siècle* (Paris: Musée des Arts Décoratifs, 1971), illus. p. 109. Franco Borsi, *Bruxelles 1900* (Bruxelles: Marc Vokaer, Editeur, 1974), illus p. 144. Erika Gysling-Billeter, *Objekte des Jugendstils* (Bern: Benteli, 1975), illus. pp. 144-5 *Important 20th Century Decorative Arts*, catalogue of sale (New York: Christie, Manson & Woods International Inc., December 16, 1983), no. 331, illus. p. 154. Derek E. Ostergard, *Mackintosh to Mollino: Fifty Years of Chair Design* (New York: Barry Friedman Ltd., 1984), cat. no. 1.

EXHIBITED: *Mackintosh to Mollino: Fifty Years of Chair Design*, Barry Friedman Ltd., New York, November 13, 1984–February 13, 1985.

5. Peter Selz and Mildred Constantine, eds., *Art Nouveau: Art and Design at the Turn of the Century* (New York: The Museum of Modern Art, 1959), p. 95.

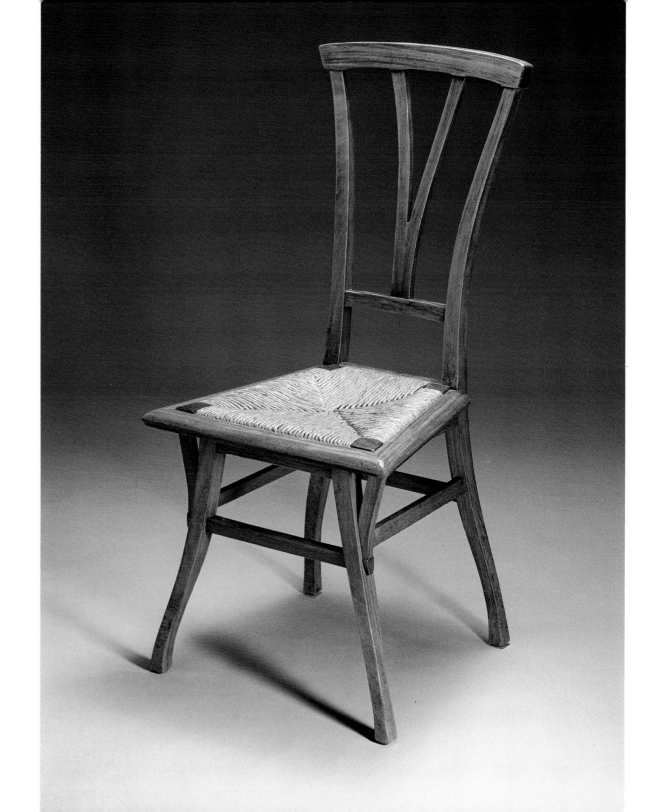

Philippe Wolfers
Belgian, 1858-1929
for the firm of
Emile Müller
French (Ivry, established 1854)

5 *Orchidées* Cachepot, ca. 1900

Stoneware
36.8 × 48.2 × 47 (14½ × 19 × 18½)
Signed on bottom: *Wolfers*; possible beginning of second
signature marred by restoration
Virginia Museum of Fine Arts Purchase, The Sydney and Frances
Lewis Art Nouveau Fund, 81.27

Philippe Wolfers was born in Brussels, where members of his family had established themselves as jewelers. He was apprenticed in his father's studio, where he first created jewelry designs based on traditional forms, later giving way to Far Eastern influences. Throughout the remainder of his long career, however, the majority of his work was based on themes from nature. By 1890, Wolfers was producing sculpture as well as jewelry.

This sculptured vessel, called *Orchidées*, represents the successful collaboration between two important artists of this period: Wolfers and the firm of ceramist Emile Müller, established in Ivry, near Paris, in 1854. Although Müller died in 1889, the factory continued under his name, and around 1897 Wolfers collaborated with the firm on this monumental flowerpot holder. In fact, Wolfers designed an entire series of large bronze cachepots which served as models for a group of ceramics produced by

Müller, whose rich, deep glazes were the perfect complement to Wolfers's deeply sculpted and modeled forms.

Wolfers's jewelry, which he produced until 1904, and his early sculpture, are related to Symbolism, which drew its inspiration from sensations and emotions, often depicting literary or religious themes in complex detail. The whole is characterized by a sense of decadence. Symbolist painters relied on the sensuous line associated with Art Nouveau. Wolfers's later sculpture, however, tended to be more classic in both theme and style. An example of this was the sculptural installation entitled *Gioconda* that he created for the Belgian pavilion in the 1925 Paris Exposition.

PROVENANCE: Galerie Félix Marcilhac, Paris, 1981.
PUBLISHED: Patricia Bayer, "Art Nouveau," *Antiques World* (October 1981), illus. p. 27.

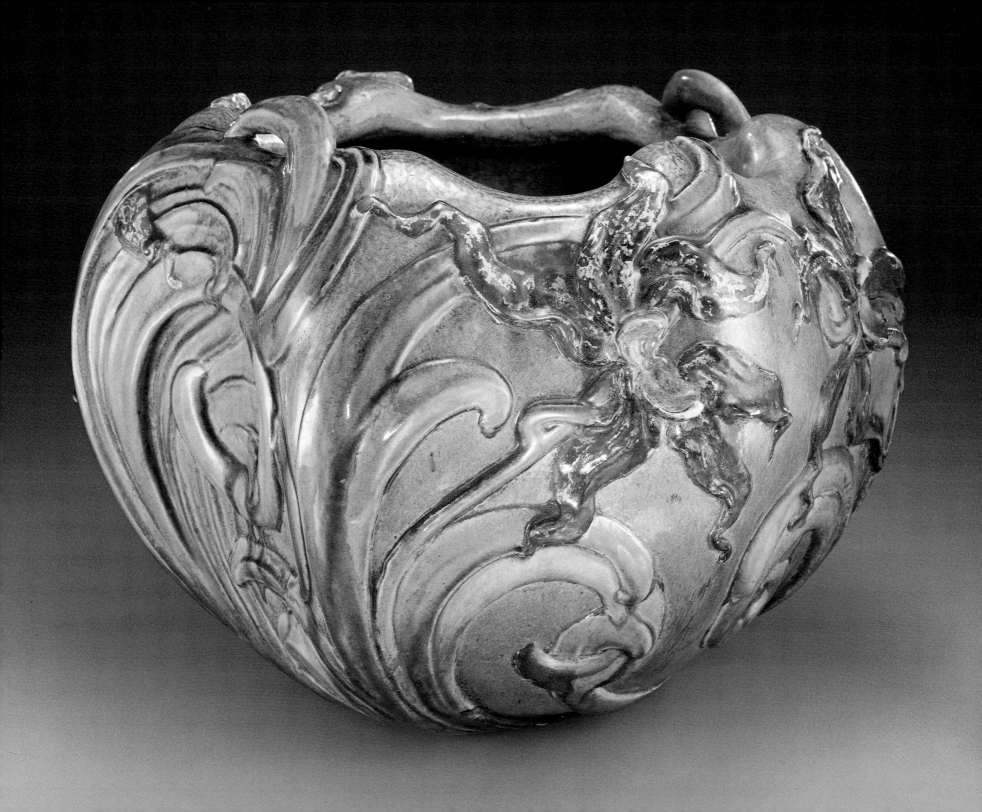

Designed by Alf Wallander
Swedish, 1862-1914
for
Rörstrand
Swedish (Stockholm) established 1726

6 Soup Tureen, ca. 1897

Porcelain 20.3 × 36.8 × 21.6 (8 × 14½ × 8½)
Signed: *Rörstrand* and three crowns on bottom
Virginia Museum of Fine Arts, Gift of Sydney and Frances Lewis,
85.56a/b

By the time Alf Wallander—a designer of metalwork, glass, lamps, tapestries, and ceramics—became art director for Rörstrand in 1895, the firm had already existed for more than 150 years. Some of its finest work had been produced in the mid to late eighteenth century in the Rococo style. Wallander, undoubtedly aware of stylistic developments in other parts of Europe, introduced the Art Nouveau line to Rörstrand wares in the late nineteenth century. Not surprisingly, his designs were prominently featured in the Swedish pavilion at the 1900 Paris Exposition.

It is interesting to compare the soft underglaze colors and more subtle forms of this porcelain piece to the brilliant colors and sharply modeled forms of the ceramics by Müller and Wolfers (see cat. no. 5).

In 1909 in the catalogue *Kunstindustriutstallningen*, C.P. Laurin stated "There were a few dinnerware sets presented at the Stockholm exposition of 1897, and the most remarkable amongst them was Wallander's large feldspar porcelain set with iris motifs in underglaze and relief."[6]

Perhaps Wallander's major contribution to Sweden's porcelain industry was to take the traditional ceramic techniques already well developed there and to combine them with the delicate modeling and colors of the Art Nouveau style, evident in his work by the use of native plant and animal life rendered in soft pastel underglazes.

The Rörstrand firm still exists today, although the designs now follow more contemporary lines.

PROVENANCE: Christie, Manson & Woods International, Inc., New York, 1979.

PUBLISHED: Em. Sedeyn, "La Céramique de Table," *L'Art Décoratif* 3 (April 1901), pp. 7-17, illus. p. 14. C.G. Laurin, *Konstindustriutstallningen* (Stockholm: P.A. Norstedt Sonner, 1909), p. 464. Elizabeth Hidemark, *Svensk Jugend* (Stockholm, 1964), illus. p. 109. *Important Art Nouveau & Art Déco*, catalogue of sale (New York: Christie, Manson and Woods International Inc., May 24, 1979), No. 290, illus. p. 114.

EXHIBITED: Stockholm, 1897.

6. C. G. Laurin, *Konstindustriaustallningen* (Stockholm: P. Norsted & Sonnen, 1909), p. 464.

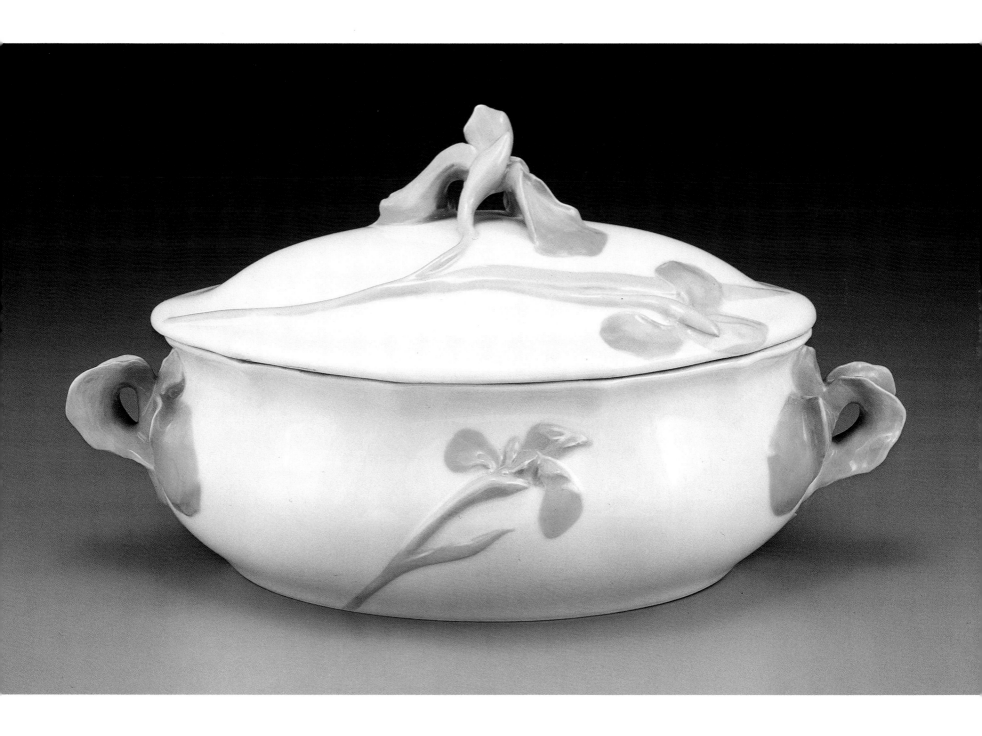

René Lalique
French, 1860-1945

7 Brooch/Pendant, ca. 1897-98

Enameled 18-carat gold, plique-à-jour enamel, glass, baroque
pearl
7.93 × 4.76 × 1.11 (3⅛ × 1⅞ × ⁷⁄₁₆)
Gold mount stamped *LALIQUE* on upper right reverse
Virginia Museum of Fine Arts, Gift of Sydney and Frances Lewis,
85.246

This magnificent brooch reflects Lalique's outstanding skill. The flower motif is an example of his lifelong interest in and dedication to natural forms, using both the human figure and, as in this case, floral forms. The brooch also displays the outstanding craftsmanship and detail that, along with the use of the rarest and most exotic materials, characterizes his work of this period. Lalique's flowers—of glass and *plique-à-jour* enamel—are exquisite miniature sculptures that almost surpass their use as jewelry. Lalique was the first jeweler to use nonprecious materials, including horn and, in this case, glass.

As Irene Sargent so poetically stated in her review in *The Craftsman* in 1903,

These articles of feminine adornment strike a note never before sounded or even attempted in what has been, until now, one of the minor arts. They do away with the last trace of suspicion, that it is a barbarous instinct which prompts the wearing of jewels and ornaments. It is not exaggeration to say that each of these little creations is a hymn in praise of Nature, composed by one who is capable of feeling the great and of rendering the small.[7]

That same year, in a review of the spring Salon of the Society of French Artists for *Art et Décoration*, a M. Verneuil singled out Lalique's work as the most important in the exhibition and refers to Lalique as "the acknowledged equal of any living French artist, painter or sculptor, and he is further adjudged to be the greatest silversmith in all history."[8]

PROVENANCE: Christie, Manson & Woods International, Inc., New York, 1979.

PUBLISHED: *Important Art Nouveau and Art Déco*, catalogue of sale (New York: Christie, Manson & Woods International, Inc., October 26, 1979), no. 508, illus. in color, p. 147.

7. Irene Sargent, "A Minor French Salon," *The Craftsman* (April-September 1903): 454.
8. As quoted in the review by Sargent, "A Minor French Salon," p. 452.

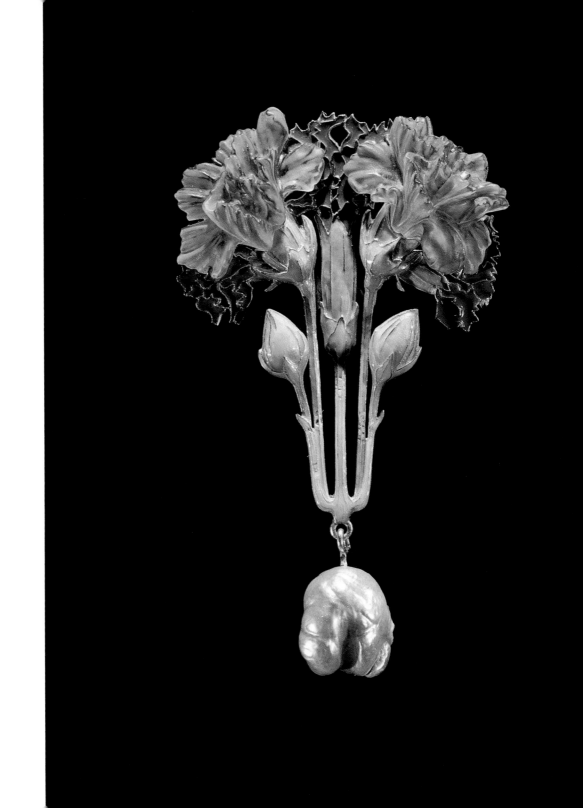

François Rupert Carabin
French, 1862-1932

8   Wash Stand, 1897-98

Walnut, stoneware, pewter
178.4 × 88.6 × 32.4 (70¼ × 34⅞ × 12¾)
Signed: on lower right side of water reservoir R *Carabin* 10
Virginia Museum of Fine Arts, Gift of Sydney and Frances Lewis,
85.94

François Rupert Carabin created perhaps the most eccentric, unusual, erotic, and interesting sculptural works of his day. Born in Saverne, Alsace, France, in 1862, Carabin moved with his family to Paris where, in 1873, he was apprenticed to an engraver of precious stones. In later years, he studied anatomy (by attending surgical operations at the Faculté de Médicine) and learned woodcarving from a furniture maker. He opened his own studio in 1889.

Throughout his lifetime Carabin worked in a variety of media, including clay, wax, bronze, precious metals, wood, and ceramics. In the vast majority of the functional and sculptural objects he created, the nude female figure predominates and is often accompanied by exotic creatures of the sea and of the earth.

For example, an early bookcase of 1890 is ostensibly a piece of furniture but its function has been nearly superseded by its carved decoration: female nudes, some perched on carved books on the top of the bookcase, others serving as the supporting elements at the feet.

A Carabin table created in the same year uses nude female figures as caryatids supporting a huge book that becomes the actual table. In other Carabin pieces, female figures support chairs, form the bases of cabinets, or comprise the legs of vitrines. In 1900-01 he even carved the case for a piano in which the side elements contain female figures and a frieze of women's portraits embellishes the upper front.

Except for the carved and molded figures on his earlier furniture, most of Carabin's sculpture is usually small in scale. Among his smaller works is a series of bronze sculptures of the 1890s depicting the American dancer Loïe Fuller. Each piece captures the rhythm of her dance in an individual pose, almost like a series of still images from a motion-picture sequence. Carabin also did two ceramic sculptures of Fuller.

This wall-hung washstand is typical of Carabin's large figural work of the late nineteenth century. At least one identical piece is known. The stoneware female figure is actually a water container, while the pond and lily pad below serve as the catch-basin and soap dishes. A towel bar in wood on the upper right completes the ensemble.

Carabin, perhaps more than any artist of the period, combines the agitated line of the Art Nouveau movement with the decadent motifs of the Symbolists.

PROVENANCE: Messrs Laurin, Guilloux, Buffetaud, Paris, 1976.

PUBLISHED: Gustav Coquiot, "Rupert Carabin," *Biographies Alsaciennes*, illus. p. 143. *Catalogue de la Société Nationale des Beaux-Arts*, Paris, 1898. *Catalogue de l'exposition Carabin*, (Paris: Musée Galliera, 1934). E Molinier, "Les Arts du Feu," *Art et Décoration* (1899), p. 137. Paul Gsel, "Rupert Carabin," *La Contemporaine* (January 1902), p. 371. *L'Oeuvre de Rupert Carabin 1862-1932*, catalogue of exhibition (Paris: Galerie de Luxembourg, 1974), no. 191, illus. p. 233. Félix Marcilhac, "Meubles 1900," *Antiquitiés, Beaux-Arts, Curiosités* (September 1977), p. 55.

EXHIBITED: Société des Beaux-Arts, Paris, 1898; Exposition, Vienna, 1898; Musée Galliera, Paris, 1934-35.

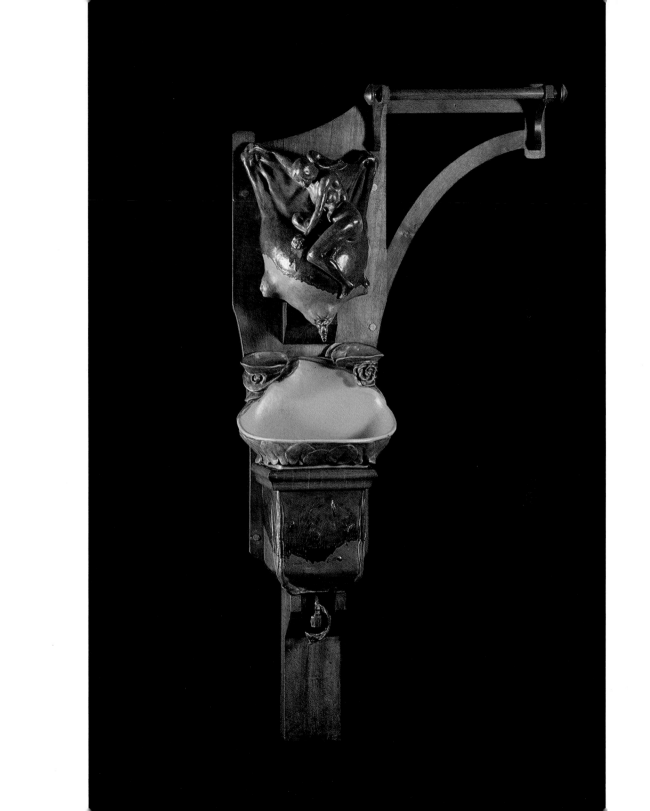

René Lalique
French, 1860-1945
and
Lamarre
French, dates unknown
and
Charles Louchet
French, dates unknown

9   Vase, 1898

Ceramic, gilt bronze, enamel
57.1 × 26.6 × 21 (22½ × 10½ × 8½)
Signed on bottom: *Lamarre, 1898/Lt Fres*; on rim of base: *Louchet*
Virginia Museum of Fine Arts, Gift of Sydney and Frances Lewis,
85.49

This baluster-shaped vessel covered with blue, brown, and green glazes is an exceptional example of the collaboration of three artists. The vase was made by the ceramist Lamarre in 1898 for the Paris Exposition, where it was awarded a first prize. Unfortunately, nothing else is known about this particular artist.

The gilt-bronze mounts, by the French sculptor Charles Louchet, depict a fantasy creature, a voluptuous female nude with dragonfly wings. It is difficult to tell whether she is being transformed into a dragonfly or whether she is simply a female figure who has some of the exotic forms of the dragonfly. She stands on a lily pad that grows from a cluster of lily pads, complete with frog, that form the bronze-doré foot. The figure's *plique-à-jour* wings are said to be the work of René Lalique (see cat. nos. 7 and 38).

PROVENANCE: Sotheby Parke Bernet, New York, 1972.

PUBLISHED: *Tiffany and Art Nouveau*, catalogue of sale (New York: Sotheby Parke Bernet Inc., November 9, 1972), no. 155, p. 23. Laurence Buffet-Challié, *The Modern Style* (New York: Rizzoli International Publications Inc., 1982), p. 147.

EXHIBITED: Paris Exposition, 1898.

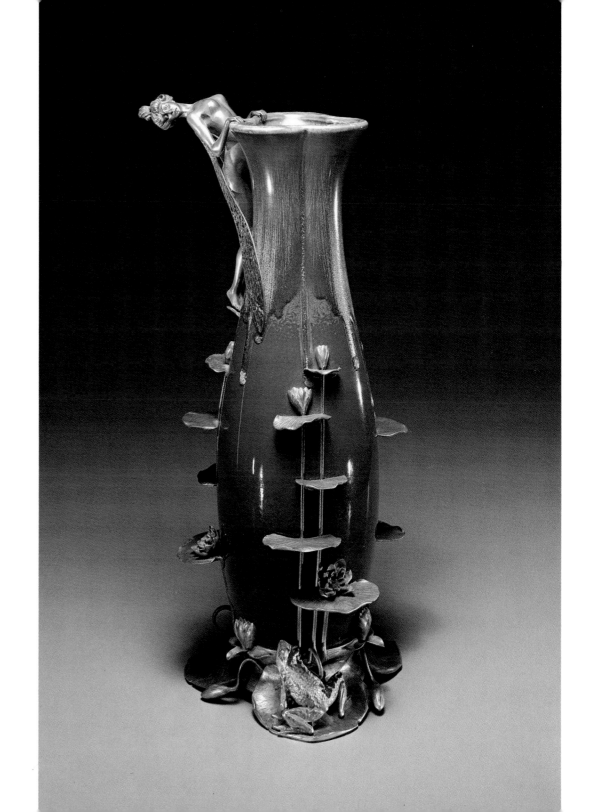

Louis Majorelle
French, 1859-1926

10 Buffet, ca. 1898

Oak, ebony, maple, chestnut, palisander, other woods
144.8 × 132 × 52 (57 × 52 × 20½)
Signed on lower right corner of cabinet door: L *Majorelle*
Virginia Museum of Fine Arts Purchase, The Sydney and Frances
Lewis Art Nouveau Fund, 73.46.2

Louis Majorelle has been called the greatest Art Nouveau cabinetmaker, both by his contemporaries and by writers of today. There is no doubt that by using a wide range of woods and woodworking methods, he had complete control over his medium.

Born in Toul, Majorelle moved with his family to Nancy in 1860. Upon the death of his father in 1879 he was forced to leave school in order to take over his father's modest furniture shop where, for the next ten years, he produced furniture in the Louis XV and XVI styles. Around 1894 his furniture style shifted to one that could be called Art Nouveau, and the following years realized his success as a master cabinetmaker in this style.

This buffet represents an early phase of his work, before he introduced his elaborate *nénuphar*, or waterlily, ormolu mounts. Perhaps because it was designed for a dining room, the buffet reflects the French gourmet's delight in food through the symbolic representation of various animals. The nutwood galleries are inlaid with maple carved to represent snails; the back

panel marquetry has rabbits and cattails; the drawer pulls are cast in the form of ducks' heads holding snakes in their mouths. The lower door panel, inlaid with various woods in a plant motif, bears the signature L *Majorelle*. In all, the marquetry and veneers employ at least eight different woods, while all of the undecorated surfaces are veneered in palisander, a type of Brazilian rosewood.

Although the Style 1900 motifs appear in the design of the marquetry, the drawer pulls, and the various veneers, the outline and overall design of this piece are very conservative, recalling earlier French styles. This is in contrast to the more innovative designs being done at this time by Gallé, and what Majorelle himself would do soon afterward (see cat. no. 57).

PROVENANCE: Dr. Hans-Jörgen Heuser & Co., Hamburg, 1973.
PUBLISHED: Patricia Bayer, "Art Nouveau," *Antiques World*, (October 1981), illus. p. 32

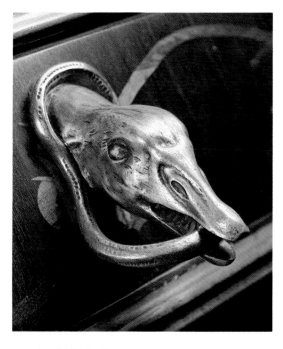

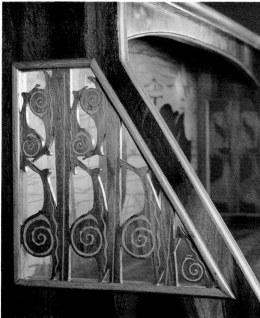

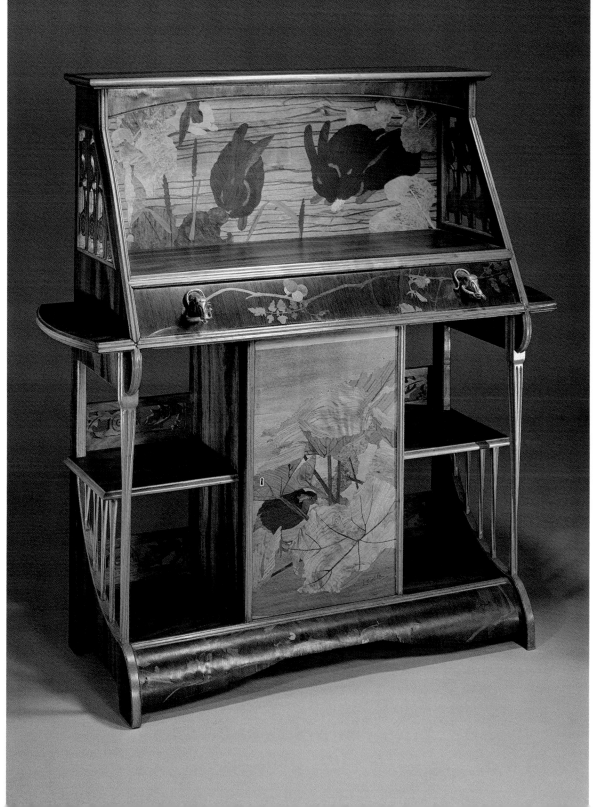

Jacques Gruber
French, 1870-1936

11 Desk and Chair, ca. 1898

Mahogany, leather, gilt bronze
Desk: 94.5 × 144.1 × 83.8 (37½ × 56¾ × 33)
Chair: 79.3 × 77.5 × 63.5 (31¼ × 30½ × 25)
Desk signed right top: *Gruber Nancy*; chair unsigned
Virginia Museum of Fine Arts, Gift of Sydney and Frances Lewis,
85.86.1/2

Like so many other members of the Ecole de Nancy, Jacques Gruber was a versatile designer and craftsman, excelling in creating objects in many different media. He enjoyed prestige as a professor at the Nancy School of Decorative Arts.

Gruber's early work is characterized by decorative flowers and other natural subjects, whether in carvings, elaborate marquetry, or veneers. He also designed etched-glass panels for his furniture.

The desk is deeply carved, with the forms seeming to emerge from the flat surfaces of the wood. The two small upper shelves seem to spring forth from their supports which, in turn, appear to grow out of the desk top. Many of Gruber's pieces appear to rise out of the ground, as if they were the result of some unusual natural growth process.

Gruber influenced the French decorative arts until his death in 1936. He excelled not only in furniture-making but also in the design and execution of stained-glass windows (see cat. no. 23).

PROVENANCE: Macklowe Gallery Ltd., New York, 1973.

PUBLISHED: Yvonne Brunhammer et al., *Art Nouveau Belgium/France* (Houston: Institute for the Arts, Rice University, 1976), illus. 351, p. 228. Alastair Duncan, *Art Nouveau Furniture* (New York: Clarkson N. Potter, 1982), pl. 38.

EXHIBITED: *Art Nouveau Belgium/France*, Rice University, Houston, March 25–June 27: Art Institute of Chicago, August 28–November 7, 1976.

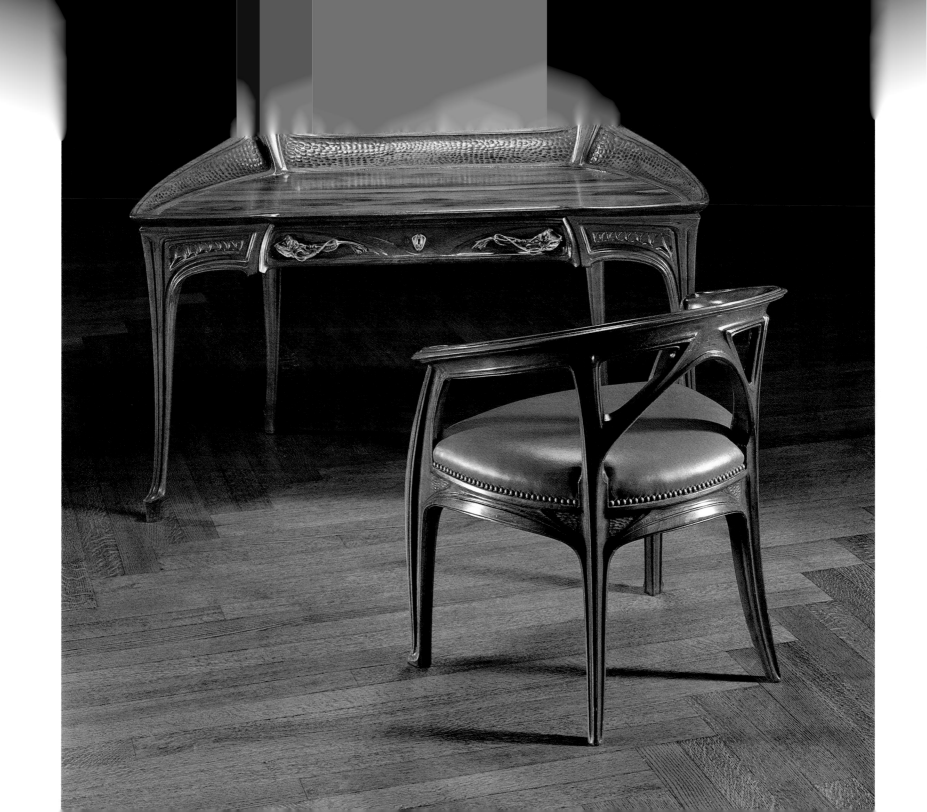

Richard Riemerschmid
German, 1868-1957

12 Chair, ca. 1898

Oak, leather
80.6 × 55.2 × 57.1 (31¾ × 21¾ × 22½)
Unsigned
Virginia Museum of Fine Arts, Gift of Sydney and Frances Lewis,
85.140

During Riemerschmid's long career, he created paintings as well as furniture, ceramics, glass, metalwork, textile designs, and architecture. He was a leader in founding the Vereinigte Werkstätten für Kunst und Handwerk in Munich, as well as the Deutscher Werkbund in that same city.

This chair, part of a set designed for a music salon for the Deutsche Kunstausstellung and later shown at the 1900 Paris Exposition, owes a great debt to traditional European furniture design while still recognizing the concepts of the new style.

In the 1900 Exposition, Riemerschmid designed a *Zimmer Eines Kunstfreundes* (Room for an Art Lover), in which he included this same chair design. The room also included works by Hermann Obrist and Bernhard Pankok, fellow artists from Munich.

Riemerschmid's desire to create objects that could be produced for mass consumption through mass production, together with his Teutonic sense of order and formality, and his apparent disinterest in the decorative qualities of French Art Nouveau, contributed to the straight lines and subtle curves of his furniture.

PROVENANCE: Modernism Gallery, New York, 1983.

PUBLISHED: Robert Schmutzler, *Art Nouveau* (New York: Abrams, 1962), p. 200. Stephan Tschudi Madsen, *Art Nouveau* (New York: World University, 1967), p. 179. Stephan Tschudi Madsen, *Sources of Art Nouveau* (New York: DaCapo Press, 1975), p. 62. Garner Read Russell, *Chair Design* (New York: Rizzoli International Publications Inc., 1980), p. 64. Winfried Nerdinger, *Richard Riemerschmid vom Jugendstil zum Werkbund Werke und Dokumente* (Munich: Prestel-Verlag, 1982), illus. p. 18, no. 142. Derek E. Ostergard, *Mackintosh to Mollino: Fifty Years of Chair Design* (New York: Barry Friedman Ltd., 1984), cat. no 18.

EXHIBITED: *Mackintosh to Mollino: Fifty Years of Chair Design*, Barry Friedman Ltd., New York, November 13, 1984–February 13, 1985.

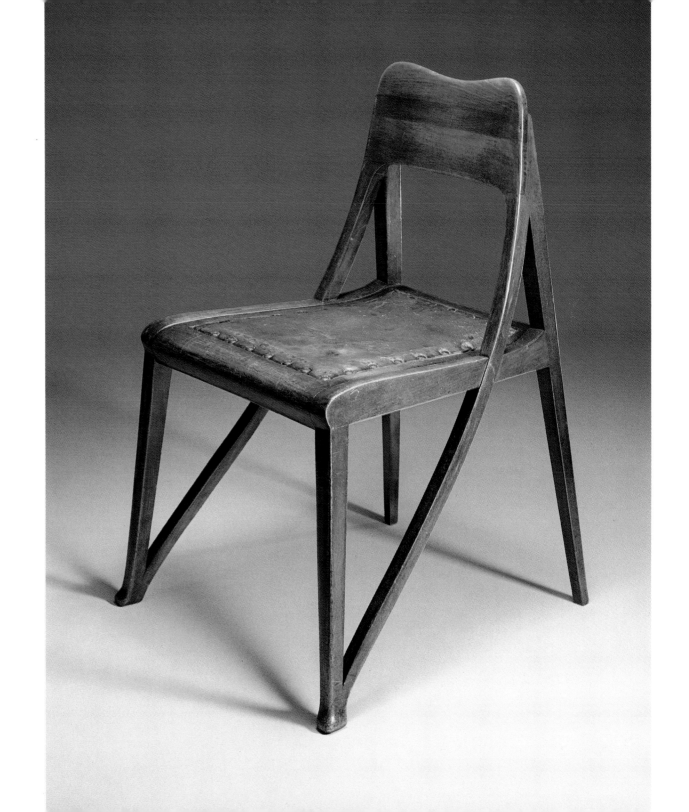

Gustave Gurschner
Austrian, 1873-?

13 Nautilus Lamp, 1899

Bronze, nautilus shell
44.4 × 18.9 × 19 (17½ × 7⅜ × 7½)
Signed on proper right of base: *Gurschner/* 7 99
Virginia Museum of Fine Arts Purchase, The Sydney and Frances
Lewis Art Nouveau Fund, 72.19

Gurschner received his early education at a technical school for wood industries in Bozen, Austria, where for three years he learned the intricacies of wood carving. In 1888 he moved to Vienna to study at the arts and crafts school in that city. He then studied sculpture with August Kühne and Otto König, and in 1894 he received his first portrait commission. After a brief stay in Munich, he left for Paris in 1897, where he absorbed the influence of the flamboyant French Art Nouveau style, so evident in this lamp. He later returned to Vienna, where he was associated with the artists of the Secession.

Unlike the classic symmetry and severity seen in the work of other Viennese artists, this lamp appears to follow the flowing, undulating motion more typical of the art of France and Belgium. The sweeping curve of the mermaid's tail, which acts as the lamp's base and stem, is especially sinuous in movement.

While many Art Nouveau artists used stylized natural forms for their motifs, Gurschner made the shade of this small lamp from an actual nautilus shell. He so expertly worked the shell into the bronze that it almost seems to be part of the base. Like Larche (see cat. no. 3), Gurschner has successfully combined sculpture in the Art Nouveau style with the ever-present interest in the new invention, electricity.

Interestingly enough, Gurschner's later style is much more rigid and geometric while this earlier piece undoubtedly owes a great debt to some of the leading French sculptors, including Jean-Auguste Dampt and Alexandre Charpentier, whom Gurschner knew during his early years of study and work in Paris. Gurschner's later geometric style seems to have been influenced by Charles Rennie Mackintosh, whose work was shown in Vienna in 1900 (see cat. nos. 44 and 61).

PROVENANCE: Knut Günther, Frankfurt-am-Main, 1972.

PUBLISHED: Similar lamp in Franz Windisch-Graetz, "Leben und Werk der Bildhauers Gustave Gurschner," *Alter und Moderne Kunst*, (July/August 1926), illus. p. 36. Patricia Bayer, "Art Nouveau," *Antiques World* (October 1981), illus. p. 32.

EXHIBITED: *Art Nouveau*, Virginia Museum Artmobile Exhibition, September 1972–May 1975.

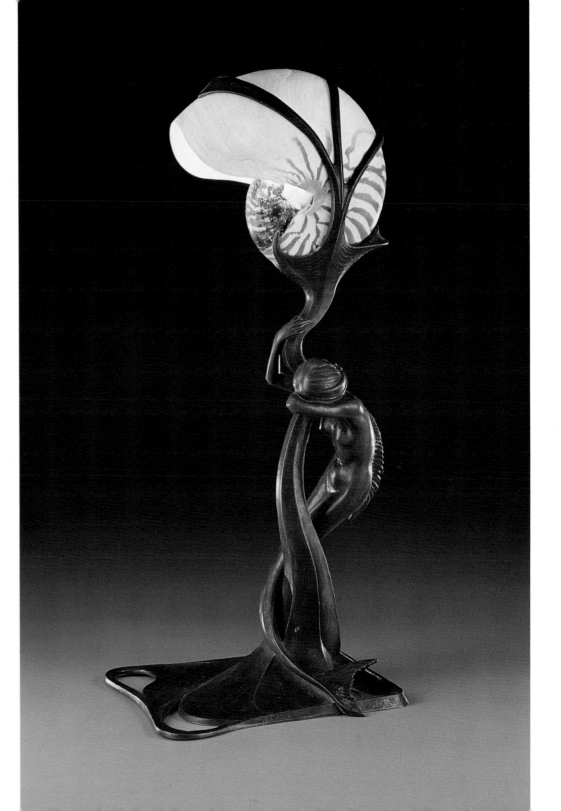

Alphonse Mucha
Czechoslovakian, 1860-1939

14 *Nature*, ca. 1900

Gilt bronze, silver, marble
69.2 × 27.9 × 30.5 (27¼ × 11 × 12)
Signed on proper right side: *Mucha*; founder's seal on
proper left side: *Bronze Garanti Au Titre PARIS*
Virginia Museum of Fine Arts Purchase, The Sydney and Frances
Lewis Art Nouveau Fund, 72.13

There has been much speculation as to the origin of this figure, what or whom it represents, and who, if anyone, collaborated on it with Mucha.

Four versions are known of the bust. Until recent years, it had been thought to be based on a portrait of Sarah Bernhardt or Cléo de Mérode. The connection with "the divine Sarah" is logical, since she played such an important role in Mucha's oeuvre. In 1895, he created his first lithograph for Bernhardt as a poster for her title role in *Gismonda* in the Théâtre de la Renaissance. Her appreciation of his work prompted a continuing professional relationship for the next six years, resulting in a great number of posters and works featuring the actress, as well as specially designed jewelry on which Mucha collaborated with the Parisian jeweler Georges Fouquet (see cat. no. 18).

There is no actual basis for the assumption that this bust is a portrait of Sarah Bernhardt. In recent years, however, this piece and three others like it have been interpreted as symbolic representations of nature. This theory is based on a photograph of a similar bust entitled *La Nature*, which was exhibited in the Austrian section of the 1900 Paris Exposition and again two years later at the Turin exposition.

Each of the four known sculptures varies slightly in detail, particularly in the disposition of the diadem with its ovoid "jewel" and in the finish of the actual figures, in some cases mat, in others more highly polished.

It is known, primarily through recollections of Mucha's son, Jiri, that the artist collaborated with Auguste Seysses on sculpture around the turn of the century. This bust was originally believed to have been part of that collaboration, but that is now questionable, primarily because of the lack of any signature or mark of Seysses, who was a fairly prominent sculptor.

Another work by Mucha that is related very closely to this one is a lithograph created in 1896-97 entitled *Zodiac*, done as a calendar for *La Plume*. The profile of an almost identical figure, albeit clothed, is depicted in the print. A similar crown capped by the ovoid "jewel" tops the figure's hair, which swirls in sinuous whiplash lines down over the shoulders and bust.

Regardless of the origin or intent of this bust, it is one of Mucha's finest, even though he was generally better known for prints and drawings. In this case, he has brought those familiar images into three-dimensional reality.[9]

PROVENANCE: Valentin Abdy, Paris; Robert Walker, Paris, 1972.

PUBLISHED: "La vie des objets: un second bronze de Mucha est retrouvé," *Connaissance des Arts* (January 1965), illus. p. 11. Jiri Mucha, Marina Henderson, Aaron Scharf, *Alphonse Mucha: Posters and Photographs* (New York: St. Martin's Press, 1971), p. 50; illus. opposite p. 34. *Art at Auction, The Year at Sotheby Parke Bernet, 1971-1972* (New York: Viking Press, 1972), p. 346. Similar cast in *Plaisir de France* (December 1972/January 1973), cover illus. Similar cast in Yvonne Brunhammer, *Art Nouveau Belgium/ France* (Houston: Institute for the Arts, Rice University, 1976), no. 439, p. 276. "Bronzes for the Age of Art Nouveau," *Discovering Antiques* (1971), no. 74, fig. 11, p. 1772. Alastair Duncan, *Art Nouveau Sculpture* (New York: Rizzoli International Publications Inc., 1978), illus. frontispiece. Patricia Bayer, "Art Nouveau," *Antiques World* (October 1981), illus. p. 24.

---

9. Different foundry marks appear on the four busts that now belong to museums in Karlsruhe and Richmond, and private collections in Brussels and Munich. For a more detailed explanation, including the contribution of Anna Dvorak to the partial solution to the mystery of these images, see *Mucha: 1860-1939* (Paris: Grand Palais, 1980), entry 145. See also Philippe Garner, "The Bronzes of Alphonse Mucha," *Art at Auction The Year at Sotheby Parke-Bernet, 1971-1972* (New York: Viking Press, 1972), pp. 432-37.

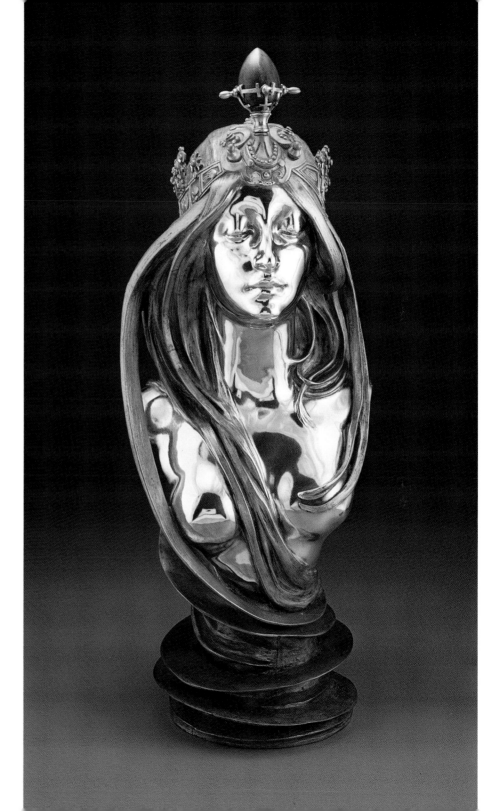

Hector Guimard
French, 1867-1942

15

Cabinet, ca. 1899

Pear and ash woods, bronze, mirrored glass
297.2 × 237.5 × 49.5 (117 × 93½ × 19½)
Unsigned
Virginia Museum of Fine Arts Purchase, The Sydney and Frances
Lewis Art Nouveau Fund, 72.12

Hector Guimard was one of the most influential architects of his day. Born in Lyons, he studied at the Ecole des Arts Décoratifs and the Ecole des Beaux-Arts. During this time, around 1885, he completed his first architectural projects. Although he received many commissions during the succeeding years, it was the Castel Béranger that brought him recognition and that is today considered his masterpiece.

This monumental sideboard was designed by Guimard for the dining room of the Castel Béranger, an apartment house at 14-16 Rue La Fontaine in Paris. The building was constructed over the period 1894 to 1898 and was outfitted about 1899.

Judging from drawings for the sideboard, Guimard originally intended the piece to have more elaborate carved projections on the sides, as well as cross-members over the glass areas. The final design resulted in a slight simplification of forms but retained the basic concept of the overall design.

It is important to remember that Guimard conceived the sideboard as part of the overall design of the dining room and not as a separate piece of furniture. It would undoubtedly have adjoined other parts of the interior, thus giving unity to the room.

As with other Guimard works of this period, the decoration of this cabinet comprises an essential part of the form; it is not just an applied extension. The contour of the projecting shapes as well as the flowing line in the upper decoration all reflect Guimard's concern with nature and its inherent asymmetry.

PROVENANCE: Castel Béranger, Paris, ca. 1899; Galerie Félix Marcilhac, Paris, 1972.

PUBLISHED: Philippe Garner, "Art Nouveau Furniture," *Discovering Antiques* (1971), no. 74, illus. p. 1776. Philippe Garner, *Twentieth Century Furniture* (New York: Van Nostrand Reinhold, Co., 1980), color illus. p. 21.

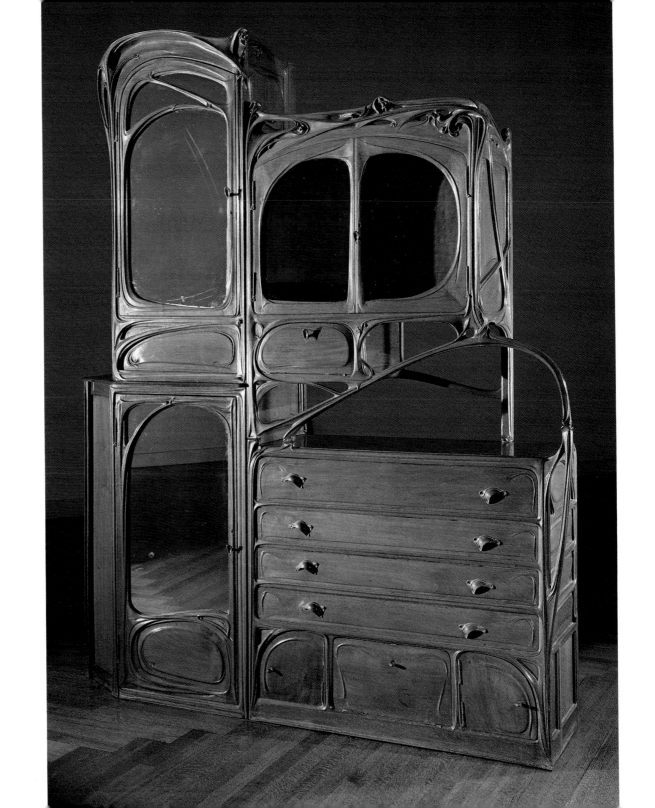

Charles Rohlfs
American, 1853-1936

16

Desk, 1898-1901

American white oak, iron, brass
142.2 × 64.7 × 60.3 (56 × 25½ × 23¾)
Unsigned
Virginia Museum of Fine Arts, Gift of Sydney and Frances Lewis,
85.66

Charles Rohlfs was one of the most creative, eccentric, and innovative artists working in the United States in the late nineteenth and early twentieth centuries. Born in New York City, he was educated at the Cooper Union School. By 1890, after working as a designer of cast-iron stoves, he began designing and producing his own oak furniture, soon establishing himself as a leader in the American Arts and Crafts movement.

Rohlfs's furniture, normally executed in dark oak, is characterized by its somewhat traditional, native sense of design and its closer ties with the English Arts and Crafts Movement than with the highly skilled cabinetry of his Gallic contemporaries, such as Gallé and Majorelle.

This fall-front desk, indisputably one of Rohlfs's masterpieces, bears a decided Gothic influence, as well as a strong affinity to the furniture of his fellow designer Gustav Stickley. The openwork elements, however, show Rohlfs's awareness of the European Art Nouveau line.

Not surprisingly, Rohlfs's philosophy was closely related to that of William Morris. He established his own workshop to produce objects that would not only enhance one's environment but also one's whole life.

In an 1899 article in *House Beautiful*, author Charlotte Moffitt describes a visit to Rohlfs's studio in Buffalo:

. . . Occasionally one hears of a tiny workshop where some earnest artist is trying by the work of his own hands to preserve ideas that to him seem worthy.

One such shop is to be found in Buffalo, New York . . . . The furniture is not turned out rapidly, for, excepting for the assistance of his wife, who was better known as Anna Katherine Green, Mr. Rohlfs does the work himself. In the collection shown in Chicago of this queer, dark, crude, medieval furniture is a desk, a very marvel of complexity, with endless delights in the way of doors, pigeon-holes, shelves, and drawers. When closed, that is when the writing-shelf is raised and fastened with its rough hasp of dark steel and crude wooden pin—all the drawers and shelves in place, and the doors closed, it looks like nothing so much as a miniature Swiss cottage. The opposite side from the writing-shelf is a support for books, and the whole desk revolves upon its base.[10]

It is interesting to note how Rohlfs applied decoration to the piece through the use of jigsaw cutouts, carved finials, decorative nailheads, and a textured surface made with a rounded hammer. These motifs, plus the use of oak, which has inherent strength and beauty, combine to form a masterpiece of the American Arts and Crafts Movement.

PROVENANCE: Jordan-Volpe Gallery, New York, 1982.

PUBLISHED: Charlotte Moffitt, "The Rohlfs Furniture," *House Beautiful* 7 (December 1899), p. 83.

---

10. Charlotte Moffitt, "The Rohlfs Furniture," *House Beautiful* 7 (December 1899) 81-85.

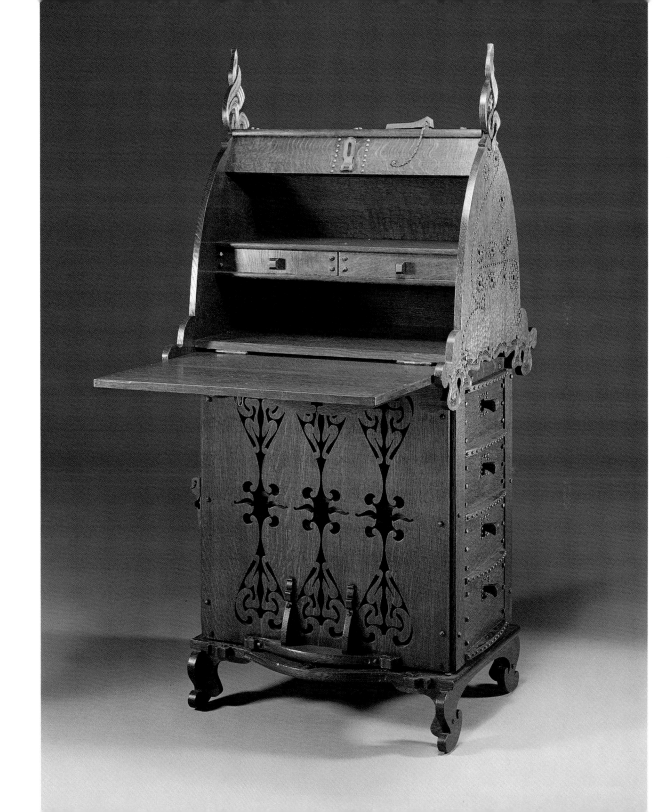

Tiffany Glass & Decorating Co.
American, 1892-1900

17 Punch Bowl with Three Ladles, 1900

Favrile glass, gilded silver
Bowl: 36.2 × 60.9 diameter (14¼ × 24)
Ladles, each: 6.3 × 8.9 × 25.4 (½ × 3½ × 10)
Marked on base: *April 1900/Tiffany / G. & D. Co./*1282
Virginia Museum of Fine Arts Purchase, The Sydney and Frances
Lewis Art Nouveau Fund, 74.16

Louis Comfort Tiffany, the son of Charles L. Tiffany, founder of Tiffany & Company, was originally trained as a painter, studying first with George Inness and later in Paris. Because of his interest in interior design, Tiffany established his own firm in 1879, producing glass, lamps, tiles, furniture, and other objects. By 1900, Tiffany Studios was well established as the leader in design and decoration and Tiffany's name had become synonymous with high quality in both design and materials. One often-used material was Favrile glass, a handmade iridescent substance which was coined and marketed by Tiffany.

In a photograph taken at the Paris Exposition in 1900, the displays of Tiffany & Company and Louis C. Tiffany can be seen side by side. In a photograph of the entrance to Louis Tiffany's booth (fig. 11), this punch bowl is visible in a display case, in the lower right corner. In her review of the Exposition, critic Florence N. Levy said:

> Among the collection of Favrile glass sent by the Tiffany Company the most important piece was a punchbowl, about 30 inches in diameter. The glass is encased in a frame of chased and wrought golden metal, the design of the base suggesting the effect of breaking waves, while from their foaming crests spring six arms of peacock-hued Favrile glass, they in turn support the uprights of the frame, becoming a richly ornamental band at the top. Three of the supports end in quaintly twisted finials of lustre glass from which hang ladles of metal and iridescent glass.[11]

Tiffany was one of the prizewinners at the Exposition, as indicated by the "Grand Prix" and "Médaille d'Or" signs in the photograph.

Since then, the punch bowl has frequently been cited as the masterpiece of Tiffany's art. Tiffany scholar Dr. Robert Koch cited it as "the weirdest, most exuberant, most Art Nouveau, most Expressionist object of its era ever produced in America."[12]

Dr. Koch also convincingly points out that the wave forms in which the bowl rests might possibly derive from the "broomcorn" motif of the designer Edward Colonna, who had previously worked for Tiffany. He also notes that the designer John T. Curran, who had already patented a "broomcorn" design for silver flatware, may have aided Tiffany in the design of the silver mounts.

PROVENANCE: Robert and Gladys Koch, Stamford, Connecticut, 1974.

PUBLISHED: *American Art Annual* III (New York: R.R. Bowker, 1900), illus. p. 21. *Nineteenth Century America: Furniture and Other Decorative Arts* (New York: The Metropolitan Museum of Art, New York Graphic Society, 1970), cat. no. 271 (illus.). Robert Koch, "Tiffany Exhibition Punch Bowl," *Arts in Virginia* 16 (Winter/Spring, 1976), pp. 32-39, illus. p. 32. Charles H. Carpenter, Jr., "The Silver of Louis Comfort Tiffany," *Antiques Magazine* (February, 1980), illus. p. 393. Patricia Bayer, "Art Nouveau," *Antiques World*, (October 1981), illus. p. 31. Carla Cerutti, *Arti Decorative del Novecento: Liberty* (Novara: Istituto Geografico de Agostini, 1985), pp. 50-51, illus. p. 51.

EXHIBITED: Exposition Universelle, Paris, 1900; *Nineteenth Century America*, The Metropolitan Museum of Art, New York, April 16–September 7, 1970.

---

11. Florence N. Levy, "Applied Arts at the Paris Exposition," *American Art Journal* 3 (1900): 21
12. Robert Koch, "Tiffany Exhibition Punchbowl," *Arts in Virginia* 16 (Winter/Spring 1976), 32-39.

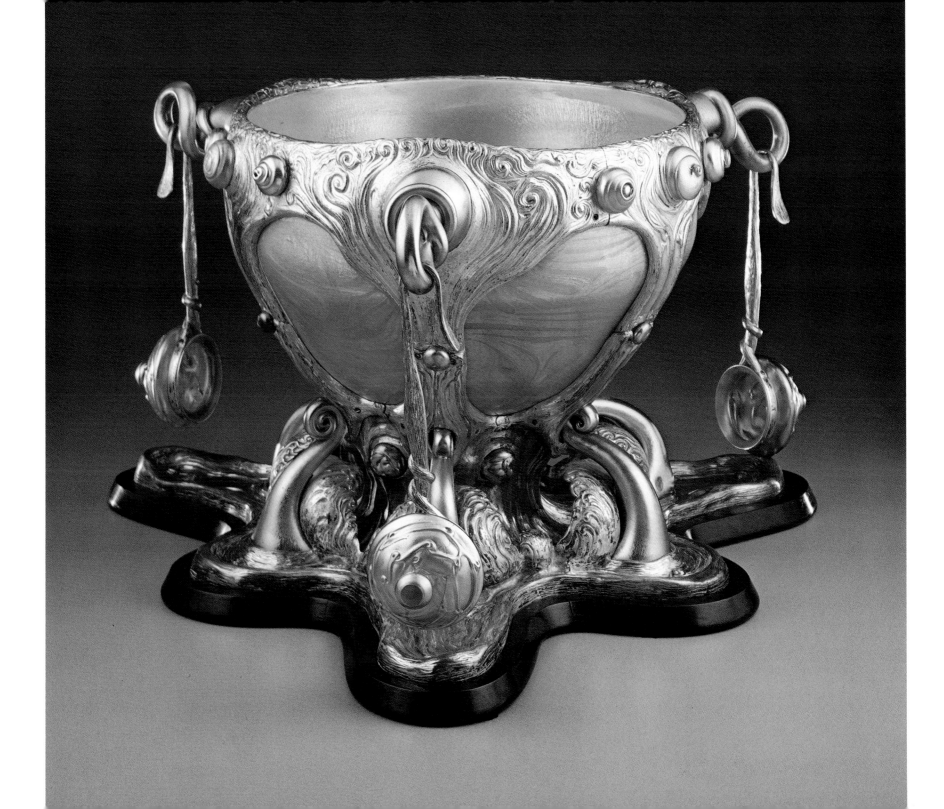

Alphonse Mucha
Czechoslovakian, 1860-1939
and
Georges Fouquet
French, 1862-1957

 18   Adornment for the Bodice, ca. 1900

Gold, enamel, emeralds, baroque pearl, watercolor, and metallic
paint on mother-of-pearl
17 × 8.6 × 7 (6¹¹/₁₆ × 3⅜ × 9/32)
Stamped on reverse: *G FOUQUET* 2873
Virginia Museum of Fine Arts, Gift of Sydney and Frances Lewis,
85.253

This piece of jewelry closely resembles another pendant by Mucha and
Fouquet that was displayed at the Paris Exposition of 1900 and that can be
seen in a photograph taken at the Exposition. Instead of a baroque pearl
suspended from its lower part, however, there is a chain holding a small,
abstract gold-and-jeweled pendant. In addition, the rings on either side of
the female figure support additional chains.

It is known that Mucha and Fouquet at times collaborated on
variations of the same piece of jewelry, but such is assumed to be the case
in this instance. The location of the object in the photograph is not
recorded after 1905 and is still unknown.[13]

The most significant difference between this piece and the one in the
photograph is that the entire pendant shown in the photograph is
suspended by chains fastened to elaborate epaulets. Because of its size,
mass, and weight, it is logical that it would need to be suspended with
some type of shoulder device rather than pinned to the delicate fabric of a
dress. Perhaps this example once had such a supporting device.

Mucha and Fouquet not only collaborated on the design of jewelry but
also on the design and decoration of Fouquet's shop. Some of the motifs in
this pendant appear in other works they produced. Another related piece is
in the collection of Lillian Nassau, while sketches for similar designs are in
a private collection in Paris, as is an original drawing for the pendant in the
Lewis Collection. A larger and more elaborate piece of jewelry, with a
female head flanked by two wings, is in the collection of Johanna Walker in
England.

Although Fouquet opened his shop around 1900-01 at 6 Rue Royale in
Paris, it is not known when he began working with Mucha. "Exactly when
my father began collaborating with Fouquet is not clear," said Jiri Mucha in
his biography of Alphonse Mucha. "The three most important pieces of
jewelry made for Sarah Bernhardt from his designs indicate that the
association started long before the shop was opened, but the dates given
for their manufacture do not agree with other evidence."[14]

PROVENANCE: Sotheby Parke Bernet Monaco S.A., 1977.

PUBLISHED: *Arts Décoratifs, Styles 1900 et 1925*, catalogue of sale (Monaco: Sotheby Parke Bernet
Monaco S.A., December 5, 1976), no. 132, p. 20. Philippe Garner, editor, *Encyclopedia of Decorative Arts*
(New York: Van Nostrand Reinhold, 1978), p. 98, illus. in color. *Mucha: 1860-1939*, exhibition catalogue,
Grand Palais (Paris: Editions de la Réunion des Musées Nationaux, 1980), pl. 147. Marie-Noël de Gary
et al, *Les Fouquet: Bijoutiers & Joailliers à Paris 1860-1960* (Paris: Musée des Arts Décoratifs, 1983), illus. p.
68.

EXHIBITED: Art Nouveau Gallery, Virginia Museum of Fine Arts, long-term loan; *Mucha: 1860-1938*,
Grand Palais, Paris, February 5-April 28, 1980; Mathildenhöhe, Darmstadt, June 8-August 3, 1980;
National Gallery of Prague, October-December 1980; *Les Fouquet: Bijoutiers & Joailliers à Paris 1860-1960*,
Musée des Arts Décoratifs, January–February 1984.

13. For the original photographs of this pendant see Marc Bascou and others, *Alfons Mucha: 1860-1939*
(Darmstadt: Mathildenhöhe, 1980), pp. 193,232,234-35.
14. Jiri Mucha, *Alphonse Mucha: The Master of Art Nouveau* (Prague: Knihtisk Artia, 1966), p. 181.

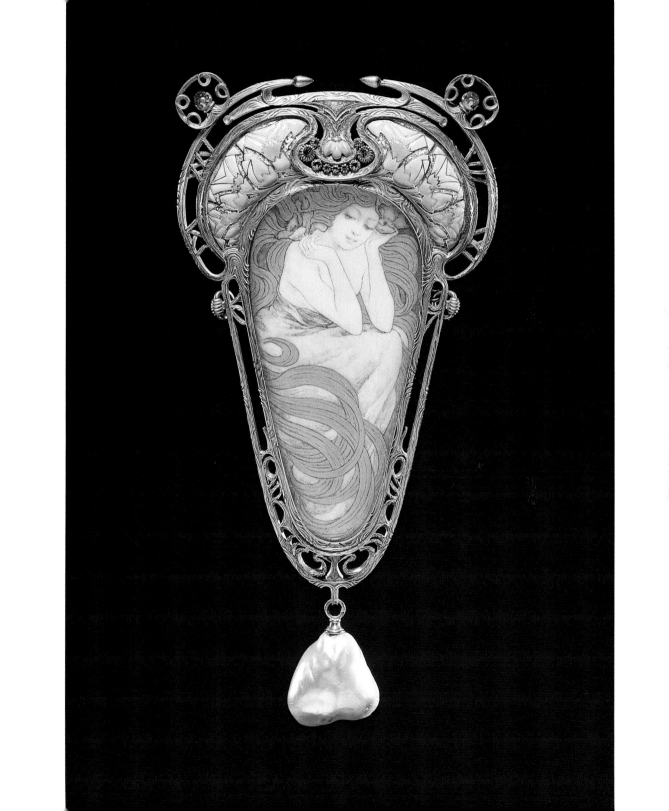

Emile Gallé

French, 1846-1904

19

Dragonfly Etagère, ca. 1900

Burl elm, maple, other woods, mirrored glass
135.8 × 83.8 × 43.8 (53½ × 33 × 17¼)
Signed on second shelf from top: *Gallé*
Virginia Museum of Fine Arts Purchase, The Sydney and Frances
Lewis Art Nouveau Fund, 73.60

Although most French Art Nouveau furniture design is derived from natural motifs, Gallé's is the most accurate in its rendering of plant forms. Gallé was a botanist by training and a firm believer in using nature's forms as direct sources for his furniture and glass. As Philippe Garner has pointed out, Gallé felt that "structural elements should be suggested by plant stems, both in the silhouette and their section."[15] Garner also observed that "his policy was to treat flat surfaces as fresh canvases on which to elaborate floral themes in a subtle juxtaposition of rich woods, to compose a graphic hymn to the glory of Nature and to her mysteries."[16]

Having successfully established himself as an innovative designer and glassmaker, Gallé began experimenting with rare woods in 1885. This early work culminated in his first major public exhibition at the Paris Exposition Universelle of 1889.

Although the inlay of this étagère depicts various forms of plant life, and the major upright structural supports are Gallé's interpretations of other plant forms, the dominant motif is the dragonfly, of which a monumental one acts as the support connecting the middle and lower shelves to the bottom shelf. Gallé incorporated the insect into a number of his most important works, including the large vitrine of 1904, now in the collection of Mr. and Mrs. Robert Walker, London, and a table of 1900 in the Musée de l'Ecole de Nancy, in which the four legs, in the form of dragonflies, rise to support the top. Gallé also used the motif extensively in the glass and mounts of various vases. These mysterious and exotic creatures served as the perfect visual embodiment of the period, since they combined the typical Art Nouveau line with images inspired by nature.

PROVENANCE: Mme Marie de Beyrie, Paris, 1973.

PUBLISHED: Patricia Bayer, "Art Nouveau," *Antiques World* (October 1981), illus. p. 24

15. Philippe Garner, *Emile Gallé* (New York: Rizzoli International Publications, Inc., 1976), p. 79.
16. Garner, p. 85.

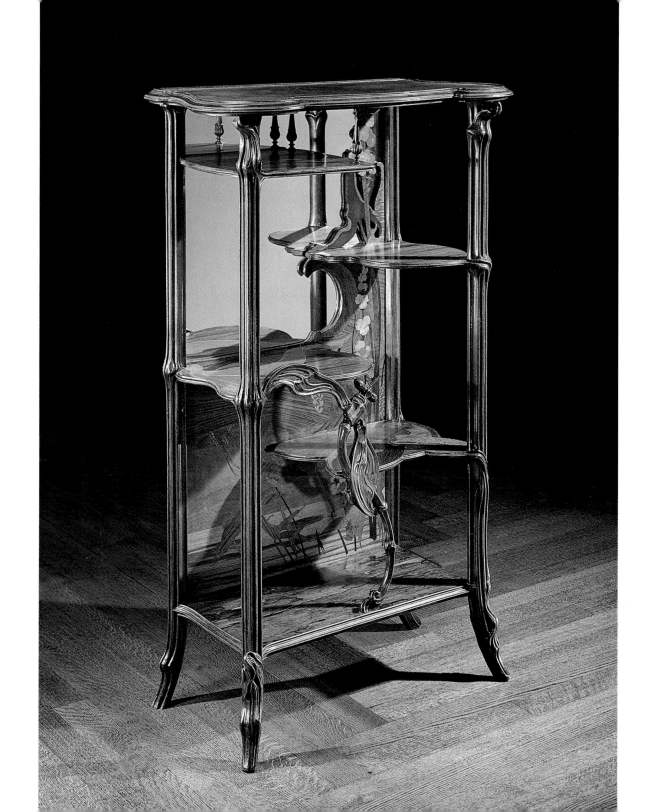

Edward Colonna
German-American, 1862-1948

20

Settee and Chair, ca. 1899

Carved maple, velvet
Settee: 99.7 × 113.6 × 53.3 (39¼ × 44¾ × 21)
Chair: 98.4 × 61 × 53.3 (38¾ × 24 × 21)
Unsigned
Virginia Museum of Fine Arts, Gift of Sydney and Frances Lewis,
85.139.1/2

For many years Edward Colonna remained an elusive yet important figure in the development of the Art Nouveau style. Only recently, through the intensive research conducted by Martin Eidelberg of Rutgers University in New Jersey, has the true picture of this remarkable designer and craftsman come to light.

Colonna was born Edouard Klönne in Mulheim-am-Rhein, Germany, in 1862. As a young man he undertook some architectural training in Brussels but soon left for the United States, arriving in New York in 1882. In the succeeding years he worked for Louis Comfort Tiffany's Associated Artists of New York and for the Barney & Smith Manufacturing Company in Dayton, Ohio. While in Dayton he designed furniture as well as interiors.

It was also in Ohio that Colonna produced a book entitled *Essay on Broom-Corn*, which included a series of drawings that set forth his concepts of design based on this plant form. The drawings exhibit a distinctive Art Nouveau style that was to characterize his work for the next fifteen years. In addition, says author Martin Eidelberg, "not only do they look forward to the curvilinear stylizations of High Art Nouveau design, but they display an originality of style which Colonna did not again attain for some time to come."[17]

In 1888 Colonna was naturalized as an American citizen. For the next few years he undertook projects in Ohio and Montreal, eventually traveling to France at the end of 1893. It was there that he began his most important work in the innovative Style 1900. During the five-year period from 1898 to 1903, Colonna was associated with S. Bing's shop, *La Maison de l 'Art Nouveau.*

During these years, Colonna was responsible for producing unique furniture and jewelry items for Bing, but it was at Bing's pavilion at the 1900 Paris Exposition that his best work was displayed. Photographs of the salon for which Colonna was responsible show a settee and a chair very much like these from the Lewis Collection (see fig. 6). They embody the same curvilinear silhouette and carved backs, the distinctive line of which descends almost to the floor between the rear legs. The fabric in the Lewis settee and chair has been replaced, but the original covering would have resembled that of the pieces in the Paris salon, with their luxurious curvilinear floral motifs.

Colonna continued to design furniture, jewelry, and porcelain for Bing until the shop was forced to close in 1903. His later years were spent trying to survive through meager sales of some of his work and as an antiques dealer. As his health declined, he became bed-ridden for the last two decades of his life; he died in southern France in 1948.[18]

PROVENANCE: Lillian Nassau Ltd., New York, 1971.

PUBLISHED: "L'Art Nouveau de M. Bing à l'Exposition Universelle," *Revue des arts décoratifs* 20 (1900), no. 9, p. 285. Gabriel P. Weisberg, "Samuel Bing: International Dealer of Art Nouveau," *The Connoisseur* (May 1971): 49-55, illus. p. 51. Connie Morningstar, "Furniture from Rococo to Art Nouveau," *The Antiques Journal* (May 1973), illus. p. 28. Frederick R. Brandt, "Serpentine Seating: Art Nouveau Chairs," *The Antiques Journal* (September 1979): 18-21, 46, 47. Martin Eidelberg, *E. Colonna* (Dayton, Ohio: Dayton Art Institute, 1983), fig. 70, p. 51.

EXHIBITED: *Art Nouveau*, Virginia Museum of Fine Arts, Richmond, November 22–December 26, 1971, nos. 14, 15; Art Nouveau Gallery, Virginia Museum of Fine Arts, long-term loan 1975-1981; *E. Colonna*, Dayton Ohio Art Institute, October 29, 1983–January 2, 1984; Musée des arts décoratifs de Montréal, January 20–March 26, 1984; The Renwick Gallery, Washington, D.C., April 27–August 19, 1984.

17. Martin Eidelberg, "The Life and Work of E. Colonna," *The Decorative Arts Society Newsletter* 7 (March 1981): p. 3.
18. The facts contained within are based primarily on the research of Martin Eidelberg, which was published in his three-part essay "The Life and Work of E. Colonna" in *The Decorative Arts Society Newsletter* 7/1, 2, 3 (March, June, September, 1981). For further detailed information see also the catalogue by Martin Eidelberg, *Edward Colonna: 1862-1948* (Dayton, Ohio: Dayton Art Institute, 1983).

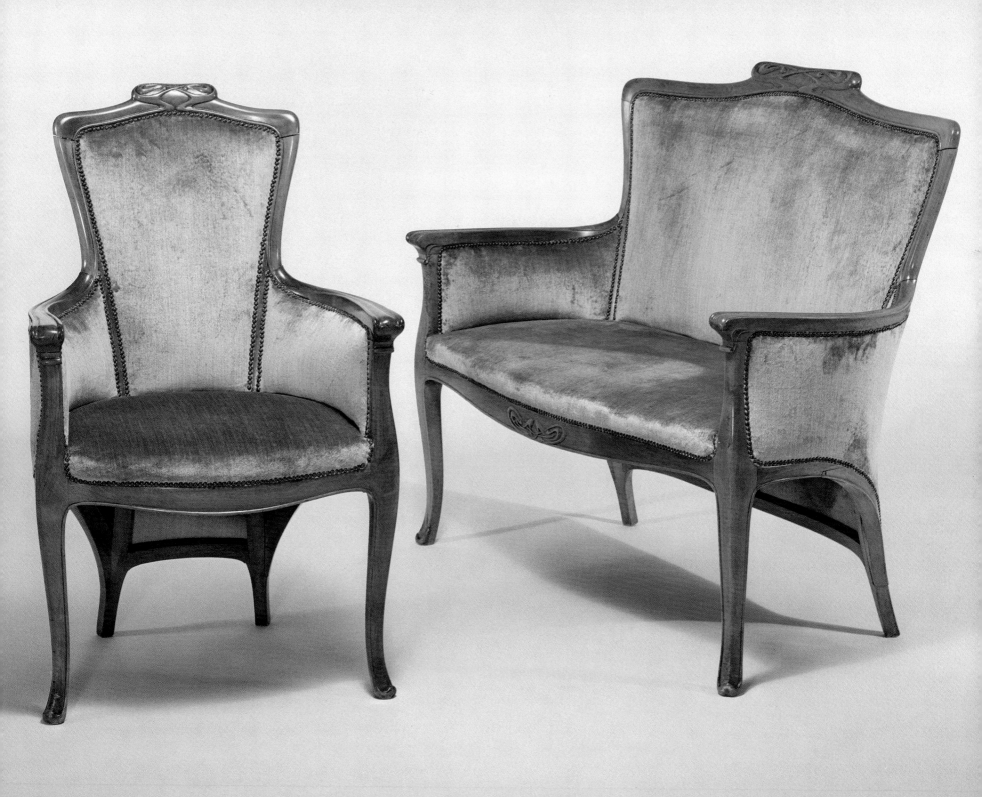

Charles Korschann
French, 1872-?

21 Table Lamp with Inkwell, ca. 1894-1906

Gilt bronze
45.7 × 44.1 × 31.7 (18 × 17⅜ × 12½)
Signed: *Charles Korschann Paris*, founder's mark on lower rear
Virginia Museum of Fine Arts, Gift of Sydney and Frances Lewis,
85.170

Although details of Korschann's life are sketchy, it is known that he lived and worked in Paris from 1894 to 1906, the period in which this remarkable lamp figure was created.

It is perhaps typical of the turn of the century that a figure as large and elaborate as this could serve not only as a piece of sculpture but also as an inkwell and as a subdued desk or table lamp. Electricity was in its infancy and many artists were fascinated by the ability to incorporate into their sculptural projects small bulbs that would literally "paint" the sculpture in light, thus highlighting forms and details (see also cat. nos. 3 and 13).

According to the founder's mark, the lamp was fabricated by Charles Louchet. Its sculptural forms represent the quintessence of Art Nouveau through the subtle play of lines in the figure's dress, which swirls around her feet to form the base. In addition, the bouquet of flowers that she holds conceals the small electric light bulb yet allows some light to illuminate her face. The flowers, in typical Art Nouveau fashion, also provide a point of reference between the fin-de-siècle archetypal Woman and Nature. In this case, as in many other Korschann bronzes, although the figure holds the flowers, they almost become part of her.[19]

The fact that this lamp-sculpture actually serves a functional as well as an aesthetic purpose carries out the philosophy of the Art Nouveau artist— that all the components of interior design should contribute to the uses of that interior. Thus, sculpture and painting should not exist as separate entities, but should play an important role as functional objects in the interior environment.

PROVENANCE: Sotheby & Co., London, 1971.

PUBLISHED: *Art Nouveau* exhibition catalogue (Richmond: Virginia Museum of Fine Arts, 1971), illus. no. 79, p. 6. "Bronzes for the Age of Art Nouveau," *Discovering Antiques* (1971) illus. no. 74, p. 1772. *Nineteenth and Twentieth Century Ceramics*, Sotheby & Co. catalogue of sale (London: Sotheby & Co., March 9, 1971), no. 354. Yvonne Brunhammer et al., *Art Nouveau Belgium/France* (Houston: Institute for the Arts, Rice University, 1976), illus. 395, p. 253.

EXHIBITED: *Art Nouveau*, Virginia Museum of Fine Arts, November 22-December 26, 1971, no. 79. *Art Nouveau Belgium/France*, Rice University, Houston, March 25-June 27, 1976; Art Institute of Chicago, August 28-November 7, 1976.

---

19. For a documentation of lighting of this period, see Alastair Duncan, *Art Nouveau and Art Deco Lighting* (London: Thames and Hudson, 1978).

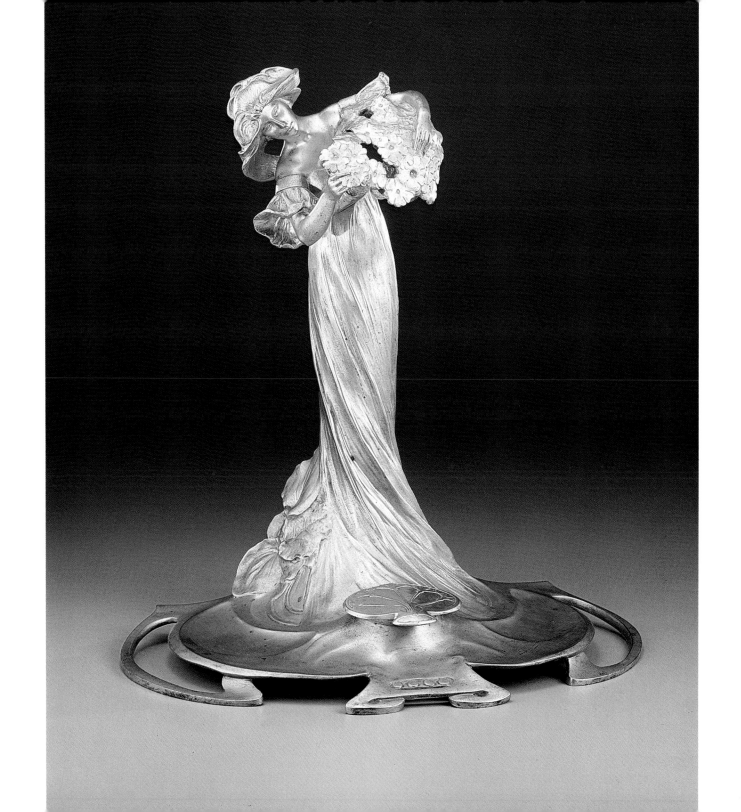

Artist Unknown
French, late 19th-early 20th century

22 "Black Peacock" Pendant, ca. 1900

166-carat black fire opal, 18-carat gold, plique-à-jour
enamel, baroque pearl
11.7 × 8.2 (4⅝ × 3½)
Marked on reverse 1 *pan d'or* 166 *ct.*, R lower right reverse
Virginia Museum of Fine Arts, Gift of Sydney and Frances Lewis,
85.228

The unknown designer of this striking pendant has created a swirling, miniature sculpture of 18-carat gold and plique-à-jour enamel to serve as a frame, or backdrop, for the magnificent Black Peacock stone.

Found in Nevada in the late nineteenth century, this sumptuous semi-transparent, multicolored opal weighs 166 carats. The black fire opal is in no way diminished by the large swirling Art Nouveau design of whiplash lines and enameled swallows that surrounds it. Its very size and color allow the opal to control the composition; the asymmetrical shape of the opal and its mount are balanced by the suspension of the baroque pearl.

Nothing is known about the creator of this fine pendant. The lower right corner on the obverse bears the initial "R" in script, but no known maker signed his work in that manner. From the inscription it can be assumed that the stone, although American, was mounted in France.

PROVENANCE: Robert C. Eldred Co., Inc., East Dennis, Massachusetts, 1974.

PUBLISHED: *Antiques & Furnishings from the Estate of the late* D.T. *Watson of Pittsburgh and others,* catalogue of sale (East Dennis, Massachusetts: Robert C. Eldred Co. Inc., August 8, 1974), no. 272. Tom Dewey II, *Art Nouveau, Art Deco, and Modernism: A Guide to the Styles,* 1890-1940, exhibition catalogue (Jackson, Mississippi: Mississippi Museum of Art, 1983), illus. 42, p. 26.

EXHIBITED: Art Nouveau Gallery, Virginia Museum of Fine Arts, long-term loan, September 1976–September 1983; *Art Nouveau, Art Deco, and Modernism: A Guide to the Styles,* 1890-1940, Mississippi Museum of Art, Jackson, September 16–November 13, 1983; Arkansas Arts Center, Little Rock, February 24–April 1, 1984; Montgomery (Alabama) Museum of Fine Arts, May 6–June 17, 1984; Tampa (Florida) Museum, July 8–October 28, 1984.

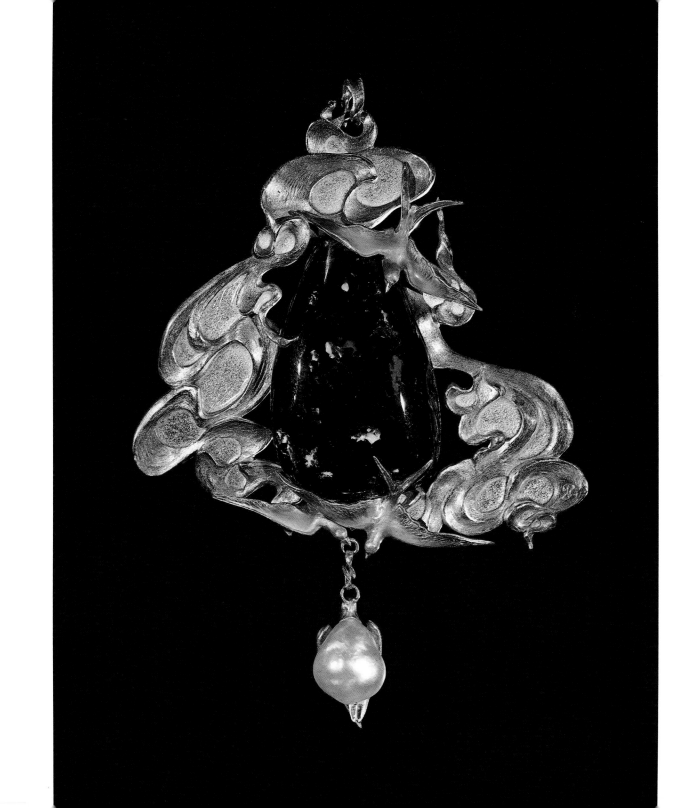

Jacques Gruber
French, 1870-1936

23 Window, ca. 1900

Stained, etched, and leaded glass
151.1 × 133.3 (59½ × 52½)
Signed: on lower left: *Jacques Gruber Nancy*
Virginia Museum of Fine Arts Purchase, The Sydney and Frances
Lewis Art Nouveau Fund, 75.26

Gruber studied at the Ecole de Beaux-Arts in Paris and later worked for Daum Frères at Nancy. He produced numerous designs for furniture, ceramics, and bookbindings, and later opened his own stained-glass studio.

Undoubtedly made for an exposition, this magnificent window is made primarily of triple-layered glass. The jewels are thick molded opalescent glass, while the waterlilies are acid-etched cameo glass, possibly *pâe-de-verre*. A lovely example of Gruber's stained-glass mastery, this work not only employs vivid colors in a great variety, but also displays a diversity of textures, as a result of the many different processes used to create it. As Nancy was a center of glassmaking in France, Gruber had all of the resources and knowledge of the finest glass craftsmen at his command.

The hanging leaves are made of glass with a rippled surface that lends definition to the plant forms. Various glass jewels occur throughout the branches at the intersections of the leading. These not only support the window but also delineate the forms. Etching also details the petals of the waterlilies and the lily pads. Finally, Gruber added layers of colored glass to the reverse, to color the light as it is transmitted through the window, much the same as a painter might build up layers of glazes in an oil painting.

Visually, the lily pads create a stepping-stone effect, leading the viewer to the distant horizon. The hanging leaves frame the window and suggest a frontal plane. The glass jewels, like fireflies in foliage, add a magical element to the dreamlike quality of the entire scene, while the border frames the window and focuses the viewer's eye on the central image.

PROVENANCE: Mrs. Tracy Rust and Mr. Richard Kaufmann, New York, 1975.
PUBLISHED: *Art et Décoration* (date unknown).

86

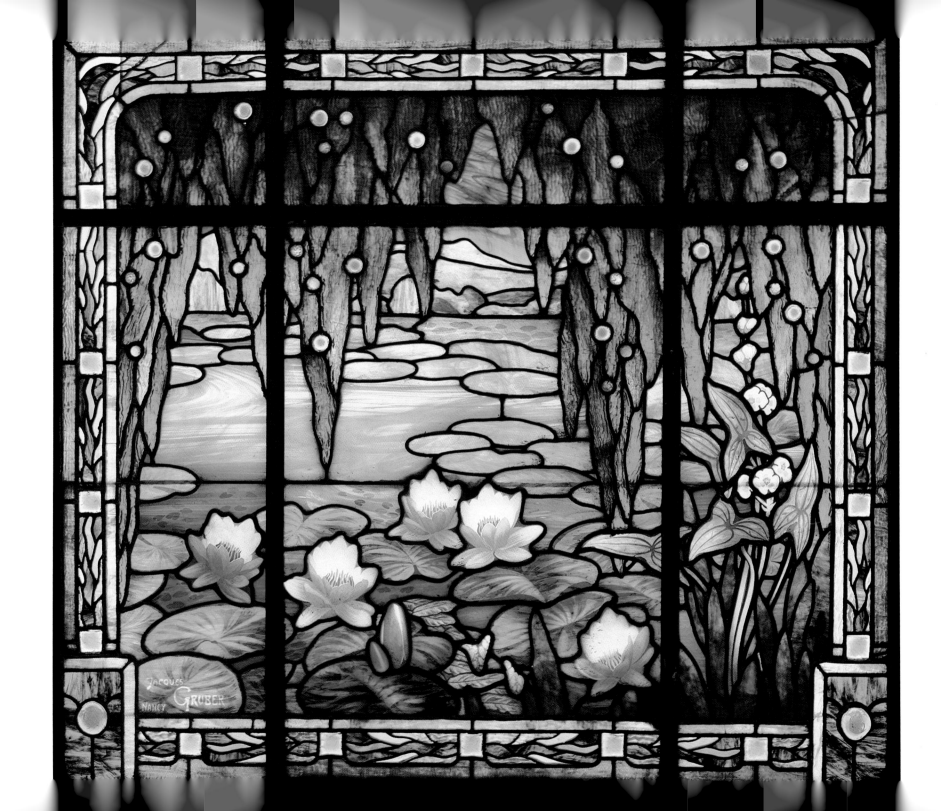

Emile Gallé
French, 1846-1904

24 Ladle, ca. 1900

Marquetry, acid-etched, engraved, and internally decorated blown glass
14.6 × 25.4 × 10.2 (5¾ × 10 × 4)
Signed on proper right front: *Gallé*
Virginia Museum of Fine Arts Purchase, The Sydney and Frances Lewis Art Nouveau Fund, 75.6

Apparently Gallé came to glassmaking through his interest in enameling and through his father's glassmaking business. In his early twenties, Gallé apprenticed at Meisenthal, a center of the glass industry in the Saar Valley, to learn the various techniques of the medium, but it was not until about 1875 that his glass designs began to express his unique vision. By the late 1880s and 1890s, Gallé glass was world renowned and had won numerous awards at major international expositions.

This internally decorated blown-glass ladle with carved applications clearly demonstrates Gallé's dedication to natural forms and his genius in handling glass as a plastic medium. The piece was formed by the conscious effort of a craftsman, but its shape and loose style imply an almost natural genesis. This natural quality is in turn emphasized by the seashell-shaped glass forms embedded in the piece, which make it look more like a geologist's find than a man-made object.

Many of Gallé's greatest glass pieces were inspired by the Symbolist poets and writers. In some cases, Gallé inscribed verses from his literary contemporaries directly into the glass. In other works, the forms convey the mystery and depth of feeling expressed by the Symbolists, put into visible and tangible form by the master glassmaker.

PROVENANCE: Galerie Félix Marcilhac, Paris, 1975.
PUBLISHED: Philippe Garner, "Emile Gallé: His Art and His Industry," *Arts in Virginia* 20 (1979), p. 31.

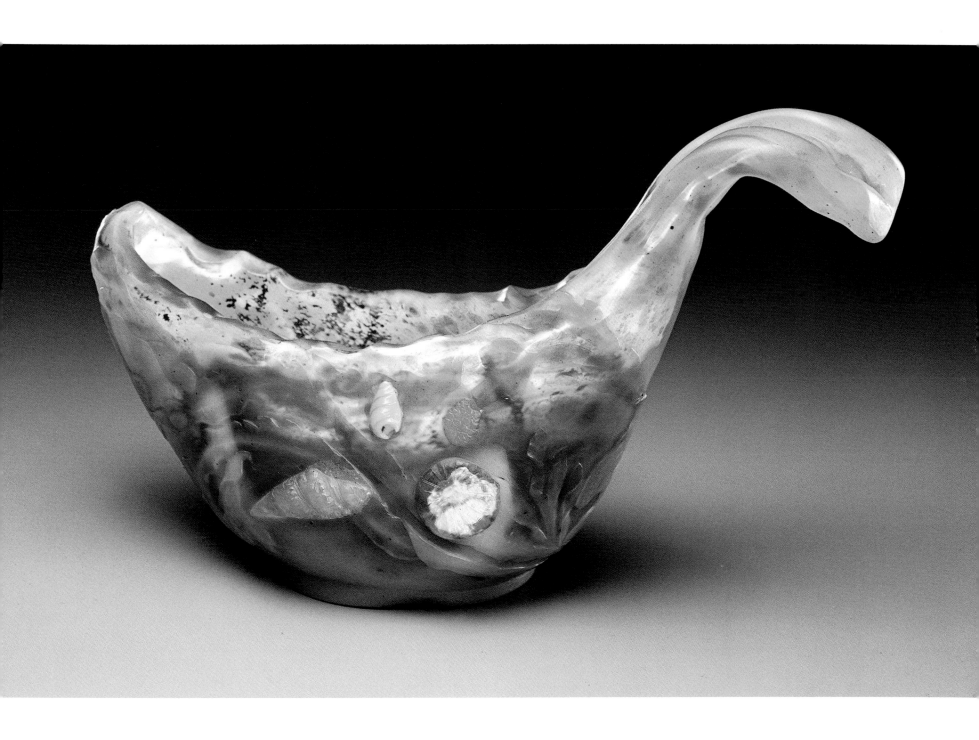

Tiffany Studios
American (New York), 1900-1938

25 Magnolia and Apple Blossom Window, ca. 1900

Stained and leaded Favrile glass
294.6 × 375.9 (116 × 148)
Unsigned
Virginia Museum of Fine Arts Purchase, The Sydney and Frances
Lewis Art Nouveau Fund, 73.47.1/9

This large window is made up of nine sections, one of which is clear glass. The design depicts apple blossoms on the left and magnolias to the right that arch up over the central window, intertwining at its apex. To achieve this remarkably realistic image, Tiffany used heavily milled or grooved came (the lead strips that hold the glass together) to simulate the bark and branches of the trees. In this way, the leading not only helps to support the various pieces of glass that comprise the composition, but also serves as a design element. By having the linear motif double as a structural element, it was no longer necessary to separate the sections by additional horizontal or vertical elements, as is usually necessary in stained-glass work. Thus, a smooth continuity of design was achieved.

The unknown artist who designed this window for Tiffany Studios employed numerous techniques for which Tiffany glass was famous. The petals of the magnolia are made up of so-called "drapery glass," which has literally been folded and bent to form thick waves of glass that give a realistic, three-dimensional effect to the petals. In addition, small, irregularly shaped pieces of fractured glass adhere to or are embedded in the reverse of the sheet glass, creating various shadings and colors, much like a painter might employ glazes. Similarly, glass plating is used on the leaves, both to lend textural richness and to vary their colors. With this technique, several layers of different colored glass, placed one behind the other, create special effects as light penetrates them.

For the original owner of this lovely window, George E. Dimock, the seasons never changed outside his paneled study. The apple tree was forever in bloom, and the magnolia continually bore its wax-like flowers. And so the artist's goal was successfully achieved: "Mr. Tiffany's commission was to preserve for the full year the spring impression of the blossoms on an apple tree and a magnolia tree that were part of the view from the window."[20]

PROVENANCE: George E. Dimock, Elizabeth, New Jersey; E.J. Dimock, Cambridge, Maryland, 1973.
PUBLISHED: Alastair Duncan, *Tiffany Windows* (New York: Simon and Schuster, 1980), illus. p. 76, color plate no. 93, p. 118. Patricia Bayer, "Art Nouveau," *Antiques World* (October 1981), illus. p. 25.

20. Letter from E.J. Dimock to Virginia Museum Curator Pinkney L. Near, undated, 1973.

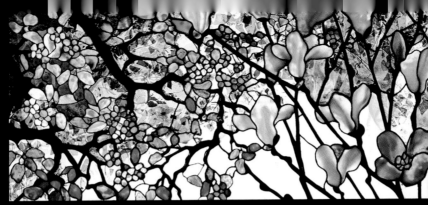
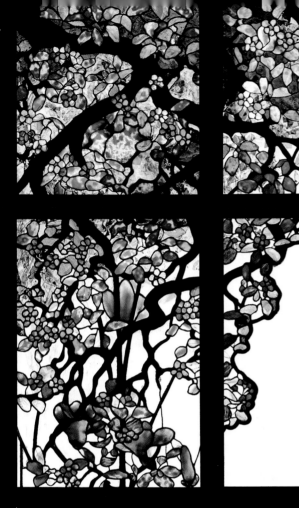
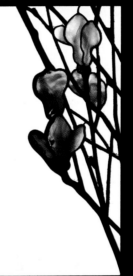
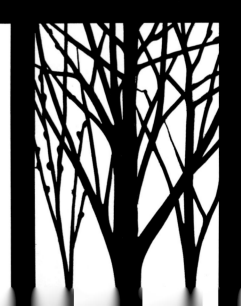
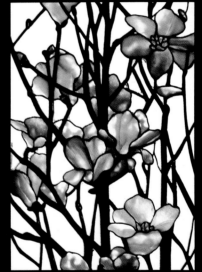
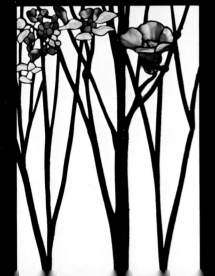

Tiffany Studios
American (New York), 1900-1938

26 Autumn Leaves Lamp, ca. 1899

Favrile glass, bronze
80 × 27.3 diameter (31½ × 10¾)
Shade unsigned; base impressed on bottom: *Tiffany Studios New York 3051*
Virginia Museum of Fine Arts, Gift of Sydney and Frances Lewis, 85.156 a/b

Unlike the vast majority of Tiffany's lamps, Autumn Leaves has a shade that forms a nearly complete globe. Totally surrounding the bulb and socket, the orb only permits transmitted light to emanate softly through the glass, without the distraction of any harsh, direct light.

The design of the shade is exceptional in that flat pieces of glass have been arranged in such a skillful and meticulous manner that they form a perfect sphere. Branches and stems rise from the central core and then merge into an ever-increasing number of varicolored leaves, terminating in a crown composed almost exclusively of leaves.

The glass globe is fitted with what Tiffany referred to as a Tyler base of patinated bronze, cast to suggest that it is an organic form growing from the foot. The base connects to branch-like extensions on the bottom of the globe.

PROVENANCE: Sotheby Parke Bernet Los Angeles, 1976.

PUBLISHED: Tiffany Studios Price List 1906; *19th and 20th Century Works of Art*, catalogue of sale (Los Angeles: Sotheby Parke Bernet Los Angeles, March 10, 1976), no. 1021, illus. on back cover; William Feldstein, Jr., and Alastair Duncan, *The Lamps of Tiffany Studios* (New York: Harry N. Abrams, 1983), pp. 58-59, illus. p. 59.

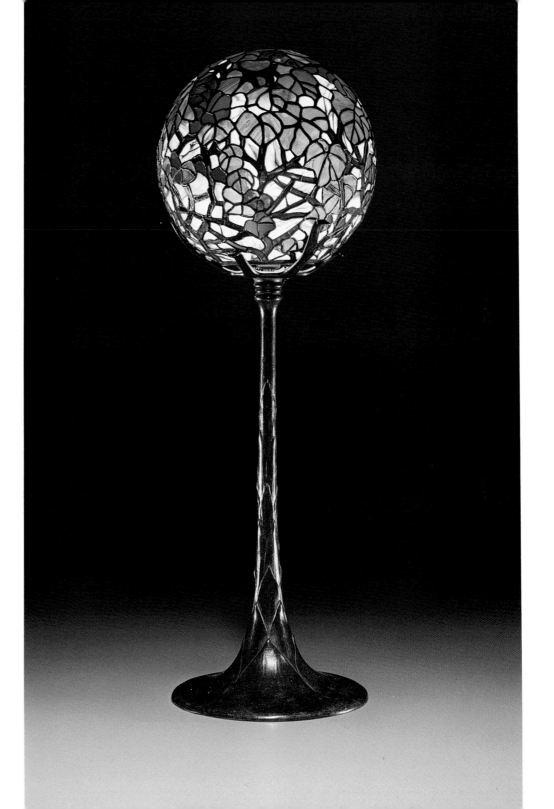

Tiffany Studios
American (New York), 1900-1938

27

Lava Vase, ca. 1900

Favrile glass
13.7 × 17.7 diameter (5⅜ × 7)
Inscribed on bottom: L.C. *Tiffany-Favrile* 22 A-Coll.
Virginia Museum of Fine Arts Purchase, The Sydney and Frances
Lewis Art Nouveau Fund, 81.195

The name Louis C. Tiffany has become synonymous with glass. Although Tiffany's enterprises began producing stained-glass windows as early as 1879, it was not until the early 1890s that they started making vases and other smaller objects.[21] The next half-century witnessed the manufacture of a plethora of glass objects bearing the Tiffany name. Tiffany's firm—not to be confused with Tiffany & Company, his father's New York jewelry firm—bore many different names during its thirty-eight-year history: Louis C. Tiffany and Co.; Lewis Comfort Tiffany and Associated Artists; Tiffany Glass Co.; Tiffany Glass and Decorating Co.; Allied Arts Co.; and Tiffany Studios.[22]

During his long career, Tiffany constantly urged his glass blowers to experiment with various techniques. One of the most incredible effects they achieved was what he called "lava glass." Named for its resemblance to volcanic lava, it was one of the most abstract of all Tiffany glass types and was one of his favorites.[23] Its rough texture, uneven surfaces and shapes, and rich, iridescent color made it appear to have been formed through natural evolution.

This particular lava-glass vase was once part of Tiffany's own personal collection, as the inscription A–Coll. on the bottom indicates. Its semitransparent body has an irregular overlay of textured glass that allows the basic form to show through. Applied to the exterior surface are heavy globules of gold-colored glass that infuse the whole piece with a mystical iridescence reminiscent of ancient glass, which Tiffany greatly admired.

PROVENANCE: L.C. Tiffany Collection, Laurelton Hall, Long Island, New York; Robert and Gladys Koch, Stamford, Connecticut, 1981.

PUBLISHED: Robert Koch, "Tiffany's Abstractions in Glass," *Antiques* (June 1974), p. 1291, illus. p. 1293, pl. 3. Robert Koch, *Louis C. Tiffany's Art Glass* (New York: Crown Publishers, Inc., 1977), illus. pl. 22.

---

21. Robert Koch, *Louis C. Tiffany's Art Glass* (New York: Crown Publishers, Inc., 1977), p.3.
22. For the definitive history of Tiffany's work see Robert Koch, *Louis C. Tiffany's Glass –Bronzes–Lamps* (New York: Crown Publishers, Inc., 1971) and Robert Koch, *Louis C. Tiffany, Rebel in Glass* (New York: Crown Publishers, Inc., 1964).
23. Robert Koch, *Louis C. Tiffany's Art Glass* (New York: Crown Publishers,Inc., 1977), p. 12.

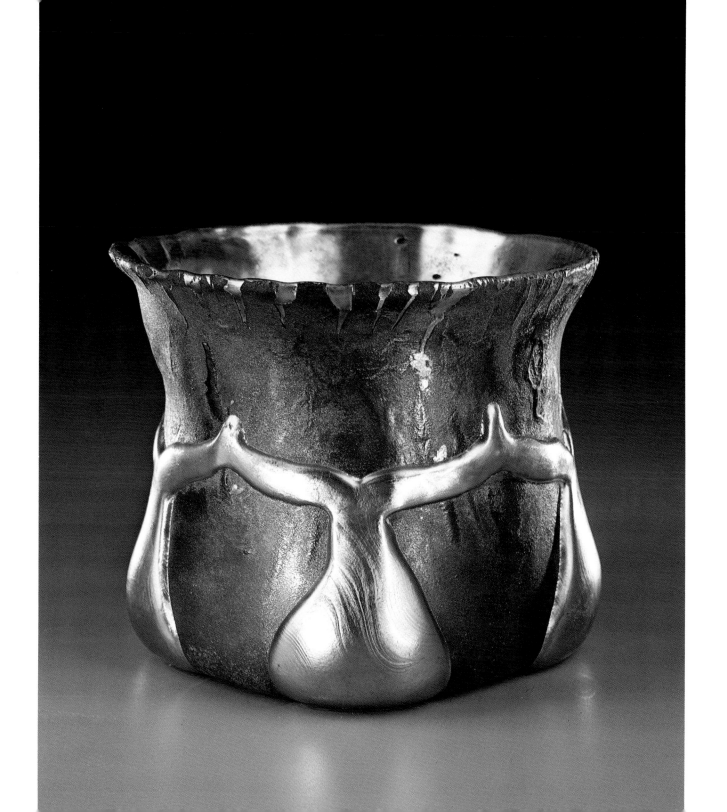

Johann Loetz Witwe Glassworks
Austrian (Klostermühle), 1836-1939

28 Vase, ca. 1900

Blown glass, applied metal decoration
12.7 × 11.4 diameter (5 × 4½)
Signed on bottom: F|?| 3049
Virginia Museum of Fine Arts, Gift of Mrs. J.F.M. Stewart, 74.15.16

A great deal of superb art glass was produced in Europe, particularly Austria, in the mid to late nineteenth century. A glass company founded in the early nineteenth century at Klostermühle was bought by Johann Loetz and, upon his death in 1848, was taken over by his widow. Renamed Glasfabrik Johann Loetz Witwe, the firm existed until the onset of World War II.

Unlike Tiffany, Loetz employed many well-known designers, including those who were working with the famed Wiener Werkstätte, among them Koloman Moser, Josef Hoffmann, Leopold Bauer, and Gustave Gurschner. Their pieces were made of iridescent, transparent, or opaque glass created either to stand alone, in metal mounts, or as parts of other objects, such as lamps.

Much of Loetz's glass was left unmarked; signed pieces were usually meant for a foreign market. Their iridescent glass was a natural rival of that produced by Louis Comfort Tiffany.

Unfortunately, the designer of this vase is unknown, but its maker's anonymity does not detract from its beauty. The delicate application of metal floral forms causes the two elements—metal and glass—to interact closely in overall design and effect. Decoration tended to be more important to the Loetz designers than the shape of the vase.

PROVENANCE: Mrs. J.F.M. Stewart, Upperville, Virginia, 1974.

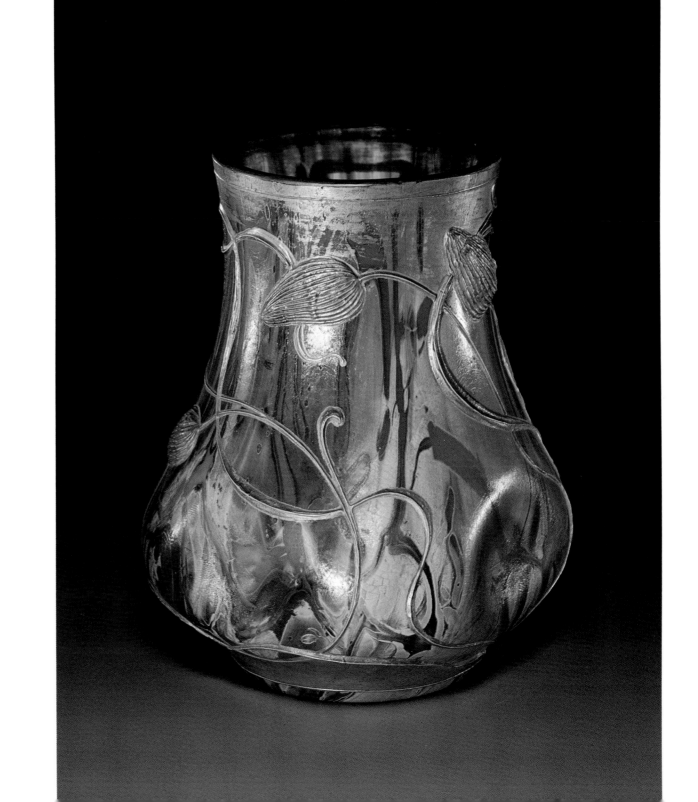

Józef Rippl-Rónai
Hungarian, 1861-1927
for
Zsolnay Ceramic Works
Hungarian (Pécs), established 1862

29 Vase, ca. 1900

Glazed ceramic
15.2 × 10.7 diameter (6 × 4¼)
Stamped on bottom: Zsolnay seal (five-spired church) and 7182
Virginia Museum of Fine Arts Purchase, The Sydney and Frances
Lewis Art Nouveau Fund, 78.144

The Zsolnay Ceramic Works of Pécs flourished under the direction of Vilmos Zsolnay, son of the factory's founder. The Zsolnay seal on the bottom of this vase depicts a five-spired church, a hallmark derived from Fünfkirchen (five churches), the original name of the town of Pécs.

Zsolnay employed a number of designers and artists to produce his marvelous and distinctive ware. One of the most famous was the painter Józef Rippl-Rónai, who had been trained in Munich and in Paris, where he became acquainted with the work of the Nabis. Their influence is apparent in much of his work.

Rippl-Rónai's philosophy of art and design was similar to that of William Morris and John Ruskin. He firmly believed that the artist's purpose was to apply his own taste and skill into industry so that manufactured objects would reflect the artist's higher taste and thus improve the lives of the consumers. He also believed that new forms, not those of the past, should define the environment of the consumer. All of this, according to Rippl-Rónai, was "to contribute to the foundation of a social life on a more individualistic basis,"[24] thus bringing order to daily life.

PROVENANCE: Modernism Gallery, San Francisco, 1978.

24. Józef Rippl-Rónai, "Extracts from His Memoirs," 1911, as quoted in *Hungarian Art Nouveau*, exhibition catalogue (Washington, D.C.: Smithsonian Institution Traveling Exhibition Service, 1977), p. 67.

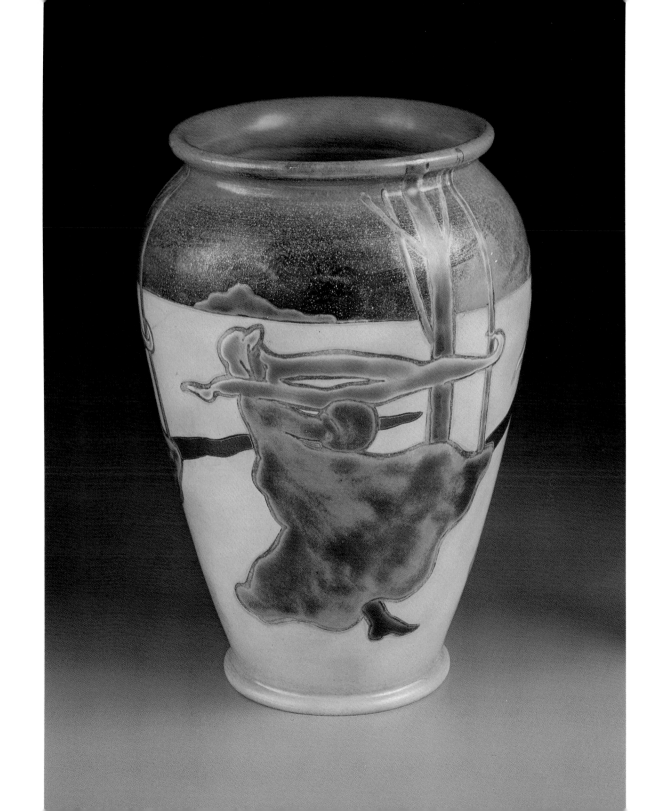

Leopold Bauer
Austrian, 1872-1938

30
Cabinet for a Postcard Collector, ca. 1900

Sycamore, maple, various other woods in marquetry, brass, felt
90.1 × 67.2 × 45.6 (35½ × 26½ × 18)
Stamped on underside in purple ink: *Schl. No:* 7013; label on
underside: L. Nr *2142* R. Nr *3.0/10-1900*; on lock plate: *Portois
& Fix/Wien* 7013
Virginia Museum of Fine Arts, Gift of Sydney and Frances Lewis
85.79

In the late nineteenth century, Austria underwent a revolution in its arts, particularly architecture. This revolution was led by Otto Wagner, whose 1895 book, translated as *Modern Architecture*, became a handbook of contemporary aesthetics at the turn of the century. Although ridiculed by architects of his own generation, Wagner was hailed as a bold innovator and leader in the field by his students and followers.

One of his students was Leopold Bauer. As with other architects of this period, Bauer designed not only buildings but also many of the furnishings to be used therein.

This architectonic cabinet was made to Bauer's specifications by the Viennese firm of Portois and Fix around 1900. Strict horizontals and verticals dominate the design, and the only decoration to which Bauer conceded is the color of the woods, the inlay on the sides, front, and rear, and the small designs on the metal-sheathed feet. The inlay pattern is reminiscent of much of the work that was being done in England, particularly the repeating patterns of Voysey. The work of English artists and architects was transmitted internationally through such journals as *The Studio*, with which Bauer was probably familiar. Because of its specific purpose, to hold a postcard collection, this cabinet is in all likelihood a commissioned piece.

By 1906 Bauer's work had undergone a transition. According to the contemporary critic Hugo Haberfeld:

> Bauer's views have undergone a marked change. Not that he has at any point diverged from modern principles, but his attitude toward the architecture of the past is no longer one of downright opposition. He has come to recognize that if architecture as an art is to be a vital force, it cannot wholly neglect tradition. He would step in where the organic evolution of Viennese architecture was suddenly interrupted at the beginning of the nineteenth century, the period of the Biedermeier style.[25]

In spite of these comments, photographs of Bauer's work in 1906 still show a strong influence of Charles Rennie Mackintosh, whose 1900 exhibition in Vienna greatly affected the work of many of the younger Viennese architects.

PROVENANCE: La Boetie, Inc., New York, 1972.

PUBLISHED: Ludwig Abels, ed., "Die Kunstgewerbeaustellung der Secession," *Das Interieur* (Vienna: Kunstverlag Anton Schroll & Co., 1901), illus. p. 20.

EXHIBITED: *Kunstgewerbeaustellung der Secession*, Vienna, 1901; Art Nouveau Gallery, Virginia Museum of Fine Arts, Richmond, long-term loan 1975-1982.

25. Hugo Haberfeld, "The Architectural Revival in Austria," *The Art-Revival in Austria*, a special issue of *The Studio* (London, 1906): C viii.

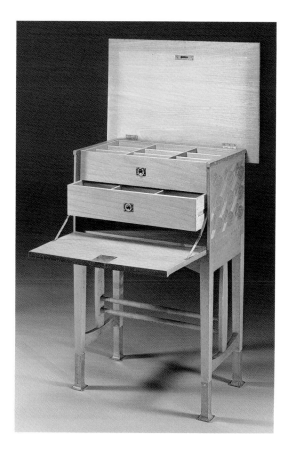
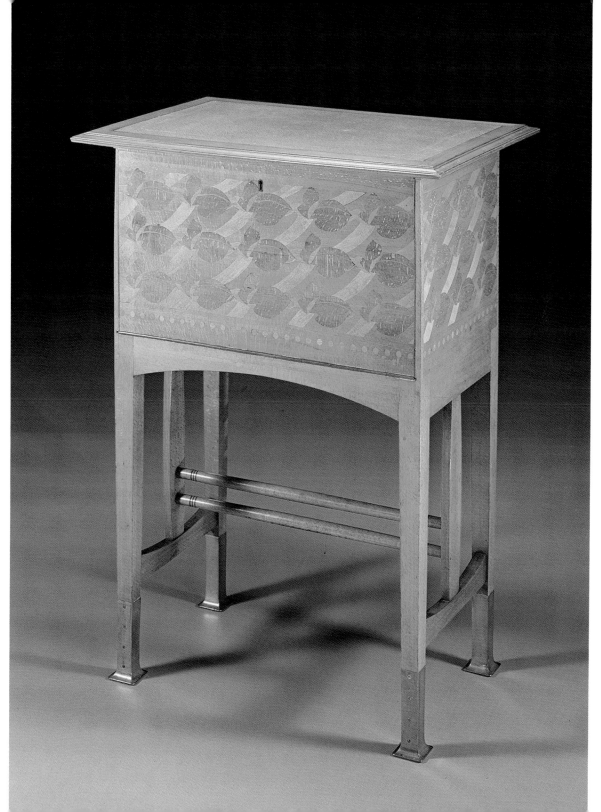

Georges de Feure
French, 1868-1943

31

Window, 1901-02

Stained and leaded glass
200 × 90.9 (78¾ × 35¹³⁄₁₆)
Unsigned
Virginia Museum of Fine Arts, Gift of Sydney and Frances Lewis,
85.349

Georges de Feure, whose surname was originally van Sluijters, was born in Paris and raised in The Netherlands. His father was the architect Jean Hendrick van Sluijters.[26]

In his review of de Feure's exhibition at Bing's *Maison de l'Art Nouveau*, Gabriel Mourey rhapsodized on the designer's work:

Georges de Feure is a fantasist of exquisite imagination, of a preciosity of endless seduction; he is the most personal and the most refined, with the gift of grace and versatility, an acuity of vision beyond excess; whether you like his art or not, it is impossible not to submit to its charm; strange charm, in truth almost a little sickly, like the perfume of the fantastic flowers which he composes, as the smile and the glance of the women which populate his work as a decorator and as a painter.[27]

Although these comments were made about a 1903 exhibition of de Feure's work in Bing's shop, they could be applied directly to the window shown here, which was included in that exhibition. The window is believed to have been made in the studio of Müller-Hickler in Darmstadt, Germany.[28]

In his research, Gabriel Weisberg has shown that many of de Feure's female images derive from literary sources, particularly the writings of Charles Baudelaire and Georges Rodenbach.[29] Although no specific source can be cited as the basis for this image, the woman's highly seductive and slightly sinister pose and gaze, as well as her floral imagery, present a provocative portrait of the elusive turn-of-the-century femme fatale.

PROVENANCE: Maison de l'Art Nouveau, Paris, 1903; Sotheby Parke Bernet Monaco S.A., 1983.

PUBLISHED: *Deutsche Kunst und Dekoration* (April 1903). *Oeuvres de Georges de Feure*, exhibition catalogue (Paris: L'Art Nouveau Bing, 1903). *Arts Decoratifs, Styles 1900 et 1925*, catalogue of sale (Monte Carlo: Sotheby Parke Bernet Monaco S.A., March 6, 1983), no. 92. Carla Cerutti, *Arti Decorative del Novecento: Liberty* (Novara: Istituto Geografico de Agostini, 1985), illus. p. 37 and cover.

EXHIBITED: "Oeuvres de Georges de Feure à l'Art Nouveau Bing," Paris, March–April, 1903.

26. Gabriel P. Weisberg, "Georges von Sluijters 'De Feure:' An Identity Unmasked," *Gazette des Beaux-Arts* (October 1974): 231-32.
27. Gabriel Mourey, "L'Exposition Georges de Feure," *Art et Décoration* 13 (January-June 1903): 162.
28. *Arts Décoratifs, Styles 1900 et 1925*, auction catalogue, March 6, 1983 (Monaco: Sotheby Parke-Bernet Monaco S.A., 1983), p. 29.
29. Gabriel P. Weisberg, "Georges De Feure's Mysterious Women," *Gazette des Beaux-Arts* (October 1974): 223-30.

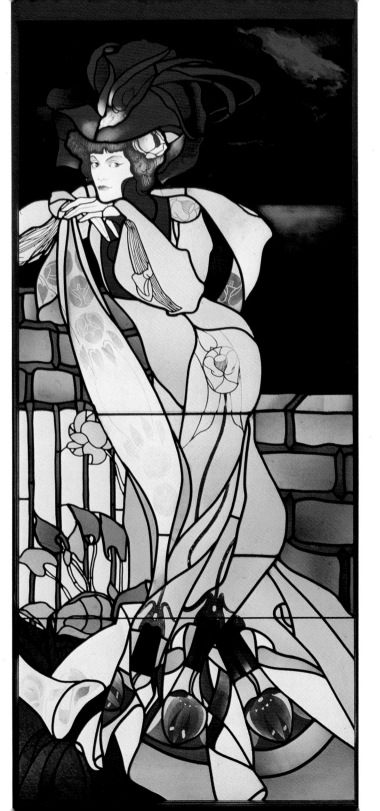

Carlo Bugatti
Italian, 1855-1940

32

Chair, 1902

Parchment over wood, copper, paint
88.9 × 41.8 × 53.3 (35 × 16½ × 21)
Unsigned
Virginia Museum of Fine Arts Purchase, The Sydney and Frances
Lewis Art Nouveau Fund, 72.10

Carlo Bugatti was the father of a family of creative people. He was himself a furniture designer and painter, while his elder son Ettore designed the famous Bugatti automobile and his younger son, Rembrandt, was a noted sculptor of animal figures. In addition, Bugatti's father, Luigi, had also been a fairly well-known sculptor and his grandson Jean created award-winning designs for car bodies in the 1930s.

Following the success of the Paris 1900 Exposition, the Italians organized the Exposizione Internazionale at Turin in 1902. Unlike its predecessors and indeed anticipating the Paris 1925 Exposition, the Turin exhibition was organized to include only those works that reflected creative innovations in design, and to exclude those that merely echoed historical precedents.

Among several outstanding rooms designed for the Exposition were three by Bugatti. This serpentine-curved chair is one of a set of four designed for the "Salle de Jeu et Conversation," a recreation room of sorts (fig. 14). In addition, Bugatti created a bedroom and a salon, designed in the same motif. Although critics reviewed his work with mixed reaction, Bugatti's furniture designs received awards both at the Paris 1900 Exposition and at Turin.

Of all Bugatti's output, the furniture he produced for the Turin 1902 Exposition is among his most outstanding, both in concept and execution. For the most part his other furniture was an eccentric variation of pseudo-Moorish. Although these idiosyncratic pieces were not derived from specific models, they owe at least a second-hand debt to designs of the Middle East.

It is not accurate to describe Bugatti's furniture as of the Style 1900. It is better to say that he was an innovative furniture designer who happened to be working during this particularly rich period of design history. His only possible relationship to Art Nouveau is his use of stylized floral and insect decorations on many of his works, including the painted decorations on this chair.

PROVENANCE: Alain Lesieutre, Paris, 1972.

PUBLISHED: Italo Geirona, Il Tempo dell' Art Nouveau (Florence: Vallechi, no date), pl. 358. Alain Lesieutre, The Spirit and Splendour of Art Deco (New York: Paddington Press Ltd., 1974), illus. p. 8. Frank Russell, ed., A Century of Chair Design (New York: Rizzoli International Publications Inc., 1980), illus no. 5, p. 88. Patricia Bayer, "Art Nouveau," Antiques World (October 1981), illus. pp. 24, 26.

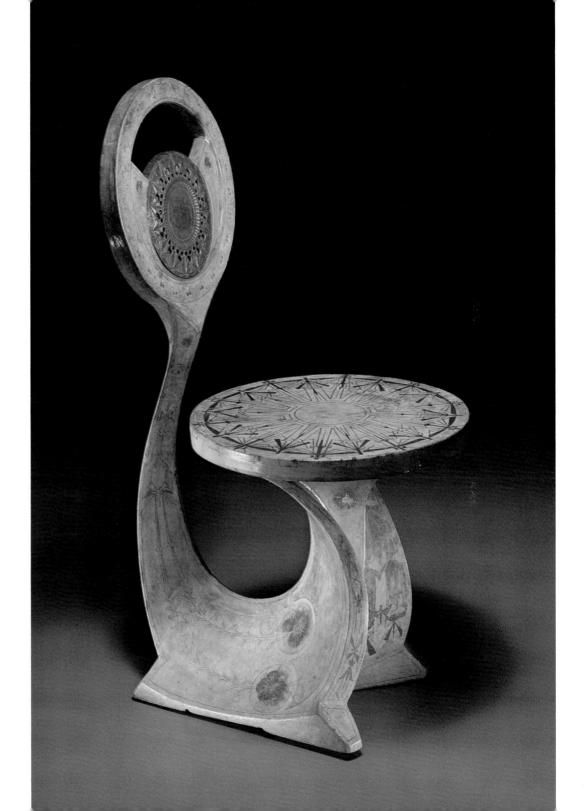

Josef Hoffmann
Austrian, 1870-1956

33 Footed Dish with Cover, 1902

Hammered silver, turquoise
16.2 × 7 diameter (6⅜ × 2¾)
Stamped with artist's mark and metalsmith's mark on foot and lid
Virginia Museum of Fine Arts Purchase, The Sydney and Frances
Lewis Art Nouveau Fund, 72.20

Josef Hoffmann studied architecture at the Vienna Academy of Art under Carl von Hasenauer and Otto Wagner, whose studio he entered in 1896. In the following year, Hoffmann was a founding member of the Vienna Secession. In 1899 he was appointed Professor at the Kunstgewerbeschule in Vienna, where he taught until 1941.

As in so many other countries around the turn of the century, Hoffmann was one of many Viennese artists who became increasingly concerned with the lack of quality in man-made objects. Echoing the earlier philosophy of Morris and Ruskin, Hoffmann wrote in 1903: "The boundless evil, caused by shoddy mass-produced goods and by uncritical imitation of earlier styles, is like a tidal wave sweeping across the world . . . . The machine has largely replaced the hand and the business-man has supplanted the craftsman."[30]

To return to the concepts of fine craftsmanship, Hoffmann became a founder of the Wiener Werkstätte in 1903, an association of artisans based in part on C.R. Ashbee's Guild of Handicraft in England. Hoffmann's aim was:

> . . . to create an island of tranquility in our own country which, amid the joyful hum of arts and crafts, would be welcome to anyone who professes faith in Ruskin and Morris . . . . We wish to create an inner relationship linking public, designer and worker and we want to produce good and simple articles of everyday use. Our guiding principle is function, utility our first condition, and our strength must lie in good proportions and the proper treatment of materials. We shall seek to decorate when it seems required but we do not feel obliged to adorn at any price.[31]

Hoffmann and his fellow artists ran into the same problems as Morris did, in that the works they produced could not be priced to be affordable to the common man but were available only to the wealthy.

This small covered dish was created in 1902, the year prior to the establishment of the Wiener Werkstätte. Although an early work, it bears many of the motifs Hoffmann used sparingly as decoration. For example, the small silver spheres at the base of the stem and interspersed with the tall, leaf-like shapes repeated on the lid supporting the turquoise are found in much of Hoffmann's early work in silver. Despite its size, the dish appears almost monumental—an obvious reflection of Hoffmann's architectural training. When he designed this dish, Hoffmann was just beginning his long career as architect, designer, and teacher.

PROVENANCE: Primavera Gallery, New York, 1972.

PUBLISHED: *Dekorative Kunst* 2 (October 1902): 40. *Art and Design in Vienna* 1900-1930, exhibition catalogue (New York: La Boetie Gallery, 1972), illus. no. 3, p. 5.

EXHIBITED: *Art Nouveau*, Virginia Museum Artmobile Exhibition, Fall 1972-Spring 1974; *Vienna Moderne: 1898-1918*, Cooper-Hewitt Museum, New York, November 27, 1978-February 4, 1979; Sarah Campbell Blaffer Gallery, University of Houston, March 2-April 29, 1979; Portland (Oregon) Art Museum, June-July 1979; Smart Gallery, University of Chicago, January 11, 1979-February 24, 1980.

---

30. Josef Hoffmann, "The Work Program of the Wiener Werkstätte 1903," as quoted in *Josef Hoffmann: Architect and Designer* 1870-1956 (New York: Galerie Metropol, no date), p. 7.
31. Hoffmann, "Wiener Werkstätte 1903," pp. 7-8.

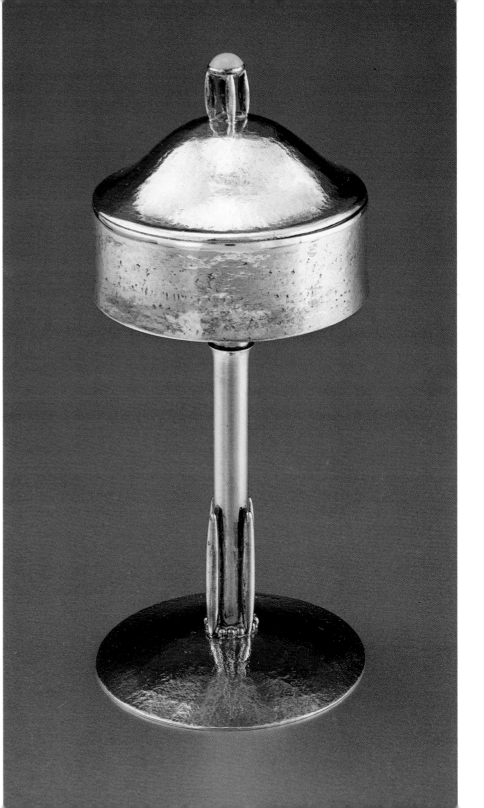

Peter Behrens
German, 1868-1940

 34 Dining-Room Chair, 1902

Polished oak, upholstery
98.4 × 45 × 46.3 (38¾ × 17¾ × 18¼)
Unsigned
Virginia Museum of Fine Arts, Gift of Sydney and Frances Lewis,
85.138

During his long and productive career, Peter Behrens was active in many branches of the arts. Born in Hamburg, he was trained as a painter at the Academy in Karlsruhe and later studied with Ferdinand Brütt in Düsseldorf. He lived in Munich where he helped establish the Sezession and later the Vereinigten Werkstätten für Kunst im Handwerk. In 1899 he was called to Darmstadt by the Grand-Duke of Hesse to form an artists' colony in that city. Behrens's first architectural project was to design his own house and all interior fittings. His work was shown at the Paris 1900 exhibition and at the Turin exhibition in 1902, the same year he created this chair.

This is one of a set of at least six chairs; the set appears in a 1903 photograph in *Deutsche Kunst und Dekoration* and is described as part of the furnishings of a modern room displayed at the A. Wertheim department store in Berlin. The chairs originally had woven seats.

A set of dining furniture by Behrens was sold at Christie's, London, on April 17, 1984. According to the catalogue of that sale, this set was identical to that from which the chair in the Lewis Collection originates.

Behrens had served as the director of several art schools, finally becoming artistic director for the firm of A.E.G. in Berlin, where he worked from 1922 to 1936. It was there that he displayed his skill as one of Germany's leading industrial designers, conceiving everyday objects that could be considered the product of a successful marriage of art and industry.

PROVENANCE: Modernism Gallery, New York, 1983.

PUBLISHED: *Deutsche Kunst und Dekoration* (1902-1903), pp. 259, 291-92. *Innendekoration* (1903), p. 6. Stephan Tschudi Madsen, *Sources of Art Nouveau* (New York: DaCapo Press, 1975), illus. p. 425. *Ein Dokument Deutscher Kunst* 4, (Darmstadt: 1977), illus. p. 3. *Peter Behrens und Nürnberg* (Nürnberg: Germanisches Nationalmuseum, 1980), illus. p. 57. Frank Russell, ed., *Chair Design* (New York: Rizzoli International Publications Inc., 1980), p. 66. Derek E. Ostergard, *Mackintosh to Mollino: Fifty Years of Chair Design* (New York: Barry Friedman Ltd., 1984), cat. no. 15.

EXHIBITED: part of a group of dining-room furniture by Behrens in the exhibition *Moderne Wohnkunst bei A. Wertheim*, Wohnraumes des Warenhauses A. Wertheim, Berlin, 1902. *Mackintosh to Mollino: Fifty Years of Chair Design:* Barry Friedman Ltd., New York, November 13, 1984-February 13, 1985.

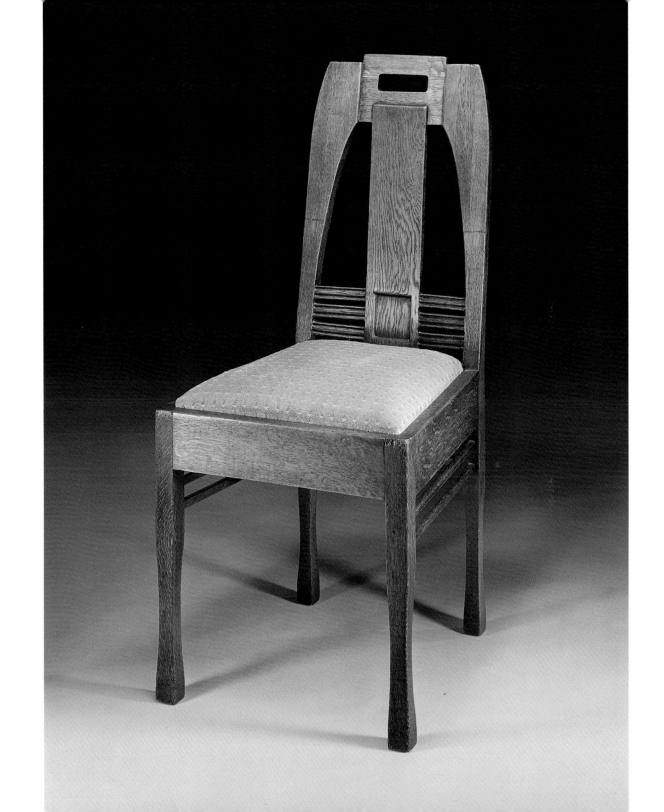

Attributed to Archibald Knox
English, 1864-1933
for
Liberty and Company
English (London), established 1875

35 Mirror with Easel Back, 1902

Silver, enamel, wood, mirror
47.6 × 22.5 × 1.2 (18¾ × 8⅞ × ½)
Signed with firm mark: *Cymric*, and hallmarks for Birmingham and 1902 on lower left
Virginia Museum of Fine Arts, Gift of Sydney and Frances Lewis, 85.292

Liberty and Company was originally founded by Arthur Lasenby Liberty as the East India House in London in 1875; the firm specialized in Oriental and Oriental-inspired fabrics, porcelains, and other goods. These accessories were suitable for followers of the Aesthetic Movement, which held Japanese design in high esteem. The shop soon became known for its wide range of decorative objects, and the name was later changed to Liberty and Company.

Around 1899, recognizing the importance of the Arts and Crafts Movement and the possibilities of mass-producing decorative objects for the market, the astute Liberty began to produce a wide range of original silverwork and jewelry. The designs of the new pieces no longer depended on the orientalizing fashion but instead blazed new artistic trails.

Unlike the true Arts and Crafts objects, such as those being produced by Ashbee's Guild of Handicraft, many items that Liberty's craftsmen turned out were actually die-cast or stamped and then reworked to give the appearance of having been fashioned by hand. Nevertheless, some stunning and indeed unique pieces were crafted by Liberty's skilled artisans. Because the name of the company and that of its founder was of primary importance, designers were not permitted to sign their works and remained anonymous. We do know, however, that such highly regarded designers as Rex Silver, Jesse M. King, and, above all, Archibald Knox, produced designs and supervised their production in silver and pewter from the years 1899 to 1926.

Liberty silver was produced under the trade name "Cymric," from the Welsh. Liberty went into partnership with W.H. Haseler, manufacturing goldsmiths and jewelers of Birmingham, in 1901. The Haseler firm produced the majority of Liberty Cymric wares, as well as all of the later pewter wares known by the trade name "Tudric."

This mirror has been attributed to Archibald Knox on the basis of its style and exquisite workmanship. Its design, as with so much of Knox's work, shows a strong kinship to Celtic ornament of the early Middle Ages. There were the remains of many Celtic monuments on the Isle of Man, where Knox was born, and Knox had selected Celtic design as the subject matter for his final examination in the last year of his education. These same Celtic motifs—notably the *entrelac*, or interlaced decoration—appear in many other works produced at Liberty's in both silver and pewter.

Knox is thought to have worked in the design studio of Dr. Christopher Dresser. He began work for Liberty around 1899, designing for approximately ten years. Unfortunately, most records have been lost or destroyed, and it is therefore impossible to date his designs for Liberty. He also taught design at art schools and even traveled to the United States in 1912, apparently to find work; the venture proved unsuccessful, since he returned a year later, to his native Isle of Man where he spent the remainder of his life.

PROVENANCE: Sotheby's Belgravia, London, 1975.

PUBLISHED: *Art at Auction, The Year at Sotheby Park Bernet, 1974-1975* (New York: Viking Press, 1975), illus. p. 448. *Decorative Arts 1880-1950*, catalogue of sale (London: Sotheby's Belgravia, 1975), illus. no. 35, p. 11. Rowland and Betty Elzea, *The Pre-Raphaelite Era 1848-1914*, (Wilmington: Society of Fine Arts, 1976), cat. no. 8-32; illus. p. 195. John Culme, *Nineteenth Century Silver* (London: Country Life Books, 1977), p. 112; illus. back cover of jacket.

EXHIBITED: Art Nouveau Gallery, Virginia Museum of Fine Arts, Richmond, January 1976; *The Pre-Raphaelite Era 1848-1914*, Delaware Art Museum, April-June 1976.

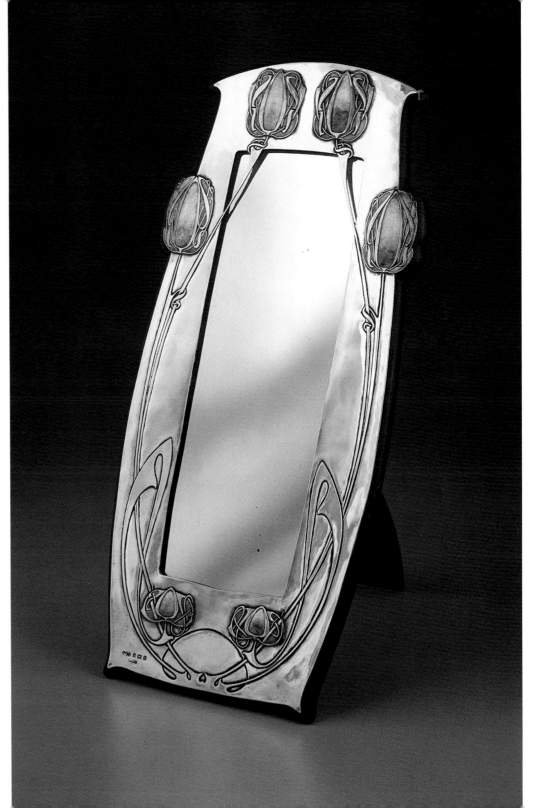

Eugène Gaillard
French, 1862-1933

36 Tea Table with Removable Tray, ca. 1902

Mahogany, brass
Table: 109.8 × 43.1 × 43.1 (43¼ × 17 × 17)
Tray: 1.9 × 41.5 × 41.5 (¾ × 16⅜ × 16⅜)
Marked on brass marker attached under top: *Modèle Déposé*
Virginia Museum of Fine Arts, Gift of Sydney and Frances Lewis,
85.111 a/b

This remarkable tea table, created for Bing's shop, shows Gaillard's mastery of combining the unwieldy Art Nouveau form with straightforward function. When closed, the table is a suitable stand for displaying objects or plants. However, by opening out the carefully sculpted and fitted shelves, it becomes a highly functional serving piece with a removable serving tray.

Gaillard was one of three major designers for Bing's shop, *La Maison de l'Art Nouveau*; Colonna and de Feure were the other two. It was Bing who first recognized Gaillard's capabilities and entrusted to him the design of furnishing a major part of his pavilion in the 1900 Paris Exhibition. Because of Gaillard's contribution, the rooms exuded a quiet charm and elegance coupled with a strong sense of design and respect for materials.

This tea table also displays the artist's ability to exploit the Art Nouveau line without allowing its strong curves to dominate either the wood or the quiet strength and elegance of its overall form. Only when the shelves are opened out do we notice the familiar asymmetrical curve that characterizes the Style 1900. The other lines of the table are quite symmetrical and are decorated only with subtle carving at the joints and the feet.

PROVENANCE: Lillian Nassau Ltd., New York, 1971.

PUBLISHED: *Album de Références de l'Art Nouveau*, a photographic inventory of Bing's shop now in the Bibliothèque des Arts Décoratifs. *Art et Décoration* 1 (1902), p. 22, no. 439. Laurence Buffet-Challié, *Le Modern Style* (Paris: Baschet et Cie., 1975), illus. p. 49. Yvonne Brunhammer et al. *Art Nouveau Belgium/France* (Houston: Institute for the Arts, Rice University, 1976), illus. no. 310, p. 208.

EXHIBITED: *Art Nouveau*, Virginia Museum of Fine Arts, Richmond, November 22-December 26, 1971, no. 29. *Art Nouveau Belgium/France*, Rice University, Houston, March 25-November 7, 1976; *Design in the Service of Tea*, Cooper-Hewitt Museum, New York, August 7-October 28, 1984.

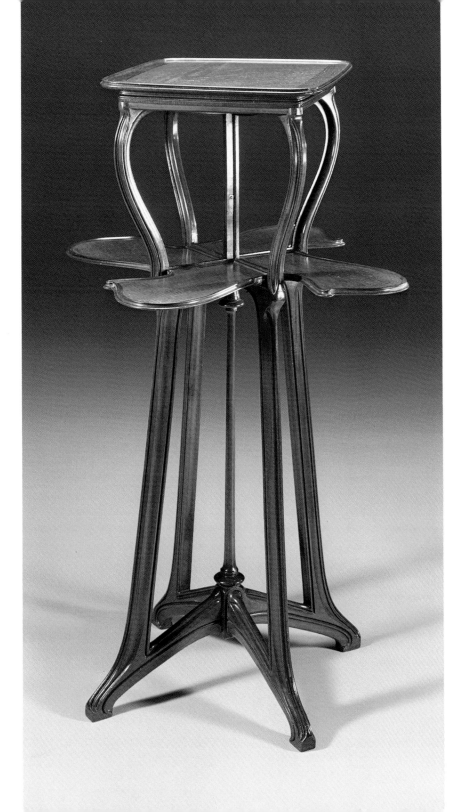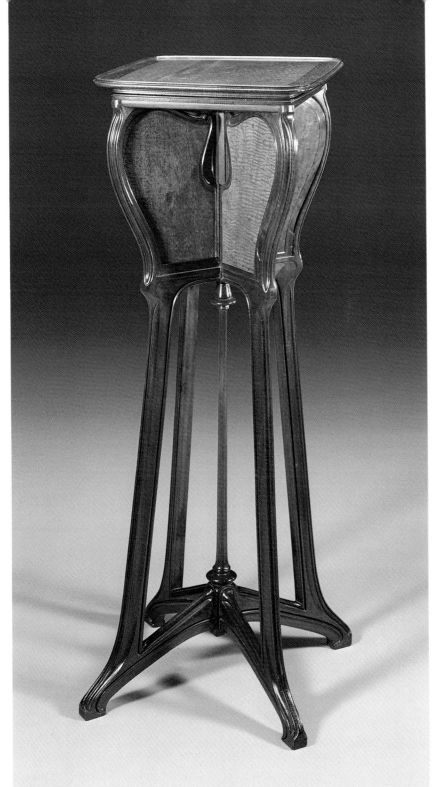

Otto Wagner
Austrian, 1841-1918

37

Chair, 1902-04

Bent beechwood, plywood, aluminum
77.5 × 55.6 × 55.9 (30½ × 21⅞ × 22)
Unsigned
Virginia Museum of Fine Arts Purchase, The Sydney and Frances
Lewis Art Nouveau Fund, 84.82

In many respects Otto Wagner is considered the father of modern architecture and design in Vienna.

Born in 1841 in Penzing, a suburb of Vienna, Wagner was educated at the Polytechnic Institute of Vienna, later the Königliche Bauakademie in Berlin, and the Viennese Academy of Fine Arts, finishing his studies in 1863. For the next twenty years he received numerous commissions for houses, apartment buildings, theatres, and, in 1880, his first bank. In 1894 he was appointed Professor at the Academy of Fine Arts, where his students included Joseph Maria Olbrich, Josef Hoffmann, and Leopold Bauer, three important members of the Viennese school of design of the early twentieth century (see cat. nos. 30, 33, 43, 45, 46, and 48).

In order to define his own theories of architecture Wagner published his famous book *Moderne Architektur* in 1895, which had a great influence on younger architects not only in Vienna but throughout Europe, culminating in a Wagnerschule, or School of Wagner. In 1899 he joined the Viennese Secession, a group of primarily younger artists and architects who had first banded together in 1897 to protest the clique of the Künstlerhaus, the Society of Artists. The Secession artists worked and exhibited together in their own building, designed by Olbrich.

In 1903, in competition with thirty-seven entries, Wagner's design for the new Austrian Postal Savings Bank in Vienna was awarded first prize. This building, constructed in two stages, from 1904 to 1906, is considered Wagner's masterpiece and is among the major monuments of modern architecture, not only in Austria but in all Europe.

This chair, which Wagner designed for the Postal Savings Bank, was manufactured by Gebrüder Thonet of Vienna. It is a perfect example of good design through economy of means. The front legs and back-rail are fashioned from one continuous piece of bent beechwood. The two back legs also form the uprights for the chair-back, and adjoining rails on the back and the legs lend support and strength. No decoration has been added. The aluminum on the feet and arm-rests, with their distinctive rivets, add style to the design while they highlight major curves and joints and lend solidity and support. The holes in the plywood seat are drilled in a pattern of diminishing diameters, but they are merely restrained decoration and have no historical design reference. Their rigid geometry could be interpreted as a debt to the spare designs of Charles Rennie Mackintosh, whose work Wagner would have seen when it was exhibited in Vienna in 1900.

PROVENANCE: Barry Friedman Ltd., New York.

PUBLISHED: *Vienna Moderne: 1898-1918* (Houston: Sarah Campbell Blaffer Gallery, University of Houston, 1978), p. 37. *Moderne Vergangenheit Wien 1800-1900* (Vienna: Künstlerhaus, 1981) p. 265, no. 206. Derek E. Ostergard, *Mackintosh to Mollino: Fifty Years of Chair Design* (New York: Barry Friedman Ltd., 1984), cat. no. 37.

EXHIBITED: *Mackintosh to Mollino: Fifty Years of Chair Design*, Barry Friedman Ltd., New York, November 13, 1984-February 13, 1985.

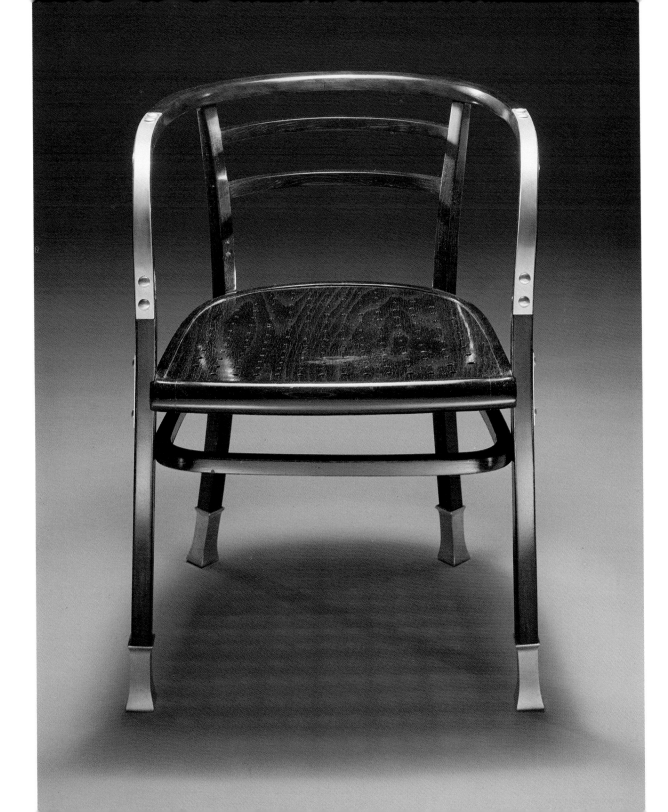

René Lalique
French, 1860-1945

38 Brooch, 1902-05

Gold, opals, baroque pearl, enamel
10.2 × 6.3 (4 × 2½)
Stamped upper edge, back: *LALIQUE*
Virginia Museum of Fine Arts Purchase, The Sydney and Frances
Lewis Art Nouveau Fund, 73.46.1

The natural curves and innate mystery of the tiny seahorse make this peculiar creature a perfect motif for an Art Nouveau designer such as René Lalique. It is characteristic of Lalique to be so observant of the world around him that he would select such an unusual creature and place it in a very natural-looking setting while using only the finest materials. The natural line of the backs and tails of the seahorses echoes the characteristic S-curve of the period. By placing these graceful creatures face to face, he produced an outline that seems so appropriate for a piece of jewelry.

The frame of this brooch was cast in gold, which also outlines the seahorses and the bezels that hold the large opal at the top and the small triangular opal at the bottom. The enameled seahorses enclose a stylized marine setting of plique-à-jour enamel dotted with five "bubbles" fashioned of cabochon opals. A pair of larger bubble-like opals is set at the top and bottom of the pendant. Appropriately, a baroque pearl, its irregular shape fashioned by Nature itself, is suspended from the brooch.

Jeweler and goldsmith C. James Meyer has observed that the opals were individually set into the bezels before being inserted into the enamel panel. Presumably this was done so that no pressure would be exerted on the enamels when setting the stones, and so that the piece could easily be disassembled for cleaning or repair.

PROVENANCE: Dr. Hans-Jörgen Heuser and Co., Hamburg, 1973.
EXHIBITED: *Treasures from the Virginia Museum Collection featuring the Fabergé Collection*, North Carolina Museum of Art, Raleigh, April 21-June 3, 1979.
PUBLISHED: Patricia Bayer, "Art Nouveau," *Antiques World* (October 1981), illus. p. 32. C. James Meyer, "René Lalique Seahorse Brooch," *Metalsmith* (Winter 1981/82), pp. 26-27.

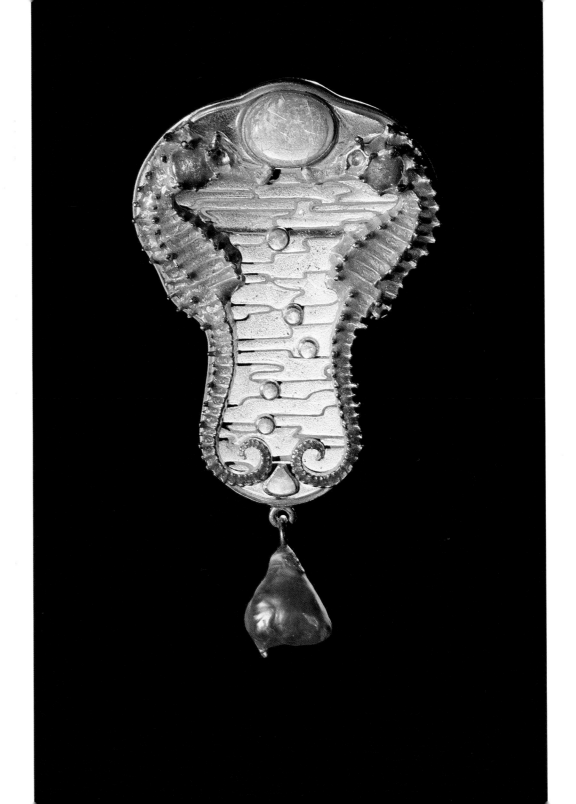

Emile Gallé
French, 1846-1904

39 Sideboard, 1903

Walnut, oak, chestnut, fruitwoods, gilt iron, glass
271.7 × 210.8 × 69.9 (107 × 83 × 27½)
Signed on bottom of proper left door: *Gallé*, and marked on
proper left side: *Salon des Beaux-Arts-1903*
Virginia Museum of Fine Arts Purchase, Sydney and Frances
Lewis Art Nouveau Fund, 77.4

As with much of Gallé's glass and furniture, this monumental sideboard reflects the artist's interest in Symbolist painting and poetry. But at the same time, its forms reflect his insistence that the structure of his furniture should be modeled on plant forms, particularly stems and trunks. Produced for the Salon des Beaux-Arts of 1903, the year before his death at the age of fifty-eight, this sideboard is also one of the most narrative pieces in Gallé's oeuvre.

It is possible to interpret the sideboard's narrative motifs as symbols of life and death, and, further, as Gallé's premonition of his own death. The massive carved wheat sheaves on the sides and the wheat tendrils and sheaves repeated in the metalwork, possibly representing fertility, were a familiar theme in Gallé's work. Likewise, the farmers working in their fields in the marquetry of the lower panels could symbolize the fertile fields of Gallé's native countryside. Foreboding elements, however, are the gilt-iron "snowflakes" at the top, which may be seen as symbolic of the coming of winter, the end of the growing season, and the end of life itself.

PROVENANCE: D. Leonard Trent, New York, 1977.

PUBLISHED: Philippe Garner, *Emile Gallé* (New York: Rizzoli International Publications Inc., 1976), illus. p. 132. Harvey Littleton, "Gallé: Transcendence in Glass and Wood," *Crafts Horizon* (August 1977), p. 32, illus. p. 36. "Art Across America: New Accessions," *Apollo* 106 (November 1977), p. 418, fig. 8. Patricia Bayer, "Art Nouveau," *Antiques World* (October 1981), illus. p. 24.

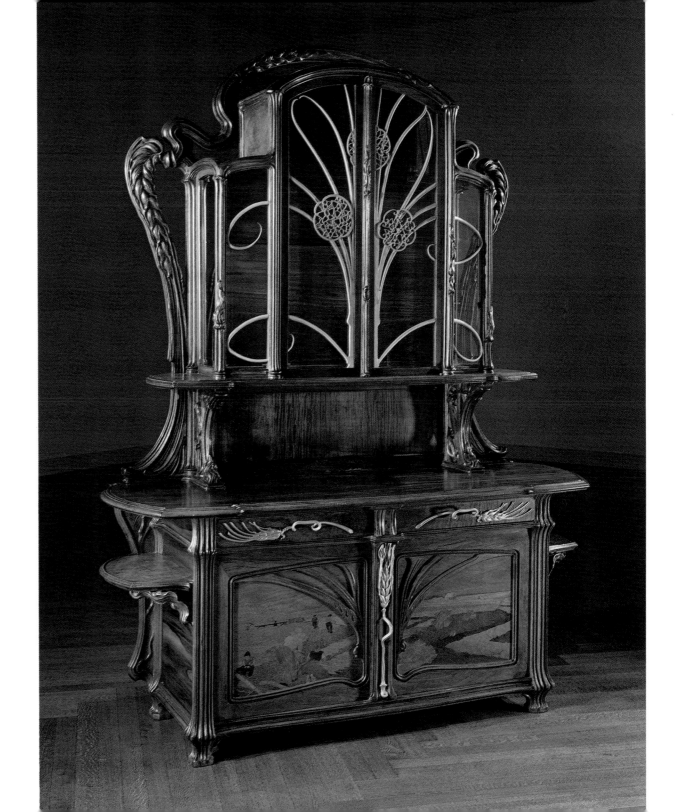

Harvey Ellis
American, 1852-1904
for
Craftsman Workshops
American (Syracuse, New York) 1900-1916

40 Fall-Front Desk, ca. 1903-04

Quarter-sawn white oak, pewter, copper, exotic wood inlays, unfinished poplar
116.8 × 106.7 × 29.2 (46 × 42 × 11½)
Marked on back, top center, with red Stickley decal and paper label: *Cobb-Eastman Co., Boston, Mass.*
Virginia Museum of Fine Arts, Gift of Sydney and Frances Lewis, 85.724

The most prominent force in the American Arts and Crafts Movement was Gustav Stickley. Born in Wisconsin, Stickley was apprenticed to Schuyler C. Brandt, who produced chairs in his Pennsylvania furniture shop. By 1898 Stickley had his own shop, the Gustav Stickley Company in Eastwood, New York, and for the next eighteen years he headed up a very successful business that not only produced furniture but also published plans for his so-called Craftsman Houses and the accompanying furnishings.

Although Stickley's furniture is constantly referred to as "Mission Oak" (either from the Franciscan missions of California or from Stickley's own dictum that his furniture fill a "mission of usefulness"), Stickley himself preferred the term "Craftsman furniture." Like Ruskin and Morris before him, Stickley wanted to create furnishings that would enhance the environment of those who purchased them. With this in mind, he formulated an entire philosophy and set it down in his magazine, *The Craftsman*. To carry out his aesthetic, the furniture had to be both practical and simple in design. In fact, Stickley was interested in creating a distinct American style.

In 1903 and 1904, some important changes occurred in the design of Stickley's furniture, primarily because he hired the gifted designer Harvey Ellis. Trained as an architect, Ellis worked for the noted architect H.H. Richardson and later started his own practice in Rochester, New York. In July 1903, the first advertisements appeared for inlaid furniture—Ellis's forte—in *The Craftsman*; the last reference to such pieces is in the June 1904 issue, just five months after Ellis's death at age 52.

Possibly hoping to attract a different, more affluent market, Stickley advertised this inlaid furniture in glowing terms: "They [the new furniture pieces] are lighter in effect and more subtle in form than any former productions of the same workshops. They have also an added color-element introduced by means of wood inlay, in designs of great delicacy, founded upon plant forms which are obscured and highly conventionalized."[32]

Scholar David Cathers believes that in the case of this particular desk the basic form had actually been worked out by Stickley before Ellis joined the Craftsman Workshops in May 1903, but that Ellis further refined the pieces he worked on through his use of inlaid decoration.[33] A similar fall-front desk appears in the May 1903 issue of *The Craftsman*, and in August of that same year a second drawing of a desk is shown. While Stickley emphasized the structural elements of his furniture, Ellis tended to play down this aspect by eliminating the visible tenons. The curved apron on the bottom shelf and the overall delicacy of the design of this desk and other Ellis pieces tended to lend lightness to Stickley's sometimes ponderous furniture designs.

Because Ellis worked with Stickley for such a short period, very few of his elegant furniture designs were produced by the Craftsman workshops. As a result, his inlaid furniture today is extremely rare and this particular desk must count among the rarest.

PROVENANCE: Richard Oliver Gallery, Kennebunk, Maine, January 1979; Jordan-Volpe Gallery, New York, April 1979.

PUBLISHED: Similar desk in *The Craftsman* (August 1903), p. 376. *Antiques*, 115 (June 1979), p. 1121 (advertisement). Beth Cathers, "Case Example: Stickley Desk," *Antique Monthly* (November 1984), illus. p. 6A. David Cathers, *Furniture of the American Arts and Crafts Movement* (New York: New American Library, 1981), pp. 188-90, illus. p. 174. David Cathers, *Genius in the Shadows: The Furniture Designs of Harvey Ellis* (New York: Jordan-Volpe Gallery, 1981), fig. 5, no. 16.

EXHIBITED: *Genius in the Shadows: The Furniture Designs of Harvey Ellis*, Jordan-Volpe Gallery, New York, March 24-April 2, 1981, no. 16.

32. David M. Cathers, *Furniture of the American Arts and Crafts Movement: Stickley and Roycroft Mission Oak* (New York: New American Library, 1981), p.48.
33. Unpublished manuscript by David Cathers in the Lewis Archives, Department of Twentieth-Century Art, Virginia Museum of Fine Arts, Richmond.

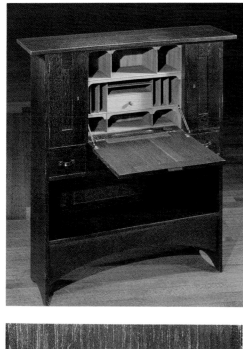

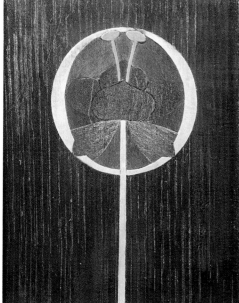

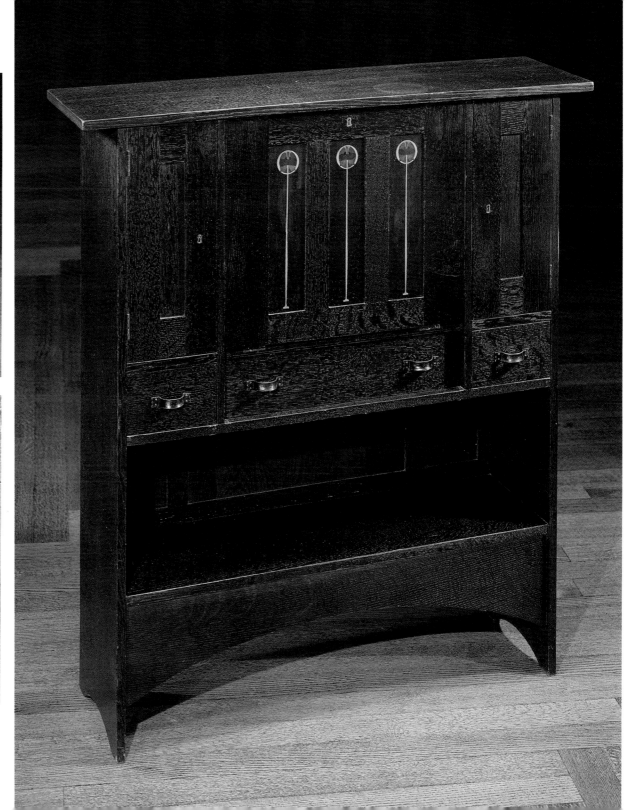

Georg Jensen
Danish, 1866-1935

 Belt Buckle, ca. 1904

Silver, opals
4.4 × 8.3 (1¾ × 3¼)
Stamped on reverse: 8263 *Georg Jensen*
Virginia Museum of Fine Arts Purchase, The Sydney and Frances
Lewis Art Nouveau Fund, 72.38

Although the Style 1900 is central European in origin, its influence was felt in other countries, especially in parts of Scandinavia. This was due in part to the wide distribution of periodicals such as *The Studio*, through which ideas and designs—primarily developed in England and on the Continent—were readily embraced and adapted elsewhere.

Scandinavian artists responded to this new style; rather than copy it outright they tended to assimilate it with their own traditional designs and materials. This was particularly true in Denmark, where the creations of Georg Jensen and others at times show a kinship to, but not slavish imitation of, Art Nouveau examples produced in France and Belgium.

This buckle is an example of such a relationship. Jensen has taken the mystical dragonfly—a favorite design motif of the Art Nouveau artist—and has intertwined its filigree wings with stylized leaves, highlighted by six opals and enclosed in an undulating and interweaving frame. Jensen's buckle shows the artist's interest in and knowledge of natural forms. At the same time, it reflects his keen ability to translate these same forms into a new idiom while retaining the traditions associated with indigenous Danish crafts.

A very early example of Jensen's work, this buckle was produced in 1904, the same year in which Jensen set up his jewelry workshop.

PROVENANCE: Martin Cohen, New York, 1972.

PUBLISHED: similar piece in Graham Hughes, *Modern Jewelry, An International Survey 1890-1967* (London: Studio Vista, 1968), fig. 202.

EXHIBITED: *Art Nouveau*, Virginia Museum Artmobile, September 1972-May 1975; *Art Nouveau*, The Columbia (South Carolina) Museum of Art and Science, September 21-October 28, 1979.

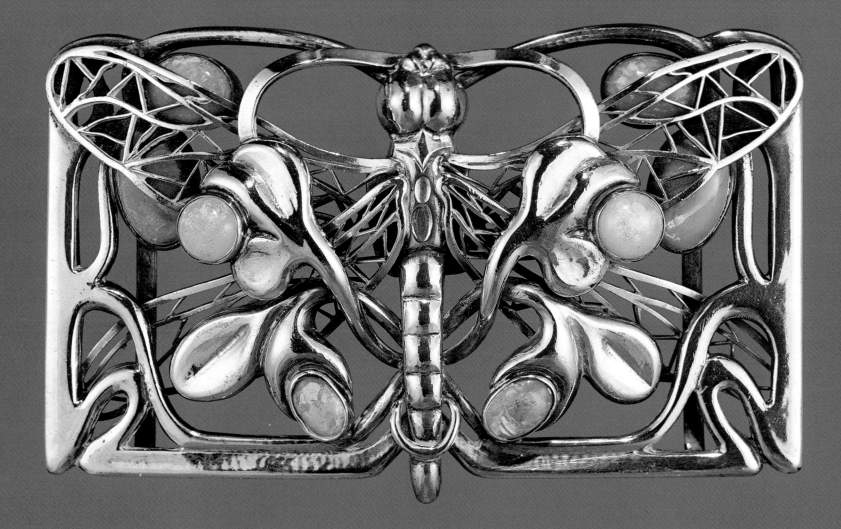

Frank Lloyd Wright
American, 1867-1959

42

Tree-of-Life Window, 1903-05

Stained and leaded glass, zinc, copper, wood
Glass: 104.8 × 66.7 (41¼ × 26¼)
Frame: 120.5 × 81.3 (42⅝ × 32)
Unsigned
Virginia Museum of Fine Arts, Gift of the Sydney and Frances
Lewis Foundation Collection, 85.347

Because Frank Lloyd Wright is considered by many to be the greatest architect America ever produced, it is not surprising that he played a key role in the development of architecture and the related arts in the early decades of the twentieth century. After serving as chief draftsman for the Chicago architect Louis Sullivan, Wright opened his own studio and soon received recognition for his work both in the United States and abroad.

In 1904 Wright designed the administration building for the Larkin Company in Buffalo, New York, a company specializing in the production and distribution of soap (fig. 13). Two years before, he had designed a house for William E. Martin, one of the founders of Larkin. Darwin Martin, Vice-President of Larkin Company and brother to William, commissioned Wright to do a similar house and furnishings for him in Buffalo, and it was constructed between 1903 and 1905. The house is considered one of Wright's early masterpieces.

The windows that Wright created for the Darwin Martin house have been called some of the most important of his designs. The "tree-of-life" design was based on three stylized plant forms, each branching out at the top in a diagonal geometric pattern. Most of the window is clear glass, its design defined by zinc and copper cames. It is known that Mathews Brothers Manufacturing Company of Milwaukee, Wisconsin, was responsible for the window's woodwork, while the glass was made by the Linden Glass Company of Chicago.

Wright had a great interest in Japanese art, and his work was profoundly influenced by it. He may have taken the idea for the window from a well-known Oriental theatre design, the arrow-sharpening scene of a

Kabuki play *Koizume Sumida Gawa*, which featured oversized arrowstands among the stage properties. According to one source, "This theme is found repeatedly in Japanese theatre prints of the 18th and 19th centuries and Wright was known to have had examples in his collection."[34]

Wright himself wrote about Japan:

"During my later years at the Oak Park [a Chicago suburb] workshop, Japanese prints had intrigued me and taught me much. The elimination of the insignificant, a process of the simplification in art in which I was myself already engaged, beginning with my twenty-third year [1890], found much collateral evidence in the print period. And ever since I discovered the print, Japan had appealed to me as the most romantic, artistic, nature-inspired country on earth. . . . I had gone there [to Japan] to rest after building the Larkin building and the Martin residence, all but tired out.[35]

PROVENANCE: Darwin Martin, Buffalo, New York; Christie, Manson & Woods International Inc., 1983.

PUBLISHED: Robert Judson Clark, *The Arts and Crafts Movement in America 1876-1916* (Princeton: Princeton University Press, 1972), p. 74. David A. Hanks, *The Decorative Designs of Frank Lloyd Wright* (New York: E.P. Dutton, 1979), p. 96, illus. pl. 8. Diane Chalmers Johnson, *American Art Nouveau* (New York: Harry N. Abrams, Inc., 1979), p. 89, fig. 96. Ernst Wasmuth, *The Early Works of Frank Lloyd Wright* (New York: Dover Publications Inc., 1982), p. 53. *Important Arts and Crafts Art Nouveau and Art Deco* (New York: Christie, Manson & Woods International, Inc., May 26, 1983), p. 38, illus. p. 41, pl. 99—(note error in catalogue, pl. 98, which accompanies entry, and pl. 99 are reversed).

34. *Important Arts and Crafts, Art Nouveau and Art Deco*, auction catalogue, May 26, 1983 (New York: Christie, Manson & Woods International, Inc., 1983), p.38.
35. Frank Lloyd Wright, *Frank Lloyd Wright: An Autobiography* (New York: Duell, Sloan and Pearce, 1943), p.195.

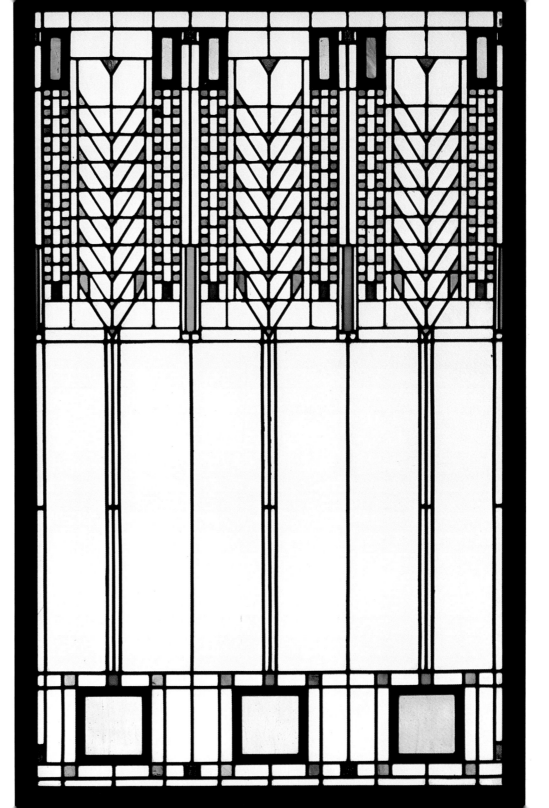

Josef Hoffmann
Austrian, 1870-1956

43

Chair, 1903-06

Beechwood, leather
98.4 × 44.4 × 43.1 (38¾ × 17½ × 17)
Unsigned
Virginia Museum of Fine Arts Purchase, The Sydney and Frances
Lewis Art Nouveau Fund, 72.18

One of the most significant and appropriate developments in furniture design at the turn of the century was the creation of bentwood furniture. This radical departure in the method of manufacturing not only permitted designs to be mass-produced—the common goal of many designers of this period—but also provided a graphic depiction of the Art Nouveau line in the simple, straightforward curves of the resultant furniture.

Thus it is not surprising that designers such as Josef Hoffmann in turn-of-the-century Vienna would apply their design skills to bentwood furniture, especially because the new manufacturing process was an Austrian invention.

As early as 1830 Michael Thonet, a cabinetmaker, began experimenting with bending wood through a steaming process. By 1842 Thonet had obtained an Austrian patent on his invention. That same year, he moved his family to Vienna, and by 1850 he was producing bentwood furniture in his own workshop. In 1853 the name of the firm was changed to Gebrüder Thonet (Thonet Brothers), after Michael Thonet's sons. The following years saw great expansion of mass production and world acclaim not only for their designs, but also for Thonet's ability to produce chairs and other furniture using a minimum of pieces. By standardization, the individual units could be mass-produced for final assembly and distribution.

The Austrian patent for Thonet lasted until 1869 and it was in that year—with the expiration of the patent—that other manufacturers began producing bentwood furniture. These manufacturers included the firm of Jacob and Josef Kohn, which made this chair to Hoffmann's design.

Between the years 1903 and 1906, the architect-designer Josef Hoffmann was commissioned to design the Pürkersdorf Sanatorium, a milestone in his work. His use of geometric shapes throughout this project would become the hallmark of his later work. This chair, one of about eighty known to have been made, was designed for the dining room. The building and all of its interior accessories were designed by Hoffmann as a unified concept. Writing in 1906 for *The Studio*, A.S. Levetus said:

> The new Sanatorium at Pürkersdorf, near Vienna, which was designed by Professor Hoffmann, is a convincing proof of what may be achieved by the united aid of artists and workmen working together in harmony for a common cause. There is no superfluous ornamentation, neither is there too little. The chief beauty lies in that due proportion which is so prominent a feature in Professor Hoffmann's works. Nowhere has he shown this better than in the Sanatorium.[36]

With simplicity of form and a minimum of parts, Hoffmann has created a classic chair. The rear legs are formed of one piece with the back of the chair, the front legs are two separate pieces, and the seat a single unit. The only decoration as such is contained in the pierced splat with circular motifs that are repeated in the nailheads of the upholstery and in the eight wooden spheres attached at the intersection of the seat with the legs.

PROVENANCE: Knut Günther, Frankfurt-am-Main, 1972.

PUBLISHED: Charles Holme, ed., *The Art Revival in Austria* (London, Paris, New York: The Studio, 1906), illus. C 10. Derek E. Ostergard, *Mackintosh to Mollino: Fifty Years of Chair Design* (New York: Barry Friedman Ltd., 1984), cat. no. 26.

EXHIBITED: *Art Nouveau*, Virginia Museum Artmobile Exhibition, September 1972–May 1975; *Mackintosh to Mollino: Fifty Years of Chair Design*, Barry Friedman Ltd., New York, November 13, 1984–February 13, 1985.

---

36. A.S. Levetus, "Modern Decorative Art in Austria," *The Art Revival in Austria*, special issue of *The Studio* (1906), D iv.

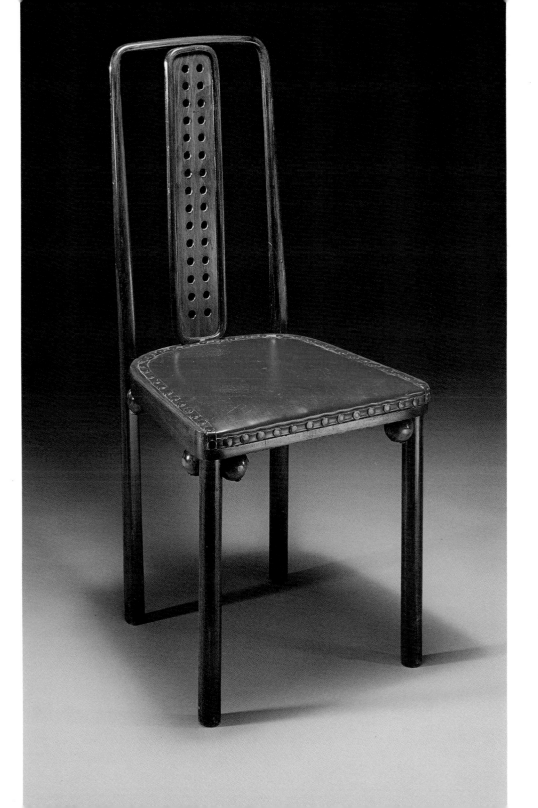

Charles Rennie Mackintosh
Scottish, 1868-1928

 44 Armchair, ca. 1904

Stained wood, glass, upholstery
119.3 × 61.5 × 63.5 (47 × 24¼ × 25)
Unsigned
Virginia Museum of Fine Arts, Gift of Sydney and Frances Lewis,
85.145

Although today Charles Rennie Mackintosh is considered one of the most brilliant architects and designers of the turn of the century, he had a great deal of difficulty finding patrons and commissions during his lifetime. One of his staunchest supporters, however, was Miss Catherine Cranston, the wife of Major John Cochrane.

Miss Cranston was the originator and owner of a series of tea rooms that she established throughout the city of Glasgow. Her aim was to provide a quiet place where one could be away from the noise of the streets and enjoy a cup of tea, a cigarette, or a friendly chat without the intrusion of alcoholic beverages. Her tea rooms were a great success, perhaps owing to Mackintosh's imaginative design and interior decoration.

In addition to the tea rooms, Mackintosh was also commissioned by Miss Cranston to refurbish and renovate "Hous'hill," her home at Nitshill, Glasgow. Between 1903 and 1919 (the majority of the work being done in the earlier years), Mackintosh refurbished the house and continued to add miscellaneous pieces of furniture. The building itself dates from the early nineteenth century; Mackintosh's task was to bring it up-to-date.

One of the outstanding elements of the house was the Music Room. Its major element was a curved screen made of thin vertical slats. The verticality of the screen was repeated in the back of this armchair, which was intended by Mackintosh to be placed with its back against the screen (see fig. 8).

Like so many of Mackintosh's chair designs, this Music Room chair has a sculptural aspect, and its importance seems to lie more in its aesthetic appeal and design than in its function or comfort. The dark-stained wood would have provided a stark contrast to the white-painted room, and the oval insets of mauve-colored glass complement the chair's overall geometric design. The subtle curve of the back again reflects the stronger curve of the vertical screen behind the chair. Three smaller low-backed chairs of similar design were also made for the room.

Much of the production of Mackintosh's furniture was accomplished by local cabinetmakers and artisans. It is recorded that Alexander Martin was paid £2.16.0d in December of 1904 for this chair; McCulloch Glass Company was paid 5.6d. for the glass inserts.[37]

PROVENANCE: Major and Mrs. John Cochrane (Miss Catherine Cranston), Hous'hill, Nitshill, Glasgow, ca. 1904; W. Ward, 1933; Sotheby's Belgravia, London, 1975.

PUBLISHED: Nicholas Pevsner, *Charles Rennie Mackintosh* (Milan, 1950), p. 113, pl. 35. Thomas Howarth, *Charles Rennie Mackintosh and the Modern Movement* (London: Routledge & Kegan Paul, 1952), pl. 46. Robert Macleod, *Charles Rennie Mackintosh* (Feltham: Country Life Books, 1968), p. 121, pl. 88. Andrew McLaren Young, *Charles Rennie Mackintosh 1868-1928: Architecture, Design and Painting* (Edinburgh: Scottish Arts Council, 1968), no. 248, illus. pl. 26. *Art at Auction, the Year at Sotheby Parke Bernet, 1974-75* (New York: Viking Press, 1975), illus. p. 312. *Decorative Arts 1880-1950 including Arts and Crafts, Art Nouveau and Art Deco*, catalogue of sale (London: Sotheby's Belgravia, March 13, 1975), no. 53, illus. p. 17. Yvonne Brunhammer et al. *Art Nouveau Belgium/France* (Houston: Institute for the Arts, Rice University, 1976), illus. 167, p. 143. Roger Billcliffe, *Charles Rennie Mackintosh: The Complete Furniture, Furniture Drawings and Interior Designs* (New York: Taplinger Publishing Co., 1979) illus. 1904G, p. 162, 1904.61, p. 169. Philippe Garner, *Twentieth Century Furniture* (New York: Van Nostrand Reinhold, 1980), illus. pp. 52, 54.

EXHIBITED: *Charles Rennie Mackintosh 1868-1928: Architecture, Design and Painting*, Royal Scottish Museum, Edinburgh, August 17-September 8, 1968; Art Nouveau Gallery, Virginia Museum of Fine Arts, Richmond, 1975-1982; *Art Nouveau Belgium/France*, Rice University, Houston, Texas, March 25-June 22, 1976; Art Institute of Chicago, August 28-November 7, 1976.

37. Roger Billcliffe, *Charles Rennie Mackintosh: The Complete Furniture, Furniture Drawings, and Interior Designs* (New York: Taplinger Publishing Company, 1979), p. 169.

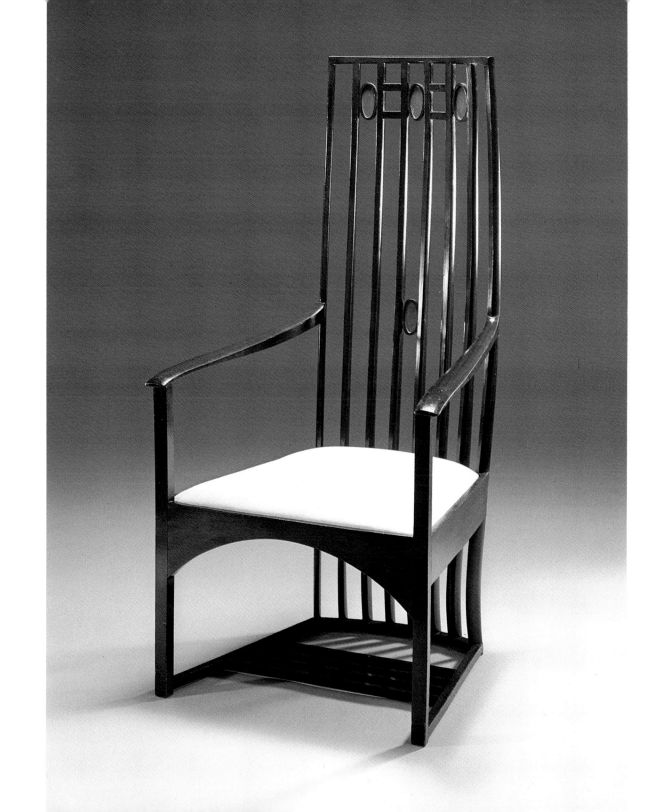

Koloman Moser
Austrian, 1868-1916

45

Chair, 1904

Rosewood, maple, mother-of-pearl
94.9 × 55.8 × 52.3 (37⅜ × 22 × 20⅝)
Unsigned
Virginia Museum of Fine Arts, Gift of Sydney and Frances Lewis,
85.80

Koloman Moser was born in 1868 in Vienna, where he was educated at the Academy of Fine Arts and later at the School of Applied Arts. In 1897, along with Gustav Klimt, Josef Hoffmann, Joseph Maria Olbrich, and Carl Moll, Moser founded the Vienna Secession.

Later, in 1901, Moser was among the founders of the Wiener Kunst im Hause. Producing quality objects for the home, this organization might be considered a predecessor to the Wiener Werkstätte, co-founded in 1903 by Moser and Hoffmann. Although the Wiener Werkstätte continued for almost three decades, Moser was only associated with that group until 1907.

This dining-room chair, created in 1904, represents the pure geometrical style evolved by the Viennese designers. It is obvious—in his use of the repeated square in the decoration and in the cross section of the arms and legs—that Moser was greatly influenced by Charles Rennie Mackintosh, whose work had been exhibited in Vienna in 1900. All proportions of the chair, in fact, are based on the square. Another element to note, and one that sets this chair above many Wiener Werkstätte designs, is its use of rare and expensive woods and inlays.[38] Its

distinctiveness becomes even more apparent when one compares the exotic woods of this chair with the plain, stained beechwood of Hoffmann's Pürkersdorf chair (cat. no. 43).

PROVENANCE: Annie Partouche, Paris; Sotheby Parke-Bernet Monaco S.A., 1977.

PUBLISHED: *Dekorative Kunst* (1904), p. 334. Yvonne Brunhammer, *Cinquantenaire de l'Exposition de 1925* (Paris: Musée des Arts Décoratifs, 1976), no. 703. *Arts Décoratifs, Styles 1900 et 1925*, catalogue of sale (Monte Carlo: Sotheby Parke Bernet Monaco S.A., October 8, 1977), no. 61, p. 44. Philippe Garner, ed., *Encyclopedia of Decorative Arts* (New York: Van Nostrand Reinhold, 1979), illus. p. 214. Philippe Garner, *Twentieth Century Furniture* (New York: Van Nostrand Reinhold, 1980), p. 66. Vera J. Behal, *Möbel des Jugendstils* (Munich: Prestel, 1981), p. 15. Patricia Bayer, "Art Nouveau," *Antiques World* (October 1981), illus. p. 33.

EXHIBITED: *Vienna Moderne: 1898-1918*, Cooper-Hewitt Museum, New York, November 27, 1978-February 4, 1979; Sarah Campbell Blaffer Gallery, University of Houston, March 2-April 29, 1979; Portland (Oregon) Art Museum, June-July 1979; Smart Gallery, University of Chicago, January 11, 1979-February 24, 1980. *Cinquantenaire de l'Exposition de 1925*, Musée des Arts Décoratifs, Paris, October 1976-February 1977, cat. no. 703.

---

38. The ornamental motif of the dove bearing an olive branch refers to the title of nobility of the original owner. See Werner Fenz, *Kolomon Moser* (Salzburg and Vienna: Residenz Verlag, 1984), p. 260.

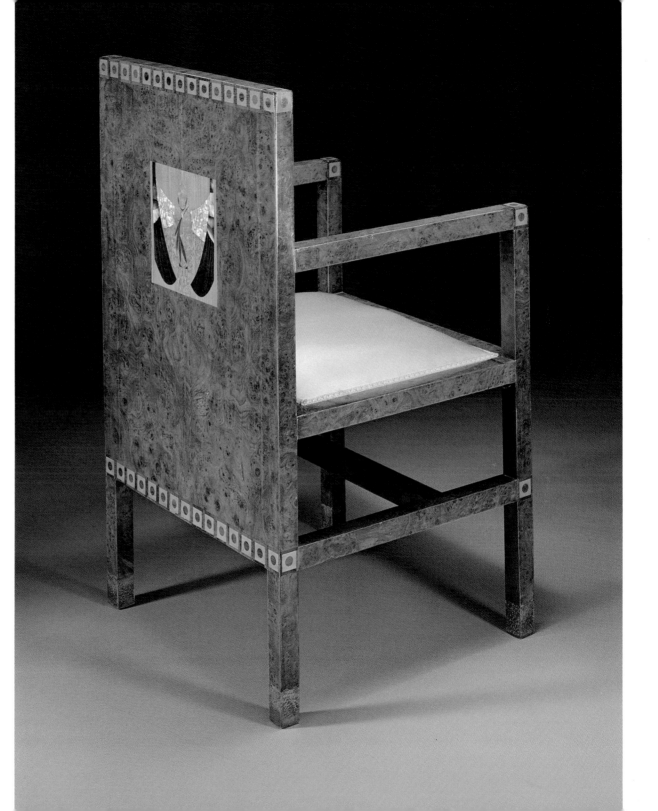

Josef Hoffmann
Austrian, 1870-1956

46 Place Setting, 1904

Sterling silver
Fish Knife: 17.9 × 1.5 × .3 (7³/₃₂ × ¹⁹/₃₂ × ⅛)
Fish Fork: 19.2 × 1.4 × .3 (7 × ⁹/₁₆ × ⅛)
Dessert Knife: 17.7 × 1.5 × .3 (7 × ⅝ × ⅛)
Dessert Fork: 18.1 × 1.5 × .3 (7⅛ × ½ × ³/₃₂)
Coffee Spoon: 13 × 1.3 × .2 (5⅛ × ½ × ³/₃₂)
Egg Spoon: 12.2 × 1.3 × .2 (4¹³/₁₆ × ½ × ³/₃₂)
Marked *JH*, hallmark, and monogram of Wiener Werkstätte on
reverse of each piece.
Virginia Museum of Fine Arts, Gift of the Sydney and Frances
Lewis Foundation, 85.289.1/6

When Josef Hoffmann first exhibited his "flaches Modell" flatware in 1906, it received very negative comments. One Hamburg reviewer called it "weird," while another Viennese critic said that what Hoffmann "makes is geometry, not art," predicting that geometry in industrial design would never become popular. These comments were prompted by the exhibition *Der gedeckte Tisch* (Table Settings) organized by the Wiener Werkstätte in 1906.

The "flaches Modell," or flat model, is in all likelihood the first set of flatware Hoffmann produced for the Wiener Werkstätte. It is quite different from much of his later work in that it was stamped from single sheets of metal and displayed an absolute minimum of decoration, in this case four small spheres at the ends of the handles. The place setting in the Lewis collection, part of a larger set, includes a dessert knife, dessert fork, coffee

spoon, egg spoon, fish knife, and fish fork.[39] Other pieces from the original set are in the collections of the Würtembergisches Landesmuseum, Stuttgart, Germany, and Osterreichisches Museum für angewandte Kunst, Vienna.

PROVENANCE: Fritz Wärndorfer, 1905; Sotheby Parke-Bernet Monaco S.A., 1984.

PUBLISHED: *Josef Hoffmann Wien*, catalogue of exhibition, Museum Bellerive, Zurich, 1983, no. 133. Waltraud Neuwirth, *Josef Hoffmann Bestecke für die Wiener Werkstätte*, Vienna, 1982, pp. 15-26, 29-33. *Arts Décoratifs Styles 1900 et 1925*, catalogue of sale (Monte Carlo: Sotheby Parke-Bernet Monaco S.A., March 11, 1984), no. 250, illus.

EXHIBITED: *Der gedeckte Tische*, Wiener Werkstätte, October 1906.

39. For further information see Waltraud Neuwirth, *Josef Hoffmann: Bestecke für die Wiener Werkstätte* (Vienna: Dr. Waltraud Neuwirth, 1982).

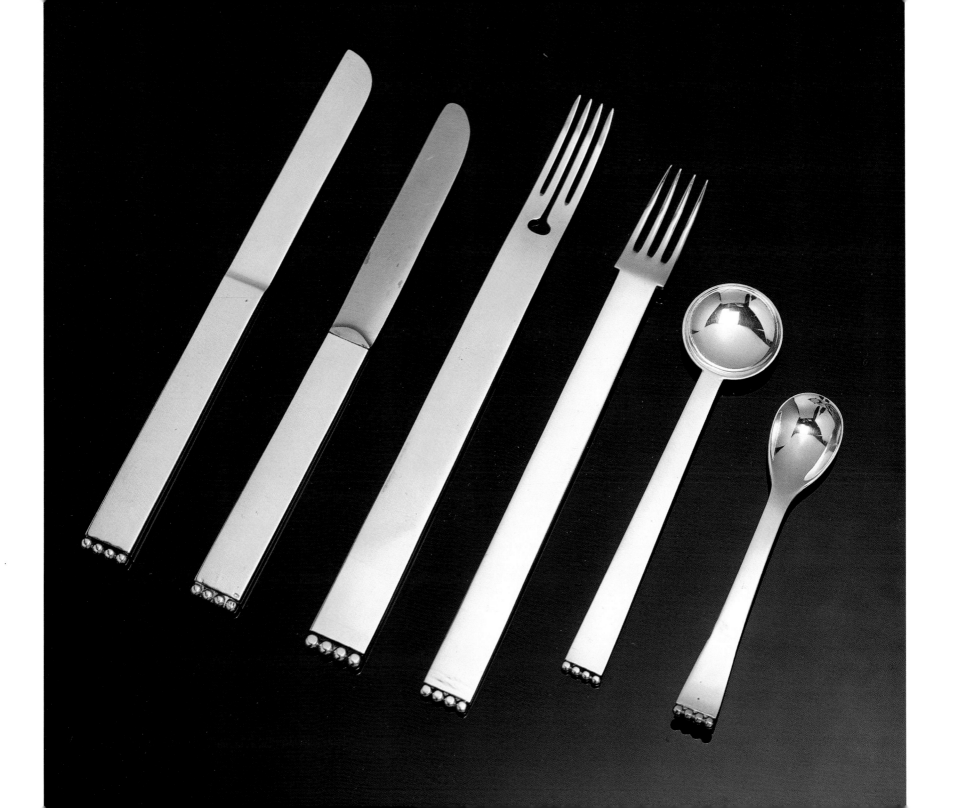

Frank Lloyd Wright
American, 1867-1959

47 Side Chair, 1904

Oak, leather upholstery
102.2 × 38.1 × 47.6 (40¼ × 15 × 18¾)
Unsigned
Virginia Museum of Fine Arts, Gift of the Sydney and Frances
Lewis Foundation, 85.74

In 1899, Frank Lloyd Wright began to build his own residence in Oak Park, Illinois, a suburb of Chicago. For the next two decades he added to the house to accommodate for its use as a studio and to serve the needs of his growing family. As with so many of his important architectural works, the studio was a complete design statement. Wright not only created the structural space, but also all of the interior details and furnishings, of which this side chair was a part.

The chair reflects both Wright's concern for structural simplicity and the relationship of his work to that of his contemporaries, Stickley and Roycroft. Its design also recalls the work of Charles Rennie Mackintosh in the use of simple, geometric shapes and in the way the back panel extends downward below the seat, almost touching the floor where it joins the stretcher. By the same token, however, it must be said that the Wright chair, with its solid plank back and post-and-lintel construction, also heralds the furniture of De Stijl, particularly the chairs of Gerrit Rietveld (see cat. no. 62).

Although this chair, unlike many of the other furnishings for Wright's studio, was not designed as a built-in unit but as a separate piece, it still bears a strong relationship to the architecture that Wright was developing during these early years in Chicago. The strict use of horizontals and verticals to support the angled plane of the back derives from his architectural vocabulary.

The same chair design was also used for several other commissions, including the Unity Temple in Oak Park, Illinois, of the same year, and the Hillside Home School in Spring Green, Wisconsin, directed by Wright's aunts.

PROVENANCE: Kelmscott Enterprises Inc., Chicago, 1981.

PUBLISHED: David Hanks, The Decorative Designs of Frank Lloyd Wright (New York: E.P. Dutton, 1979), illus. p. 38. Frank Lloyd Wright (Chicago: Kelmscott Gallery, 1981), pl. 112, p. 19. H. Allen Brooks, Frank Lloyd Wright and the Prairie School (New York: George Braziller, Inc., 1984), illus. p. 61. Derek E. Ostergard, Mackintosh to Mollino: Fifty Years of Chair Design (New York: Barry Friedman Ltd., 1984), cat. no. 32.

EXHIBITED: Frank Lloyd Wright, Kelmscott Gallery, Chicago, May-October 1981; Frank Lloyd Wright: Early Years, Early Associates, Cooper-Hewitt Museum, New York, May 17-October 4, 1983. Mackintosh to Mollino: Fifty Years of Chair Design, Barry Friedman Ltd., New York, November 13, 1984-February 13, 1985.

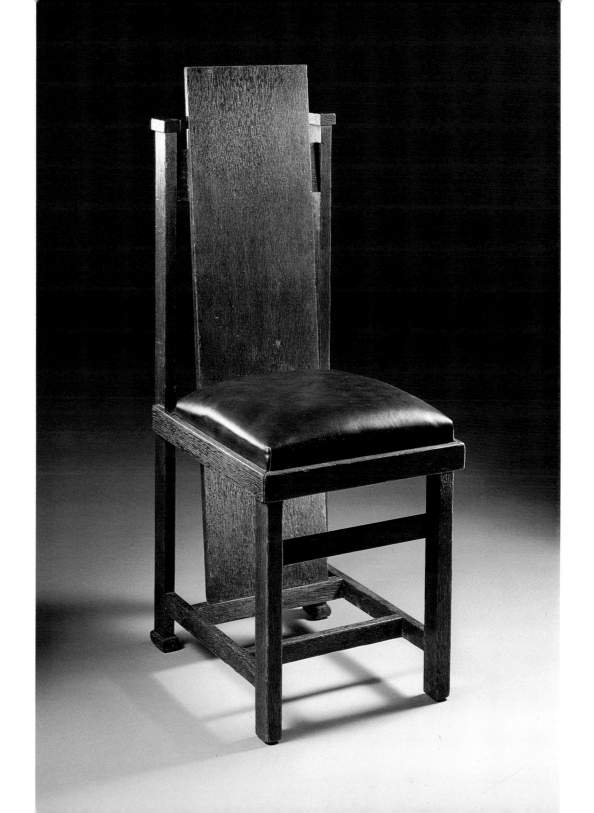

Joseph Maria Olbrich
Austrian, 1867-1908

48

Coffee and Tea Service, ca. 1904

Pewter, teak
Coffee Pot: 19.1 × 11.4 × 17.1 (7¾ × 4½ × 6¾)
Teapot: 23.5 × 10.1 × 20.3 (9¼ × 4 × 8)
Sugar: 13 × 11.1 × 11.1 (5⅛ × 4⅜ × 4⅜)
Tray: 4.1 × 57.8 × 37.7 (1⅝ × 22¾ × 14⅞)
Each piece (except tray) marked *Edelzinn/1930* on bottom; coffee
pot and teapot also have artist's monogram on side; tray
unmarked
Virginia Museum of Fine Arts, Gift of Sydney and Frances Lewis,
85.280.1/4

Like Josef Hoffmann, Olbrich was a student of architect Otto Wagner. In 1897, Olbrich co-founded the Vienna Secession with Hoffmann, Koloman Moser, and Gustav Klimt. One of Olbrich's first major commissions was the exhibition building for the Secession, built in Vienna in 1898. This remarkable edifice has long been considered a classic example of turn-of-the-century architecture. According to *The Studio* reviewer Hugo Haberfeld, "His |Olbrich's| first effort was the 'Secession' building, erected during the space of a few months, a work vigorous and fresh in conception, sober yet impressive, well-proportioned and graceful, and withal a personal creation yet dictated by 'purpose.' The particular problems presented by an exhibition building have never been better solved."[40]

In 1899, at the command of the Grand-Duke of Hesse, Olbrich moved to Darmstadt to help form the artists' colony there, and he was responsible for the design and construction of the majority of the buildings.

Like so many other architects of his generation, Olbrich not only designed buildings, but also created interior accessories in metal, wood, and other materials. This coffee and tea service is typical of Olbrich's work in pewter; its minimal decoration is based on conventionalized organic forms. The artist has perceptively combined materials; of special note is the tray of pewter and teak, which looks toward streamlined concepts in later Scandinavian design.

Olbrich's brilliant career was cut short by his death of leukemia at the age of forty-one.

PROVENANCE: Macklowe Gallery Ltd., New York, 1972.

PUBLISHED: Gerhard Bott, *Kunsthandwerk um 1900* (Darmstadt: Eduard Roether Verlag, 1965), p. 68.

EXHIBITED: *Design in the Service of Tea*, Cooper-Hewitt Museum, New York, August 7, 1984-September 28, 1984.

---

40. Hugo Haberfeld, "The Architectural Revival in Austria," *The Art-Revival in Austria*, a special issue of *The Studio* (London, 1906): C vi.

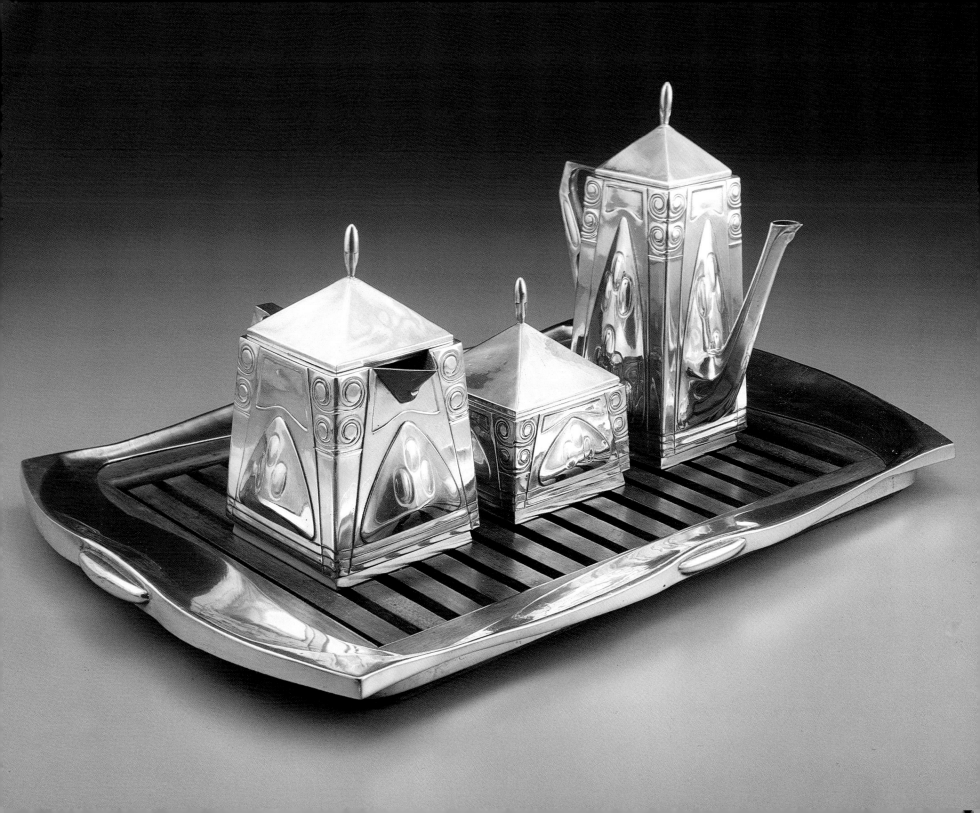

Georges Fouquet
French, 1862-1957

 49   Brooch, 1904

Gold, enamel, opal, unidentified ivory-colored stones, engraved
glass, diamonds, pearls
9.5 × 19.6 (3¾ × 7¾)
Marked on top of proper left wing: G. *Fouquet 5473*
Virginia Museum of Fine Arts, Gift of Sydney and Frances Lewis,
85.242

Georges Fouquet was the son of a master jeweler, Alphonse, and the father
of Jean, also a jewelry designer. Fouquet joined his father's firm in 1880 and
had achieved international renown on his own by the turn of the century.
Much of this fame was due to the brilliant jewelry designs he executed for
the actress Sarah Bernhardt, in collaboration with the Czechoslovakian
artist Alphonse Mucha (see cat. no. 18).

Fouquet's work has been likened to that of René Lalique. Both artists'
created stunning designs in a wide variety of materials, including precious
stones, gold, silver, ivory, and glass, as well as enamel. Also like Lalique,
Fouquet created jewelry that epitomized the fin-de-siècle style in his use of
the symbols and images of the Art Nouveau vocabulary. In this brooch he
combined a woman's head, surrounded by flowing tresses, with fantastic
wings from some incredible bird or insect. Radiating from the aureole
around the head are four glass flowers. In addition to acting as a unifying
design element, the aureole also adds a quasi-mystical or religious aspect
to the piece by suggesting that the female is more than human. Indeed, she
becomes an angelic creature, perhaps a madonna.

Jewelry on a scale such as this raises the question as to whether
Fouquet or Lalique actually intended these pieces to be worn, or whether
they considered them as miniature sculptures or display pieces. Although
not consciously an imitator or follower of Lalique, Fouquet assuredly owed
a debt to his colleague for his use of glass in this and other creations.

PROVENANCE: Sotheby Parke Bernet Monaco S.A., 1978.

PUBLISHED: *Arts Décoratifs 1900 et 1925* (Monaco: Sotheby Parke Bernet Monaco S.A., September 24,
1978), no. 214, illus. p. 92. "Brooch of Gems Lent to Museum," *Richmond Times Dispatch*, March 2, 1979.
Art at Auction: The Year at Sotheby Parke Bernet, 1978-1979 (London: Sotheby Parke Bernet, 1979), p. 424.
Vivienne Becker, *Antique and Twentieth Century Jewelry: A Guide for Collectors* (New York: Van Nostrand
Reinhold, 1982), illus. p. 198. Marie-Noël de Gary et al., *Les Fouquet: Bijoutiers & Joailliers à Paris 1860-1960*
(Paris: Musée des Arts Décoratifs, 1983), illus. p. 74.

EXHIBITED: Art Nouveau Gallery, Virginia Museum of Fine Arts, Richmond, March 1979; *Les Fouquet:
Bijoutiers & Joaillers à Paris 1860-1960*, Musée des Arts Décoratifs, Paris, January 18-March 26, 1984;
Museum Bellerive, Zurich, May 23-August 12, 1984.

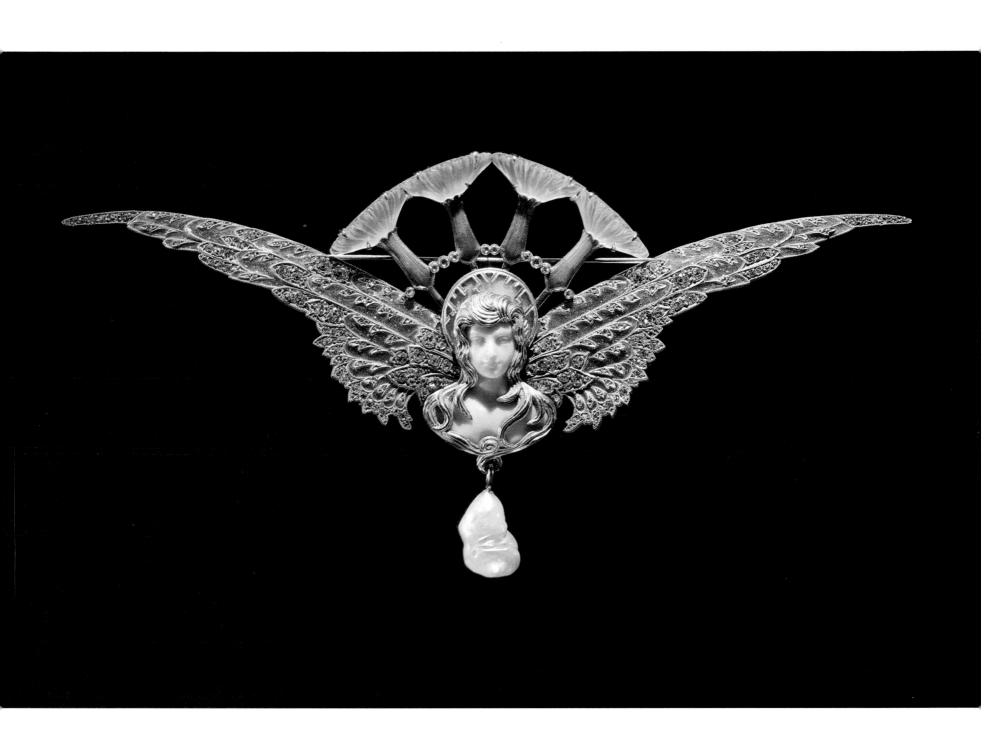

Roycroft Shops
American (East Aurora, New York), 1893-1938

50 Bookcase, 1905-10

Oak, painted copper
167 × 140.3 × 40 (65¾ × 55¼ × 15¾)
Signed with mark of the Roycroft Shops, center front
Virginia Museum of Fine Arts, Gift of Sydney and Frances Lewis,
85.69

One of the most visible proponents of the American Arts and Crafts Movement was Elbert Hubbard. A prolific writer and speaker, Hubbard could entrance his audiences with his own brand of opinionated philosophy on a variety of subjects. He is perhaps best known for his short essay "A Message to Garcia," in which he espoused the work ethic and summed up his philosophy of life.

After establishing himself as a successful partner in the Larkin Company, a soap manufacturer, Hubbard sold his interest in the firm and in 1893 founded the Roycroft community in East Aurora, New York, a suburb of Buffalo. In the previous year Hubbard had gone to Europe where he had a brief but profoundly meaningful visit with William Morris. Fascinated by the Englishman's philosophy and particularly by his Kelmscott Press, Hubbard was determined to establish a craftsmen's community of his own, where he could produce an Americanized version of Arts and Crafts books. Eventually his printing venture led him to establish the Roycroft Shops, an entire community of artisans who created not only books, but also metalwork and furniture.

Roycroft furniture was distinctly American in character, emphasizing simplicity of line and structural detail; note the mortise-and-tenon construction on the sides of this double-door bookcase. A hallmark of Roycroft furniture is the prominent display of the Roycroft mark, in this case carved into the front of the bookcase. The mark consists of an orb enclosing a distinctive "R" surmounted by a cross.

During the years of Roycroft production, many artists who later earned renown in other areas worked in the Roycroft Shops. Among them were the metalsmith Karl Kipp, the graphic designer and papermaker Dard Hunter, and the illustrator W. W. Denslow, later known for his illustrations for L. Frank Baum's *The Wizard of Oz*.

The Roycroft Shops continued successfully, even after Hubbard's untimely death in 1915—he and his wife perished in the sinking of the *Lusitania*. The firm was managed by Hubbard's son, Elbert Hubbard II, until it was dissolved in 1938.

PROVENANCE: The Artsman, Bryn Mawr, Pennsylvania, 1982.

PUBLISHED: Robert Edwards, "The Roycrofters: Their Furniture and Crafts," *Art and Antiques* (November-December 1981), pp. 80-87, illus. p. 82.

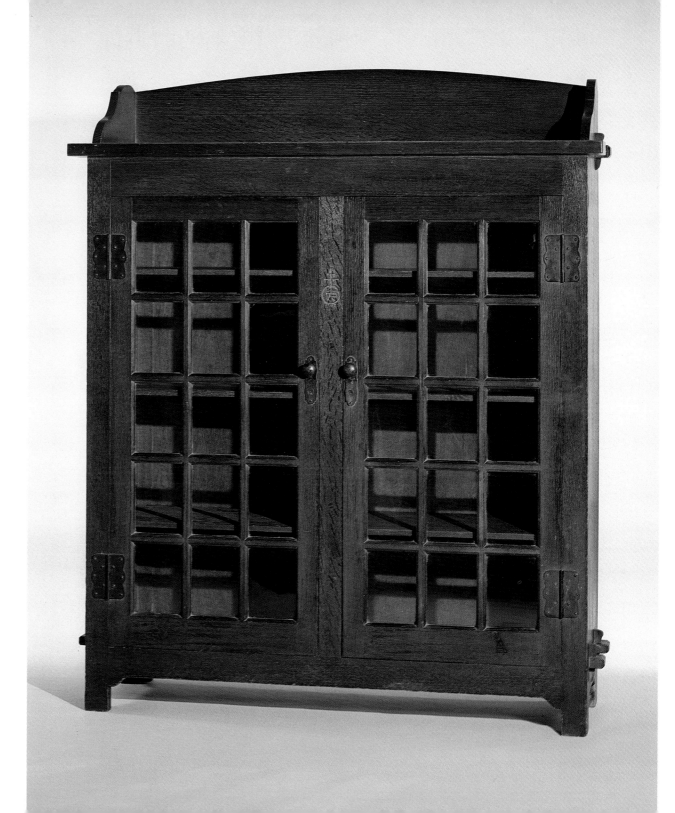

Tiffany Studios
American (New York), 1900-1938

 51

Cobweb Lamp, ca. 1904

Leaded glass, glass mosaic tiles, bronze
74.9 × 50.8 diameter (29½ × 20)
Unsigned
Virginia Museum of Fine Arts, Gift of Sydney and Frances Lewis,
85.164 a/b

This lamp appeared as the frontispiece for the small catalogue of bronze lamps published by Tiffany Studios around 1904, then located at 331-341 Fourth Avenue, New York.

Because the lamp's extremely complex shade is fully integrated with a special base, it must have been very expensive to produce and equally costly to buy. A 1906 price list shows the shade on the mosaic floral base for sale at $500, an amount equivalent to the average yearly earnings for many Americans that year.

Because most Tiffany lamp bases were patinated bronze, this one of mosaic glass is exceptional and greatly enhances the color and configuration of the lamp. Through the skillful use of both clear and colored glass in the shade, the Tiffany Studios artisans created a beautiful overall pattern of cobwebs and flowers supported by bronze branches emerging from the base.

An illustrated brochure produced by Tiffany Studios around 1905 extols the virtues of Tiffany glass and lamps with an impressive fervor:

The bronze lamps made by the artist-craftsmen at the Tiffany Studios today are constructed of the same striving for the artistic and beautiful that has marked the evolution of the Tiffany glass, and they have a distinction and individuality which the Studios impress upon all their work.

The ability of the Studios to work and finish bronze in combination with the beautiful effects in Favrile and leaded glass shades permits the production of lamps to harmonize with any scheme of architecture and decoration, and lamps can always be made in special designs to meet special requirements.[41]

PROVENANCE: Lillian Nassau Ltd. New York, 1972.

PUBLISHED: *Bronze Lamps* (New York: Tiffany Studios, no date), frontispiece. Tiffany Studios Price List, 1906. Robert Koch, *Louis C. Tiffany's Glass, Bronzes, Lamps* (New York: Crown Publishers Inc., 1971), cover illustration and frontispiece. Egon Neustadt, *The Lamps of Tiffany* (New York: Fairfield Press, 1970), pl. 235, p. 169.

41. Tiffany Studios, *Bronze Lamps* (New York: Tiffany Studios, no date), p. 7.

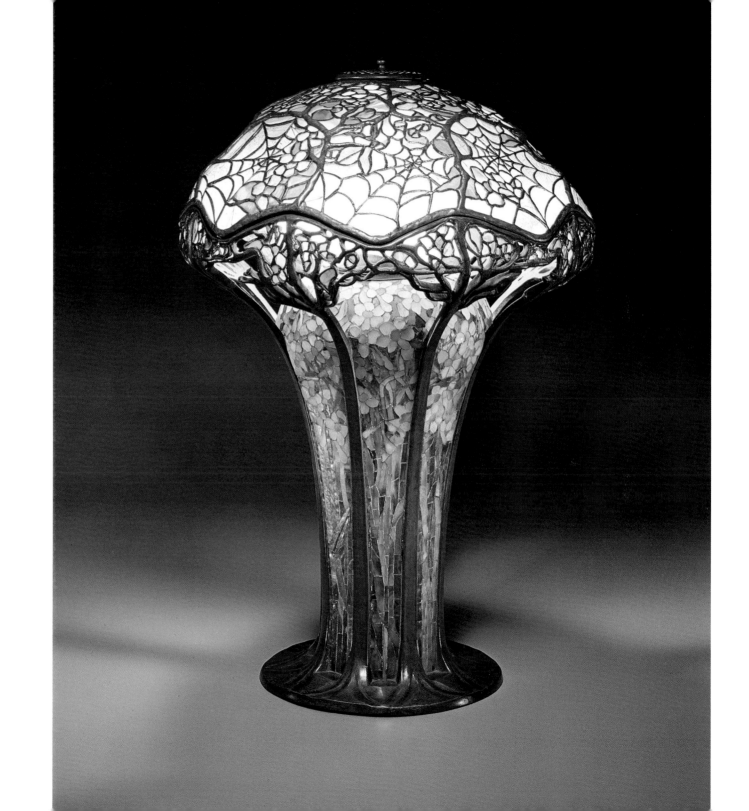

Tiffany Studios
American (New York), 1900-1938

52 Squash Lamp, ca. 1906

Leaded glass, Favrile glass, bronze
80 × 73.6 diameter (31½ × 29)
Globes inscribed *L.C.T.*; bottom of base impressed: *Tiffany Studios New York 28278*
Virginia Museum of Fine Arts, Gift of the Sydney and Frances Lewis Foundation, 85.151 a/h

A photograph in the original Tiffany Studios album shows this unique lamp. The shade is created from a series of overlapping leaf-shaped pieces; the top is open, revealing six iridescent Favrile-glass squash-blossom globes. Both the shade and the globes are supported by a finely detailed cast-bronze base that terminates in a foot in the shape of squash leaves and vines.

The shade exemplifies what Dr. Egon Neustadt, in his book *The Lamps of Tiffany*, describes as Tiffany's "diochroic" glass, the color of which is dependent upon either transmitted or reflected light. When the lamp is lit, the leaves each take on a different tonality, although they all appear to be similar in color under reflected light.

PROVENANCE: Christie, Manson & Woods International Inc., New York, 1982.

PUBLISHED: Tiffany Price List, 1906. Egon Neustadt, *The Lamps of Tiffany* (New York: Fairfield Press, 1970), fig. 272, p. 200. *Important Tiffany Lamps and Windows*, catalogue of sale (New York: Christie, Manson & Woods International, Inc., December 11, 1982), no. 380, illus. p. 31. William Feldstein, Jr., and Alastair Duncan, *The Lamps of Tiffany Studios* (New York: Harry N. Abrams Inc., 1983), pp. 134-35, illus. p. 135.

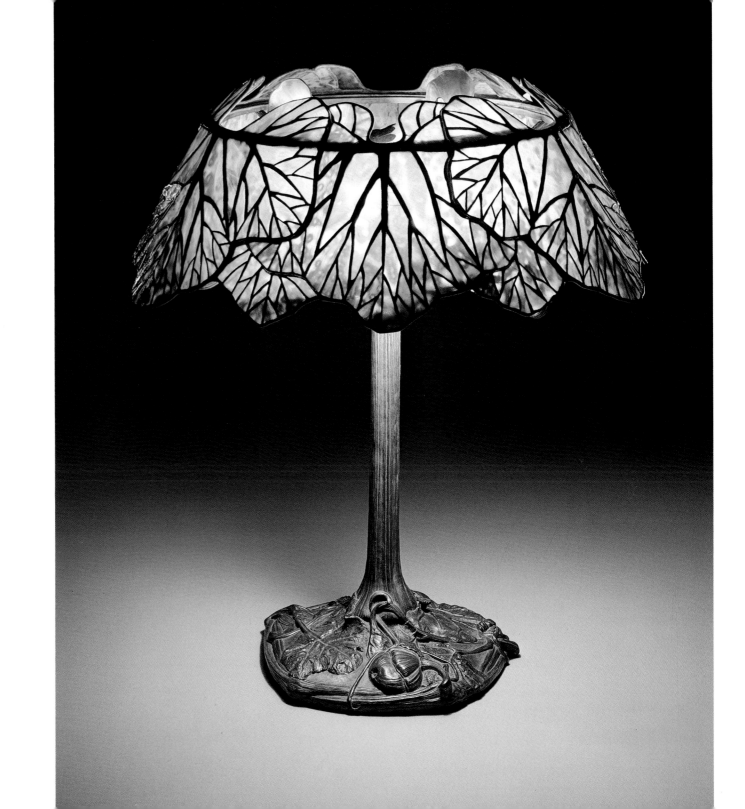

Lucia K. Mathews
American, 1870-1955
for
The Furniture Shop
American (San Francisco), 1906-1920

53

Covered Jar, ca. 1906

Painted and gilded wood
31.7 × 25.4 diameter (12½ × 10)
Signed in frieze band: *Lucia K. Mathews*
Virginia Museum of Fine Arts, Gift of the Sydney and Frances
Lewis Foundation, 85.299 a/b

The Furniture Shop represents a unique collaboration that was founded just after the great San Francisco fire of 1906. The principal artists were Arthur F. Mathews and his wife, Lucia K. Mathews, both well-established artists at that time. The fire had destroyed much of the city, including the Mathews studio and several public and private collections containing many of their paintings. During the rebuilding of the city, the Mathewses opened The Furniture Shop, where they proposed to produce quality, custom-designed furniture and accessories. In addition, they began to publish *Philopolis*, a monthly magazine devoted to art and related issues.

Arthur Mathews served as chief designer for The Furniture Shop, devoting his time to buildings, interiors, and furniture. Lucia Mathews was responsible for decorating, painting, and carving the furniture and accessories. The result of their work is a distinct approach that combines the premier traits of the English Art and Crafts Movement with those of the modern style. Because the objects they created were not mass-produced,

pieces such as this covered jar are unique. The jar was designed and decorated around 1906 by Lucia Mathews, as a wedding gift for her sister. The decoration consists of a continuous frieze of figures in a landscape: the lower band is a series of stylized flowers, while the lid repeats the motif in carved figures decorated in polychrome enamels. The Furniture Shop closed in 1920.[42]

PROVENANCE: Mrs. Margaret R. Kleinhaus (Lucia Mathews's sister), San Francisco, on the occasion of her wedding, from Arthur and Lucia Mathews; Christie, Manson & Woods International Inc., 1983.

PUBLISHED: Harvey L. Jones, *Mathews Masterpieces of the California Decorative Style* (Oakland, California: Oakland Museum, 1972), cat. no. 164, p. 102. *Important 20th Century Decorative Arts* (New York: Christie, Manson & Woods International, Inc., December 16, 1983), no. 153, illus. p. 73.

EXHIBITED: *Mathews Masterpieces of the California Decorative Style*, Oakland Museum, May 12-July 30, 1972.

---

42. For a complete history of the Mathewses and their shop see Harvey L. Jones, *Mathews: Masterpieces of the California Decorative Style* (Oakland, California: The Oakland Museum, 1972).

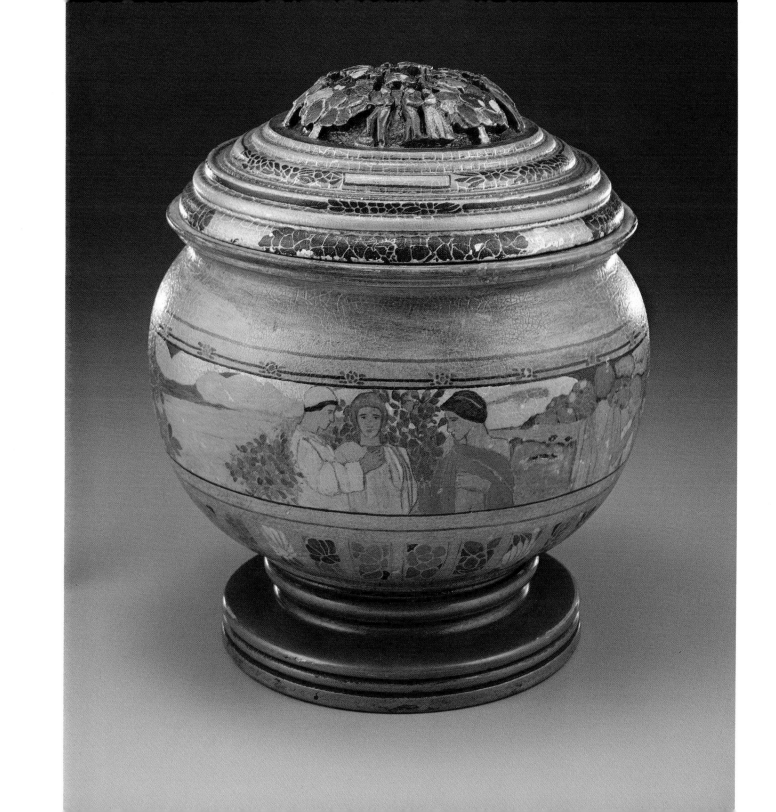

Charles Sumner Greene
American, 1868-1957
and
Henry Mather Greene
American, 1870-1954

54

Table, ca. 1909

Honduras mahogany, ebony, silver
74 × 137.2 × 91.5 (29⅛ × 54 × 36)
Signed under each end of table top and under drawer bottom:
Sumner Greene his true mark
Virginia Museum of Fine Arts, Gift of the Sydney and Frances
Lewis Foundation, 85.63

The Greene brothers, whose architecture and design are often cited as the archetype of West Coast Arts and Crafts, were born in Cincinnati. Following their studies at the Manual Training High School in St. Louis and their graduation from the Massachusetts Institute of Technology, they set up their own architectural firm in Pasadena, California, in 1893.

Most likely because of their location, significant Oriental design influence is apparent in their work, particularly in the stylized motifs, the simplicity of line and form, and the use of mortise-and-tenon joinery. The Greene brothers had been aware of the British Arts and Crafts principles through *International Studio* magazine, and through the work of its American proponent, Gustav Stickley (see cat.no.40), especially in his periodical *The Craftsman*. It was Stickley, in fact, who described the Japanese influences in their work:

> In [their] homes . . . Green & Green [sic] have attempted to naturalize in a new world environment the usable and livable features of Japanese architecture. . . . Although the motif is picturesque, it is not carried to extremes, but an effect of simplicities is obtained in a composition which is in itself rather loose and uncomplicated by the simple treatment of detail.[43]

By 1905, when their commissions expanded to include not only architecture but also furnishings and complete interior designs, they sought the assistance of two Swedish craftsmen, John and Peter Hall, whose cabinetmaking skills added greatly to the refinement and distinction of Greene & Greene furniture.

The table shown here, from the living room of the Charles Pratt residence in Ojai, California, displays an elegance of line and economy of design that represents the pinnacle of the Greene brothers' work. The octagonal top is edged with a strip of wood, and is joined by ebony splines and pegs at the angles. Beneath the top is a drawer than can be opened from either side, its pulls inlaid with silver in parallel wavy lines—a motif that is repeated in the pierced apron of the lower shelf. The signatory joinery on the drawer is reminiscent of Japanese architectural construction.

PROVENANCE: Charles M. Pratt, Ojai, California; Jennie E. Culbert; Christie, Manson & Woods International, Inc., New York, 1985.

PUBLISHED: Randall L. Makinson, *Greene & Greene: Furniture and Related Designs* (Santa Barbara, California: Peregrine Smith, 1979), illus. p. 96.

43. Henrietta P. Keith, "The Trail of Japanese Influence in Our Modern Domestic Architecture," *The Craftsman* 12 (July 1907), no. 4, p. 446.

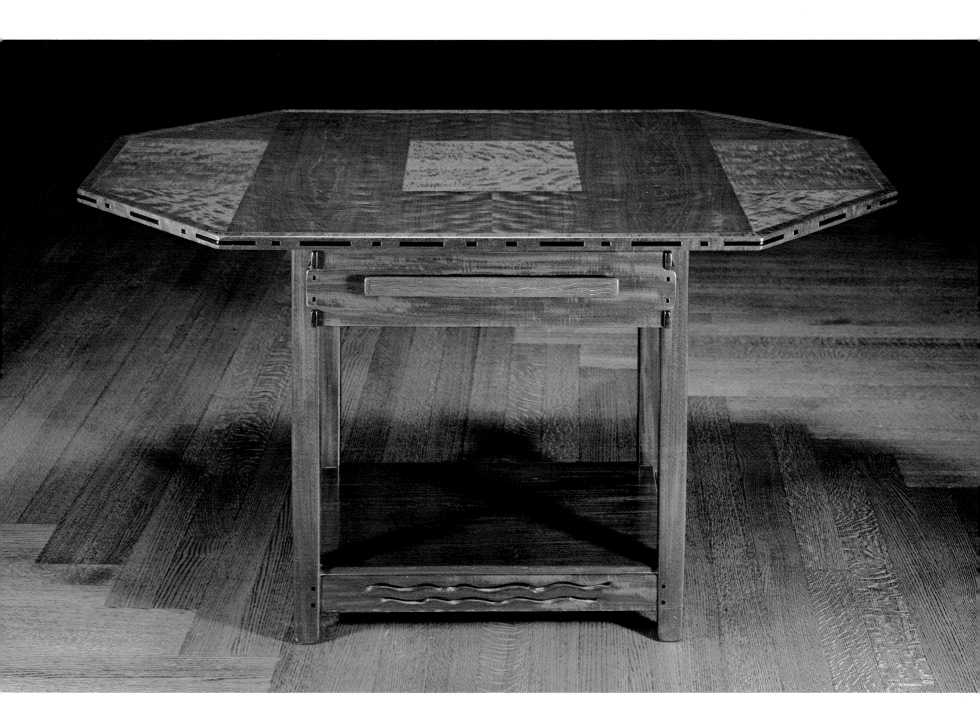

Hector Guimard
French, 1867-1942

55 Office Suite, 1909

Pearwood, mahogany, bronze, upholstery, glass, leather
Desk: 96.5 × 191.4 × 70.5 (38 × 75⅜ × 27¾)
Files (2), each: 191.1 × 78.1 × 37.8 (75¼ × 30¾ × 14⅞)
Armchair: 88.9 × 66.6 × 52 (35 × 26¼ × 20)
Chairs (2), each: 83.8 × 43.8 × 52 (33 × 17¼ × 20½)
Signed: *Hector Guimard* 1909 (on chairs, front right; files, lower
right; desk, lower left)
Virginia Museum of Fine Arts, Gift of Sydney and Frances Lewis,
85.87.1/6

Hector Guimard was a significant force in the period of the Style 1900, creating complete buildings and their interiors in a manner that became hallmarks of his own personal and unmistakable style.

Basing his botanical motifs on the "lower" system—the stem and roots of plant life—as opposed to the "upper"—the leaf-and-flower motifs favored by other artists—Guimard created a wide repertoire of furniture in fine woods and leathers, with metal accessories. Representing the highest quality in cabinetmaking, many pieces carried Guimard's flamboyant signature and date of production.

The carved decoration here, though in very high relief, actually serves to unify the structure of the furniture. The carved elements are so well integrated with the subtle curves and outlines of the design at strategic points that each piece almost looks as if it had been carved from one large block of wood.

PROVENANCE: Hôtel Drouot Auction, Paris, date unknown; Robert Walker, Paris, 1975.

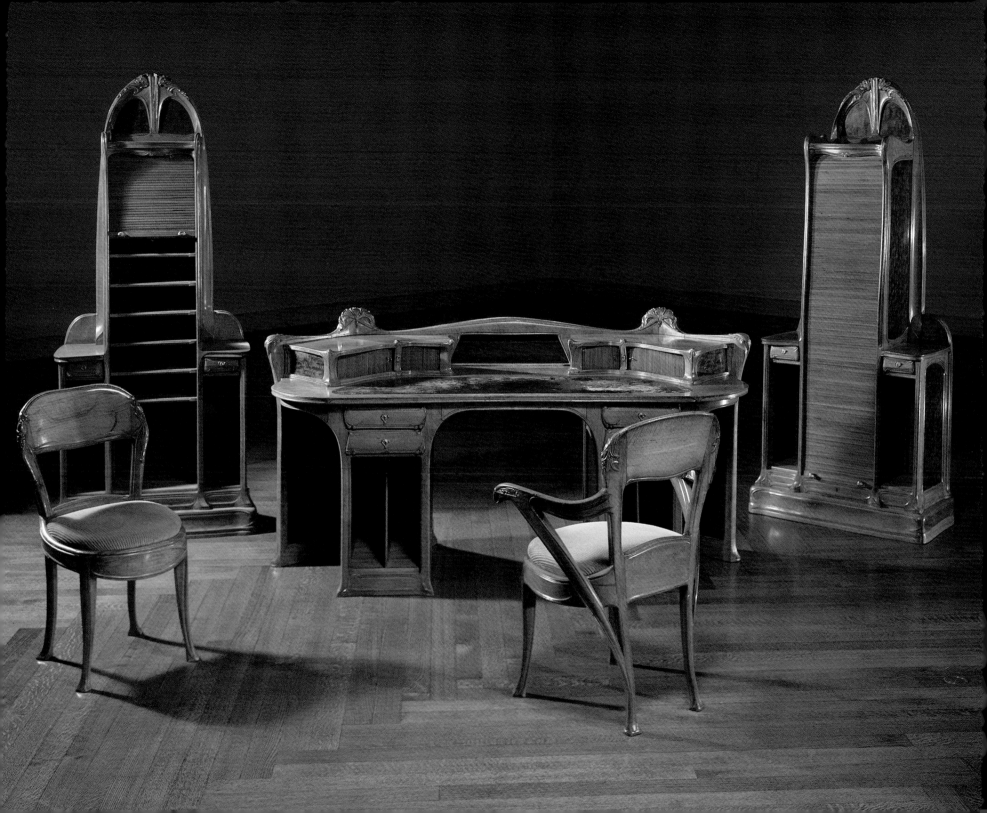

Margaret Macdonald
Scottish, 1865-1933

56

Panels, *The Four Queens*, 1909

Paint and gesso on wood panels
58.1 × 40 (22⅞ × 15¾)
Signed lower right with monogram *MMM* and *1909*
Virginia Museum of Fine Arts, Gift of Sydney and Frances Lewis,
85.143.1/4

When Miss Catherine Cranston and her husband Major John Cochrane commissioned Charles Rennie Mackintosh to redecorate their home, "Hous'hill," Mackintosh was aided in the project by his wife Margaret Macdonald (see cat. no. 44). These four panels were created for the Card Room in 1909.

Margaret and her sister Frances were students in the drawing classes at the Glasgow School of Art from 1891 to 1894. Some time during that period, possibly in 1893, they met Mackintosh and Herbert MacNair, future architects who were enrolled in evening courses at the Glasgow School. The result was both a romantic and professional collaboration among the four artists; Mackintosh married Margaret, and MacNair married Frances.

The Macdonald sisters developed a unique and often eerie style that may have been derived from the works of the English designer-illustrator Aubrey Beardsley and the Dutch Symbolist painter Jan Toorop. In any case, the Macdonald sisters' mature style included distinctive personal motifs and images.

Margaret Macdonald painted many of the stenciled and gessoed pictures for the tea rooms that Mackintosh designed for Miss Cranston. In addition, she did special embroideries for furniture and designed various other projects in the Cranston home.

In these four panels, which were probably originally set into the wall of

the Card Room, Macdonald depicted the queens of the four card suits. Each panel shows a queen in fine robes flanked by two court pages, and the dominant motif varies according to the card suit represented. The linear style is emphasized not only by the artist's use of color but also by the use of outlines in relief, as in leaded glass or cloisonné.

PROVENANCE: Major and Mrs. John Cochrane (Miss Catherine Cranston), Hous'hill, Nithill, Glasgow, 1909; William Ward, 1933. Sotheby's Belgravia, London, 1972.

PUBLISHED: *Studio Yearbook of Decorative Art*, 1917, pp. 63, 79. *Artwork* 6 (Spring 1930), p. 29. Thomas Howarth, *Charles Rennie Mackintosh and the Modern Movement* (London: Routledge & Kegan Paul, 1952), pp. 115-16. *Decorative Arts 1880-1939 including Arts and Crafts, Art Nouveau and Art Déco*, catalogue of sale (London: Sotheby's Belgravia, November 16, 1972), no. 163, illus. p. 42. *Connoisseur* (February 1973), fig. 7, p. 145. Annamaria Edelstein, ed., *Art at Auction: The Year at Sotheby Parke Bernet, 1972-1973* (New York: Viking Press, 1973), illus. p. 378. James Mackay, *Turn of the Century Antiques, An Encyclopedia* (New York: E.P. Dutton & Co., Inc., 1974), pp. 175-76. *The Random House Collectors' Encyclopedia: Victoriana to Art Deco* (New York: Random House, 1974), illus. p. 179. Rowland and Betty Elzea, *The Pre-Raphaelite Era 1848-1914* (Wilmington, Delaware: Wilmington Society of Fine Arts, 1976), illus. 8-93, p. 214. Diana L. Johnson and George P. Landow, *Fantastic Illustration and Design in Britain: 1850-1930* (Providence: Museum of Art, Rhode Island School of Design, 1979), pp. 74, 182-83.

EXHIBITED: *Charles Rennie Mackintosh–Margaret Mackintosh Memorial Exhibition*, McLennan Galleries, Glasgow, 1933; *Charles Rennie Mackintosh: Architecture, Design and Painting*, Royal Scottish Museum, Edinburgh, August 17-September 8, 1968; *The Pre-Raphaelite Era 1848-1914*, Delaware Museum of Art, April-June 1976; *Fantastic Illustration and Design in Britain: 1850-1930*, Rhode Island School of Design, Providence, March 28–May 13, 1979; Cooper-Hewitt Museum, New York, June 5–September 2, 1979.

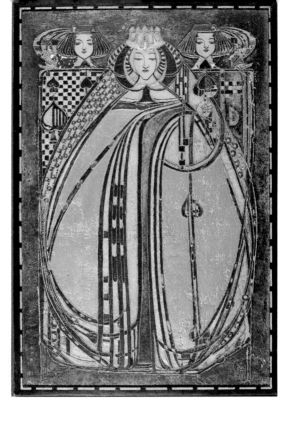
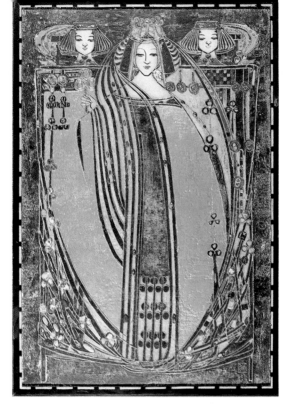
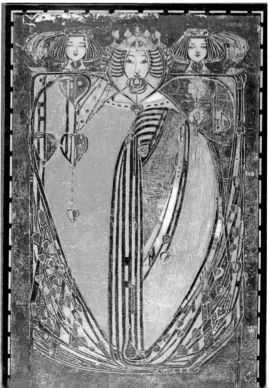
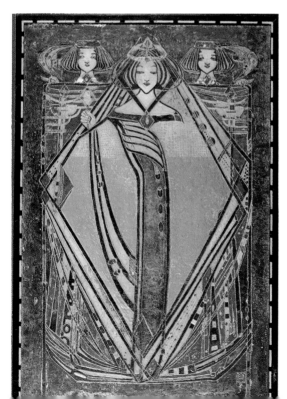

Louis Majorelle
French, 1859-1926

57 Bedroom Suite, before 1909

Cuban mahogany, rosewood, various inlaid woods, gilt bronze, upholstery
Bed: 200.1 × 204.5 × 228.6 (79 × 80½ × 90)
Nightstands (2), each: 119.3 × 55.8 × 44.5 (47 × 22 × 17½)
Armoire: 223.5 × 243.8 × 78.7 (88 × 96 × 31)
Side Chairs (2), each: 100.3 × 41.2 × 47 (39½ × 16¼ × 18)
Armchairs (2), each: 113 × 66.6 × 64.1 (44½ × 26¼ × 25¼)
Unsigned
Virginia Museum of Fine Arts, Gift of Sydney and Frances Lewis, 85.90.1/8

Majorelle's mature style dates from about 1898-99, when he began to use the ormolu *nénuphar* (waterlily) mounts as decorative motifs on his furniture. This bedroom suite dates well after that but before 1909, the year it appeared in *Art et Industrie*. Oral tradition has it that the suite was made for Germaine Paillet, a famous courtesan of the period who was mistress of the Crown Prince of Germany, son of Kaiser Wilhelm.

Whatever its origin, the suite represents a high point in Majorelle's *oeuvre*. Designed and executed with remarkable skill, it shows the craftsmanship for which Majorelle and his artisans were so famous. Fine woods, soft, undulating curves, gilt-bronze mounts and pulls, inlaid panels in abstract patterns—all contribute to define the suite as a masterpiece. The upward and outward flair of the nightstands is repeated on a more elaborate scale in the armoire.

Typical of the furniture-makers of Nancy, the organic lines of the design are derived from flower forms. Majorelle's exquisite cabinetry was a logical continuation of the great tradition of French furniture-makers of the eighteenth century.

PROVENANCE: Galerie Félix Marcilhac, Paris, 1975.

PUBLISHED: *Art et Industrie revue*, 1909. Laurence Buffet-Challié, *Le Modern Style* (Paris: Baschet et Cie., 1975), pp. 28, 39. Félix Marcilhac, "Meubles 1900," *Antiquités, Beaux-Arts, Curiosités* (September, 1977), pp. 58-59. Philippe Garner, *Twentieth Century Furniture* (New York: Van Nostrand Reinhold, 1980), p. 24. Alastair Duncan, *Art Nouveau Furniture* (New York: Clarkson N. Potter, 1982), pl. 42.

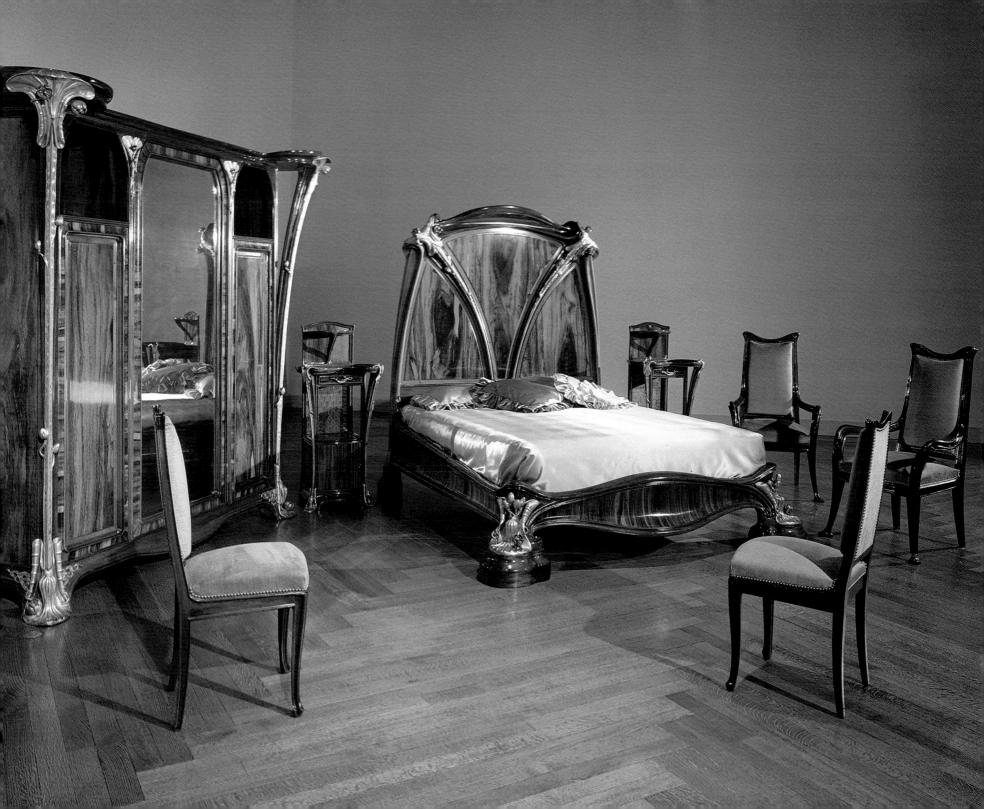

Fulper Pottery Company

American (Flemington, New Jersey), 1805-1929

58 Mushroom Lamp, ca. 1910

Pottery, glass
45.7 × 33. diameter (18 × 13)
Stamped on bottom: *FULPER*
Virginia Museum of Fine Arts, Gift of Sydney and Frances Lewis,
85.150 a/b

The Fulper Pottery Company had its roots in the Samuel Hill Pottery, possibly founded as early as 1805 for the manufacture of drainage tiles and other industrial products. It was not until 1909, however, that Fulper introduced his Vasekraft line and entered the American art pottery market. For the next two decades, this Flemington, New Jersey, pottery produced outstanding wares in the Arts and Crafts tradition, with emphasis on unusual forms and glazes.

Advertisements in Arts and Crafts periodicals of the time, such as Elbert Hubbard's *The Fra* and Gustav Stickley's *The Craftsman*, extolled the virtues of Vasekraft pottery, especially the Fulper Vasekraft lamps, first introduced in 1910. One advertisement called the lamp "the very latest in interior decoration, [adding] beauty to every home." Another remarked on its "originality and beauty of design, wonderful workmanship."

This lamp has a *verte antique* glaze with cucumber-green highlights in an extraordinary combination of form and materials—glass and glaze. Because of the different heating and cooling characteristics of pottery and glass, combining the two materials in this way was a difficult process that often led to disaster. Nonetheless, many lamps were successfully produced and were highly sought after.

Fulper pottery was considered a perfect accompaniment for Arts and Crafts furniture, especially the sort produced by Stickley's Craftsman Shops

(see cat. no. 40). In fact, Fulper shared a pavilion with Stickley at the Panama-Pacific International Exposition in San Francisco in 1915. For its display, Fulper Pottery won the Medal of Honor.

William Hill Fulper II, the grandson of Abraham Fulper, who had first acquired the firm, was credited with establishing the Vasekraft line of production. He hired J. Martin Stangl as the main technical consultant, and it was probably Stangl who was responsible for the development of Fulper's unique glazes. The success of the Fulper Pottery was relatively short-lived. After a fire destroyed the plant in 1929, the company was moved to Trenton. Stangl took over the firm and renamed it the Stangl Pottery Company, shifting production from art pottery to more commercial wares for the home.

PROVENANCE: R. A. Ellison; Jordan-Volpe Gallery, New York.

PUBLISHED: Kirsten Keen, *American Art Pottery, 1875-1930* exhibition catalogue (Wilmington, Delaware: Delaware Art Museum, 1978), cat. no. 152, illus. p. 69. Robert W. Blasberg and Carol L. Bohdan, *Fulper Art Pottery: An Aesthetic Appreciation 1909-1929* exhibition catalogue (New York: The Jordan-Volpe Gallery, 1979), pp. 1, 85, illus. p. 3.

EXHIBITED: *American Art Pottery, 1875-1930*, Delaware Art Museum, Wilmington, March 10-April 23, 1978, cat. no. 152; *Fulper Art Pottery: An Aesthetic Appreciation 1909-1929*, Jordan-Volpe Gallery, New York, March 21-May 30, 1979, cat. no. 144.

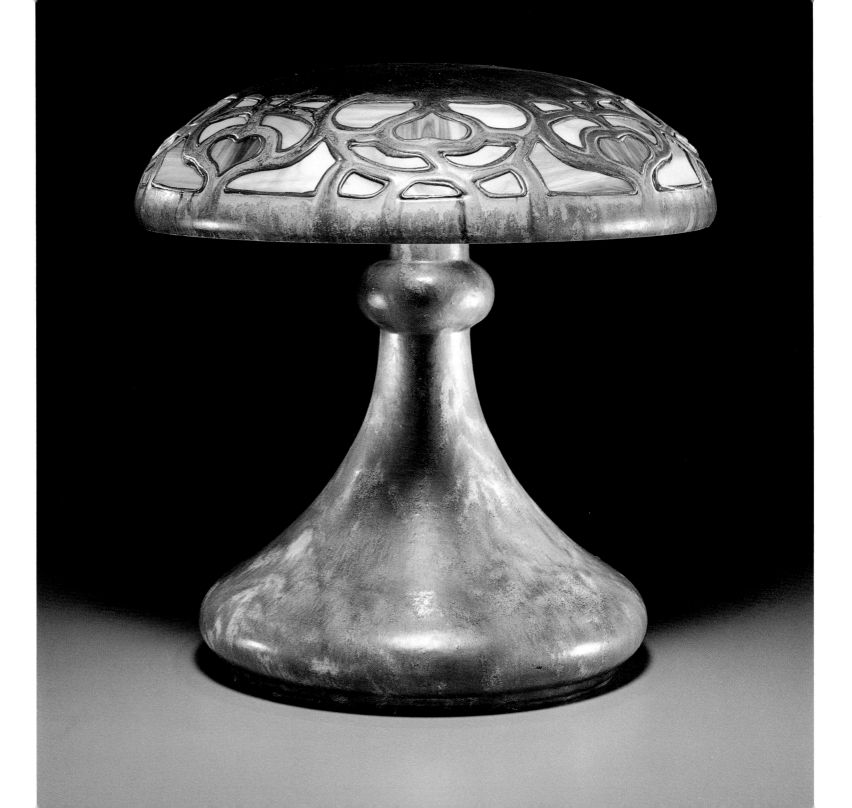

Tiffany Studios
American (New York), 1900-38

59 Gould Peacock Lamp, before 1914

Favrile glass, enamel over copper
102.9 × 33 diameter (40½ × 13)
Base unsigned; globe signed: *M 3460* inside rim
Virginia Museum of Fine Arts, Gift of the Sydney and Frances
Lewis Foundation, 85.152 a/b

Some time before 1914, Charles Winthrop Gould, son of Charles and
Henrietta Saltanstall Gould and a relative of the noted financier Jay Gould,
commissioned Louis Comfort Tiffany to do some interior decorating in his
New York residence using the peacock as a central motif. Almost four
decades earlier, in 1876, James Abbott McNeill Whistler had completed the
famous Peacock Room for British industrialist F. R. Leyland, and perhaps
either Gould or Tiffany was familiar with this extravagant commission. (The
room is now installed in the Freer Gallery of Art in Washington, D.C.) This
lamp, along with a matching newel-post and wall sconces, was created for
Gould. This lamp is especially important in the context of the Tiffany
oeuvre, since, being a private commission, it allowed the artist more
freedom of expression.

Unlike the normal production lamps of Tiffany Studios, the base of this
lamp is not patinated bronze but glass in the peacock-tail motif. The base is
supported by a flared enamel-on-copper foot that repeats the peacock-tail
motif and that has a band of enameled scarabs around the top edge.
Projecting from the shoulder of the base are three enameled peacocks with
their backs arched, seemingly to support the large, iridescent Favrile globe
on the top of the lamp. The peacocks with scarab necklaces are also enamel
on copper.

Charles Gould died in 1931, bequeathing all his furnishings to the
Louis Comfort Tiffany Foundation in Long Island. When the Tiffany
Foundation auctioned the contents of Tiffany's home at Laurelton Hall in
1946, this lamp sold for $225. At that time it was the highest auction price
ever paid for a piece of Tiffany glass.

PROVENANCE: Charles W. Gould, before 1914; Louis C. Tiffany Foundation, 1931-46; Richard Barnett, 1946-68; Oscar Schroeder, 1968-78; Christie, Manson & Woods International Inc., New York, 1978.

PUBLISHED: Charles DeKay, *The Artwork of Louis C. Tiffany* (New York: Doubleday, Page & Co., 1914), illus. opposite p. 34. *The Objects of Art of the Louis Comfort Tiffany Foundation*, catalogue of sale, no. 789 (New York: Parke-Bernet Galleries, September 24-28, 1946), front cover and no. 288. Gertrude Speenburg, *The Arts of the Tiffanys* (Chicago: Lightner Publishing Corp., 1956), pp. 69-70. Robert Koch, *Louis C. Tiffany: Rebel in Glass* (New York: Crown Publishers, 1964), pp. 187, 206. Henry Winter, *The Dynasty of Louis Comfort Tiffany* (Boston: privately printed, 1971), pp. 242-43. *Fine Art Nouveau & Nineteenth Century Sculpture*, catalogue of sale (New York: Christie, Manson & Woods International Inc., December 1, 1978), no. 293, illus. p. 87 and on cover. *Review of the Season, Christie's Yearbook* (London: Studio Vista, 1979), p. 359. Patricia Bayer, "Art Nouveau," *Antiques World*, (October 1981), illus. p. 24. Alastair Duncan, *Tiffany at Auction* (New York: Rizzoli International Publications Inc., 1981), no. 316, p. 17. William Feldstein, Jr., and Alastair Duncan, *The Lamps of Tiffany Studios* (New York: Harry N. Abrams, 1983), pp. 76-77, illus. p. 77.

EXHIBITED: The Louis C. Tiffany Foundation, Laurelton Hall, Long Island, New York. The Dayton (Ohio) Art Institute, October 21-November 20, 1966; Art Nouveau Gallery, Virginia Museum of Fine Arts, Richmond, long-term loan, 1978-1985.

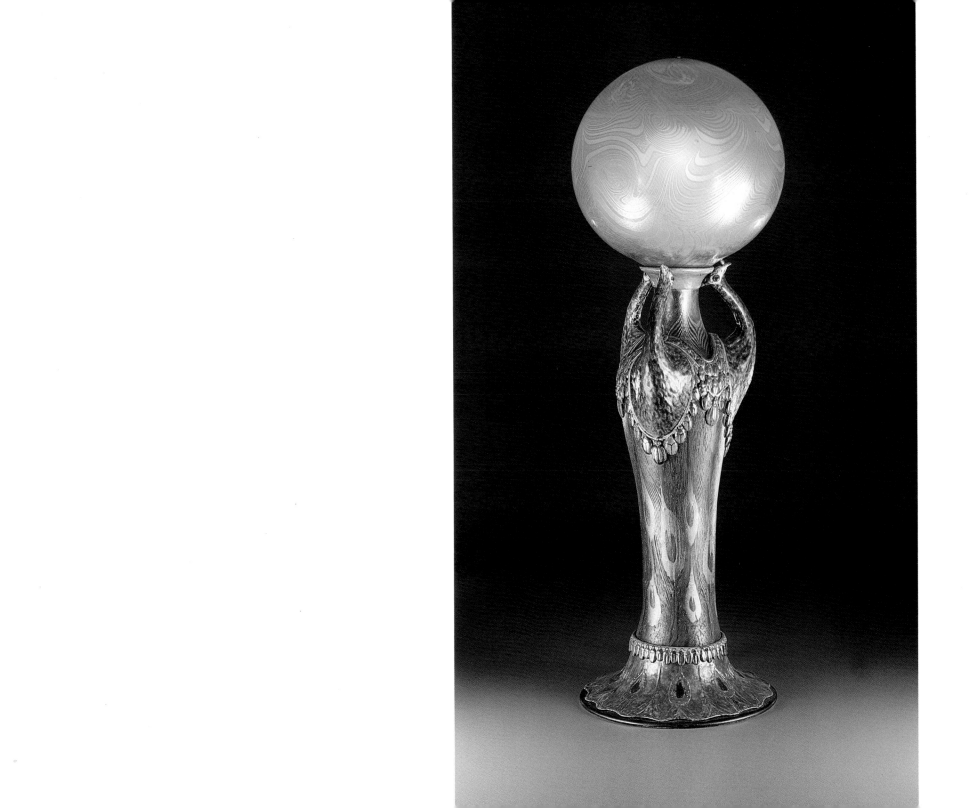

Emile-Jacques Ruhlmann
French, 1879-1933

 60 Corner Cabinet, 1916

Lacquered rosewood, ivory, rare woods
128.3 × 85 × 60.3 (50½ × 33½ × 23¾)
Unsigned
Virginia Museum of Fine Arts, Gift of Sydney and Frances Lewis,
85.135

Emile-Jacques Ruhlmann is considered one of the greatest of the French cabinetmakers of the twentieth century and is often compared to such great *ébénistes* as Jean-Henri Riesener, who worked for Louis XVI. During the two decades of his work, Ruhlmann brought elegance, refinement, and taste to French cabinetmaking, qualities unequaled by his contemporaries and unsurpassed by his successors.

Ruhlmann was born in Paris in 1879, but little else is known about his early life. It is believed that he was self-trained as a cabinet designer, which makes his success all the more exceptional. He is said to have designed the furniture for his own home after his marriage in 1907, but it was not until 1913 that he first exhibited at the Salon d'Automne in Paris, where his work was highly acclaimed. By 1919 Ruhlmann had taken on a partner, Pierre Laurent, and their firm was considered outstanding in France.

Although this cabinet is extraordinary in its sense of refinement and its adherence to many of the principles of the Style 1925, there is little question that its design owes much to Ruhlmann's predecessors. The opulent inlaid vase design, which serves as the central motif on the door, was used often by Ruhlmann and has its origins in eighteenth-century furniture design. But the way Ruhlmann adapted this motif—with a profusion of flowers rendered in rare woods and ivory—clearly distinguishes this piece.

The door is outlined in small dots of ivory, which are also used to accent the feet and the scrolls on the legs, and in rectangular insets along the top edge. This use of fine detail, combined with exquisite cabinetry and finish, all became trademarks of Ruhlmann's work, which he constantly developed and refined until his death in 1933.

Ruhlmann's furniture was made for an exclusive clientele who sought and could afford items of great luxury and exorbitant cost. Under such circumstances, he was able to fulfill his creative fantasy of using the finest and rarest materials, sparing no expense in finish or detail.

PROVENANCE: Palais Galliera, Paris, 1972.

PUBLISHED: Emile Bayard, L'Art Appliqué Français d'Aujourd'hui (Paris: Ernest Gründ, no date), illus. p. 12. De 1900 à 1930, catalogue of sale (Paris: Palais Galliera, November 24, 1972), no. 67, illus. p. 31. Marvin D. Schwartz, "Art Nouveau & Art Deco, The Avant-garde Antiques," Art News 71 (December, 1972), p. 63. "Le Mobilier des 'Années 25': Petit lexique des principaux ornemanistes," Gazette de l'Hôtel Drouot (February 2, 1973), p. 12. "Conseils aux Acheteurs: folies pour le style 'Art Deco'," Connaissance des Arts 252 (February, 1973), p. 113. Philippe Garner, ed., Encyclopedia of Decorative Arts (New York: Van Nostrand Reinhold, 1979), illus. p. 63. Pierre Kjellberg, "La Curiosité. 'Les Maîtres de l'Art Deco: Jacques Emile [sic] Ruhlmann," La Gazette de l'Hôtel Drouot (July 4, 1980), illus. p. 74. Pierre Kjellberg, Art Deco: Les Maîtres du Mobilier (Paris: Les Editions de l'Amateur, 1981), p. 158. Karen Davies, At Home in Manhattan: Modern Decorative Arts, 1925 to the Depression (New Haven: Yale University Art Gallery, 1983), illus. no. 2, p. 17. Alastair Duncan, Art Deco Furniture (New York: Holt, Rinehart and Winston, 1984), p. 104, illus. pl. 52.

EXHIBITED: At Home in Manhattan: Modern Decorative Arts, 1925 to the Depression, Yale University Art Gallery, New Haven, November 10, 1983-February 5, 1984.

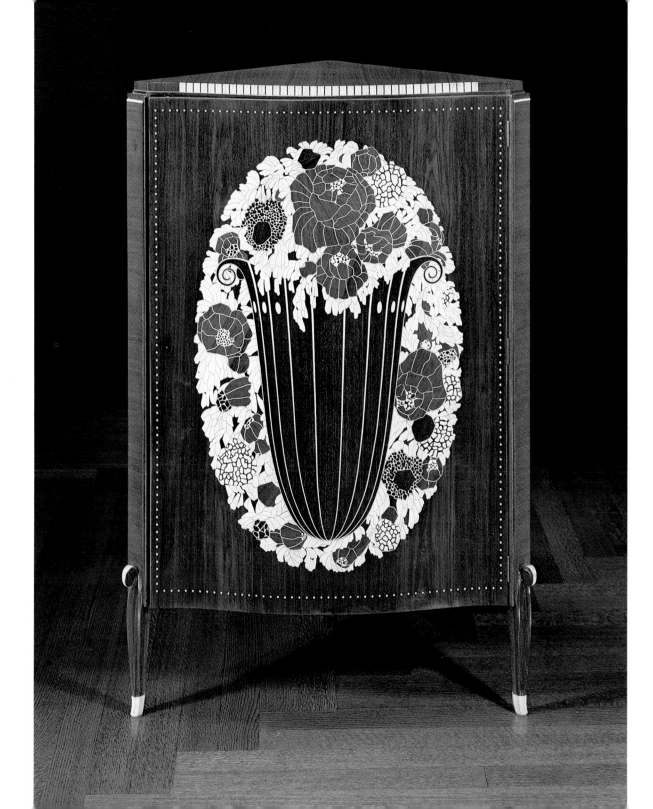

Charles Rennie Mackintosh
Scottish, 1868-1928

61 Mantel Clock, 1917

Ebonized wood, ivory, green Erinoid
23.7 × 13 × 11.3 (9¹¹/₃₂ × 5⅛ × 4⁷/₁₆)
Unsigned
Virginia Museum of Fine Arts, Gift of Sydney and Frances Lewis, 85.222

In 1914, Mackintosh was greatly disappointed by a lack of commissions and critical support in his native Glasgow, and it is thought that he was planning to leave Scotland for the more sympathetic atmosphere of Vienna when World War I began. He settled first in Walberswick, then in London.

Mackintosh was sought out in 1916 by W.J. Bassett-Lowke to make alterations on his small townhouse at 78 Derngate in Northampton. Bassett-Lowke was the manufacturer of precision scale models and a member of the Design & Industries Association, founded in 1915 to reconcile good design with machine-made household goods. Because he was familiar with various design activities in other countries, Bassett-Lowke was much more knowledgeable than any of Mackintosh's previous clients.

One of the pieces that Mackintosh designed and had fabricated for the dining room of Bassett-Lowke's townhouse was this clock. A simple design, it consists of a cube supported by ten uprights, all of ebonized wood. The numerals are inlaid in ivory around a twelve-sided slab of green Erinoid, an early synthetic material made from resin or protein plastic. A small ivory triangle is set at the base of each of the ten square supports, which rest on a stepped base inlaid with alternating strips of ivory and wood.

Although unique, the clock bears a definite relationship to other mantel, hanging, and tall-case clocks Mackintosh designed for various clients. In 1905 he created a clock for Hill House in Helensburgh, Scotland; its design was a similar cube mounted on legs of ebony and stained sycamore, but the face was painted rather than inlaid.

In 1917, Mackintosh created another clock for Bassett-Lowke that resembles the clock shown here. Known as the "Domino Clock," it is a cube supported on six columns. Again, the primary material is ebonized wood,

and the numerals and face are inlaid ivory with green and purple Erinoid. Each numeral is represented by a stylized domino block containing one to twelve dots.

Mackintosh designed a third clock for Bassett-Lowke in 1919, for the guest bedroom at 78 Derngate. This one is quite different from the earlier two, being more closely related to Viennese design, especially the work of Otto Prutscher.[44]

The work Mackintosh did for Bassett-Lowke at 78 Derngate was his final design commission. He later moved to France, where he devoted his life to painting watercolors. He returned to London in 1927 and died there the following year.

PROVENANCE: W.J. Bassett-Lowke, 1917; Osborne Robinson; Colin Robinson; Sotheby's Belgravia, London, 1977.

PUBLISHED: *The Ideal Home* (October 1920), pl 131. Thomas Howarth, *Charles Rennie Mackintosh and the Modern Movement* (Feltham: Country Life Books, 1968), pp. 203-04, pl. 77. Andrew McLaren Young, *Charles Rennie Mackintosh 1868-1928: Architecture, Design and Painting* (Edinburgh: Scottish Arts Council, 1968), no. 252, illus. pl. 29. *Decorative Arts 1880-1950 including Art Nouveau and Art Deco*, catalogue of sale (London: Sotheby's Belgravia, July 20, 1977), no. 130, illus. p. 24. Philippe Garner, "Charles Rennie Macintosh as Designer," *Art at Auction, 1976-1977* (London: Sotheby Parke Bernet, 1977), pp. 474-80, illus. p. 480. Isabelle Anscombe and Charlotte Gere, *Arts and Crafts in Britain and America* (New York: Rizzoli, International Publications, Inc., 1978), p. 181. Roger Billcliffe, *Charles Rennie Mackintosh: The Complete Furniture, Furniture Drawings and Interior Designs* (New York: Taplinger Publishing Co., 1979), illus. 917.1, p. 229. Sylvia Katz, *Classic Plastics: From Bakelite to High Tech* (London: Thames and Hudson, 1984), illus. p.33.

EXHIBITED: *Historical Clocks*, Northampton (England) Art Gallery, 1966; *Charles Rennie Mackintosh 1868-1928: Architecture, Design and Painting*, Royal Scottish Museum, Edinburgh, August 17-September 8, 1968.

44. Billcliffe, *Charles Rennie Mackintosh*, p. 247.

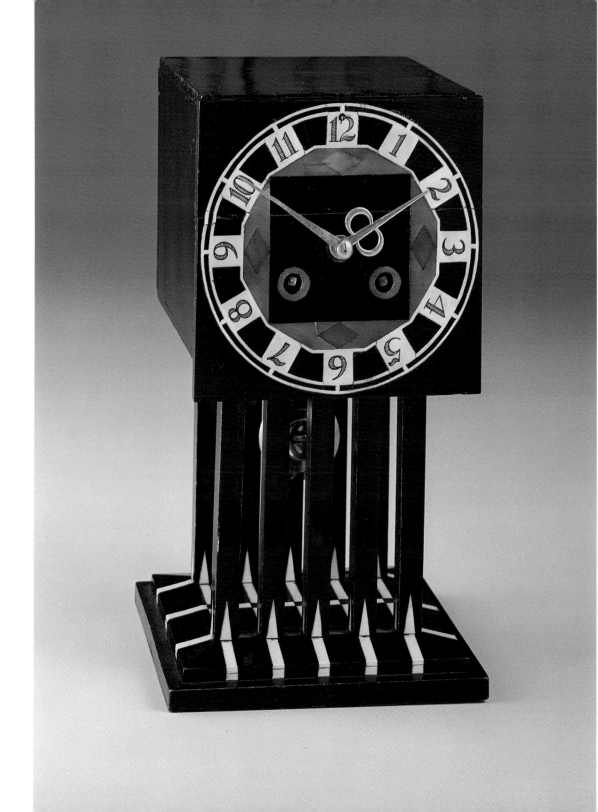

Gerrit Rietveld
Dutch, 1888-1964

 62

Chair, 1917

Painted wood
87.5 × 60.3 × 82.5 (34⁷⁄₁₆ × 23¾ × 32½)
Unsigned
Virginia Museum of Fine Arts, Gift of Sydney and Frances Lewis,
85.83

The De Stijl movement was named after a periodical of the same name first published in October of 1917. The purpose of the magazine was to document the aims and the work of a group of Dutch painters, sculptors, writers, and architects, led by Theo Van Doesburg who, like the French artists of the Art Nouveau period, sought to break down the distinctions between the so-called fine and applied arts. In addition, foreshadowing the later Bauhaus movement in Germany, they sought ways to make all art forms, including literature and music, interactive with one another by way of a universal visual language in which each artist could create without inflicting his or her own personality into the aesthetics.

De Stijl combined simple geometric shapes, horizontal and vertical lines, and primary colors to create this new visual vocabulary. Both the movement and the style remained active for fourteen years, until 1931.

Although Gerrit Rietveld designed this chair in 1917—two years before he joined the De Stijl movement—he incorporated many of De Stijl's design principles. Executed in black and white, the chair can be seen as the prototype of what is perhaps Rietveld's most famous creation, the "Rood Blauwe Stoel" (red-and-blue chair) of 1918.

According to Rietveld scholar Daniele Baroni, this chair comprises seventeen basic elements "crisscrossing each other vertically and horizontally to imprint a reciprocal dynamism and concluding in a carrying structure. Two planes which rest very lightly and do not touch each other act as the seat and the back."[45]

In 1971 Rietveld described his motives and methods. The chair, he said,

. . . was created with the intention of demonstrating that an aesthetic and spatial object could be constructed with linear material and made by machinery. I therefore sectioned the central part of the plank into two, obtaining a seat and a back; then, with lintels of varying lengths, I constructed a chair. When I made it, I did not realize that it would have such an enormous significance for me and also for others, nor did I imagine that its effect would be so overwhelming even in architecture. When the opportunity arose for me to build a house |Schröder Huis| based on the same principles, I naturally did not let it pass me by.[46]

PROVENANCE: Paul Citroën; Piet Moget; Galerie Jean Chauvelin, Paris; Donald Karshan; Sotheby Parke Bernet Monaco S.A., 1977.

PUBLISHED: Plaisir de France (June 1974), p. 30. Arts Décoratifs Styles 1900 et 1925 catalogue of sale (Monte Carlo: Sotheby Parke Bernet Monaco S.A., October 8, 1977), p. 49, illus. pl. 64.

45. Daniele Baroni, Gerrit Thomas Rietveld Furniture (London: Academy Editions, 1978), p. 42.
46. As quoted in Baroni, Rietveld Furniture, p. 43.

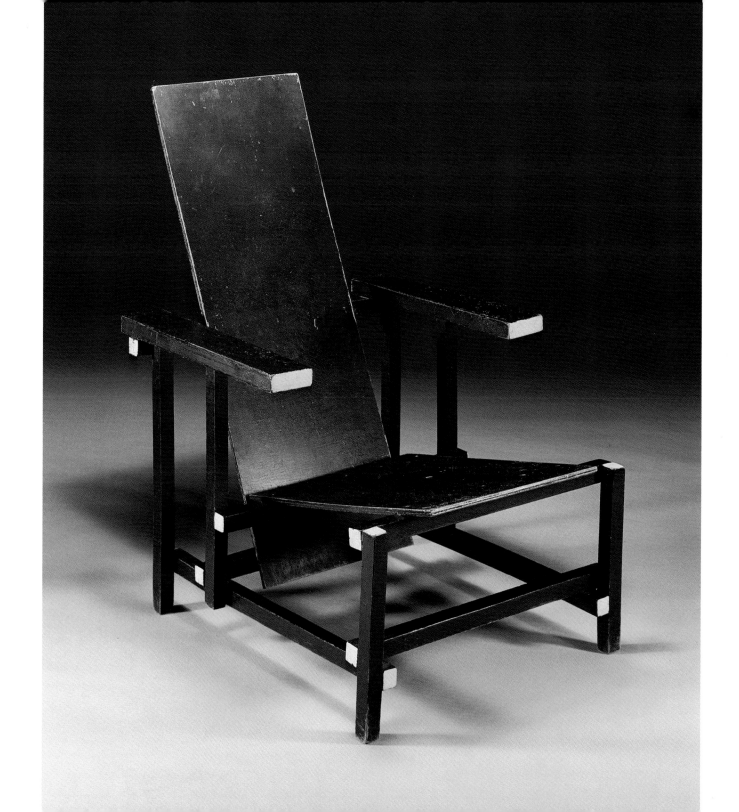

Eileen Gray
French (born in Ireland), 1879-1976

63 "Canoe" Sofa, ca. 1919-20

Lacquered wood, silver leaf
72.1 × 270 × 64.9 (28⅜ × 106⁵/₁₆ × 25⁹/₁₆)
Unsigned
Virginia Museum of Fine Arts, Gift of Sydney and Frances Lewis,
85.112

One of the most ambitious and comprehensive decorating commissions undertaken by the Irish designer Eileen Gray was the apartment for Suzanne Talbot (Mme Mathieu Lévy), a successful Parisian couturière. Gray not only designed the accessories for the apartment but also redesigned the walls of the space itself. Among the most extravagant pieces of furniture was a sofa in the shape of a canoe.

Although there is no documentation on the origin of her design, Gray must have been aware of the Polynesian and Micronesian dugout canoe, the shape of which is strongly evoked in this sumptuous piece. Indeed, Gray and many of her colleagues—including Pierre Legrain (see cat. no. 89)— were familiar with the arts of Africa and other exotic lands, and they showed little hesitancy in adapting some of these forms for their own furniture designs.

The *pirogue* (canoe) sofa in this collection is very similar to the one Gray designed for Suzanne Talbot. It is not known for whom this particular sofa was intended, but it was made around the same time as the Talbot design, that is, 1919-20.

Like so much of Gray's furniture, the sofa is lacquered, an extremely difficult finishing process. Gray was familiar with the lacquer technique from her earlier work in the shop of D. Charles, a London craftsman who specialized in repairing lacquer screens.[47] She later worked with the Japanese lacquer master, Sugawara, and by 1913 she was exhibiting lacquered furniture. A true master of the medium, Gray was able to produce a wide variety of lacquer textures and colors, as well as to combine lacquer with other materials, in this case silver leaf.

Amazingly, for a designer with such an impressive output, Gray had no formal training in furniture-making. She had originally studied painting but abandoned it in order to redirect her energies into making what she felt were more useful objects.

PROVENANCE: Enghien Hôtel des Ventes, Enghien-les-Bains, France, 1982.

PUBLISHED: Similar model in J. Stewart Johnson, *Eileen Gray* (London: Debrett's Peerage for the Museum of Modern Art, 1979), pp. 18-19. *Art 1900-1925*, catalogue of sale (Enghien-les-Bains, France: March 21, 1982), no. 157, cover illus.

47. J. Stewart Johnson, *Eileen Gray: Designer 1879-1976* (London: DeBrett's Peerage Ltd., 1979), p. 11.

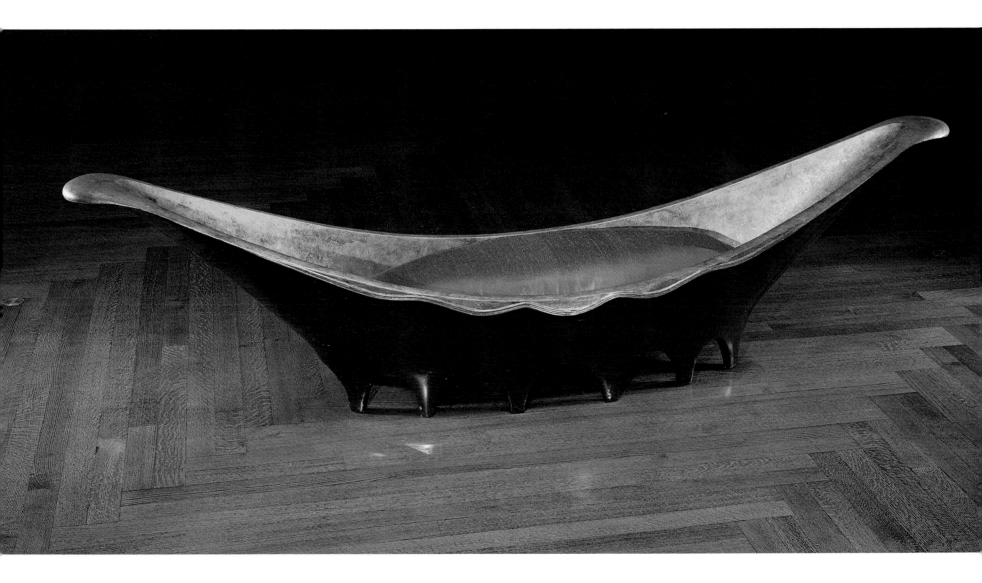

Louis Cartier
French, 1875-1942

 64   Pendant, 1921

Jade, onyx, rubies, emeralds, sapphires, pearls, diamonds,
silver
10.5 × 2.86 diameter (4⅛ × 1⅛)
Unsigned
Virginia Museum of Fine Arts, Gift of Sydney and Frances Lewis,
85.234

The name Cartier has been synonymous with fine jewelry since 1847, the year that Louis François Cartier began his firm. The company continued under Louis's son Alfred, but it was his grandson, also named Louis, with whom we associate a special phase of modern jewelry-making.

Louis Cartier joined the family firm in 1898. By the turn of the century he was already recognized for his skill and for the unique creativity he brought to the art of the goldsmith. In his most successful designs, as in this pendant, Cartier abandoned traditional stone-setting methods and instead combined precious and semiprecious stones in harmonious combinations and a dazzling display of colors. His style was obviously influenced by the jewelry he saw in other lands, as well as by the products of the modern movement in Europe during the 1920s.

This pendant features several tiers of pear-shaped jade, with a cabochon ruby and a pearl at the bottom, all hanging from an onyx dome set with cabochon rubies, emeralds, sapphires, pearls, and diamonds. The suspension link is jade, pearl, and ruby, and the ring at the top is silver mounted with diamonds.

In addition to his innovative jewelry, Cartier was also known for his remarkable designs for clocks and watches, including the famous "Mystery Clock," with hands that seem to float in a glass case, the works concealed in the base. He is credited with the invention of the first wristwatch, created in 1907. Louis Cartier died in 1942, but the firm of Cartier continues to this day.

PROVENANCE: H. Robert Greene; Christie's International S.A., Geneva, 1978.

PUBLISHED: The H. Robert Greene Collection of Art Deco, catalogue of sale (Geneva: Christie's International S.A., November 16, 1978), no. 518, illus. p. 42.

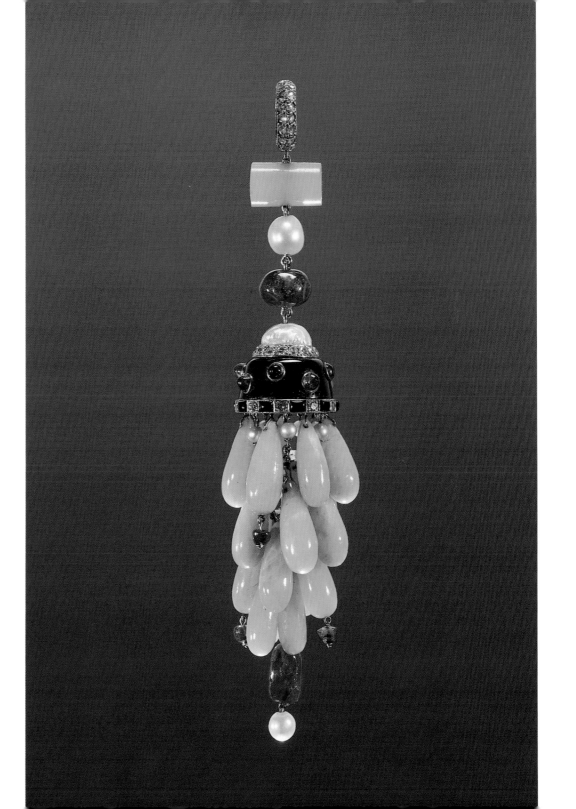

Eileen Gray
French (born in Ireland), 1879-1976

65 Floor Lamp, 1923
Lacquered wood, painted parchment
185.4 × 52 diameter (73 × 20½)
Unsigned
Virginia Museum of Fine Arts, Gift of Sydney and Frances Lewis,
85.169 a/c

For the fourteenth *Salon des Artistes Décorateurs* in Paris in 1923, Eileen Gray created a "bedroom-boudoir for Monte Carlo" (see fig. 20). The room was a total design entity that included carpets, tables, sofas, screens, and several lighting fixtures. Among them was the floor lamp shown here, a brilliant example not only of Gray's mastery of technique but also her ability to design furniture that was well ahead of her time.

Born in Ireland, Gray moved to Paris in 1902 and lived there until her death. She had no formal training in furniture design but had studied drawing at London's Slade School of Art. By teaching herself the difficult art of lacquering, Gray produced enough of her own furniture to exhibit it in a gallery of her own design in Paris in 1922. She called the gallery *Jean Désert*. Although Gray's furniture, like the Monte Carlo bedroom-boudoir, was not well received by French critics, many others responded positively to her work.

In 1924, at the urging of the architectural writer Jean Badovici, Gray designed her first house in the south of France at Roquebrune. As with her other projects, she filled the house with furniture and other accoutrements she designed herself. By the beginning of World War II, she had designed several other private dwellings, including a second, smaller house for herself. During the war she was interned in Paris, and much of her work was looted and destroyed. She went into semi-retirement after the war, and it was only recently that her furniture and architectural concepts have been recognized for their freshness and intelligence of design.

It is believed that because she was a woman working in what had been a predominantly male profession she did not receive the accord due her in her lifetime.

PROVENANCE: Michel Perinet, Paris, 1973.

PUBLISHED: Yvonne Brunhammer, *Cinquantenaire de l'Exposition de 1925* (Paris: Musée des Arts Décoratifs, 1976), cat no. 487. Brigitte Loye Deroubaix, *Eileen Gray: Architecture Design 1879-1976*, (Paris: Direction de l'architecture, Ministère de l'urbanisme et du logement, 1983), illus. pp. 25, 33. Alastair Duncan, *Art Deco Furniture* (New York: Holt, Rinehart and Winston, 1984), p. 32, illus. pl. 29.

EXHIBITED: *Salon des Artistes Décorateurs*, Paris, 1923. *Cinquantenaire de l'Exposition de 1925*, Musée des Arts Décoratifs, Paris, October 15, 1976–February 2, 1977.

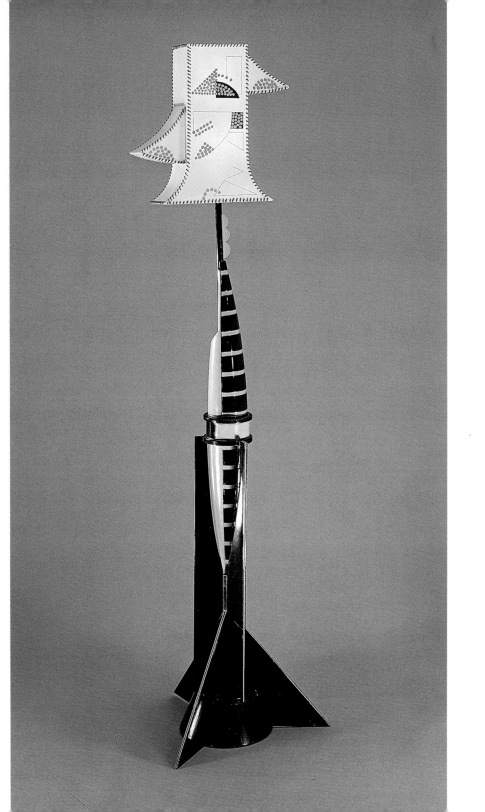

Waldemar Raemisch
German, 1888-1955

 66
Pair of Table Lamps, 1923

Brass
69.2 × 16.5 × 20.3 (27¼ × 6½ × 8)
Signed on each base, rear: *Raemisch*
Virginia Museum of Fine Arts, Gift of Sydney and Frances Lewis,
85.172.1/2

In 1898, Karl Schmidt established the Deutsche Werkstätten in Dresden, Germany, to create well-designed objects for commercial production. (Richard Riemerschmid was among the other major designers involved in the Werkstätte, see cat. no. 12.)

Waldemar Raemisch designed these lamps for the Deutsche Werkstätten. In *Modern Applied Art* (1948) the lamps are shown with pleated fabric shades with a chevron design on the upper and lower edges. On each lamp, a figure holds an oversized torch and is flanked by an animal. The sculptures have smooth, rounded forms, a stylization typical of the period.

Raemisch was born in Berlin in 1888 and had a long career as a painter and sculptor. From 1923 to 1927, as professor at the State Academy of Art in Berlin, he was responsible for a number of important commissions, including design of the currency for the German Republic in 1923. Raemisch also designed the massive outdoor sculpture for the stadium of the Berlin Olympic Games in 1936. Forced to give up his professorship in 1937, Raemisch fled to the United States, where he joined the faculty of the Rhode Island School of Design. One of his most important public commissions in this country was the sculpture in front of the Youth Detention Center in Philadelphia. Raemisch died in Rome in 1955.

PROVENANCE: Cranbrook Academy of Art, Bloomfield Hills, Michigan; Sotheby Parke-Bernet, New York, 1972.

PUBLISHED: Rudolph Rosenthal and Helen Ratzka, *Modern Applied Art* (New York: Harper Bros., 1948), illus. following p. 42. *The Cranbrook Collections*, catalogue of sale (New York: Sotheby Parke-Bernet, May 2-5, 1972), no. 116, illus. p. 24.

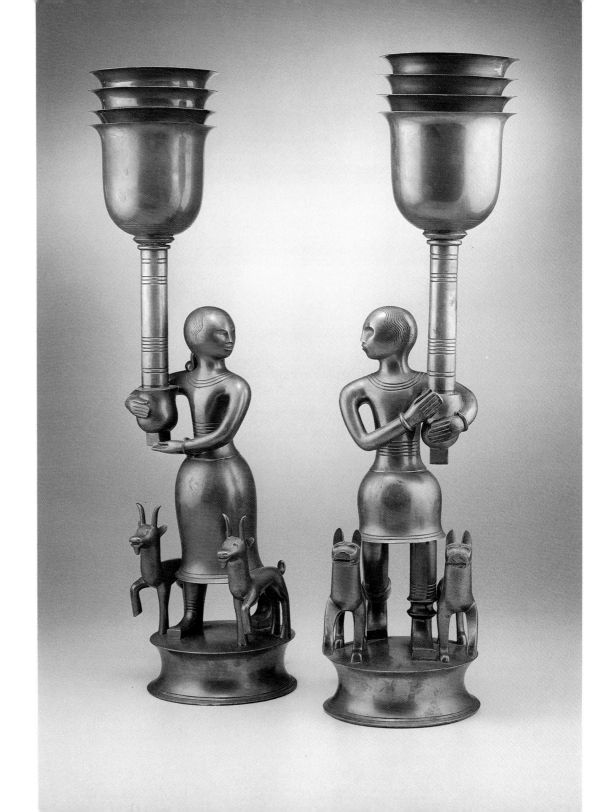

René Joubert
French, died 1931
and
Philippe Petit
French, died 1945
for
Décoration Intérieure Moderne
French (Paris), established 1919

67

Lady's Writing Desk, 1924

Palisander, ivory
119.4 × 80 × 41.9 (47 × 31½ × 16½)
Unsigned
Virginia Museum of Fine Arts, Gift of Sydney and Frances Lewis,
85.119

Décoration Intérieure Moderne was founded after World War I by René Joubert, a furniture designer, and Georges Mouveau, a theatre designer, who was replaced by Philippe Petit in 1924. The purpose of the firm was to produce furniture and interior designs.

Joubert and Petit are known for their use of rare veneers and other extraordinary materials. This exceptional desk was originally displayed in 1924 in a furniture group described as "bedroom for Mme de G." The following year it was included in the firm's shop at the Paris Exposition; it was also part of a traveling exhibition that toured New York at the close of the Exposition.

Using a minimum of decoration, Joubert and Petit created a sumptuous piece of furniture highlighted by inlaid ivory, both at the top of the slanted lid and on the front of the two long drawers. The long, slender, tapering legs end in stylized claw feet.

The stepped pyramid on the upper part of the desk could be attributed to the current interest in Indian art of the Americas, specifically the Mayan temples of Mexico.

PROVENANCE: Society of Arts and Crafts; Cranbrook Academy of Art, Bloomfield Hills, Michigan; Sotheby Parke Bernet, New York, 1972.

PUBLISHED: *Art et Décoration*, July-December 1924, illus. pp. 1, 6. *L'Art Décoratif Français 1918-1925* (Paris: Editions Albert Lévy, 1926), illus. pp. 17, 55. Pierre Olmer, *Le Mobilier français d'aujourd'hui (1920-1925)* (Paris: publisher unknown, 1926), illus. pl. 29. *Mobilier et décoration*, May 1928. Waldemar George, *Intérieurs d'aujourd'hui* (Paris: publisher unknown, 1928), p. 6. Judith Applegate, *Art Deco* (New York: Finch College Museum of Art, 1970), catalogue of exhibition, cat no. 233. Bevis Hillier, *The World of Art Deco*, catalogue of exhibition, Minneapolis Institute of Art (New York: E.P. Dutton & Co. Inc., 1971), cat. no. 63. *The Cranbrook Collections*, catalogue of sale (New York: Sotheby Parke Bernet, May 2-5, 1972), lot 118, illus. p. 25. Katherine Morrison McClinton, *Art Deco: A Guide for Collectors* (New York: Clarkson N. Potter, Inc., 1972), p. 32. Pierre Kjellberg, *Art Deco: Les Maîtres du Mobilier* (Paris: Les Editions de l'Amateur, ca. 1981), p. 52. Alastair Duncan, *Art Deco Furniture* (New York: Holt, Rinehart and Winston, 1984), illus. p. 79.

EXHIBITED: *Exposition Internationale des Arts Décoratifs et Industriels Modernes*, Paris, 1925. Traveling exhibition of the Paris Exposition, 1926; *Art Deco*, Finch College Museum of Art, New York, October 14-November 30, 1970, no. 223. Cranbrook Academy of Art, Bloomfield Hills, Michigan, January 19-February 28, 1971; *Art Deco*, Minneapolis Institute of Art, July-September 1971, cat. no. 63.

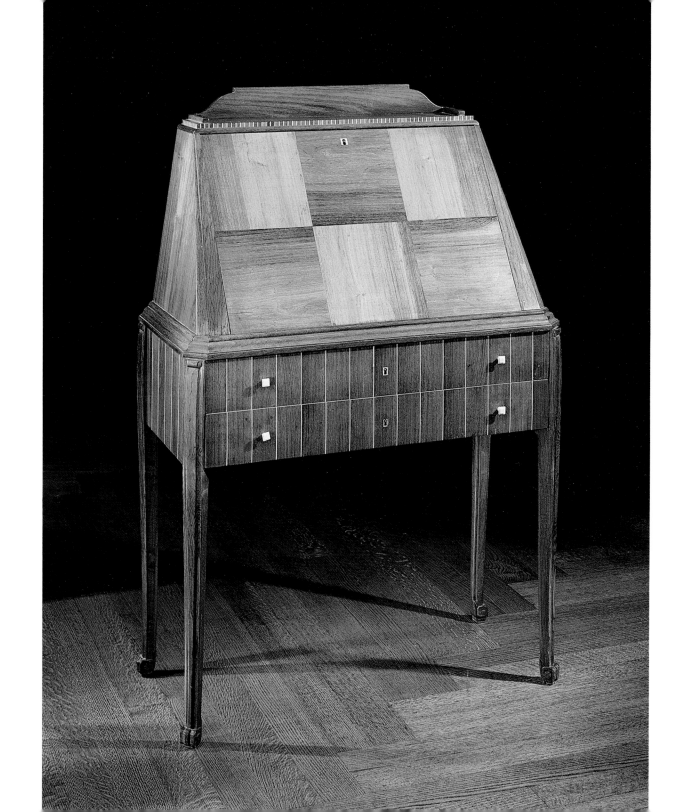

Rose Adler
French, 1892-1959
and
Marcel Vertes
French (born in Hungary), 1895-1962

68 Bookbinding and Illustrations for *Chéri* by Colette, 1925

Edition number 48/100, Editions de la Roseraie, Paris
Binding: Morocco leather, stamped and foiled
Illustrations: wood engravings
28 × 22.9 × 4.8 (11 × 9 × 1⅞)
Signed inside front cover at bottom: *Rose Adler 1931*
Virginia Museum of Fine Arts, Gift of Sydney and Frances Lewis,
85.37 a/b

The fine art of bookbinding reached a new peak in the 1920s. Following innovative concepts developed in the late nineteenth century, the artists of this period created elegant leather bindings that in many cases reflected or complemented the text within. In addition, the front and back covers took on equal importance, with a narrative scene often continuing from one to the other.

Chéri can be thought of as a collaboration between three very talented artists of the period: the text is by Colette; the engravings are by Marcel Vertes, and the binding is by Rose Adler.

Colette (1873-1954), born Sidonie Gabrielle Colette, was one of the most famous French writers of her day and was known for novels that reflected life in her own time. She wrote *Chéri* in 1920, later transforming it into a play in which she herself performed. Perhaps her most famous novel was *Gigi*, which she wrote in 1944, and which was later produced as a motion picture.

Marcel Vertes, who was born in Hungary, established himself as a graphic artist in Vienna, and came to Paris in 1925. His early work in Paris,

which reflected the seamy side of life, met with much criticism. In the late 1930s he moved to the United States, where he pursued a successful career as a painter.

Rose Adler studied bookbinding at the École d'Art Décoratif under Pierre Legrain from 1917 to 1925. She also studied with the bookbinder Noulhac. She first came to the attention of the art patron Jacques Doucet when she exhibited some of her student work in 1923. Legrain was working for Doucet at this time, and Adler became familiar with both Legrain's furniture and his bookbindings. She produced work for Doucet and, after his death in 1929, continued to work for the Jacques Doucet Literary Foundation.

PROVENANCE: Jeanne Dor; Sotheby Parke-Bernet Monaco S.A., 1977.

PUBLISHED: *Arts Décoratifs, Styles 1900 et 1925*,catalogue of sale (Monte Carlo: Sotheby Parke-Bernet Monaco S.A., October 8, 1977), lot 177, illus. p. 75. *Art at Auction, The Year at Sotheby Parke-Bernet*, 1977-1978 (London: Sotheby Parke-Bernet, 1978), p. 464. Philippe Garner, ed., *Encyclopedia of Decorative Art* (New York: Van Nostrand Reinhold, 1978), illus. p. 111.

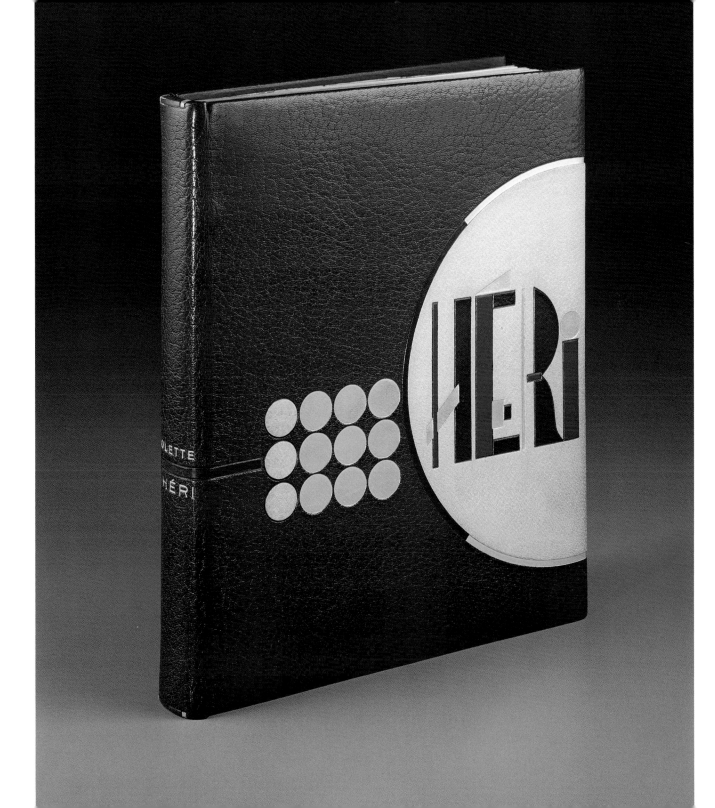

Emile-Jacques Ruhlmann
French, 1879-1933

69 Desk, ca. 1925-27

Macassar ebony, snakeskin, ivory, silvered bronze
72.4 × 134.6 × 72.4 (28½ × 53 × 28½)
Signed under proper right drawer section: *Ruhlmann*; *B* under
proper left drawer section
Virginia Museum of Fine Arts, Gift of Sydney and Frances Lewis,
85.136

In Ruhlmann's Paris workshops, a staff of craftsmen made working drawings from the many small sketches he produced for his furniture designs, and Ruhlmann himself personally supervised every phase of production.

Although it is not known for whom this particular desk was made, it is thought to be unique. Using his favorite material, Macassar ebony, Ruhlmann designed a tour de force of cabinetmaking. Silvered bronze mounts both accent and protect the delicate tapered legs with Ruhlmann's characteristic sabot or "shoe." Ivory is used for the side-drawer pulls, as well as for the small sliding tray that serves as a writing surface. Exotic snakeskin both contrasts and complements the bold grain of the ebony.

Indeed, the woodgrain on the top has been so expertly matched to the grain on the drawer-fronts that the entire desk seems to be carved from a single block of wood.

Unlike Ruhlmann's 1916 corner cabinet (see cat. no. 60), this desk is more distinctive for its straightforward shape than its decorative motifs. On the whole, it is more streamlined and anticipates Ruhlmann's later work, which approaches Modernism. Characteristically, the desk has many subtle convex surfaces that underscore its grace and elegance.

PROVENANCE: Alain Lesieutre, Paris, 1972.
PUBLISHED: Florence Camard, *Ruhlmann* (Paris: Editions du Regard, 1983), illus. p. 161.

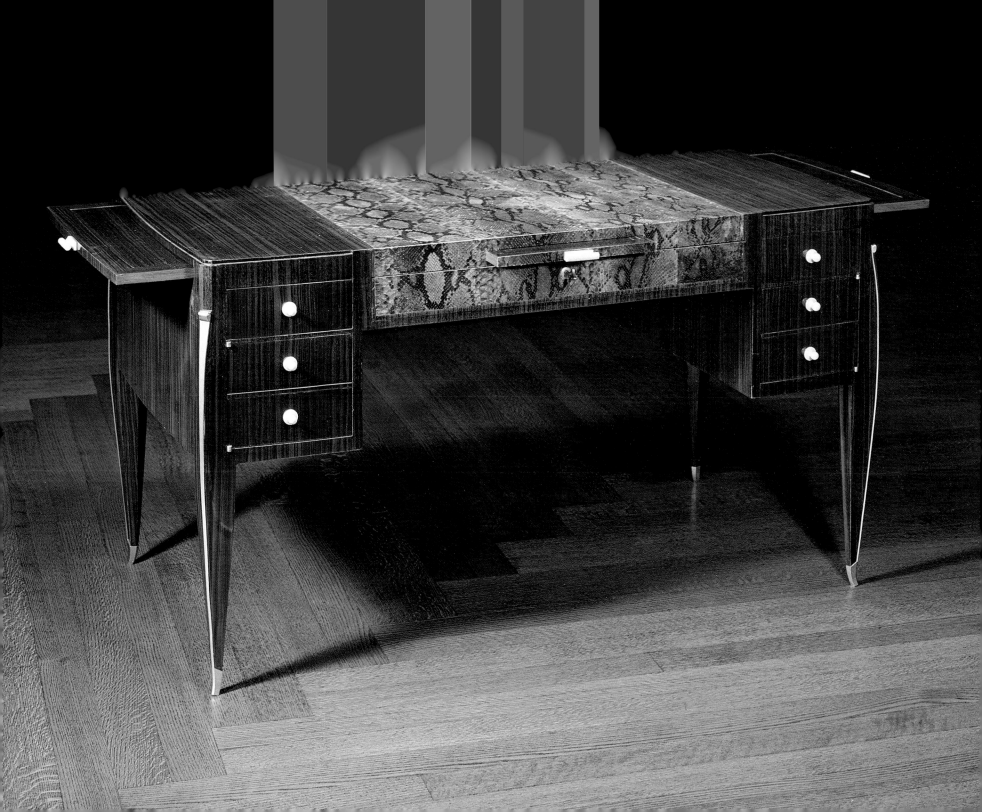

Clément Rousseau
French, 1872-?

 70 Pair of Chairs, ca. 1925

Rosewood, sharkskin, upholstery, mother-of-pearl
92.7 × 43.2 × 52.1 each (36½ × 17 × 20½)
Signed on inside front frame of seat supports: Clément Rousseau
Virginia Museum of Fine Arts, Gift of Sydney and Frances Lewis,
85.128/129

Clément Rousseau was an extraordinary designer of the Style 1925. Examples of his work, unfortunately, are quite rare. Rousseau was trained both as a sculptor and furniture designer, and he exhibited his work at the Salon des Artistes Françaises during the 1920s.

These chairs, both of similar design, differ in the treatment of the backs. The major decorative motifs are created through the use of shagreen (sharkskin), both dyed green and natural gray. A very durable and beautiful material, sharkskin was favored by Rousseau and other designers, including Jean-Michel Frank, Pierre Legrain, and André Groult. Because artists like Rousseau knew that shagreen has a particular imbrication or grain that usually radiates from a certain point, they would direct the design as one would work with wood grain. Rousseau accented shagreen with ivory in small fillets and other details. Stylized flower petals decorate the back of one chair, while petals and volutes are on the back of the other. Both have a sunray pattern, a favorite motif of Rousseau's, on the front and sides of the seat.

PROVENANCE: Alain Lesieutre, Paris, 1972.

PUBLISHED: "Salle de Ventes: Conseils aux Acheteurs," *Connaissance des Arts* (July, 1972), p. 82. Gérald Schurr, "Collecting," *Réalités* (October, 1972), pp. 8-10, illus. p. 8. Gérald Schurr, "Le Mobilier des 'Années 25': Petit lexique des principaux ornemanistes," *Gazette de l'Hôtel Drouot* (January 1973), p. 9. Alastair Duncan, *Art Deco Furniture* (New York: Holt, Rinehart and Winston, 1984), p. 104, illus. pl. 50.

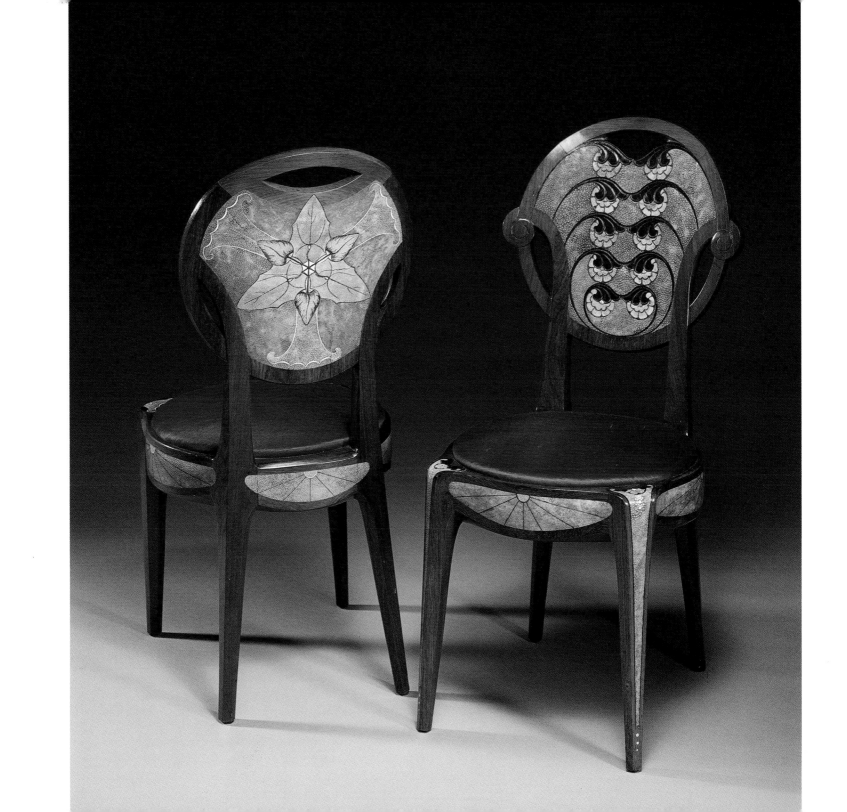

Clément Mère
French, 1870-?

71

Armchair, ca. 1925

Macassar ebony, repoussé leather, upholstery
72.4 × 63.5 × 55.9 (28½ × 25 × 22)
Signed on proper right side: C. Mère
Virginia Museum of Fine Arts, Gift of Sydney and Frances Lewis,
85.125

Clément Mère was one of several artists, including Lalique, who made a successful stylistic transition from Art Nouveau to Art Deco. By l900, after studying under the painter and sculptor Jean-Léon Gérôme and pursuing a profession as a landscape painter, Mère became associated with Julius Meier-Graefe's La Maison Moderne, which opened in 1898 on the Rue des Petits Champs in Paris. This shop served as a showcase for the modern ideas of talented designers, much as Bing's more successful Maison de l'Art Nouveau had begun to do three years earlier. Mère created many small decorative items, eventually turning to furniture in which, during the 1920s, he began to incorporate elements of Eastern exoticism.

Mère's style is apparent in this chair. The back and arms create a continuous line broken only by the ivory inlay and ending in long, slender, tapered legs. The back and side panels are tooled and dyed leather in a stylized floral motif. The rare carved wood—Macassar ebony—combined with the rich colors and textures of leather and ivory, defines Mère's stylistic preferences and sensibilities. In general, his style is somewhat reminiscent of the exoticism, opulence, and color of the Ballets Russes which, under the direction of Serge Diaghilev, had captivated Paris in 1909.

The form of the chair, however, also includes elements from earlier French prototypes. The overall floral pattern was a key motif in the decorative vocabulary of some of the Art Deco designers. Paul Iribe is said to have popularized the use of the flower as a decorative motif to the extent that it was frequently transformed into repetitive patterns, as Mère has done here. The stylized flower became a highly visible symbol of the Style 1925, just as the Glasgow rose, through its use by Mackintosh, had been adapted throughout Europe and the United States by artists of the Style 1900.

PROVENANCE: Alain Lesieutre, Paris, 1972.

PUBLISHED: "Salles de Ventes: Conseil aux Acheteurs," *Connaissance des Arts* 245 (July 1972), p. 82. Gérald Schurr, "Le Mobilier des 'Année 25 ,'" *Gazette de l'Hôtel Drouot* (January 1973), p. 8. Alain Lesieutre, *The Spirit and Splendor of* Art Deco (New York: Paddington Press, 1974), illus. no. 138. Pierre Kjellberg, *Art Déco: Les Maîtres du Mobilier* (Paris: Les Editions de l'Amateur, 1981), p. 126. Alastair Duncan, *Art Deco Furniture* (New York: Holt, Rinehart and Winston, 1984), illus. p. 139.

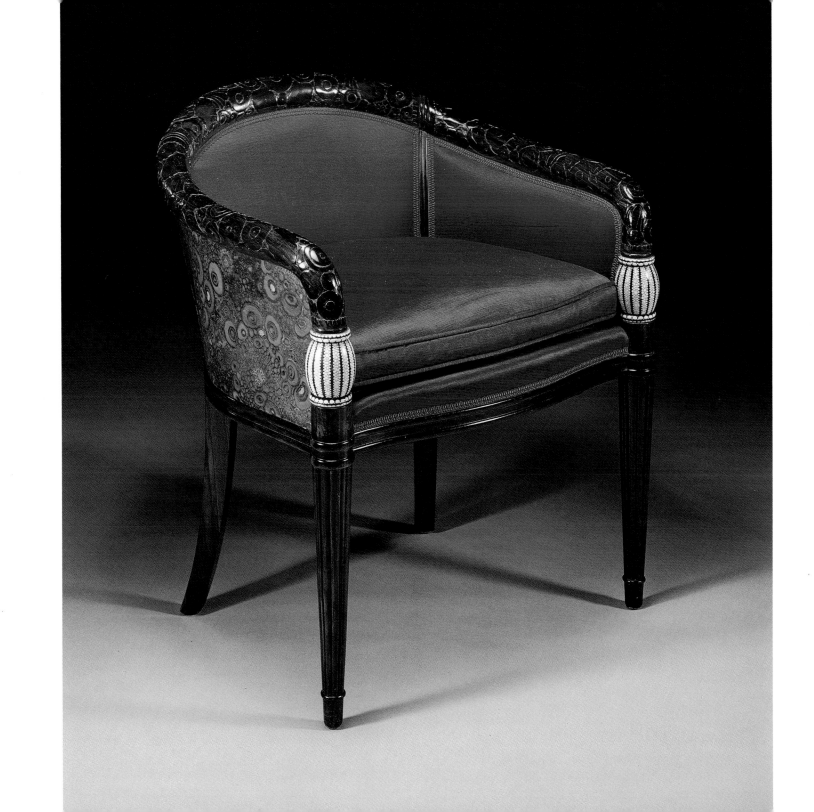

André Groult
French, 1884-1967

72

Chair, 1925

Sharkskin over wood, upholstery
80 × 49.5 × 52 (31½ × 19½ × 20½)
Unsigned
Virginia Museum of Fine Arts, Gift of Sydney and Frances Lewis,
85.116

The focal point of one of the main axes of the 1925 Paris Exposition was a U-shaped building representing a French embassy. The building's twenty-five rooms, arranged around the Cour des Métiers, were furnished with the work of noted designers of the Société des Artistes Décorateurs; the architecture was designed by Michel Roux-Spitz, Pierre Selmersheim, and Pierre-Louis Sezille.

This chair, designed by André Groult, was for the bedroom of the wife of the imaginary French ambassador. All the furnishings had softly rounded forms and were covered in sharkskin, while delicate paintings by Marie Laurençin complemented the décor.

Groult often used sharkskin to accent furniture. In the bed, chair, and cabinet of this room, however, it became the dominant feature, covering almost the entire surface of each piece. Groult's use of delicate color and convex, "feminine" forms makes his furniture aptly suited for its theoretical occupant.

In addition to his work on the French embassy, Groult also designed several other projects for the Exposition, including pavilions for Fontaine, Christofle et Baccarat, and the Art of the Garden.

PROVENANCE: Pierre Cornette de Saint-Cyr, Paris, 1981.

PUBLISHED: Art Nouveau/Art Deco, catalogue of sale (Paris: Pierre Cornette de Saint-Cyr, 1981), no. 142, illus. p. 142.

EXHIBITED: "Chamber for the wife of the Ambassador of France," Exposition Internationale des Arts Décoratifs et Industriels Modernes, Paris, 1925.

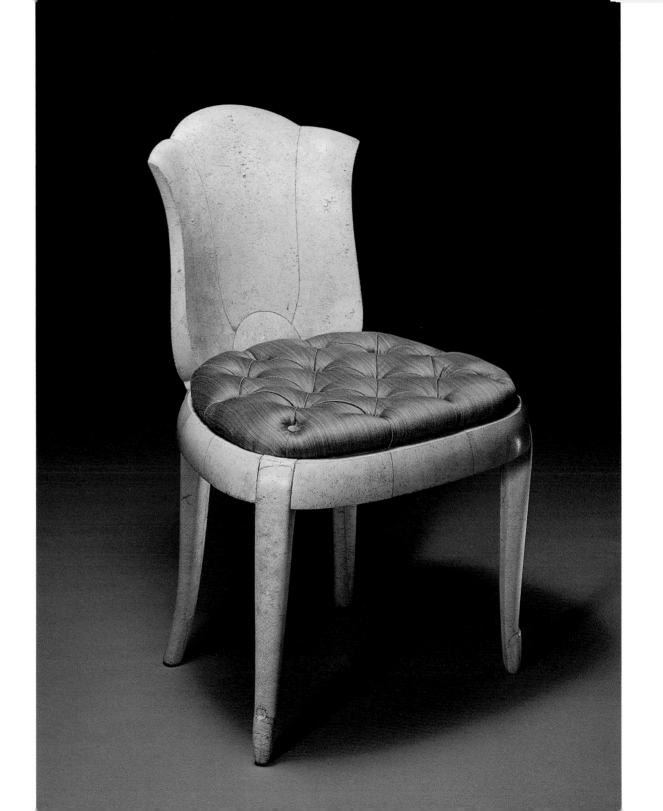

Jean Dunand
French, 1877-1942

73

Table, ca. 1925

Lacquered wood, eggshell
69.8 × 59.6 × 35.5 (27½ × 23½ × 14)
Signed under top: *Jean Dunand Lacquer*
Virginia Museum of Fine Arts, Gift of Sydney and Frances Lewis,
85.103

The ancient art of lacquer became very important to the master furniture designers of the 1920s, particularly in France. A group of Indo-Chinese lacquer specialists had been brought to France during World War I to lacquer and preserve the wooden propellers of the French Air Force. At the end of the war, many of these lacquerers remained in France and found work in cabinetry shops, where their craftsmanship was highly valued.

Natural lacquer is prepared from the sap of certain trees, the *rhus succedanea* and *rhus vernicifera*. Various colors are obtained by adding different pigments, minerals, metal foils or powders, mother-of-pearl, or crushed eggshell (*coquille d'oeuf*), the latter a technique revived by Jean Dunand.

Lacquering is a very slow, tedious, and precise technique. The artisan must apply successive coats of lacquer with a brush, allowing each coat to dry very slowly in a humid room for up to three weeks. In addition, each coat must be carefully polished with pumice before the next is applied. Once the final coat is polished, the piece must be set out to dry in the sunlight for a certain period of time.[48]

In 1912 the Japanese lacquer-master Sugawara shared the secrets of his profession with Dunand. Beginning in 1921, when Dunand first exhibited his own lacquer work, he used the technique for a wide range of furniture and miscellaneous objects, not only those of his own design but also on pieces designed by Legrain, Ruhlmann, Schmied, and others.

Born in Switzerland, Dunand studied at the School of Industrial Arts in Geneva, and moved to Paris by 1897. Until he learned the art of lacquer, his major work comprised hammered metal vases and other pieces. As with lacquer, working with metal is a very demanding technique that involves complex and precise manipulation of the material.

After World War I, with the availability of Indo-Chinese laborers, Dunand worked in lacquer, eventually creating a workshop that employed hundreds of craftsmen. By 1925, his work had become so well recognized that he was asked to design the smoking-room for the French embassy at the Paris Exposition. Later in his long and active career, Dunand was awarded commissions for some parts of the interiors of two transatlantic steamships: the *Atlantique* (1931) and the ill-fated *Normandie* (1935).

This table, an excellent example of Dunand's lacquerware, draws its strength from its delicate form combined with the bold geometric design of the red squares and the random pattern of the crushed eggshell.

PROVENANCE: Michel Perinet, Paris, 1973.

---

48. Yvonne Brunhammer, *Jean Dunand/Jean Goulden* (Paris: Galerie du Luxembourg, 1973), p. 40.

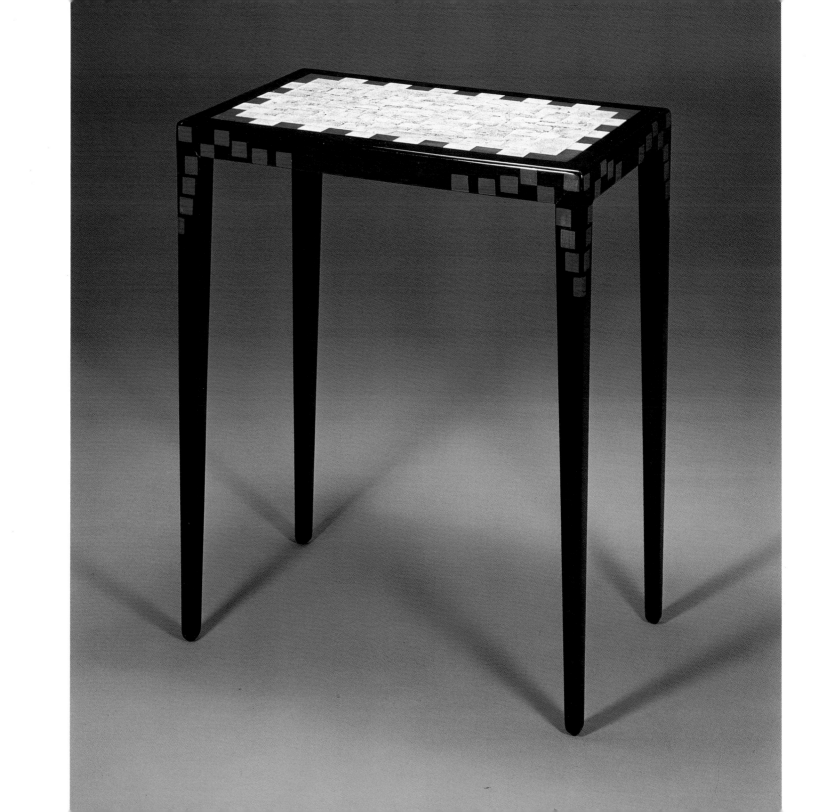

Camille Fauré
French, 1872-1956

74

Vase, ca. 1925

Enamel on copper
12.7 × 12 diameter (5 × 4¾)
Signed on side: C. *Fauré/Limoges*
Virginia Museum of Fine Arts, Gift of Sydney and Frances Lewis,
85.60

By the 1920s, the art of enameling had undergone a long and gradual development. Although used somewhat sporadically since ancient times, it did not reach full importance until the early Middle Ages, particularly in Byzantium. Gradually, new techniques were developed for ornamenting religious objects, and by the twelfth century Limoges, France, had become an important enameling center. A major revival occurred in the mid nineteenth century and continued in the Fabergé workshops of St. Petersburg, Russia; but in the twentieth century enameling reached a new peak, primarily through the work of Camille Fauré.

For more than fifty years, Fauré practiced his art in Limoges, creating a multitude of vases, jars, and other forms in enamel. His elaborate abstract and representational designs were done in the Style 1925.

For this bulbous vase, Fauré used a stylized floral motif. The traditional glossy surface of the leaves, stems, and background contrasts with a crystalline-textured enamel to define the petals and to highlight the thick cylindrical neck. Additional droplets of clear enamel resemble jewels set into the surface.

The basic technique of enameling consists of mixing pulverized glass with various chemical pigments. The enamel powder is then mixed with a temporary liquid adhesive and applied to a metal base, usually copper. Finally, while it is baked in an enameling kiln at temperatures ranging from 1300° to 1600°F, the enamel powder melts and fuses to the surface of the metal.

PROVENANCE: Sotheby's Belgravia, London, 1972.

PUBLISHED: *Decorative Arts 1880-1939 including Arts and Crafts, Art Nouveau, and Art Deco*, catalogue of sale (London: Sotheby's Belgravia, March 8, 1972), no. 6, p. 5.

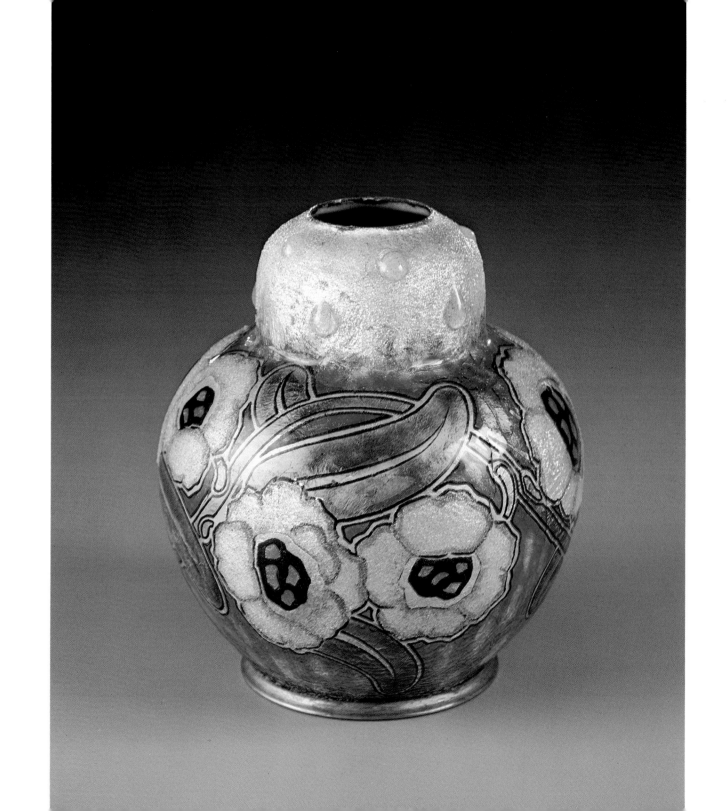

Pierre Chareau
French, 1883-1950

75 Club Armchair, ca. 1925

Rosewood, metal, upholstery
60 × 70 × 80 (23⅝ × 27⁹⁄₁₆ × 31½)
Unsigned
Virginia Museum of Fine Arts, Gift of Sydney and Frances Lewis,
85.95

Although trained as an architect, Pierre Chareau is better known for his furniture designs. His masterpiece is the Maison de Verre, on the Rue St.-Guillaume in Paris. Chareau worked with the Dutch architect Bernard Bijvoet on the project for Dr. and Mme Jean Dalsace between 1928 and 1932.

When Chareau had first exhibited his work at the Salon d'Automne in 1919, his relatively plain furniture was not fully appreciated by all of the critics. In 1923, he exhibited at the Salon des Artistes Décorateurs, and later, for the 1925 Paris Exposition, he was one of only a few French architect-designers who were invited to participate in the conception of the French embassy. Chareau, in collaboration with Jean Lurçat and Hélène Henry, designed the embassy library, which featured books bound by Pierre Legrain.

A distinctive feature of Chareau's furniture is the concern for form as it relates to architecture. Completely ignoring the traditional French design formula—tall legs, rounded backs, and applied decoration—this club armchair shows a mastery of form that could only have come from one trained in architecture. Because of its low center of gravity, the chair seems to hug the floor and becomes part of any architectural scheme in which it is placed. Like some of Chareau's earlier furniture, the chair shows the designer's interest in the angular planes of Cubism and his disregard for decoration of any sort.

PROVENANCE: Galerie Félix Marcilhac, Paris, 1976.

PUBLISHED: René Herbst, L'Architecte Pierre Chareau (Paris: Union des Artistes Modernes, 1954), pp. 74, 78. Philippe Jullian, "The Collectors: Félix Marcilhac in Paris," Architectural Digest (July/August 1977), illus. p. 59. Pierre Kjellberg, Art Deco: Les Maîtres du Mobilier (Paris: Les Editions de l'Amateur, ca. 1981), p. 43.

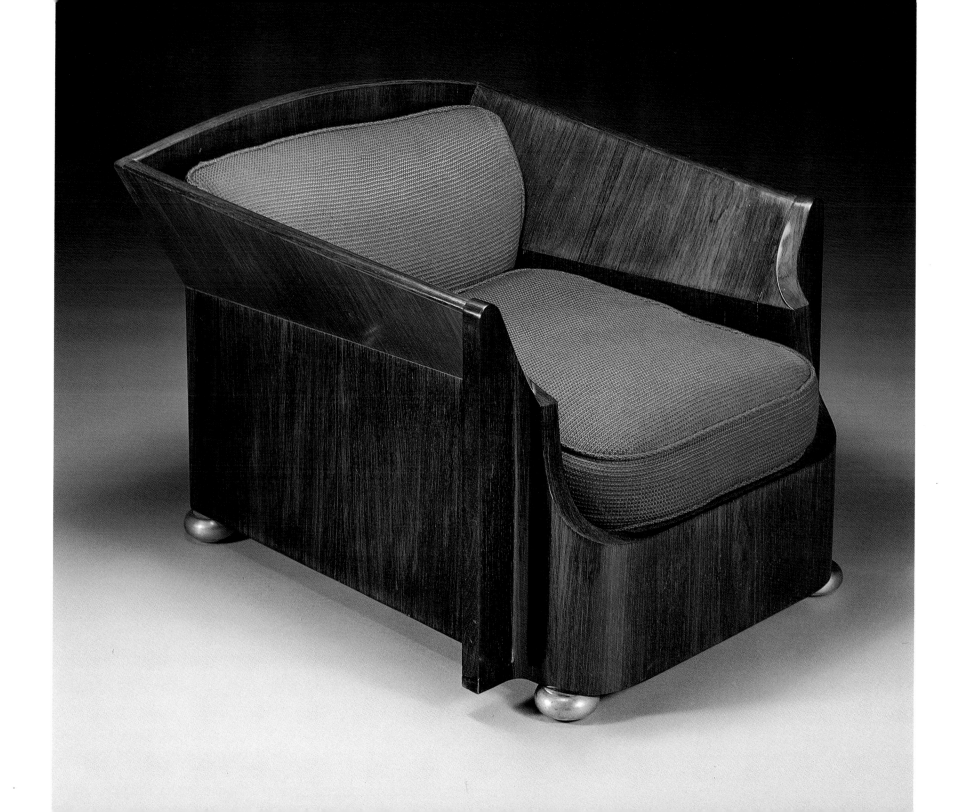

Raymond Templier
French, 1891-1968

76 Bracelet with Brooch, ca. 1925-30

Silver, platinum, gold, onyx, diamonds
5.3 × 5.8 × 6.4 (2⅛ × 2¼ × 2½)
Signed under brooch on outside of bracelet: *Raymond Templier*; on
edge of bracelet: *30141*; on reverse of brooch: hallmarks and
30141
Virginia Museum of Fine Arts, Gift of the Sydney and Frances
Lewis Foundation, 85.257 a/b

Raymond Templier was the son of Paul Templier, whose father Charles had founded the family jewelry firm in Paris in 1849. In 1912 Raymond entered the firm, and he later opened his own company under the name of Paul and Raymond Templier. He was a co-founder of the Union des Artistes Modernes in 1930, and served as the vice-president of the Salon d'Automne. Throughout his long career, Templier created many extraordinary jewelry designs based on geometric shapes, employing a combination of both precious metals and stones, as well as other rare materials.

This bracelet is a perfect example of Templier's pioneering use of abstract patterns and geometric shapes. The central brooch, of platinum and white gold, can be removed from the wide silver band, or both pieces can be worn together as an ornate bracelet.

PROVENANCE: Christie's International S.A., Geneva, 1984.

PUBLISHED: Alain Lesieutre, *The Spirit and Splendour of Art Déco* (New York: Paddington Press, 1974), illus. pp. 278, 297. Philippe Garner, ed., *Encyclopedia of Decorative Arts* (New York: Van Nostrand Reinhold, 1979), illus. p. 104. *Magnificent Jewels*, catalogue of sale (Geneva: Christie's International S.A., May 17, 1984), no. 442, illus. p. 129.

EXHIBITED: *Sieraad 1900-1972/Eerste Triennale*, cat. no 156, Museum Flehite, Amersfort, The Netherlands, 1972.

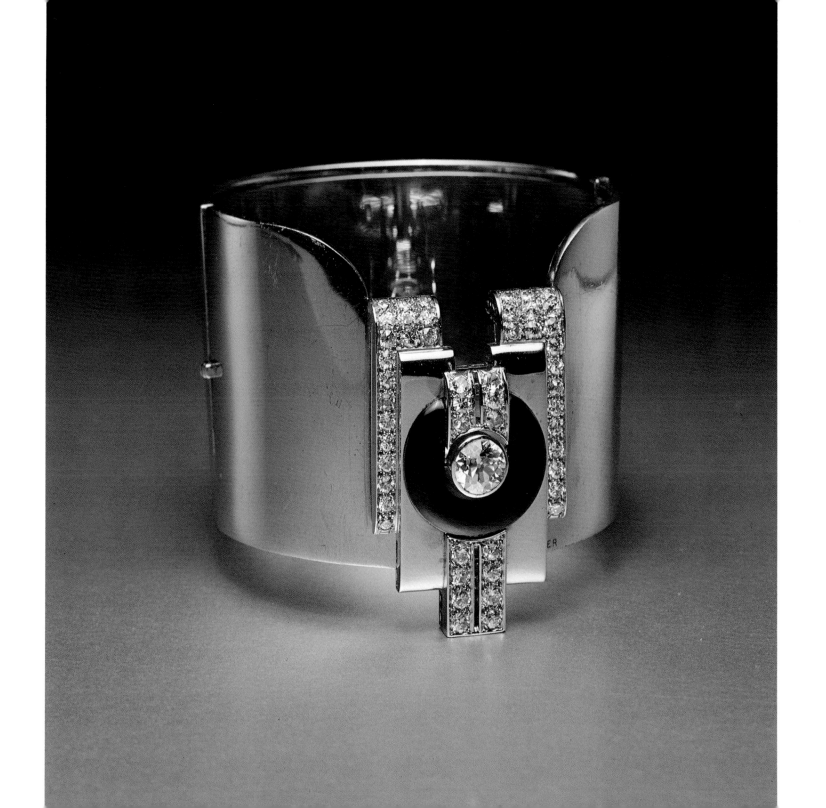

Alexander Kelety
Hungarian, dates unknown

77 *Affection*, ca. 1925-30

Silvered and cold-painted bronze, ivory, marble
34.9 × 18.4 × 12.7 (13¾ × 7¼ × 5)
Signed on top of base: *Kelety*
Virginia Museum of Fine Arts, Gift of Sydney and Frances Lewis,
85.328

Kelety was a Hungarian sculptor who studied and exhibited his work in France. While not as prolific as many of his contemporaries, Kelety is known for the exquisite detail, grace, and craftsmanship of his figures.

Like his colleagues, Kelety worked in ivory and cold-painted bronze. In keeping with the current vogue, Kelety produced figurines that reflected the tastes and interests of his time. Though in many cases these figures are depicted in contemporary costume, they represent timeless allegories of virtue and strength.

One of the main reasons for the frequent use of ivory in small sculptures during this period was that Belgian merchants, eager to export it from the Congo, made it available to European artists and craftsmen in great quantities at a relatively low price. Many chryselephantine pieces (those made in ivory and metal, traditionally gold) were produced in Austria and Germany, where they were exported to fashionable shops throughout Europe and abroad. Depending on the complexity of the figure and the type and amount of metal used, the works varied greatly in cost. Because of their widespread production, the quality of such pieces varies greatly, often even within one sculptor's oeuvre.

PROVENANCE: John Jesse, London, 1976.

PUBLISHED: Similar piece in Bryan Catley, *Art Déco and Other Figures* (Woodbridge, Suffolk, England: Antique Collectors' Club, 1978), p. 185.

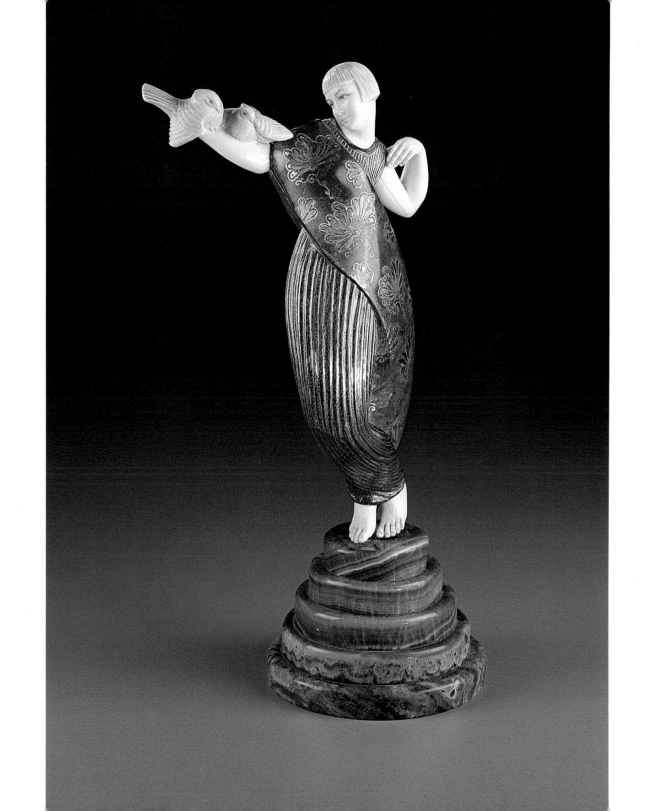

Demêtre Chiparus
Romanian, dates unknown

78 *Dancer*, ca. 1925-30

Ivory, cold-painted bronze, onyx
56.3 × 31.9 × 9.2 (22³⁄₁₆ × 12⅝ × 3⅝)
Signed on top of base: *Chiparus*
Virginia Museum of Fine Arts, Gift of Sydney and Frances Lewis, 85.336

In addition to the German sculptor Johann Ferdinand Preiss (see cat. no. 97), the best-known sculptor of chryselephantine figures is Demêtre Chiparus, a Romanian-born artist who lived and worked in Paris.

Chiparus's work reflects the influence of the exotic Ballets Russes on Western European consciousness and aesthetics in general, and on the development of the Style 1925 in design. His figures, usually larger than those of Preiss, often represent costumed dancers. They are of cast bronze that has been painted; the hands and faces are carved ivory. Chiparus also produced small figurines of children, and nudes made entirely of carved ivory.

The Etling Foundry in Paris cast Chiparus's early statuettes, while the LN & JL Foundry made his later works. As with the work of his contemporaries, many of the Chiparus's sculptures are mounted on elaborate plinths and bases of onyx or marble. Often, but not always, the bases are inscribed with the signature of the artist.

PROVENANCE: O.K. Harris, New York, 1971.

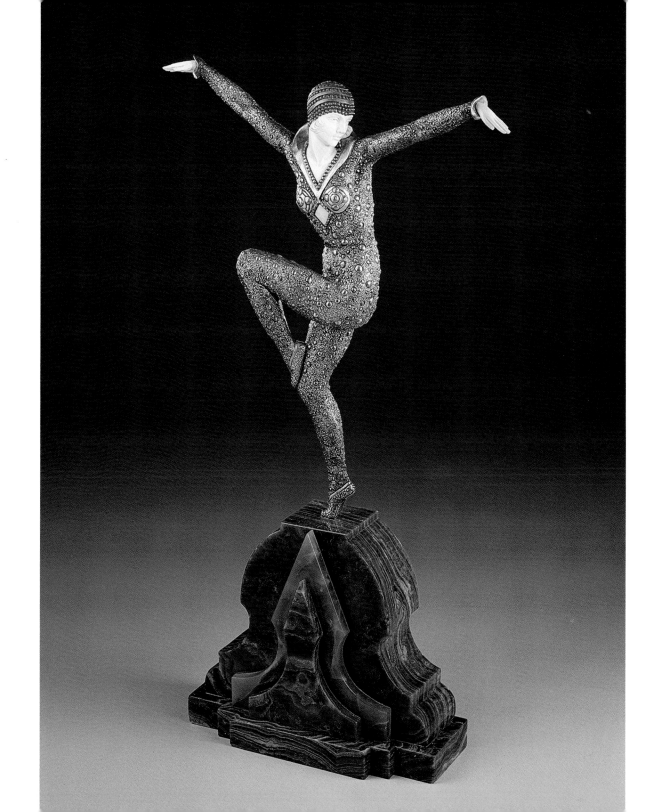

Félix Del Marle
French, 1889-1952

 79 Suite for Madame B., 1926

Painted wood, frosted glass, painted metal, upholstery,
metallic paint
Sofa: 75 × 168 × 70 (29½ × 66⅛ × 27⁹/₁₆)
Bar/Coffee Table: 56 × 67 × 41 (22¹/₁₆ × 26⅜ × 16⅛)
Armchair: 62.9 × 83.8 × 76.5 (24¾ × 33 × 30⅛)
Armchair: 62.9 × 83.5 × 76.4 (24¾ × 32⅞ × 30¹/₁₆)
Armchair: 62.9 × 83.8 × 76.8 (24¾ × 33 × 30¼)
Chandeliers (2), each: 55 × 67 × 52 (22¹/₁₆ × 26⅜ × 20½)
Lamp: 165 × 45 × 25 (64¹⁵/₁₆ × 17¾ × 9⅞)
Unsigned
Virginia Museum of Fine Arts, Gift of Sydney and Frances Lewis,
85.101.1/8

In 1909 the poet Emilio F. T. Marinetti published his *First Futurist Manifesto* in the Parisian newspaper *Le Figaro*. He subsequently became associated with a group of Italian painters, poets, sculptors, and architects who glorified war, conflict, and change, as well as various aspects of modern life. The Futurists rebelled against the glorification of Italy's past and spoke out against the Italians' complaisance toward life in general. In July 1913, the French painter Félix Del Marle published his *Manifeste Futuriste de Montmartre*, in which he railed against the Bohemianism of his fellow Parisians. Enthusiastically welcomed by Marinetti and the Futurists, Del Marle became the first non-Italian among them.

By the time of his *Manifeste Futuriste*, Del Marle's painting style had taken on strong overtones of Cubism. Having shared a studio with the Futurist painter Gino Severini, Del Marle was familiar with the style and theories of the group. But it was Del Marle's experiences in World War I that turned him against the brutality of Futurism and caused him to seek other styles and philosophies.

After the war, Del Marle met several members of the Dutch De Stijl movement (see cat. no. 62), and eventually adopted the forms, if not all the theories, of De Stijl. Working with these newer ideals of form, Del Marle was commissioned to design a suite of furniture in 1926 for a Mme B. in Dresden (see fig. 15), including a wall tapestry, a carpet, two chandeliers, a sofa, three chairs, a bar/table, and a floor lamp. Each piece was composed of rectangles and squares in black, white, and tones of gray, with accents in the primary colors—blue, red, and yellow. De Stijl painter Piet Mondrian responded enthusiastically to Del Marle's furniture: "I am very happy to tell you how much I like your work." he wrote. "I've found it to be the best application of Neo-Plasticism."[49]

PROVENANCE: Mme B. of Dresden, 1926; Robert Walker, Paris; Enghien Hôtel des Ventes, Enghien-les-Bains, France 1982.

PUBLISHED: Valentin Bresle, *Del Marle peintre* (Paris: Lillie, 1933), p. 85. Andréi Nakov, *Félix Del Marle* exhibition catalogue (Paris: Galerie Jean Chauvelin, 1973), illus. pp. 15, 17. *Art 1900-1925*, catalogue of sale (Enghien-les-Bains, France: Enghien Hôtel des Ventes, March 21, 1982), no. 153, illus. p. 43.

EXHIBITED: *Félix Del Marle*, Galerie Jean Chauvelin, Paris, June 6-July 15, 1973.

---

49. As quoted in Andréi B. Nakov, *Félix Del Marle* (Paris: Galerie Jean Chauvelin, 1973), p. 16.

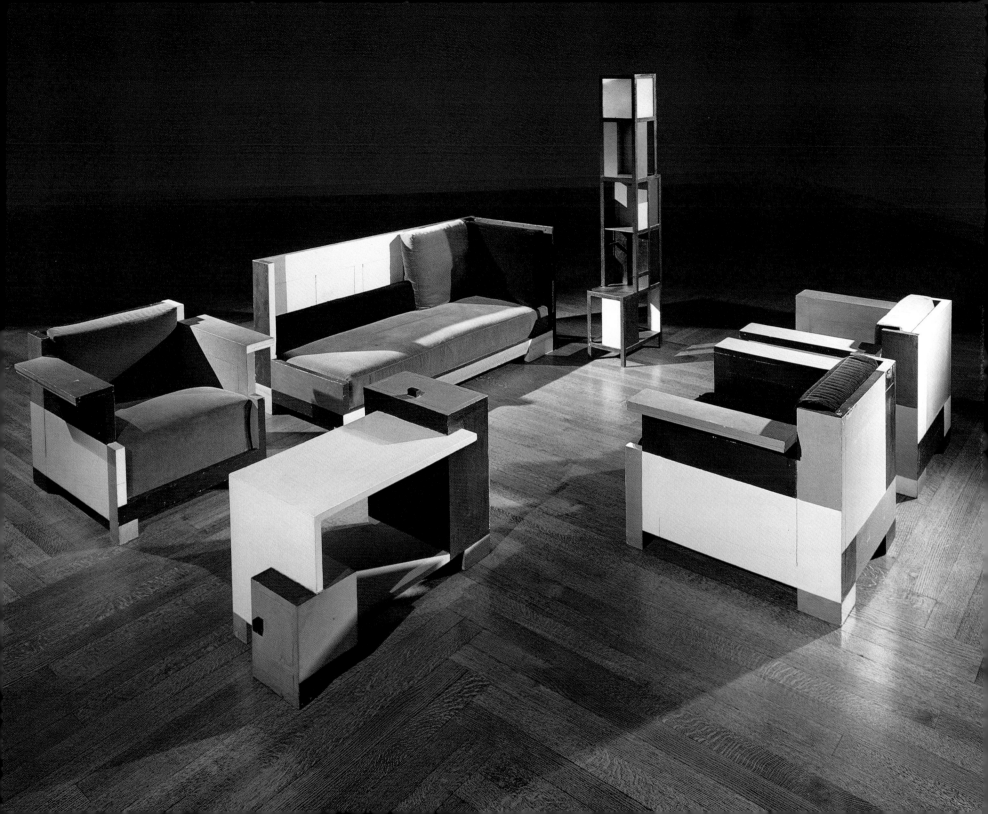

Louis Marcoussis
French, 1883-1941

 80 Carpet, ca. 1926
Wool
252 × 140 (99 × 55)
Unsigned
Virginia Museum of Fine Arts, Gift of Sydney and Frances Lewis,
85.343

This carpet by Louis Marcoussis was featured in a stairwell on the ground floor of Jacques Doucet's studio at Neuilly. The bannister of the stairwell was by the Hungarian sculptor Joseph Csáky, and both the entrance and the landing contained important furniture and sculptures, including one of the latter by Constantin Brancusi.[50]

Marcoussis, who was born in Poland as Lodwicz Markous, studied at the Cracow Academy and the Académie Julian, Paris, before he met the French poet Guillaume Apollinaire in 1910. Through him, Marcoussis also met Georges Braque and Pablo Picasso, and became familiar with the work of the Cubists. In 1929, he was among those invited by a Mme Cuttoli to submit carpet designs to the Aubusson Workshops. As a patron and friend of avant-garde artists, she was seeking ways to bring new creativity and vitality to the looms of Aubusson.

A superb draftsman, Marcoussis was also known as an illustrator and printmaker. He touched on the style and content of the Surrealists in the late 1920s, but his work is generally considered a variation of Cubism.

Although the flat, geometric shapes that dominate the design of this carpet could be construed as related to the Cubist's planes, the design seems better understood as a precursor of American Abstract Expressionism.

PROVENANCE: Jacques Doucet, Neuilly; Hôtel Drouot, Paris, 1972; Sotheby Parke-Bernet Monaco S.A., 1982.

PUBLISHED: Jean Gallotti, "Les Salons d'une Maison de Couture," Art et Décoration 51 (January-June 1927), p. 96. André Joubin, "Le Studio de Jacques Doucet," L'Illustration (May 3, 1930), illus. p. 17. Ancienne Collection Jacques Doucet (Paris: Hôtel Drouot, November 8, 1972), lot 53. Deco: 1925-1935, exhibition catalogue (Canada: Rothmans of Pall Mall Canada Limited, 1975), no. 236. Yvonne Brunhammer, Le Style 1925 (Paris: Baschet et Cie, no date), p. 76. Yvonne Brunhammer, Cinquantenaire de l'Exposition de 1925 (Paris: Musée des Arts Décoratifs, 1976), no. 665, p. 92. Arts Décoratifs Styles 1900 et 1925, catalogue of sale (Monte Carlo: Sotheby Parke-Bernet Monaco S.A., October 24-25, 1982), no. 348, cover illus. and illus. p. 112.

50. For an illustration of this stairwell and photographs of other areas of Doucet's apartment, see André Joubin "La Studio de Jacques Doucet," in L'Illustration (May 3, 1930): 17-20.

Rose Adler
French, 1892-1959

81 Table, ca. 1926

Ebony, sharkskin, metal, enamel
75.5 × 70.5 × 39.7 (29¾ × 27¾ × 15⅝)
Unsigned
Virginia Museum of Fine Arts, Gift of Sydney and Frances Lewis,
85.93

Rose Adler worked frequently for the great couturier and art patron Jacques Doucet in both furniture design and bookbinding, a craft for which she is best known today (see cat. no. 68).

Her furniture designs, though rare, show an exceptionally sensitive use of exotic materials and geometric designs. To decorate the top of this table, Adler used sharkskin set into a stylized cityscape of stairs, arches, and street lights in forced perspective. The black of the ebony is accented by silvered metal and enamel on the drawer pull and on the sabots of the legs.

The table, with Gustave Miklos's rock crystal sculpture (cat. no. 82), appears prominently in a photograph of Doucet's apartment. It stands in front of a lacquer-and-silver window blind by Hecht, and next to it is a chair by Pierre Legrain. Above this furniture group hang paintings by several prominent artists of the period, including Marie Laurençin and Pablo Picasso.

PROVENANCE: Jacques Doucet, Neuilly; Hôtel Drouot, Paris, 1972; Michel Perinet, Paris, 1976.

PUBLISHED: André Joubin, "Le Studio de Jacques Doucet," L'*Illustration* (May 3, 1930), illus. p.30. *Ancienne Collection Jacques Doucet*, catalogue of sale (Paris: Hôtel Drouot, November 8, 1972), lot 37, illus. Yvonne Brunhammer, Le *Style 1925* (Paris: Baschet et Cie, no date), illus. p. 92. Philippe Garner, *Twentieth Century Furniture* (New York: Van Nostrand Reinhold, 1980), illus. p. 87.

EXHIBITED: *Fastes et décors de la vie, 1909-1929*, Musée Galliera, Paris, June-August 1957, cat. no. 1.

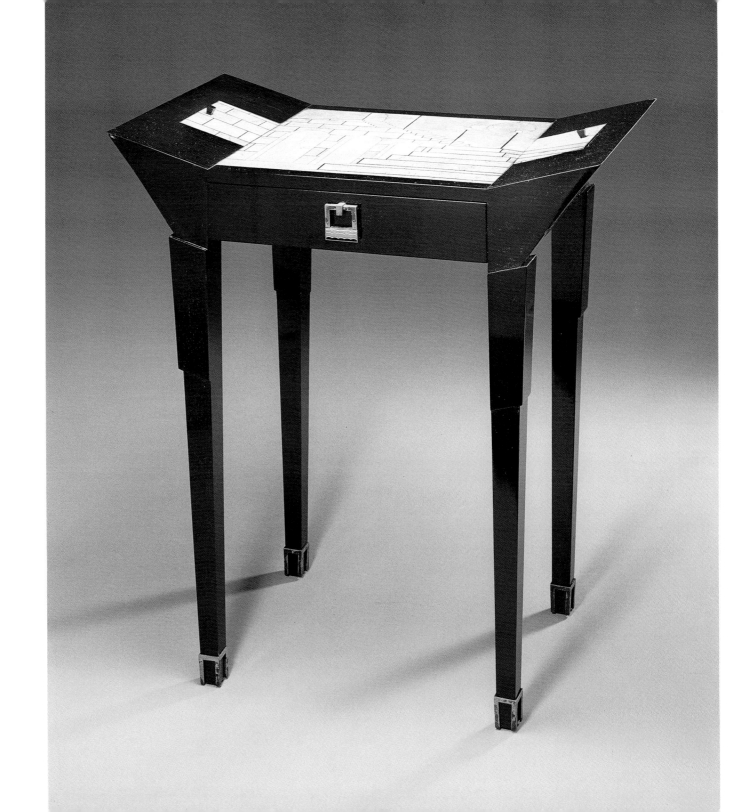

Gustave Miklos
Hungarian, 1888-1967

 82 Sculpture, ca. 1926

Rock crystal, silver, silver gilt, enamel
33.7 × 25.4 × 10.1 (13¼ × 10 × 4)
Unsigned
Virginia Museum of Fine Arts, Gift of Sydney and Frances Lewis,
85.329

Gustave Miklos was born in 1888 in Budapest, where he studied at the Ecole Royale des Arts Décoratifs. In 1909 he left for Paris, where he exhibited at the Salon d'Automne. The early work he showed there reflected definite traces of Cubism, possibly influenced by his friendship with the Cubist sculptor Joseph Csáky. In 1913 and 1914, Miklos exhibited at the Salon des Indépendants. When World War I began, he joined the French Foreign Legion and was sent to North Africa. It was there that he discovered the art of Byzantium, which was to have a profound influence on his later work. In fact, his work was sometimes even referred to as "modern Byzantine."

Upon his return to Paris in 1919, Miklos met the art patron Jacques Doucet, for whom he executed various works, including this extraordinary piece. Doucet commissioned Miklos to create a sculpture of rock crystal, silver, and enamel, to be placed on a table made for him by Rose Adler (see cat no. 81). In this example, as in much of Miklos's work, the early influence of Cubism is apparent. Although this sculpture is totally abstract, many of his other major works are recognizable depictions of animals and/or people, the most familiar of which are his tall, elongated figures.

PROVENANCE: Jacques Doucet, Neuilly; Galerie Félix Marcilhac, Paris, 1976.

PUBLISHED: André Joubin, "Le Studio de Jacques Doucet," L'Illustration (May 3, 1930), illus. p. 20. Yvonne Brunhammer, Cinquantenaire de l' Exposition de 1925 (Paris: Musée des Arts Décoratifs, 1976), no. 698. Philippe Garner, Twentieth Century Furniture (New York: Van Nostrand Reinhold, 1980), illus. p. 87.

EXHIBITED: Art Déco Année 25, Musée des Arts Décoratifs, Paris, 1976. Cinquantenaire de l'Exposition de 1925, Musée des Arts Décoratifs, Paris, October 1976-February 1977.

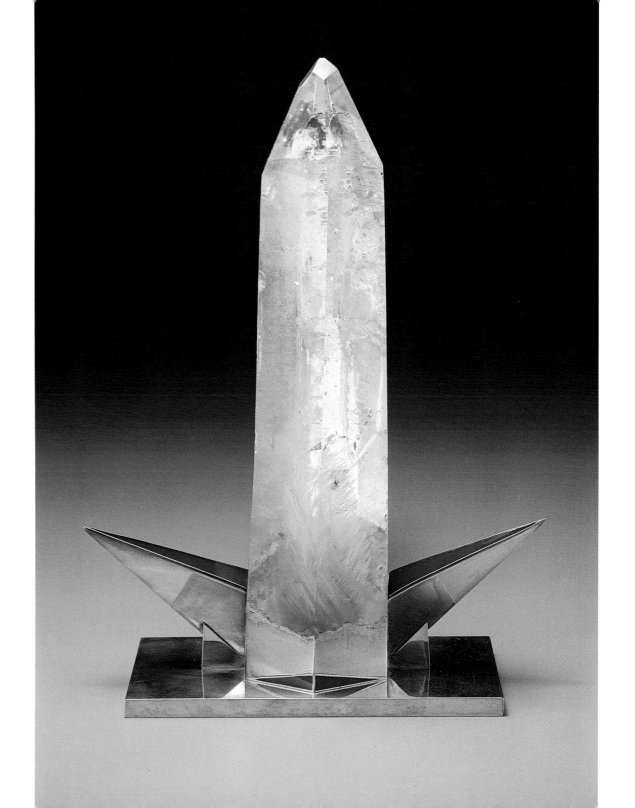

Louis Süe
French, 1875-1968
and
André Mare
French, 1885-1932

 Cabinet, 1927

Ebony, mother-of-pearl, silver
156.6 × 89.8 × 40 (61⅞ × 35⅜ × 15¾)
Paper label on back: *Chenue Emballeur, 5 Rue de la Terrasse Paris*
Virginia Museum of Fine Arts, Gift of the Sydney and Frances
Lewis Foundation, 85.137

In 1927, Louis Süe designed a villa at 2 Rue Buzenval in Saint-Cloud for the French actress Jane Renouardt (see Ruhlmann bed, cat. no. 95). In addition, the architectural firm of Süe et Mare decorated and furnished the villa, employing a large team of designers and decorators. This cabinet was made for that house.

Süe had first opened a studio called L'Atelier Français in Paris in 1912, but his work was interrupted by World War I. In 1919, together with the painter-decorator André Mare, Süe formed the Compagnie des Arts Français, more commonly referred to now as Süe et Mare. The company, which lasted until 1928, became one of the largest interior decorating firms in France, second only to that of Ruhlmann.

The two artists gained considerable fame in their time and produced some extraordinary interiors through judicious teamwork with other talented artists and designers. Their furniture is based on earlier traditional French furniture styles, particularly those from the reigns of Louis XIV, Louis XV, and Louis-Philippe.

In 1925 Süe et Mare received a commission to produce two buildings for the Paris Exposition: a Museum of Contemporary Art and a pavilion for the Maison Fontaine, a firm specializing in decorative ironwork. After the partnership was dissolved in 1928, André Mare devoted his time to painting, while Louis Süe continued working as an architect, decorator, and teacher.

PROVENANCE: Jane Renouardt, Saint-Cloud, France, 1927; Hôtel Drouot, Paris, May 5, 1972; Sotheby Parke-Bernet Monaco S.A., March 11, 1984.

PUBLISHED: *Objets d'Art et Meubles 'Art Déco'*, catalogue of sale (Paris: Hôtel Drouot, May 5, 1972), no. 160, cover illus. "Salles de Ventes: Conseils aux acheteurs," *Connaissance des Arts* (July 1972), illus. p. 82. Yvonne Brunhammer, *Cinquantenaire de l'Exposition de 1925* (Paris: Musée des Arts Décoratifs, 1976), no. 825. Raymond Foulk, *The Extraordinary Work of Süe et Mare*, exhibition catalogue (London: Foulk Lewis Collection, 1979), pp. 47, 49. Victor Arwas, *Art Déco* (New York: Harry N. Abrams, Inc., 1980), p. 53. Philippe Garner, *Twentieth Century Furniture* (New York: Van Nostrand Reinhold, 1980), illus. p. 76. *Arts Décoratifs Styles 1900 et 1925*, catalogue of sale (Monte Carlo: Sotheby Parke-Bernet Monaco S.A., March 11, 1984), no. 212, illus. pp. 58-59.

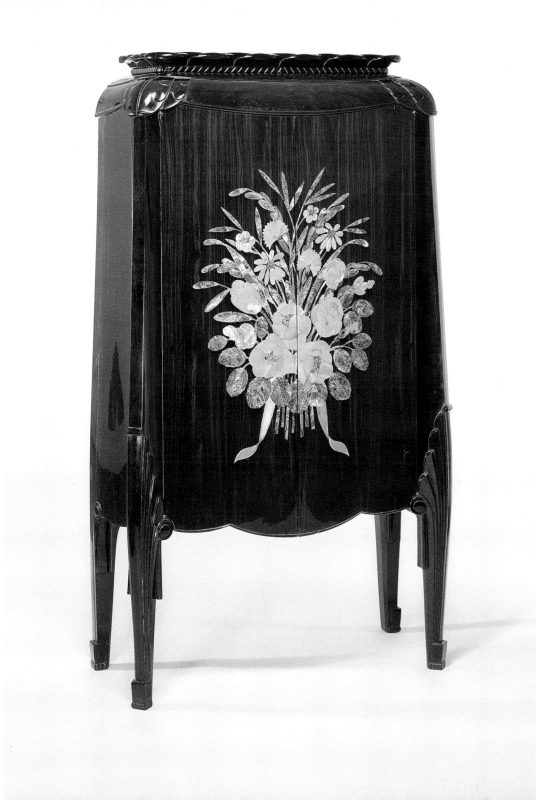

Jean-Michel Frank
French, 1895-1941

 84 Pair of Armchairs, ca. 1927

Sharkskin over wood, upholstery
67.3 × 68.9 × 73.6 each (26½ × 26¾ × 29)
Unsigned

Table, ca. 1927

Sharkskin over wood
50.8 × 60.3 diameter (20 × 23¾)
Unsigned

Virginia Museum of Fine Arts, Gift of Sydney and Frances Lewis,
85.106.1/2; 85.107

Born in 1895, Jean-Michel Frank was a successful designer and decorator who maintained a shop on the Faubourg Saint-Honoré in Paris. His clients included many European and American notables, including Mr. and Mrs. Nelson Rockefeller, Templeton Crocker of San Francisco, and the fashion designer Elsa Schiaparelli.

Frank's work, which seems to belong more to 1930s Modernism than to Style 1925, is characterized by simple elegance detailed with exquisite design and texture: color is played down, natural materials emphasized. In addition, he subordinated the importance of individual pieces of furniture to the design of the entire room.

In these chairs, Frank emphasized the graceful curve of the back, which flows forward and down to form the front legs. The frame is covered in shagreen (sharkskin), used here in its natural color. Its irregular pattern appealed to Frank and other designers of the period and, of course, the material was very much in vogue for its exoticism. The table, also covered in sharkskin, is simply a circle supported by four square legs.

Frank often created furniture designs to be executed by other artists and craftsmen. Many of his metal pieces, for example, were executed by sculptors Alberto and Diego Giacometti, including lamps, andirons, tables, and vases. Driven from his homeland during World War II, Frank first settled in South America, then in New York, where he died in 1941.

PROVENANCE: Galerie Félix Marcilhac, Paris, 1971.

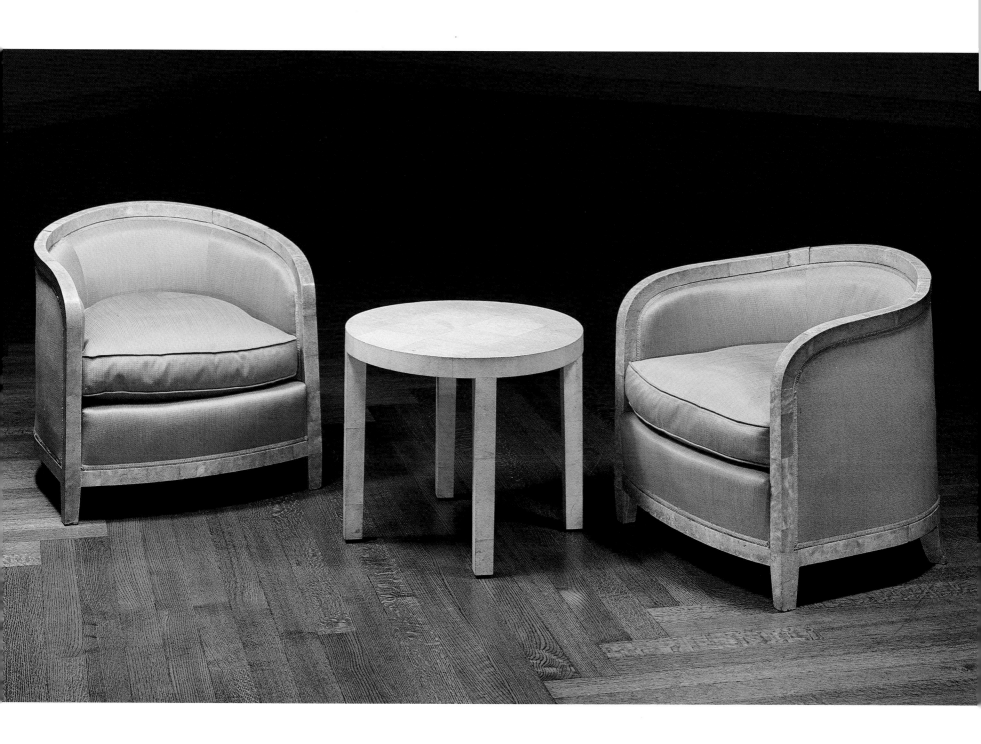

Eugène Printz
French, 1889-1948
and
Jean Dunand
French, 1887-1942

 85 Bookcase, ca. 1927-28

Palmwood, sycamore, copper, silver
144.7 × 308.9 × 50.2 (57 × 121⅝ × 19¾)
Unsigned
Virginia Museum of Fine Arts, Gift of Sydney and Frances Lewis,
85.126

This extraordinary bookcase is the result of a successful collaboration between Eugène Printz and the master lacquerer Jean Dunand. Designed by Printz, it has seven doors, designed by Dunand, that are copper inlaid with silver. The doors, mounted on pivots, revolve to expose sycamore-lined adjustable shelves within. This piece is very similar to one in a private collection in Paris, except that the Parisian cabinet has only five doors.[51]

Printz was a frequent exhibitor at the Salon des Artistes Décorateurs and the Salon d'Automne. He received numerous commissions from notable patrons such as Jeanne Lanvin, and also worked on the interior decoration of the luxury liner *Normandie*. He later helped form the design group Décor de France.

PROVENANCE: Galerie Félix Marcilhac, Paris, 1976.

PUBLISHED: Yvonne Brunhammer, *Cinquantenaire de l'Exposition de 1925*, exhibition catalogue (Paris: Musée des Arts Décoratifs, 1976), no. 729. Yvonne Brunhammer, *Le Style 1925* (Paris: Baschet et Cie, no date), p. 43. Pierre Kjellberg, *Art Déco: Les Maîtres du Mobilier* (Paris: Les editions de l'Amateur, ca. 1981), p. 141.

EXHIBITED: *Cinquantenaire de l'Exposition de 1925*, Paris, Musée des Arts Décoratifs, October 1976-February 1977, no. 729.

---

51. For an illustration of the Parisian bookcase, see Victor Arwas, *Art Deco* (New York: Harry N. Abrams, Inc., 1980), p. 84.

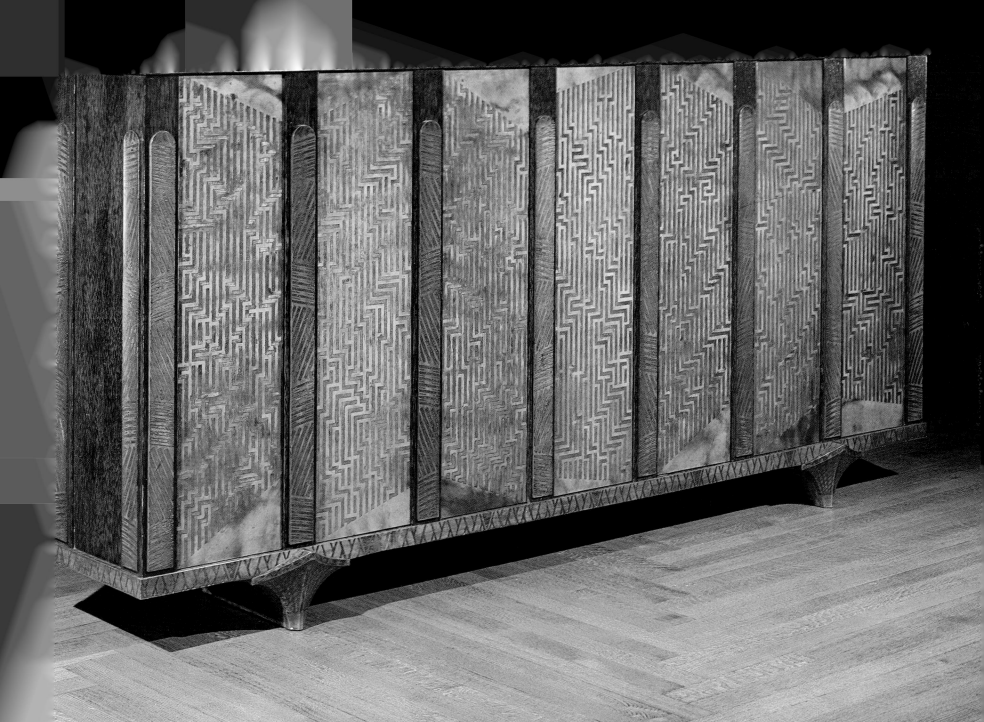

Gérard Sandoz
French, born 1902

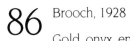 Brooch, 1928

Gold, onyx, enamel, two ½-carat diamonds
6.5 × 5.4 × 1.6 (2⁹⁄₁₆ × 2⅛ × ⅝)
Signed on reverse: *Gérard Sandoz*
Virginia Museum of Fine Arts, Gift of Sydney and Frances Lewis,
85.254

Gérard Sandoz began designing jewelry at the age of eighteen in the firm established by his grandfather, Gustave. Over a period of only about ten years, he designed a remarkable collection.

This brooch is characteristic of Sandoz's work, which included bold geometric shapes in both precious metals and stones, and designs inspired by Cubist and industrial forms. Sandoz was not only included in the Paris 1925 Exposition, he was also a regular contributor to the other various design salons, and was himself a founding member of the Union des Artistes Modernes in 1930.

Sandoz later abandoned jewelry design to concentrate on filmmaking and painting.

PROVENANCE: Primavera Gallery, New York, 1974.

PUBLISHED: *Bijoux et Orfevrerie présenté par Jean Fouquet* (Paris: Editions d'Art Charles Moreau, no date), pl. 33.

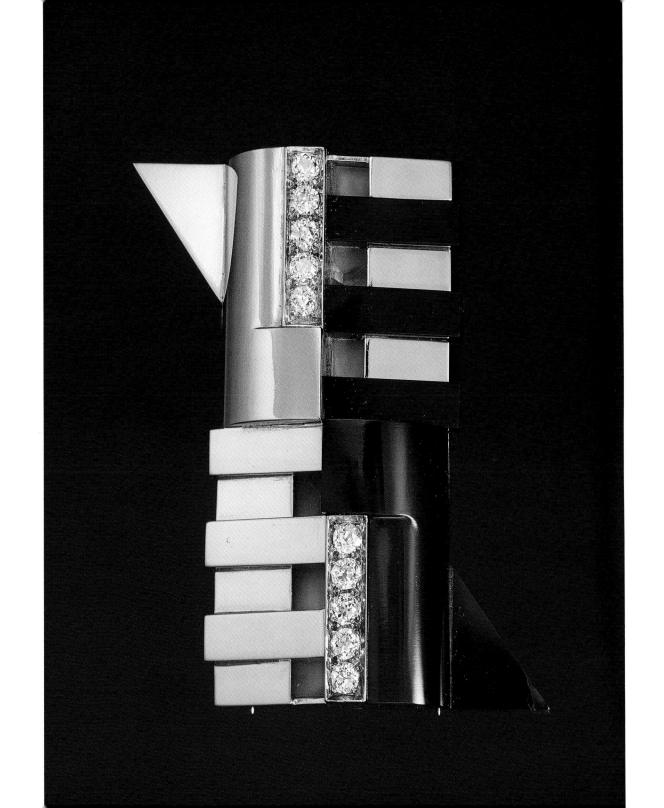

Jean Fouquet
French, born 1899

87 Bracelet, 1928-29

White gold, diamonds, jade
2.7 × 20.3 × .95 (1 1/16 × 8 × 3/8)
Signed inside: *Jean Fouquet*
Virginia Museum of Fine Arts, Gift of Sydney and Frances Lewis,
85.237

At the age of twenty, Paris-born Jean Fouquet began to work for his father, the famous jeweler Georges Fouquet (see cat. nos. 18 and 49). Jean's work was first exhibited at the 1925 Paris Exposition, and for the next thirty-five years he produced a wide variety of brilliant designs.

Unlike his father, Fouquet used simple, abstract, geometric shapes, and he set large precious and semiprecious stones into oversized mounts of jade, enamel, and metals. Figurative images played no part in his jewelry design.

In this handsome bracelet, Fouquet contrasts the jade cabochons, set in enamel and white gold, with panels of small diamonds, also mounted in white gold. He does not give the diamonds their traditional prominence, but instead subordinates them to the other materials. Thus the total design becomes well integrated. Fouquet continued to design jewelry until his failing health forced him to stop working in 1960.

PROVENANCE: Michel Perinet, Paris, 1975.

PUBLISHED: *Bijoux et Orfèvrerie présenté par Jean Fouquet* (Paris: Editions d'Art Charles Moreau, no date), pl. 2. Jean Gallotti, "Exposition de joaillerie et d'orfèvrerie au Musée Galliera," *Art et Décoration* (August 1929), pp. 33-50. Theodore Menten, *The Art Déco Style* (New York: Dover Publications, Inc., 1972), p. 155. Marie-Noël de Gary et al., *Les Fouquet: Bijoutiers & Joailliers à Paris 1860-1960* (Paris: Musée des Arts Décoratifs, 1983), illus. p. 171.

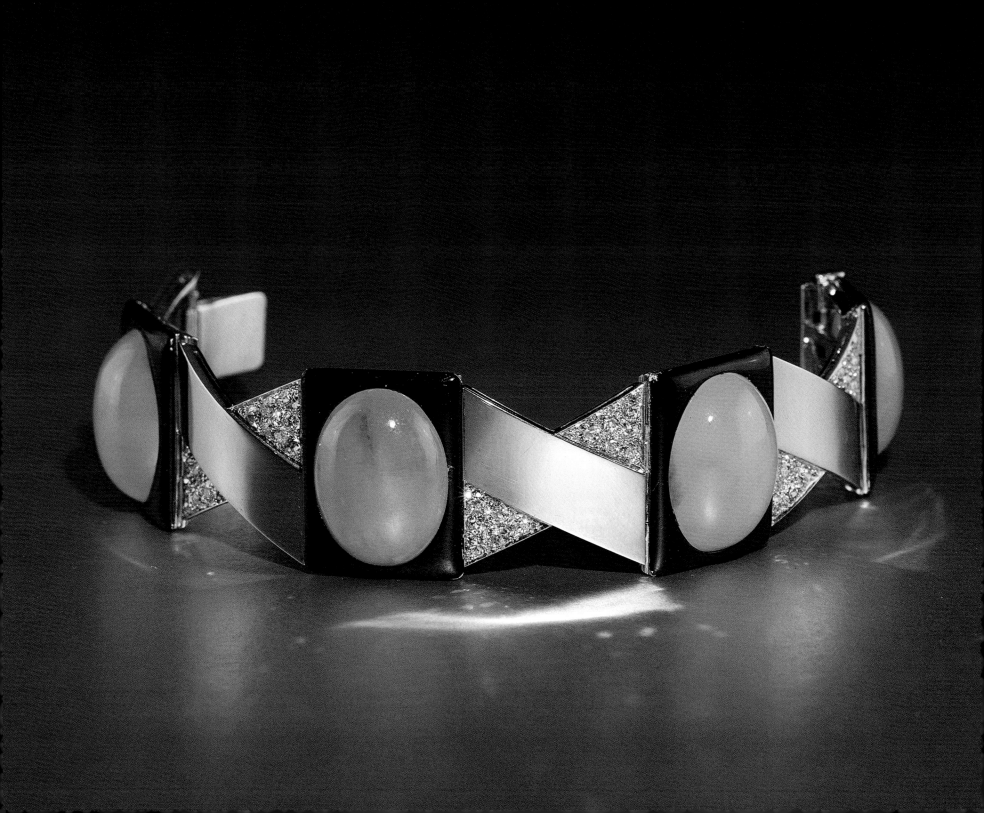

Marcel Coard
French, 1889-1975

 88 Sofa, before 1929

Rosewood, leather, ivory
87.6 × 243.8 × 91.5 (34½ × 96 × 36)
Signed back right edge: M. *Coard*
Virginia Museum of Fine Arts, Gift of Sydney and Frances Lewis, 85.99

Marcel Coard was born into a well-to-do Parisian family in 1889. An early trip to London kindled his interest in the work of William Morris and the artists represented in Arthur Liberty's shop. Coard studied architecture at the Ecole des Beaux-Arts, but his education and career were disrupted by World War I. He began to design furniture while convalescing in a military hospital, and at war's end he opened a shop as a *décorateur* on the Boulevard Haussmann in Paris, specializing in reproductions of period furniture but also creating pieces in the new style for special clients like Jacques Doucet.

One wall of Doucet's apartment at Neuilly was dominated by a niche into which this monumental sofa was placed (see fig. 17). Above it hung Henri Rousseau's *The Snake Charmer*, now in the collection of the Louvre. Other furnishings in the room included pieces by Eileen Gray and Pierre Legrain, with paintings and sculptures by Modigliani, Picasso, and Braque.

The sofa is carved in rosewood to simulate rattan; the edges are highlighted with bands of ivory. Its form, like much of Coard's other furniture, reflects his interest in the arts of Africa and the Far East.

PROVENANCE: Jacques Doucet, Neuilly; Hôtel Drouot, Paris, 1972.

PUBLISHED: André Joubin, "Le Studio de Jacques Doucet," L'*Illustration* (May 3, 1930), illus. p. 17. J.F. Revel, "Jacques Doucet, Couturier et Collectionneur," L'*Oeil* (December 1961), p. 47. *Maison et Jardin* (December 1961), p. 110. *Ancienne Collection Jacques Doucet*, catalogue of sale (Paris: Hôtel Drouot, November 8, 1972), no. 52, illus. Françoise de Perthuis, "L'Art Deco en flèche," *Gazette de l'Hôtel Drouot* (December 22, 1972), illus. p. 5. "Conseils aux Amateurs: folies pour le style 'Art Déco'," *Connaissance des Arts* 252 (February 1973), p. 113. "Die Schönen von gestern," *Stern* (March 21, 1974), illus. p. 48. *The Random House Collectors' Encyclopedia: Victoriana to Art Deco* (New York: Random House, 1974), illus. p. 75. Alain Lesieutre, *The Spirit and Splendour of Art Déco* (New York: Paddington Press, 1974), p. 23. Thomas Hoving, *The Chase, The Capture* (New York: Metropolitan Museum of Art, 1975), p. 228. Philippe Garner, ed., *Encyclopedia of Decorative Arts* (New York: Van Nostrand Reinhold, 1979), illus. p.71. Gabriele Sterner and Albrecht Bangert, *Jugendstil-Art Déco* (Munich: Batternberg Verlag, 1979), illus. no. 20. Philippe Garner, *Twentieth Century Furniture* (New York: Van Nostrand Reinhold, 1980), illus. p. 86. Pierre Kjellberg, "La Curiosité: Les Artistes d'avant-garde: Marcel Coard, Djo Bourgeois," *Gazette de l'Hôtel Drouot* (December 12, 1980), illus. p. 40. Pierre Kjellberg, *Art Deco: Les Maîtres du Mobilier* (Paris: Les Editions de l'Amateur, ca. 1981), pp. 11, 47. Alastair Duncan, *Art Deco Furniture* (New York: Holt, Rinehart and Winston, 1984), p. 16, illus. pl. 7.

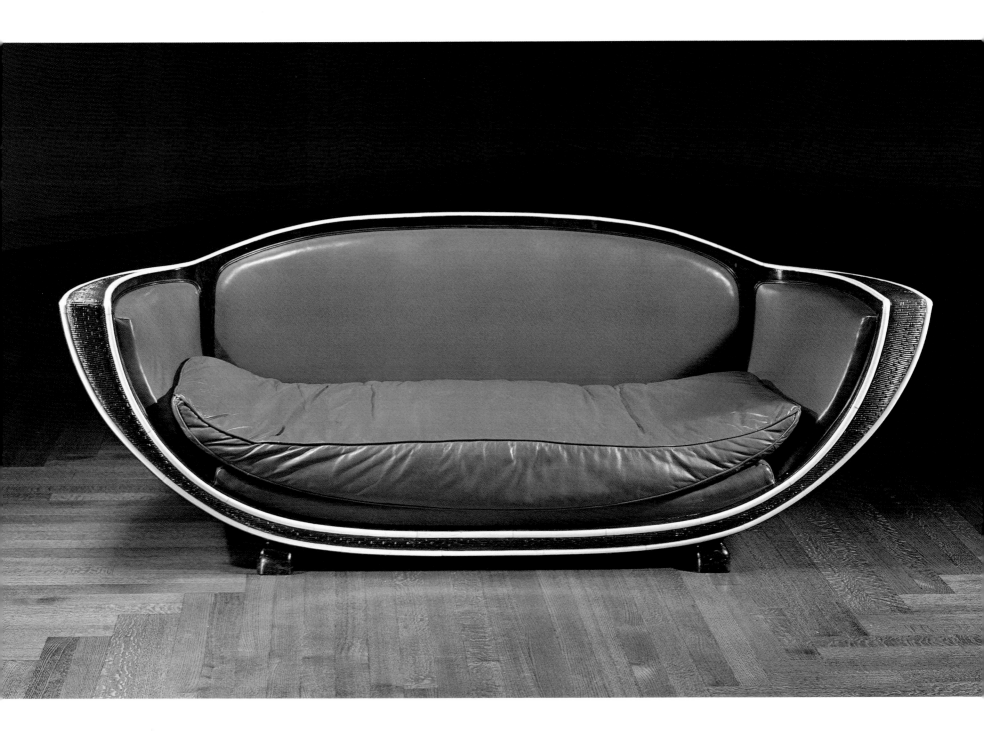

Pierre Legrain
French, 1889-1929
and
Jean Dunand
French, 1877-1942

 89 Cabinet, before 1929

Lacquered wood, pewter, bronze
86 × 74 × 33.7 (33⅞ × 29⅛ × 13¼)
Unsigned
Virginia Museum of Fine Arts, Gift of Sydney and Frances Lewis,
85.12.1

L'*art nègre* played a significant role in the stylistic development of Pierre Legrain. Important exhibitions of African art had been held in Europe in the 1920s and African forms are readily apparent in many of Legrain's furniture designs, particularly in his small chairs and stools. At the same time, however, other significant Legrain pieces show no influence of African art but instead reveal a tendency toward the clean lines of Modernism.

This cabinet, commissioned by the couturier and art patron Jacques Doucet, is a result of a collaboration between Legrain and Jean Dunand. Executed in deep red lacquer, the cabinet has two doors that close by means of a pivoting pewter lock in a stylized floral design. The interior comprises twenty-four small file drawers in a lighter red lacquer. Each drawer has a metal handle with a designated letter of the alphabet (the final two are marked "w/x" and "y/z"). Judging from its unusual design, and the fact that it was a commissioned piece, the cabinet was likely intended to hold certain of Doucet's business records.

It was Legrain who played the most influential role in redecorating Doucet's Neuilly apartment. When Paul Iribe left for the United States in 1914, Doucet turned to Legrain—well known as a talented designer and bookbinder—to complete the decoration of his home; the project lasted for the next fifteen years.

Legrain frequently exhibited at various salons, both individually and with other designers. He was a member of the Groupe des Cinq, which also included Pierre Chareau, Jean Puiforcat, Raymond Templier, and the design group Dominique. Both Doucet and Legrain died in 1929.

PROVENANCE: Jacques Doucet, Neuilly; Hôtel Drouot, Paris, 1972.

PUBLISHED: *Ancienne Collection Jacques Doucet* (Paris: Hôtel Drouot, November 8, 1972), no. 30, cover illus. Pierre Kjellberg, *Art Déco: Les Maîtres du Mobilier* (Paris: Les Editions de l'Amateur, ca. 1981), p. 92. Alastair Duncan, *Art Deco Furniture* (New York: Holt, Rinehart and Winston, 1984), p. 84, illus. pl. 38.

EXHIBITED: *Fastes et décors de la vie, 1909-1929*, Musée Galliera, Paris, June-August 1957.

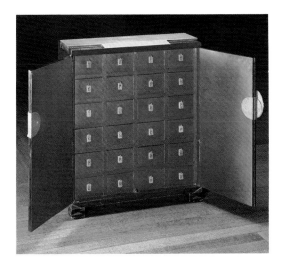

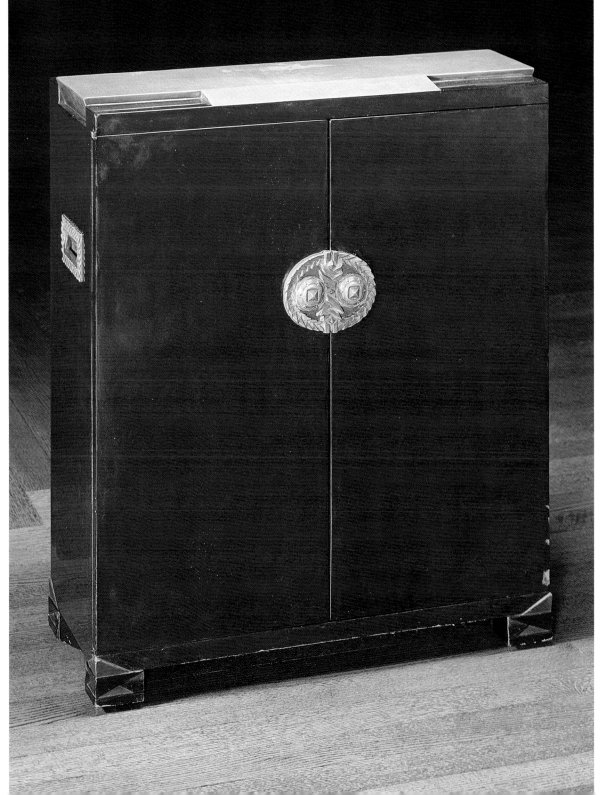

René Lalique
French, 1860-1945

90 Panel for a Pullman Car on the *Côte d'Azur*, 1929

Molded and acid-decorated glass, sycamore
Central panels (3), each: 45 × 14.5 (17¾ × 5¹¹⁄₁₆)
Top and bottom panels (6), each: 11 × 14.5 (4⅜ × 5¹¹⁄₁₆)
Including frame: 93.3 × 79.4 (36¾ × 31¼)
Unsigned
Virginia Museum of Fine Arts, Gift of Sydney and Frances Lewis,
85.350

Lalique's name is immediately associated with art glass; however, this was actually his second career, his first being that of goldsmith (see cat. nos. 7 and 38). As early as 1890 Lalique began experimenting with glass, using a small furnace he set up in Paris. During the next decade he established himself as one of the great Art Nouveau jewelers, often combining precious metals and stones with glass.

According to Lalique's biographer, Christopher Vane Percy, 1907 was important in the transformation of his career, for that was the year:

> . . . he first experimented [at his estate at Clairefontaine] with making the scent bottles for [the *parfumeur*] François Coty, which were to become one of the most enduringly successful of all his commercial ventures. Those first bottles were manufactured elsewhere and by another company, Legras & Cie de St.-Denis; but two years later, when Lalique opened his second factory, at Combs-la-Ville, about forty miles east of Paris on the edge of the forest of Sénart, he was already equipped to manufacture the bottles himself. His career as *verrier* had begun.[52]

By 1911, when he moved his shop to the Rue Royale, Lalique began to feature glass in his displays. He had to close his factory during World War I, but resumed his work in 1921, reaching what many consider to be his greatest triumph in the Paris Exposition of 1925. There, Lalique was represented not only in a pavilion for his own shop but also in the pavilions of other firms and designers.

Frank Scarlett and Marjorie Townley witnessed the 1925 Exposition first-hand as members of the staff of the British section. "Of almost equal prominence [to Ruhlmann's pavilion] on the Esplanade," they wrote, "was the Lalique pavilion, naturally exploiting the full use of glass . . . . In fact, Lalique glass, together with decorative metalwork by Brandt, pervaded the

French sections and, to most people, typified the style of the period."[53]

Reviewer Roger Gilman wrote: "Gray glass of dull finish, touched with brown or black, under the hands of its guiding genius, Lalique, has proved itself one of the discoveries of modern decoration."[54]

It was Lalique more than any other designer who made glass such an important architectural element. Among his other such commissions were designs for the Compagnie Internationale des Wagons-Lits, for the sleeping car of the President of France (1923), and the interior of a Pullman car on the luxurious *Côte d'Azur* train in 1929.

The panel shown here, from this latter commission, served as a partition at one end of the car. In keeping with the train's exotic luxury, the design features Bacchantes surrounded by grapes and grapevine motifs.

Later, Lalique was to receive a major architectural commission in the decoration of the first-class dining room for the luxury ship *Normandie*. Although Lalique died in 1945, his firm continues to produce fine glass to this day.

PROVENANCE: Compagnie Internationale des Wagon-Lits, 1929; Sotheby Parke-Bernet Monaco S.A., 1977.

PUBLISHED: *Arts Décoratifs, Styles 1900 et 1925*, catalogue of sale (Monte Carlo: Sotheby Parke-Bernet Monaco S.A., October 8, 1977), pp. 14-15. Christopher Vane Percy, *The Glass of Lalique: A Collectors Guide* (New York: Charles Scribner's Sons, 1977), p. 119, illus. p. 117.

52. Christopher Vane Percy, *The Glass of Lalique: A Collector's Guide* (New York: Charles Scribner's Sons, 1977), p. 13.
53. Frank Scarlett and Marjorie Townley, *Arts Décoratifs 1925: A Personal Recollection of the Paris Exhibition* (London: Academy Editions, 1975), p. 37.
54. Roger Gilman, "The Paris Exposition: A Glimpse into the Future," *The Art Bulletin* 8 (September 1925): 34.

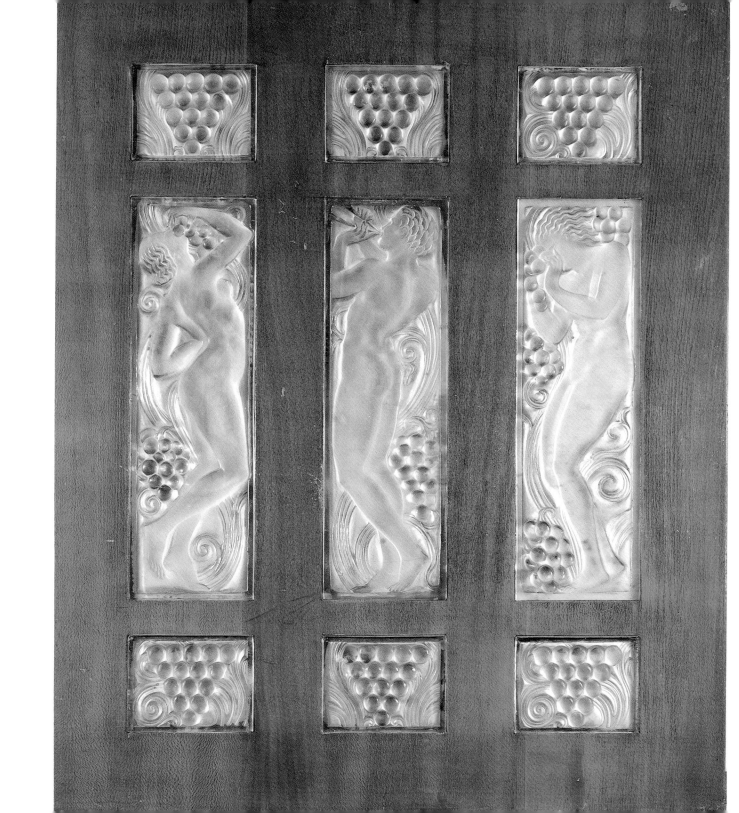

Jean Goulden
French, 1878-1947

91

Clock, 1929

Silvered bronze, enamel, marble
49.5 × 20.3 × 19 (19½ × 8 × 7½)
Signed on lower reverse: XLVII 27 *Jean Goulden*
Virginia Museum of Fine Arts, Gift of Sydney and Frances Lewis,
85.219

This clock, which seems more like a Cubist sculpture than a decorative accessory, displays Jean Goulden's mastery of metalwork and enamel.

Born in 1878 to a wealthy family of Charpentry, Meuse, Goulden studied medicine in Paris just after the turn of the century. While in Paris, he joined a circle of artists, and during World War I he served as a doctor in the army, spending several months at Mount Athos in Greece. Fascinated by the Byzantine enamels he saw there, Goulden convinced the master enamelist and lacquerer Jean Dunand to teach him the art of enameling. Because he was financially independent, Goulden was able to devote himself to his design work after the war, and he continued to do so until his death in 1947. He is thought to have produced approximately 150 pieces during his lifetime.

Stylistically his work reflects the avant-garde art of the period, particularly Cubism and, in some cases, Russian Constructivism. From 1921 to 1932, Goulden exhibited his work at the Galerie Georges Petit with that of his close friends Jean Dunand, Paul Jouve, and the bookbinder François-Louis Schmied.

PROVENANCE: Galerie du Luxembourg, Paris, 1973.

PUBLISHED: Yvonne Brunhammer, *Le Style 1925* (Paris: Baschet et Cie, no date), p. 26. *Jean Dunand, Jean Goulden*, catalogue of exhibition (Paris: Galerie du Luxembourg, 1973), illus. p. 116. Paul Maenz, *Art Déco 1920-1940* (Cologne: Verlag M. DuMont Schauberg, 1974), pp. 4, 112, illus. p. 113. Alastair Duncan, *Art Deco Furniture* (New York: Holt, Rinehart and Winston, 1984), p. 32, illus. pl. 25.

EXHIBITED: *Cinquantenaire de l'Exposition de 1925*, Paris, Musée des Arts Décoratifs, October 1976–February 1977. *Jean Dunand, Jean Goulden*, Paris, Galerie du Luxembourg, May–June 1973.

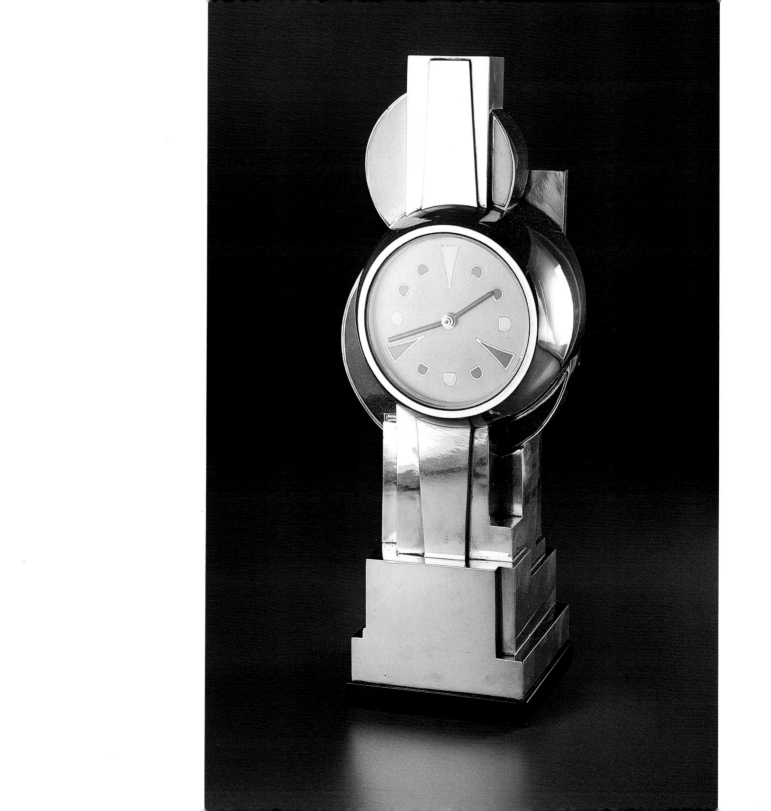

Donald Deskey
American, born 1894

92 Screen, ca. 1929

Oil paint and metal leaf on canvas, wood
197.5 × 149.2 × 2.9 (77¾ × 58¾ × 1¼)
Signed on reverse, on paper label, lower right: *Modern Decorative Art, Deskey-Vollmer, New York*
Virginia Museum of Fine Arts, Gift of the Sydney and Frances Lewis Foundation, 85.62

Deskey was one of a small group of American designers who, in the 1920s, recognized the importance of the new European styles and sought to incorporate them into their own designs. Trained in architecture and painting, Deskey worked on the West Coast and in Chicago before settling in New York. His trip to the 1925 Paris Exposition was probably the deciding factor steering him to a career in interior design. Upon his return to New York, he received several important commissions, one of them the design for the interior of Radio City Music Hall.

In 1929 Mr. and Mrs. Glendon Allvine commissioned Warren Shephard Matthews to design and build a house at Long Beach, Long Island. Newspaper accounts of the day labeled the house "America's First Modernistic Home." To decorate their house, the Allvines enlisted the aid of leading contemporary American designers, among them Deskey. This screen, probably acquired in 1929 for the Allvine dining room, reflects the color scheme of the room.[55] The Deskey-Vollmer label on the screen refers to the partnership Deskey established with Phillip Vollmer in 1927.

Paul Frankl, a contemporary of Deskey's, defined various concepts of Modernism that apply to this screen:

Today we try to express rhythm and the sharp Modernistic effects which are characteristic of our time. . . . There is also the modern movement in furniture design which, as in all previous periods, is influenced by the architecture of its day. But colour comes from the trend in fashions. At the same time ornament has been largely done away with and has been displaced by flat colours and all-over designs. Modern furniture has several strong characteristics. It is built in flat surfaces and strong lines. The angles are decided and sharp. The proportions are well considered and the finish is beyond reproach. Sentimental mouldings and panelling are avoided as much as possible in order to gain the effect of extreme and severe simplicity.[56]

PROVENANCE: Mr. and Mrs. Glendon Allvine, Long Beach, New York; The De Lorenzo Collection; Christie, Manson & Woods International Inc., New York, 1980.

PUBLISHED: American Designers' Gallery exhibition catalogue, New York, no date. *Art et Décoration* 43, no. 2, p. 9 (October 1931), p. 323. *America's First Modernistic Home*, catalogue of sale (New York: Christie, Manson & Woods International, Inc., October 4, 1980), no. 426, illus. p. 12. Michael Komanecky and Virginia Fabbri Butera, *The Folding Image: Screens by Western Artists of the Nineteenth and Twentieth Centuries* (New Haven: Yale University Art Gallery, 1984), pp. 243-45, pl. 26.1.

EXHIBITED: American Designers' Gallery, New York, dates unknown. *The Folding Image*, National Gallery of Art, Washington, D.C., March 4–September 3, 1984; Yale University Art Gallery, New Haven, October 11–January 6, 1985.

55. For a recent commentary on the house see Michael Komanecky and Virginia Fabbri Butera, *The Folding Image: Screens By Western Artists of the 19th and 20th Centuries* (New Haven: Yale University Art Gallery, 1984), p. 243.
56. Paul T. Frankl, *New Dimensions: The Decorative Arts of Today in Words & Pictures* (New York: Payson & Clarke Ltd., 1928), p. 18.

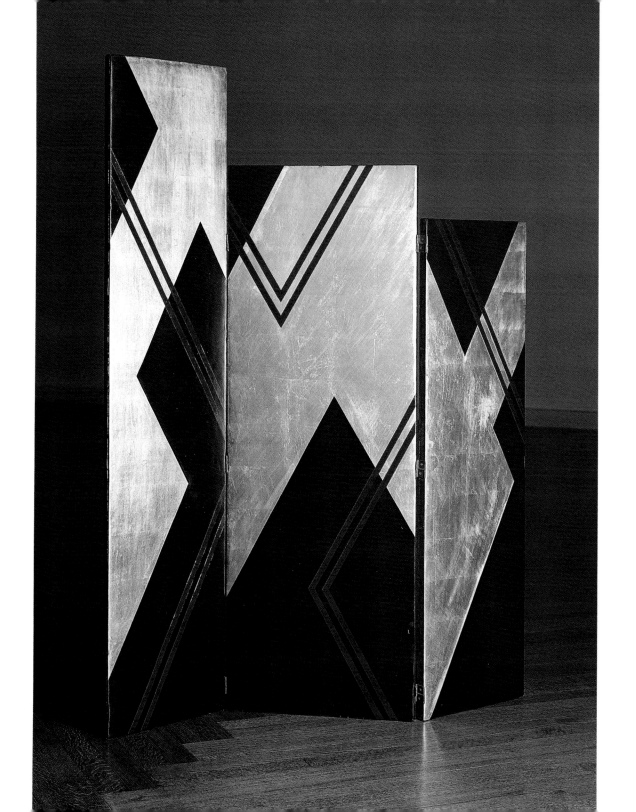

Edgar Brandt
French, 1880-1960

93 Pair of Gates, ca. 1929

Wrought iron
106.7 × 182.9 each (42 × 72)
Impressed on each side of gate, on upper corner near hinge:
E. *Brandt*
Virginia Museum of Fine Arts, Gift of Sydney and Frances Lewis,
85.277.1/2

The art of the ironsmith was vigorously revived during the late nineteenth century. Architects such as Hector Guimard incorporated ironwork in many of their architectural designs, since it was a material that, when forged, could easily take on the serpentine line of the Style 1900.

By the 1920s decorative ironwork in the hands of the artist Edgar Brandt had reached its zenith as a viable expressive material. A student of the master ironworker Emile Robert, Brandt set up his own studio in 1919 and several years later began collaborating with the architect Louis Favier. By 1925 his reputation had been established: he was invited to participate in the Paris Exposition, for which he designed ironwork for a number of pavilions, as well as for his own showroom. His reputation had expanded sufficiently by the following year to allow him to open a shop in New York. His vast output included lamps, andirons, gates, radiator grills, architectural ironwork, and other items that could be incorporated into the interiors and showrooms of the master *ensembliers*.

In an illustration in the February 1929 issue of *Les Echos d'Art*, this pair of gates is shown at the entrance to a building designed by Michel Roux-Spitz on the Rue Geynemer. Although made of wrought iron of considerable weight, the gates have a light, airy quality made possible by their thin, interlacing tendrils. A central medallion of cast iron in each gate depicts a stylized female face in low relief: one with flowing hair and a crown of stylized flowers and leaves; the other with down-cast eyes, her hands drawing a hood over her head. Although the symbolism of the two faces is uncertain, they may represent day and night or two seasons.

Brandt not only received important commissions from private patrons, but was also honored with major public projects including work at the Louvre and at the Tomb of the Unknown Soldier in Paris. Although Brandt was the outstanding *ferronier* of the period, others included Paul Kiss, Raymond Subes, Nics Frères, Robert Mallet-Stevens, Richard Desvallières, and Fred Perret.

PROVENANCE: Christie, Manson & Woods International, Inc., New York, 1981.

PUBLISHED: F.S., "Ferronnerie d'Art," *Les Echos d'Art* (February 1929), p. 22. *Mobilier et Décoration* (1931), p. 180. *Nineteenth Century Sculpture, Art Nouveau & Art Déco*, catalogue of sale (New York: Christie, Manson & Woods International Inc., March 20, 1981), no. 331, illus. p. 97.

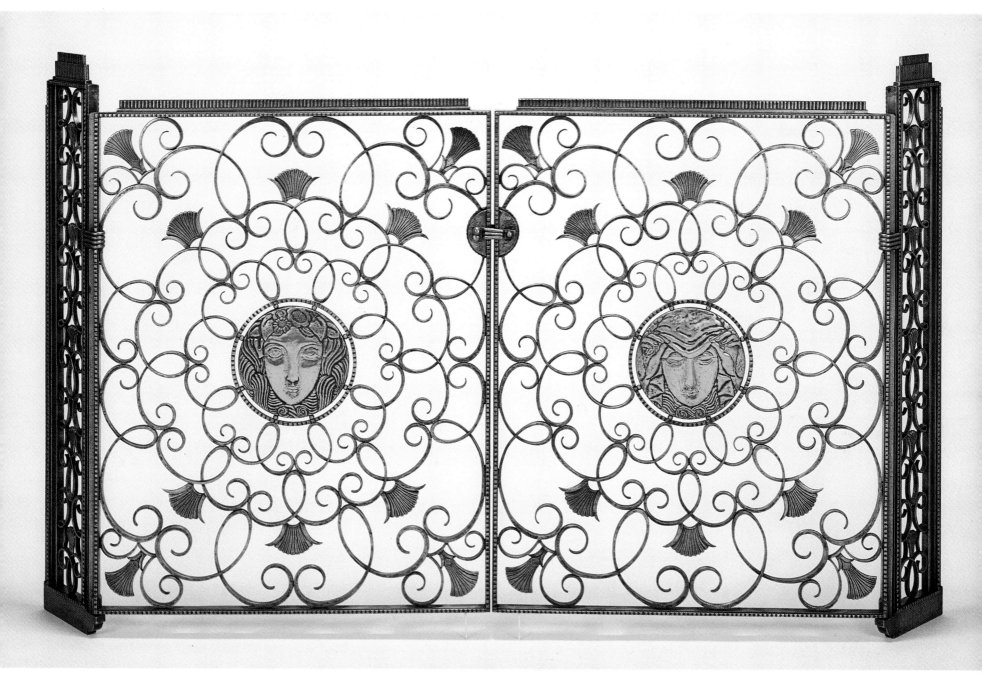

François-Louis Schmied
French, 1873-1941
and
Jean Dunand
French, 1877-1942

94

Book, *Ruth et Booz*, 1930

Edition 13/155, published by F.-L. Schmied, Paris
Illustrations: wood engravings
Binding: Levant morocco, lacquer
14½ × 12¼ × 2½ (36.9 × 31.1 × 6.4)
Cover initialed lower left: *JD*, lower right: *FLS*
Engravings signed: *Schmied*
Virginia Museum of Fine Arts, Gift of Sydney and Frances Lewis,
85.39 a/b

François-Louis Schmied was born in Geneva, Switzerland, where he was educated at the School of Industrial Arts. By 1895 he had moved to Paris, where he made engravings for book illustrations, and exhibited his work at the annual salons of the Société Nationale des Beaux-Arts from 1904 to 1914.

One of Schmied's first major commissions was to cut the blocks for Paul Jouve's drawings illustrating Rudyard Kipling's *Jungle Book*, a project that took him fourteen years to complete. The book, finally published in 1919, received much critical acclaim, and Schmied soon became a major figure in French book illustration and design. He maintained full control in all his publications because he understood and had mastered all aspects of book production, including printing the texts on his own press.

His books were shown in the Paris Exposition of 1925 and in a series of exhibitions at the Galerie Georges Petit with the group that included Jean Dunand, Jean Goulden, and Paul Jouve. Many of his works were the result of his collaboration with Dunand and Goulden. Dunand, the master French lacquerer, created the polychromed lacquered panel Schmied designed for the cover of this book.

Around 1934 or 1935 Schmied moved to Morocco to concentrate on painting; he died there in 1941.

PROVENANCE: Christie, Manson & Woods International Inc., New York, 1983.

PUBLISHED: *An Important Collection of Art Nouveau*, catalogue of sale (New York: Christie, Manson & Woods International Inc., May 26, 1983), no. 444, illus. p. 47.

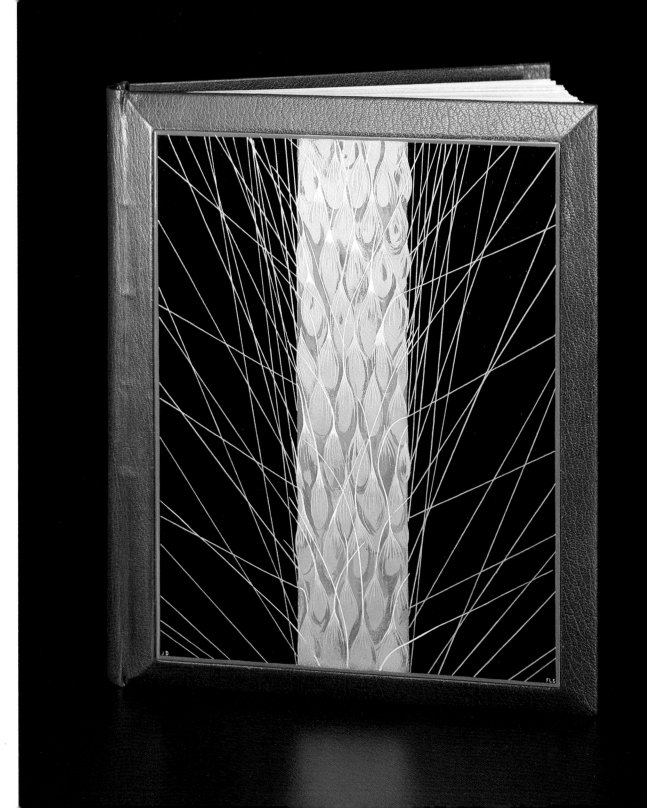

Emile-Jacques Ruhlmann
French, 1879-1933

 95 "Sun" Bed, 1930

Macassar ebony, white oak
195.6 × 212.1 × 217.8 (77 × 83½ × 85¾)
Signed *Ruhlmann* on back of headboard and twice on inside of
footboard
Virginia Museum of Fine Arts, Gift of Sydney and Frances Lewis,
85.130

A copy of a Certificate of Authenticity from Emile-Jacques Ruhlmann now in the Lewis Archives shows that this bed was executed in studio B in June 1930 for the residence of Madame Jane Renouardt at 2 Rue Buzenval, St.-Cloud. It is listed as "bed (sun) model no. 807, example no. 2" and the letterhead bears Ruhlmann's title and address, "Meublier à Paris, 27 Rue de Lisbonne." It also bears the stamp of his signature and studio B.

Jane Renouardt, a former milliner, became a well-known actress on the French stage and was eventually a director of the Théâtre Danou. The firm of Süe et Mare designed and built her house at St.-Cloud in 1924 (see Süe et Mare cabinet, cat. no. 83).

This bed employs Ruhlmann's favorite wood, Macassar ebony, on a white oak base with a brilliant cellulose finish. The headboard is a remarkable example of the skill of Ruhlmann's craftsmen. The "sun bed" was eventually moved from St.-Cloud to Madame Renouardt's apartment in Paris at 24 Avenue Gabriel. A second "sun bed," similar in design but lacking the two small built-in side tables, was also made for Madame Renouardt and her husband Fernand Gravey.

Ruhlmann had an elite and extravagant clientele. Because his work required a great deal of time and skill to complete, and because he used rare materials, Ruhlmann's furnishings were very expensive. For example, it is recorded that one of his craftsmen worked 252½ hours to make this bed, which was sold in 1930 for the exorbitant sum of 11,375 francs, equivalent to about one-half of the workman's annual salary.[57]

PROVENANCE: Jane Renouardt, St.-Cloud, France, 1930; Hôtel Drouot, Paris, 1972.

PUBLISHED: *Auction catalogue of sale* (Paris: Hôtel Drouot, May 5, 1972), no. 158. "Salles des Ventes: Conseils aux acheteurs," *Connaissance des Arts* 245 (July 1972), p. 82. "Les Meubles de Ruhlmann: un retour en force," *Gazette de l'Hôtel Drouot* (March 9, 1979), p. 2.

---

57. Florence Camard, *Ruhlmann, Master of Art Deco* (New York: Harry N. Abrams, Inc., 1984), p.225.

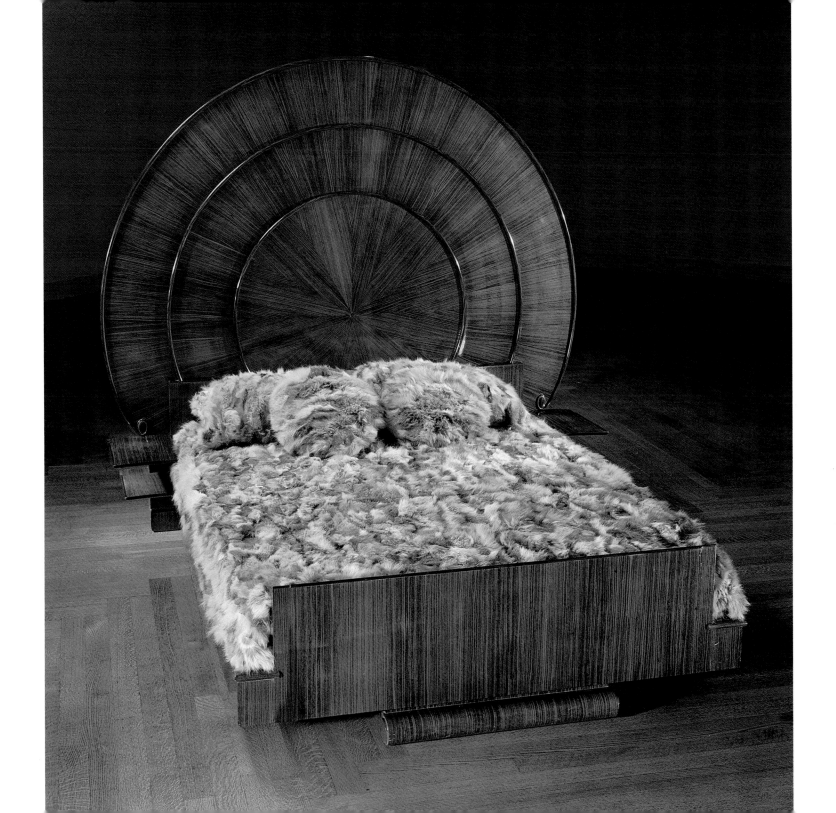

Albert Cheuret
French, dates unknown

96
Clock, ca. 1930

Silvered bronze, onyx
15.9 × 41.9 × 10.1 (6½ × 16½ × 4)
Inscribed lower right of face: *Albert Cheuret*
Virginia Museum of Fine Arts, Gift of Sydney and Frances Lewis,
85.218

In 1922, as the world read of that awesome moment when Howard Carter first set eyes on the interior of the tomb of King Tutankhamen, a craze for Egyptian styles and motifs began. Interest in Egyptian art was not new; motifs from the ancient art of that country are found throughout history, particularly in the early nineteenth century, when scientific data were published following Napoleon's invasion of Egypt. It was not until the early twentieth century, however, that such an astounding treasure trove was brought to light, and that news of its discovery could be readily transmitted to all areas of the globe.

The interest of Art Deco artists in the Egyptian style was appropriate to their quest for the exotic, and in adapting the styles and forms of this colorful and dramatic aesthetic to their own designs, they revealed their sensitivity to the drama and flair of such events.

One of the most famous objects created in the Egyptian style during this period is this mantel clock by Albert Cheuret. Fashioned of silvered bronze and onyx, its form resembles that of an Egyptian headdress or wig, the stylized tresses sweeping down and out in a pyramidal shape to frame the face of the clock.

Many other objects created in the Egyptian Revival style are of lesser taste and weaker aesthetics. It was the proliferation of objects of weak design and cheap materials that eventually led to the demise of the Style 1925.

PROVENANCE: Christie, Manson & Woods International Inc., New York, 1983.

PUBLISHED: Yvonne Brunhammer, *Le Style 1925* (Paris: Baschet et Cie, no date), p. 141. Bevis Hillier, *The World of Art Deco* (New York: E.P. Dutton, 1971), p. 32, no. 338. *Important 20th Century Decorative Arts,* catalogue of sale (New York: Christie, Manson & Woods International Inc., December 16-17, 1983), no. 340, illus. p. 159.

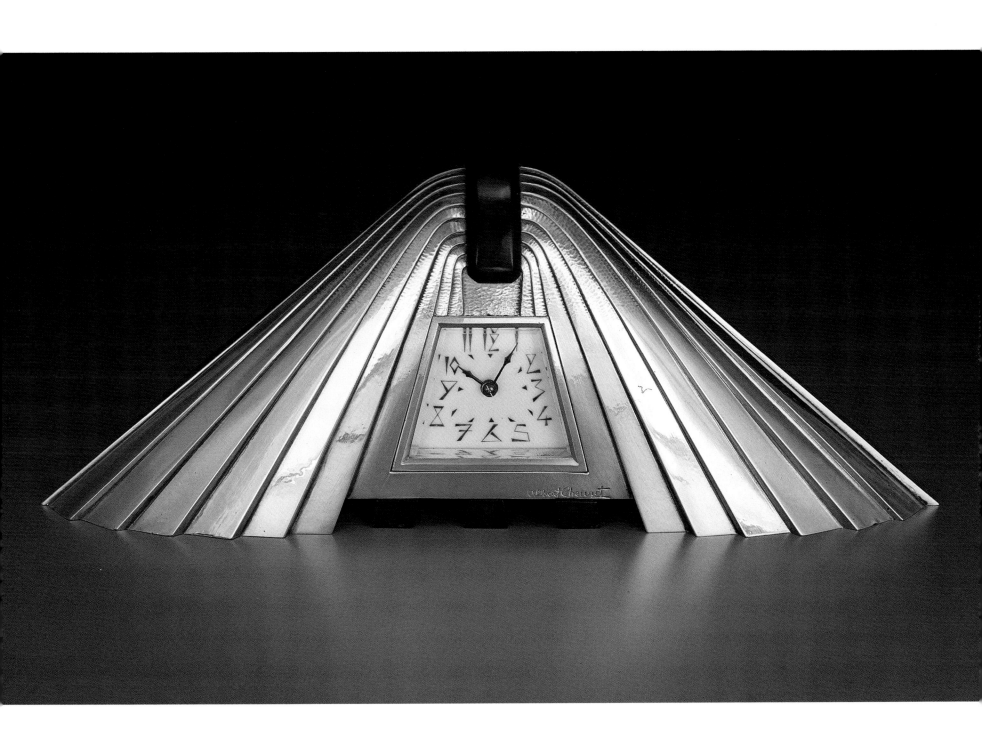

Johann Ferdinand Preiss
German, 1882-1943

 97 *Breasting the Tape*, ca. 1930s

Cast by Preiss-Kassler, Berlin
Cold-painted bronze, ivory, onyx
26.7 × 12.7 × 27.9 (10½ × 5 × 11)
Signed on front of onyx base: *PK* and *F Preiss*; under front of skirt:
monogram *PK*
Virginia Museum of Fine Arts, Gift of Sydney and Frances Lewis,
85.311

The 1920s, particularly in Europe, saw the increased manufacture and distribution of small statuettes or sculptures in ivory and cold-painted bronze. One of the best known makers of these figures was the German Johann Ferdinand Preiss.

Although Preiss's sculptures are usually associated with the Style 1925, he was producing work as early as 1906 in partnership with Walter Kassler. The Preiss-Kassler firm bought out its rival workshop, Rosenthal und Maeder, in 1929, and thus the monograms of both firms often appear as the identifying marks on Preiss's work.

Preiss's mature style of the 1920s reflects popular interests of the period. His figures usually depict women, many in athletic poses, of the type we might associate with pre-war Germany. In some ways an inventory of Preiss's sculptures is also an inventory of the manners, morals, and fashions of the 1920s.

PROVENANCE: Sotheby's Belgravia, London, 1972.

PUBLISHED: *Decorative Arts 1880-1939 including Arts and Crafts, Art Nouveau and Art Deco*, catalogue of sale (London: Sotheby's Belgravia, November 16, 1972), no. 150. Victor Arwas, *Art Déco Sculpture* (London: Academy Editions/New York: St. Martin's Press, 1976), illus. p. 97. Bryan Catley, *Art Deco and Other Figures* (Woodbridge, Suffolk, England: Antique Collectors' Club, 1978), p. 272.

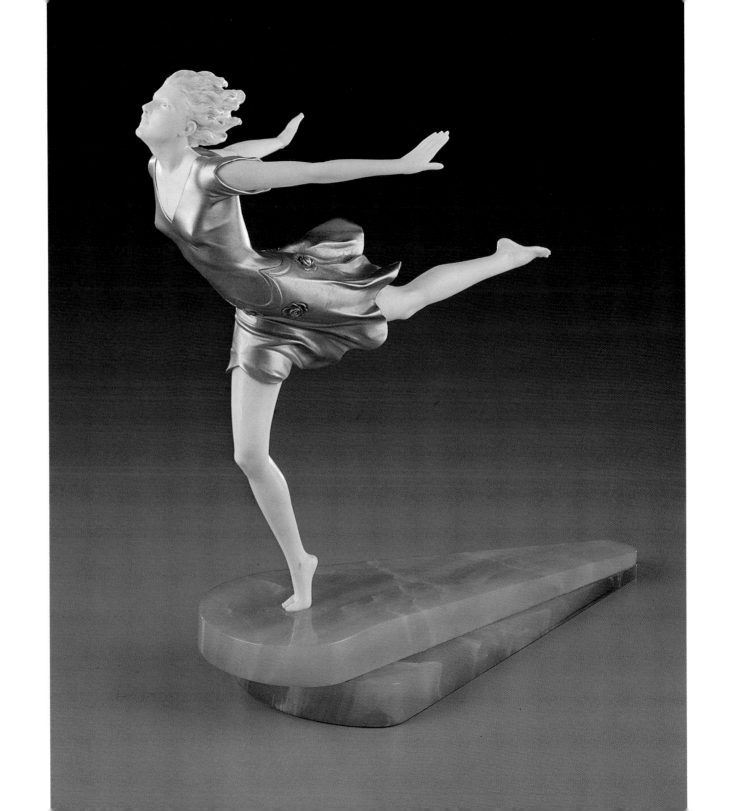

Marie Laurençin
French, 1885-1956

 98   Carpet, 1934

Tufted wool
325 × 350 (129 × 138)
Unsigned
Virginia Museum of Fine Arts, Gift of Sydney and Frances Lewis,
85.340

Marie Laurençin was one of the few easel painters whose work adorned the walls of French interiors in the Art Deco period. Most French designers during that time tended to favor wall murals that would not visually intrude on the total design effect. Laurençin's images, with their delicate coloring and graceful, slender figures, perfectly suit the feminine qualities that often characterized these luxurious interiors.

Born in Paris in 1885, Laurençin studied at the Académie Humbert. She soon became part of Picasso's circle in Montmartre, but developed a personal style that never reflected a strong Cubist influence.

Although she is today considered more successful as a painter, she contributed significantly to the overall concept of interiors of the period. Her work was especially favored by the designer André Groult (see cat. no. 72).

Laurençin's style can be seen as a somewhat light-hearted version of the theatre designs for the Ballets Russes and, in fact, in 1924 Serge Diaghilev invited her to design Poulenc's ballet Les Biches, which was to be choreographed by Nijinsky. She also worked with the firm of Süe et Mare, La Compagnie des Arts Français (see cat.no. 83).

This wool carpet—with motifs of sirens, doves, stylized fish, and ribbons—is a unique piece that was designed in 1925 for a friend who was director of a music salon in Paris. The rug is typical of Laurençin's work, both in its use of pastel pinks and blues and its depiction of imaginary, dreamlike figures.

PROVENANCE: Private collection, Paris; Sotheby Parke Bernet Monaco S.A., 1977.

PUBLISHED: Arts Décoratifs, Styles 1900 et 1925, catalogue of sale (Monte Carlo: Sotheby Parke Bernet Monaco S.A., October 8, 1977), no. 60, illus. p. 43. Victor Arwas, Art Deco (New York: Harry N. Abrams, Inc., 1980), illus. p. 68.

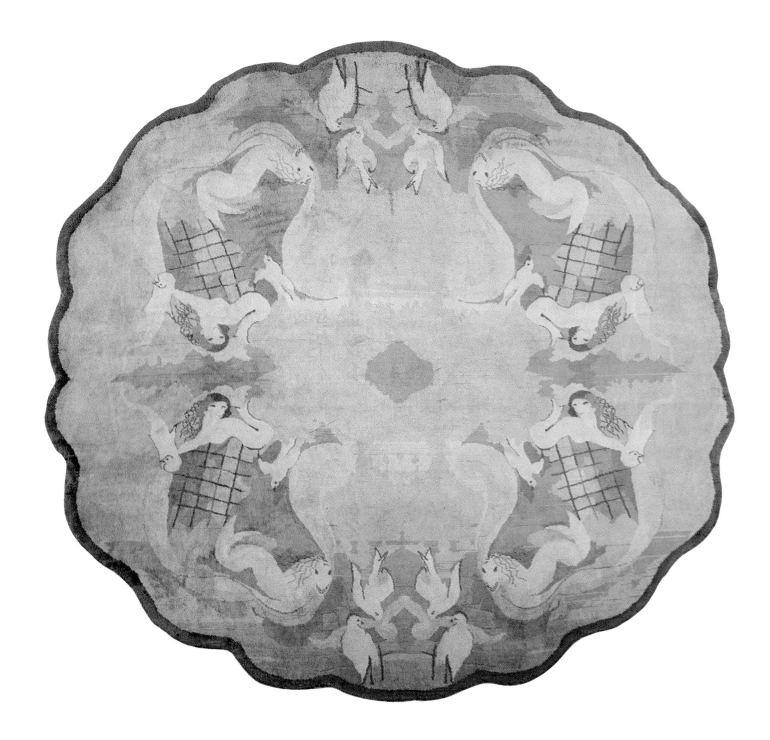

Emile Just Bachelet
French, born 1892

 Venus et l'Amour, ca. 1934

Ivory, gilt bronze, marble
124.4 × 33 diameter (49 × 13)
Signed on rear of base: E. J. *Bachelet*
Virginia Museum of Fine Arts, Gift of the Sydney and Frances
Lewis, 85.314

Ivory has been a favorite medium of craftsmen and sculptors in all civilizations and cultures. In fact, the ivory tusks of the Indian and African elephants have been in such demand that today the animals are endangered species, and various countries now prohibit the export of this exotic material.

The use of ivory as an artist's medium was promoted vigorously in the early years of the twentieth century by those countries that had colonies in Africa. Ivory was an extremely important export, especially to Belgium and France. An obvious result of this promotion during the 1920s was the evolution of chryselephantine figures (see cat. nos. 77, 78, 97). Other sculptors also used ivory as a medium for important large-scale sculptures, such as this carved tusk by Emile Just Bachelet.

While preserving the inherent shape of the tusk, Bachelet has skillfully carved it in the form of a nude Venus holding above her a small figure of Amour, or Eros. Both the form and the surface of the material lend an erotic quality that is appropriate to the subject.

Bachelet was best known for his stylized, life-sized animal carvings in stone and bronze depicting ducks, guinea hens, and chickens. Many of these were exhibited in the Salon des Artistes Décorateurs.

PROVENANCE: Galerie Félix Marcilhac, Paris; Christie, Manson & Woods International Inc., New York, 1983.

PUBLISHED: *Mobilier et Décoration* (1934), p. 210. Victor Arwas, *Art Deco* (New York: Harry N. Abrams Inc., 1980), p. 137. *Important 20th Century Decorative Arts*, catalogue of sale (New York: Christie, Manson & Woods International Inc., December 16-17, 1983), no. 329, illus. p. 150.

EXHIBITED: Salon des Arts Décoratifs, Paris, 1934; "Pavillon Société des Artistes Décorateurs," Exposition Internationale, Paris, 1937.

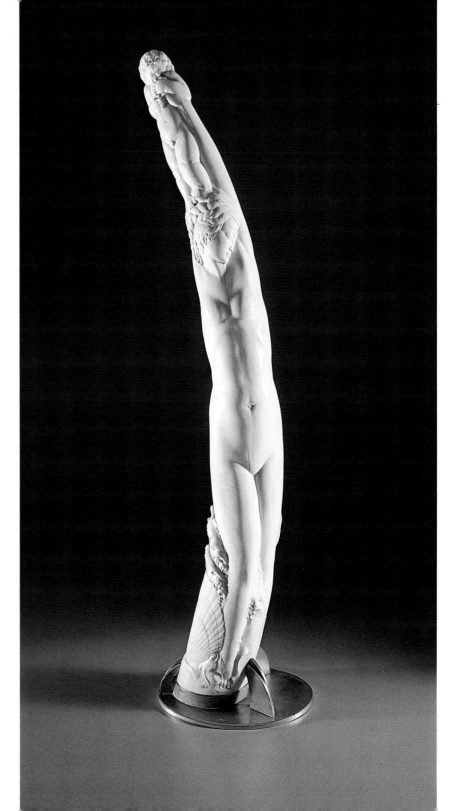

Jean Puiforcat
French, 1897-1945

100 Tea Set, 1937

Sterling silver, rosewood
Teapot: 13.6 × 17.8 × 10 (5⅜ × 7 × 4)
Coffee Pot: 13.6 × 17.8 × 10 (5⅜ × 7 × 4)
Creamer: 7.6 × 12.1 × 8 (3 × 4¾ × 3⅛)
Sugar: 7.6 × 11.4 × 8 (3 × 4½ × 3⅛)
Tray: 85.7 × 22.2 × 3.2 (33¾ × 8 ¾ × 1½)
Artist's mark and hallmark under handle, bottom, and on side
of each piece
Virginia Museum of Fine Arts, Gift of Sydney and Frances
Lewis, 85.295.1/5

Born in Paris in 1897, Puiforcat joined the French Army during World War I. After returning a hero with the *Croix de Guerre* in 1918, he went to work in his father's silver workshop. By 1921 Jean's work was recognized for its skillful, geometric designs, and by 1925 he was cited at the Paris Exposition as a master of his craft. He was represented in a number of pavilions and interiors at that fair, and a separate area was devoted to his work.

Because art of the goldsmith and silversmith has always played an important role in the history of French art, it is only natural that such luxurious materials should be used to a great extent during the 1920s, when master craftsmen strove to satisfy the extravagant tastes of their wealthy patrons.

Although a number of acclaimed artists worked in precious metals, it is Jean Puiforcat who is considered to be the greatest French silversmith of the century. His work is characterized by an almost total lack of ornament that allows the slick, smooth surfaces of silver to contrast with elements of wood and stone carved in the same geometric forms. In this case, the circular handles of the coffee pot, teapot, creamer, and sugar echo both the circular shape of the pieces themselves and the design of the rosewood tray. Nowhere are we aware of the hand of the silversmith, who would traditionally apply elaborate flourishes and other fancy designs. Instead, Puiforcat presents only smooth, unembellished surfaces.

Puiforcat felt that by applying the harmony and geometry of the ancient Greek mathematicians he could achieve the ideal in design. By studying the Platonic theory regarding the correspondence of geometric shapes to the four elements (tetrahedron/fire, octahedron/air, icosahedron/water, and cube/earth), Puiforcat felt he had found the key to art. He based the relationship of his forms to one another on the ideal arithmetic proportions, "the golden section, without which" he observed, "any of the ancients could not work. And each time they disregarded it, decadence. The end of Egypt, the end of Greece, of Rome."[58] This ideal mathematical proportion is especially apparent in Puiforcat's drawings.

As the great French jeweler Jean Fouquet observed, "the secret of Jean Puiforcat . . . is the construction and rational accord of the object and its function; it is the harmony of proportions of the volumes and the materials which join the silver according to the best traditions (ivory, precious stones, lapis, et cetera)."[59]

PROVENANCE: Primavera Gallery, New York, 1974.

EXHIBITED: In the Service of Tea, Cooper-Hewitt Museum, New York, August 7-October 28, 1984.

58. Jean Puiforcat: Orfèvre Sculpteur (Paris: Flammarion, 1951), p. 19.
59. Puiforcat, p. 30.

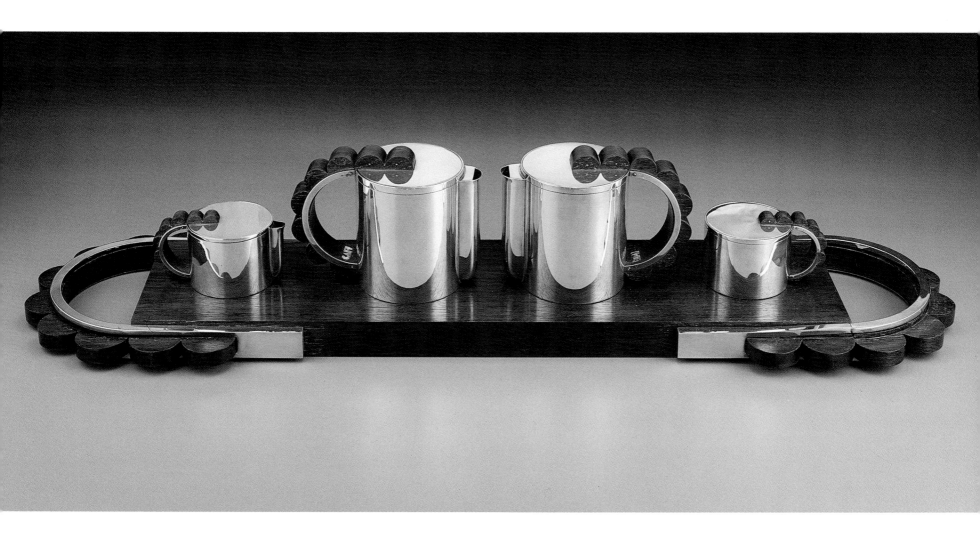

Checklist

Late 19th and Early 20th Century Decorative Arts
at the Virginia Museum of Fine Arts, Richmond

All objects on the following list indicated as being gifts from Sydney and Frances Lewis were originally part of their personal collection. Those objects identified by the prefix SLD were purchased by the Lewises for their personal collection and remain in their possession.

Additionally, a great number of objects were given to the Museum by other generous benefactors. Their names are listed with the objects they contributed.

Finally, certain other works were purchased by the Virginia Museum through the Sydney and Frances Lewis Art Nouveau Fund, the Arthur and Margaret Glasgow Fund, the Adolph D. and Wilkins C. Williams Fund, the Council Graphic Arts Fund, and the Mary Morton Parsons Collection of American Decorative Arts Fund. The objects are so designated on the list.

This list is arranged in alphabetical order by the last name of the designer. Those items for which the artist is not known are listed at the end, under the heading "Artist Unknown," according to country of origin.

Measurements are given in centimeters, then inches; height precedes width.

J. Abschlag
German (dates unknown)

1. Statuette, *Woman with Sword*, ca. 1900

    Bronze
    27.3 × 8.9 × 6.1 (10¾ × 3½ × 2⅜)
    Gift of Sydney and Frances Lewis, 85.327

Rose Adler
French (1892-1959)

2. Table, ca. 1926

    Ebony, sharkskin, metal, enamel
    75.5 × 70.5 × 39.7 (29¾ × 27¾ × 15⅝)
    Gift of Sydney and Frances Lewis, 85.93
    Catalogue no. 81

Rose Adler
French (1892-1959)
and
Marcel Vertes
French
(1895-1962)

3. Book, *Chéri* by Colette, 1929-31

    Morocco leather binding, engravings, 48/100
    28 × 23 × 4.8 (11 × 9 × 1⅞)
    Gift of Sydney and Frances Lewis, 85.37a/b
    Catalogue no. 68

Betzy Ählström
Swedish, 1860-1944
for
Reijmyre Glasbruk
Swedish (Reijmyre; founded 1810)

4. Waterlily Vase, ca. 1905

    Marquetry and applied glass, internally decorated
    21 × 14.5 diam. (8¼ × 5¹¹⁄₁₆ diam.)
    Museum Purchase, The Glasgow Fund, 85.32

242

Amphora Porzellanfabrik
Austrian (founded 1892)

5. Bowl, ca. 1900

   Ceramic
   4.4 × 14.2 × 10.2 (1¾ × 5⅝ × 4)
   Gift of Mrs. Peter Knowles, Richmond, Va., 84.10

6. Vase, ca. 1920

   Ceramic
   36.2 × 21 diam. (14¼ × 8¼)
   Gift of Mrs. Peter Knowles, Richmond, Va., 84.9

Gabriel Argy-Rousseau
French (1885-1953)

7. Vase, ca. 1900

   Pâte-de-verre
   6.7 × 8.9 diam. (2⅝ × 3½)
   Gift of Sydney and Frances Lewis, 85.204

Arnould
French (dates unknown)

8. Walking Cane, ca. 1900

   Metal, wood
   86.4 × 3.5 × 4.5 (34 × 1⅜ × 1¾)
   Gift of Sydney and Frances Lewis, 85.264

Charles Robert Ashbee
English (1863-1942)
for
Guild of Handicraft
English (London; 1888-1908)

9. Buckle/Cloak Clasp, ca. 1902

   Silver, enamel, amethysts
   6.35 × 13.8 × 1.75 (2½ × 5⅐₁₆ × 1¹⁄₁₆)
   Gift of the Sydney and Frances Lewis Foundation,
   85.223a/b

Emile Just Bachelet
French (1892-?)

10. *Venus et l'Amour*, ca. 1934

    Ivory, gilt bronze, marble
    124.4 × 33 diam. (49 × 13)
    Gift of the Sydney and Frances Lewis
    Foundation, 85.314
    Catalogue no. 99

Hannah B. Barlow
English (1851-1916)
for
Doulton & Co.
English (London; founded 1815)

11. Biscuit Barrel, 1881
    Stoneware
    11.7 × 14.3 (4⅝ × 5⅝)
    Gift of Sydney and Frances Lewis, 85.46

12. Jardinière, 1884

    Stoneware
    11.4 × 14 diam. (4½ × 5½)
    Gift of Sydney and Frances Lewis, 85.45

L. Barthélémy
French (dates unknown)

13. Statuette, ca. 1900

    Bronze, ivory, marble
    21.3 × 14 × 3.8 (8⅜ x 5½ x 1½)
    Gift of Sydney and Frances Lewis, 85.315

Leopold Bauer
Austrian (1872-1938)

14. Cabinet, 1900

    Sycamore, maple, marquetry, brass, felt
    90.1 × 45.6 × 67.2 (35½ × 18 × 26½)
    Gift of Sydney and Frances Lewis, 85.79

Peter Behrens
German (1868-1940)

15. Dining-Room Chair, 1902

    Oak, upholstery
    98.4 × 45 × 46.3 (38¾ × 17¾ × 18¼)
    Gift of Sydney and Frances Lewis, 85.138
    Catalogue no. 34

Peter Behrens
German (1868-1940)
for
Gebrüder Bauscher
German (Weiden; dates unknown)

16. Pair of Serving Dishes and Covers, 1901

    Porcelain
    11.4 × 29.2 × 23.5 each (4½ × 11½ × 9¼)
    Gift of the Sydney and Frances Lewis
    Foundation, 85.54 .1a/b, .2a/b

Franz Bergman
Austrian (dates unknown)

17. Statuette, *Dancing Girl*, ca. 1900

    Bronze, marble
    18.4 × 8.9 × 7.6 (7¼ × 3½ × 3)
    SLD 375

Antoine Bofill
Spanish (dates unknown)

18. Lamp, ca. 1900

    Bronze
    55.2 × 17.8 × 15.2 (21¾ × 7 × 6)
    Gift of Sydney and Frances Lewis, 85.173

Boin-Taburet
French (Paris; founded 1870)

19. Bowl, 1925

    Silver, lapis, ivory
    12.7 × 38.1 × 25.4 (5 × 15 × 10)
    Gift of Sydney and Frances Lewis, 85.294

Auguste Bonaz
French (dates unknown)
after design by
Paul Iribe
French (1883-1935)

20. Necklace, ca. 1925

    Bakelite
    12.1 × 14.6 × .63 (8⁵/₁₆ × 5¾ × ¼)
    SLD 665

Robert Bonfils
French (1886-1972)

21. Poster Design for Paris Exposition, 1925

    Lithograph
    59.7 × 39.7 (23½ × 15⅝)
    Gift of Mrs. Jean Brown, Tyringham, Mass.
    73.71.3

Pierre Bonnard
French (1867-1947)

22. Poster, *La Revue Blanche*, 1894

    Lithograph
    78.8 × 60.9 (31 × 24)
    Museum Purchase, The Sydney and Frances
    Lewis Art Nouveau Fund, 74.5.2

Bonni
French, (dates unknown)

23. Stickpin, ca. 1900

    Gold, diamond
    7.6 × 1.6 × 1.6 (3 × ⅝ × ⅝)
    Gift of Sydney and Frances Lewis, 85.230

Hyppolyte Boulanger (pseudonym H. Gray)
French (1858-?)

24. *Le Tréport-Mers*, ca. 1900

    Lithograph
    127.0 × 92.7 (50½ × 36½)
    Museum Purchase, The Arthur and Margaret
    Glasgow Fund, 72.9.2

Marcel Bouraine
French (active ca. 1918-1935)

25. *Amazon*, ca. 1928

    Silvered and patinated bronze
    14.6 × 37 × 5.1 (5¾ × 14½ × 2)
    Gift of Sydney and Frances Lewis, 85.316

Will Bradley
American (1868-1962)

26. Cover, *The Chapbook, Thanksgiving Number*, 1894

    Lithograph
    50.8 × 34.9 (20 × 13¾)
    Museum Purchase, The Sydney and Frances
    Lewis Art Nouveau Fund, 74.5.1

Edgar Brandt
French (1880-1960)

27. Letter Opener, ca. 1925

    Bronze
    27.6 × 3.1 × 6 (10⅞ × 1³/₁₆ × ¼)
    SLD 166

28. Pair of Andirons, ca. 1920

    Bronze
    66 × 91.4 × 48.3 each (26 × 36 × 19)
    Gift of Sydney and Frances Lewis, 85.265.1/3

29. Pair of Gates, ca. 1929

    Wrought iron
    106.7 × 182.9 (42 × 72)
    Gift of Sydney and Frances Lewis, 85.277.1/2
    Catalogue no. 93

Sir Frank Brangwyn
English (1867-1956)
for
Alexander Morton & Co.
Scottish (1862-1984)

30. Carpet, ca. 1898

    Wool
    408.9 × 787.4 (169 × 310)
    SLD 40

Louis Brouhot
French (dates unknown)

31. Table, ca. 1900

    Mahogany, satinwood, exotic wood veneers and
    inlays, marble, bronze
    102.8 × 119.4 × 52 (40½ × 47 × 20½)
    Gift of Sydney and Frances Lewis, 85.353

Ivan Da Silva Bruhns
French (dates unknown)

32. Carpet, ca. 1930

    Tufted wool
    350 × 260 (138 × 102)
    SLD 811

33. Carpet, ca. 1925

    Wool
    145. × 73.5 (57 × 29)
    SLD 795

34. Carpet, ca. 1925

    Wool
    335.2 × 548.6 (132 × 216)
    SLD 658

35. Carpet, ca. 1926

    Wool
    293.5 × 402.5 (115½ × 158½)
    Gift of the Sydney and Frances Lewis
    Foundation, 85.520

Carlo Bugatti
Italian (1855-1940)

36. Chair, ca. 1902

    Parchment over wood, copper, paint
    88.9 × 41.8 × 58.3 (35 × 16½ × 21)
    Museum Purchase, The Sydney and Frances
    Lewis Art Nouveau Fund, 72.10
    Catalogue no. 32

37. Table, ca. 1900

    Ebonized walnut, tin, parchment
    73 × 55.2 × 55.2 (28¾ × 21¾ × 21¾)
    Gift of Sydney and Frances Lewis, 85.141

Buval
French, (dates unknown)
for
A. Lontermer and Company
French (Limoges, dates unknown)

38. Creamer and Sugar, ca. 1907

    Porcelain, porcelain enamels
    Creamer: 7.3 × 9.5 × 10.1 (2⅞ × 3¾ × 4)
    Sugar: 9.5 × 14.3 × 10.1 (3¾ × 5⅝ × 4)
    Gift of Sydney and Frances Lewis, 85.50.1, 2a/b

Caillet
French (dates unknown)

39. Cigarette Holder, ca. 1930

    Jade, white gold, diamonds, Bakelite
    14.9 × 1.8 × 1.8 (5⅞ × ½ × ½)
    Gift of Mr. Furman Hebb, New York, 84.62

E.F. Caldwell & Co.
American (dates unknown)

40. Clock, ca. 1925

    Crystal, lapis, carnelian, onyx or sardonyx,
    enamel, gilt bronze
    31.1 × 20.3 × 11.8 (12¼ × 8 × 4⅝)
    SLD 774

François Rupert Carabin
French (1862-1932)

41. *Loïe Fuller*, ca. 1896-97

    Bronze
    18.5 × 20.3 × 8.9 (7¼ × 8 × 3½)
    Museum Purchase, The Sydney and Frances
    Lewis Art Nouveau Fund, 78.11

42. *Loïe Fuller*, ca. 1896-97

    Bronze
    19 × 19 × 12.7 (7½ × 7½ × 5)
    Museum Purchase, The Sydney and Frances
    Lewis Art Nouveau Fund, 78.12

43. *Loïe Fuller*, ca. 1896-97

    Bronze
    20.3 × 14 × 14.3 (8 × 5½ × 5⅝)
    Museum Purchase, The Sydney and Frances
    Lewis Art Nouveau Fund, 78.13

44. Washstand, 1897-98

    Walnut, stoneware, pewter
    178.4 × 88.6 × 32.4 (70¼ × 34⅞ × 12¾)
    Gift of Sydney and Frances Lewis, 85.94
    Catalogue no. 8

Louis Cartier
French (1875-1942)

45. Pendant, 1921

    Jade, onyx, rubies, pearls, emeralds, sapphires,
    diamonds, silver
    10.5 × 2.86 diam. (4⅛ × 1⅛)
    Gift of Sydney and Frances Lewis, 85.234
    Catalogue no. 64

46. Purse, ca. 1925

    Platinum, diamonds, lacquer, enamel, crystal
    16.5 × 15.9 × 2.54 (6½ × 6¼ × 1)
    Gift of Sydney and Frances Lewis, 85.231

47. Watch, ca. 1914

    Gold, glass
    7.3 × 4 × 1.1 (excluding strap) (2⅞ × 1⁹⁄₁₆ × ⁷⁄₁₆)
    Gift of Sydney and Frances Lewis, 85.232

Pierre Chareau
French (1883-1950)

48. Club Armchair, ca. 1925

    Rosewood, metal, upholstery
    60 × 70 × 80 (23⅝ × 27⁹⁄₁₆ × 31½)
    Gift of Sydney and Frances Lewis, 85.95
    Catalogue no. 75

49. Armchair, 1925

    Bleached mahogany, suede
    83.2 × 67.3 × 62.2 (32¾ × 26½ × 24½)
    Gift of Sydney and Frances Lewis, 85.96

Jules Cheret
French (1836-1932)

50. Poster, *Benzo-Moteur*, ca. 1900

    Color lithograph
    123.2 × 88.2 (48½ × 34¾)
    Museum Purchase, The Arthur and Margaret
    Glasgow Fund, 72.9.3

Serge Chermayeff
Russian (born 1900)

51. Cabinet, ca. 1930

    Gold leaf over wood, lacquer
    128.3 × 85.7 × 34.3 (51½ × 33¾ × 13½)
    Gift of Sydney and Frances Lewis, 85.97

Albert Cheuret
French (dates unknown)

52. Clock, ca. 1930

    Silvered bronze, onyx
    15.9 × 41.9 × 10.1 (6¼ × 16½ × 4)
    Gift of Sydney and Frances Lewis, 85.218
    Catalogue no. 96

53. Floor Lamp, ca. 1925

Silvered bronze, alabaster
174.6 × 59 diam. (68¾ × 23¼)
Gift of the Sydney and Frances Lewis
Foundation, 85.166

Demetre Chiparus
Roumanian (dates unknown)

54. *Ballets Russes*, ca. 1925-30

Cold-painted bronze, ivory, marble
59 × 29.2 × 15.2 (23¼ × 11½ × 6)
Gift of Sydney and Frances Lewis, 85.331

55. *Dancer*, ca. 1925-30

Ivory, bronze
56.3 × 31.9 × 9.2 (22³/₁₆ × 12⅝ × 3⅝)
Gift of Sydney and Frances Lewis, 85.336
Catalogue no. 78

56. *Dourga*, ca. 1925-30

Cold-painted bronze, ivory
63. × 16. × 12. (24¾ × 6¼ × 4¾)
Gift of Sydney and Frances Lewis, 85.337

57. *Eternal Friends*, 1931

Cold-painted bronze, ivory, onyx
42 × 42.5 × 9.8 (16½ × 16¾ × 3⅞)
Gift of Sydney and Frances Lewis, 85.332

58. *Girl Carrying a Doll*, ca. 1925-30

Silvered bronze, ivory
25.4 × 10.3 diam. (10 × 4)
Gift of Sydney and Frances Lewis, 85.335

59. *Innocence*, ca. 1925-30

Ivory, onyx
15.6 × 4.1 × 4.1 (6⅛ × 1⅝ × 1⅝)
Gift of Sydney and Frances Lewis, 85.334

60. *Snake Dancer*, ca. 1925-30

Cold-painted bronze, ivory, onyx
51.1 × 23.8 × 14 (20⅛ × 9½ × 5½)
Gift of Sydney and Frances Lewis, 85.333

Georges-Jules-Victor Clairin
French (1843-1919)

61. *Portrait of Sarah Bernhardt*, 1888
Pencil on paper
54 × 36.8 (21½ × 14½)
Museum Purchase, Council Graphic Arts Fund,
72.24

Clinton Co.
English, 20th century

62. Pair of Carpets, ca. 1930

Wool
155 × 91.5 each (61 × 36)
SLD 37-38

Marcel Coard
French (1889-1975)

63. Bedroom Suite
Designed for the artist/poet Jean Cocteau, 1929

Leather, pine, mirrored glass, brass
Bed: 88.9 × 217.8 × 153.7 (35 × 85¾ × 60½)
Armoire: 189.9 × 157.5 × 50.8 (74¾ × 63 × 20)
Desk: 76.2 × 99. × 68.5 (30 × 39 × 27)
Pair of Night Tables: 52.7 × 50.2 × 32.4 each
(20¾ × 19¾ × 12¾)
Gift of Sydney and Frances Lewis, 85.98.1/5

64. Sofa, before 1929

Rosewood, ivory, leather
87.6 × 243.8 × 91.5 (34½ × 96 × 36)
Gift of Sydney and Frances Lewis, 85.99
Catalogue no. 88

Edward Colonna
German-American (1862-1948)

65. Chair, ca. 1899

Carved maple, velvet
98.4 × 61 × 53.3 (38¾ × 24 × 21)
Gift of Sydney and Frances Lewis, 85.139.2
Catalogue no. 20

66. Settee, ca. 1899

Carved maple, velvet
99.7 × 113.6 × 53.3 (39¼ × 44¾ × 21)
Gift of Sydney and Frances Lewis, 85.139.1
Catalogue no. 20

Auguste Daum
French (1853-1909)
and
Antonin Daum
French (1864-1930)
for
Daum Frères
French (Nancy; founded 1878)

67. Lamp, ca. 1896

Cameo glass, bronze
35.4 × 17.7 diam. (15½ × 7)
Gift of Sydney and Frances Lewis, 85.167 a/b

68. Vase, ca. 1910

Acid-etched cameo glass
22.9 × 15.8 diam. (9 × 6¼)
Gift of Sydney and Frances Lewis, 85.206

69. Vase, ca. 1900

Acid-etched, wheel-faceted cameo glass
17.7 × 19 diam. (7 × 7½)
Gift of Sydney and Frances Lewis, 85.207

70. Vase, ca. 1900

Mould-blown, acid-etched, overlaid glass
28.2 × 11.4 diam. (11⅛ × 4½)
Gift of Sydney and Frances Lewis, 85.205

D'Avesn (?)
French (dates unknown)

71. Vase, ca. 1925

    Mould-blown glass
    22 × 30.5 diam. (8⅝ × 12)
    Gift of Sydney and Frances Lewis, 85.208

Frédéric J. Debon
French (dates unknown)

72. Pair of Jardinières ca. 1900

    Gilt bronze
    41.9 × 26.7 × 18.4 each (16½ × 10½ × 7¼)
    Gift of Sydney and Frances Lewis, 85.266.1/2

François-Emile Decorchemont
French (1880-1971)

73. Vase, ca. 1925

    Mould-blown glass
    11.6 × 9.5 diam. (4⁹⁄₁₆ × 3¾)
    Gift of Sydney and Frances Lewis, 85.209

Georges de Feure
French (1868-1943)

74. Box with Lid, ca. 1900-01

    Porcelain
    Box: 5.7 × 17.8 × 17.8 (2¼ × 7 × 7)
    Lid: 6.4 × 19.0 × 19.0 (2½ × 7½ × 7½)
    Museum Purchase, The Sydney and Frances
    Lewis Art Nouveau Fund, 77.48 a/b

75. *Isita*, ca. 1900

    Lithograph
    116.8 × 87.7 (46 × 34½)
    Museum Purchase, The Sydney and Frances
    Lewis Art Nouveau Fund, 76.5

76. Window, 1901-02

    Stained glass, lead, wood
    200. × 90.9 (78¾ × 35¹³⁄₁₆)
    Gift of Sydney and Frances Lewis, 85.349
    Catalogue no. 31

Félix Del Marle
French (1889-1952)

77. Suite for Madame B., 1926

    Painted wood, frosted glass, metal, paint,
    upholstery
    Sofa: 75. × 168. × 70. (29½ × 66⅛ × 27⁹⁄₁₆)
    Bar/Coffee Table: 56. × 67. × 41. (22¹⁄₁₆ × 26⅜
    × 16⅛)
    Armchair: 62.9 × 83.8 × 76.5 (24¾ × 33 × 30⅛)
    Armchair: 62.9 × 83.5 × 76.4 (24¾ × 32⅞ ×
    30¹⁄₁₆)
    Armchair: 62.9 × 83.8 × 76.8 (24¾ × 33 × 30¼)
    Chandeliers (2) each: 55. × 67. × 52. (22¹⁄₁₆ × 26⅜
    × 20½)
    Lamp: 165. × 45. × 25. (64¹⁵⁄₁₆ × 17¾ × 9⅞)
    Gift of Sydney and Frances Lewis, 85.101.1/8
    Catalogue no. 79

Donald Deskey
American (1894-?)

78. Mirror, ca. 1929

    Lacquer, steel, mirrored glass
    62.2 × 31.7 × 2.5 (24½ × 12½ × 1)
    Gift of the Sydney and Frances Lewis
    Foundation, 85.175

79. Three-Panel Screen, ca. 1929

    Oil paint on canvas, metal leaf, wood
    197.5 × 149.2 × 2.9 (77¾ × 58¾ × 1¼)
    Gift of the Sydney and Frances Lewis
    Foundation, 85.62
    Catalogue no. 92

Jean Desprès
French (1889-?)

80. Brooch, ca. 1925

    Silver, lapis lazuli
    5.7 × 1.9 × .635 (2¼ × ¾ × ¼)
    Gift of Sydney and Frances Lewis, 85.235

E. Diot
French (active ca. 1900-05)

81. Cabinet, 1903

    Mahogany, other woods, glass
    182.9 × 109.2 × 42 (72 × 43 × 16½)
    SLD 243

Marion Dorn
English (1899-1964)

82. Carpet, ca. 1930

    Wool
    198.1 × 144.8 (78 × 57)
    SLD 203

83. Carpet, ca. 1930

    Wool
    182.9 × 142.2 (72 × 56)
    SLD 204

Doulton & Co.
English (London; 1901-1956)

84. Set of Six Cups and Saucers, 1924-26

    Enameled porcelain
    Cups: 5.1 × 6.4 × 4.8 (2 × 2½ × 1⅞)
    Saucers: .95 × 9.5 diam. (⅜ × 3¾)
    Gift of Sydney and Frances Lewis,
    85.47.7a/b-13a/b

85. Six Dinner Plates, 1924-26

    Enameled porcelain
    2.2 × 27.6 × 27.6 each (7/8 × 10⅞ × 10⅞)
    Gift of Sydney and Frances Lewis, 85.47.1/6

Drobil
French (dates unknown)

86. Pin Tray, ca. 1900

    Bronze
    3.2 × 16.5 × 9.5 (1¼ × 6½ × 3¾)
    Gift of Sydney and Frances Lewis, 85.267

Duffner & Kimberly Company
American (ca. 1900-1916)

87. Waterlily Lamp, ca. 1907

Bronze, glass
62.2 × 50.8 diam. shade (24½ × 20)
Gift of Mrs. Peter Knowles, Richmond, Va.
79.96 a/c

Maurice Dufrêne
French (1876-1955)

88. Box, ca. 1899-1905

Tooled leather, bronze
12.4 × 8.9 × 8.9 (4⅞ × 3½ × 3½)
Museum Purchase, The Sydney and Frances
Lewis Art Nouveau Fund, 78.69 a/b

Attributed to Maurice Dufrêne
French (1876-1955)

89. Carpet, ca. 1925

Wool
305. diam. (120)
Gift of Sydney and Frances Lewis, 85.341

Dunaime
French (dates unknown)

90. Three Ashtrays, ca. 1925

Bronze and enamel
2.5 × 15.2 × 8.2 each (1 × 6 × 3¼)
Gift of Sydney and Frances Lewis, 85.268.1/3

Jean Dunand
French (1877-1942)

91. Mirror, 1927

Lacquer, mirrored glass
100 × 63.5 × 7.4 (39⅜ × 25 × 2⅞)
Gift of Sydney and Frances Lewis, 85.176.2

92. Mirror, 1927

Lacquer, mirrored glass
100 × 72.5 × 8.6 (39⅜ × 28½ × 3⅜)
Gift of Sydney and Frances Lewis, 85.176.1

93. Pair of Chairs, ca. 1925

Lacquered wood, upholstery, silver
81.3 × 71.1 × 76.8 each (32 × 28 × 30¼)
Gift of Sydney and Frances Lewis, 85.102.1/2

94. Table, ca. 1925

Lacquered wood, eggshell
51. × 80. × 52. (20 × 31½ × 20½)
Gift of Sydney and Frances Lewis, 85.103

95. Table, ca. 1925

Lacquered wood
48.2 × 80. (19 × 31½)
Gift of Sydney and Frances Lewis, 85.105

96. Table, ca. 1925

Lacquered wood, eggshell
69.8 × 59.6 × 35.5 (27½ × 23½ × 14)
Gift of Sydney and Frances Lewis, 85.104
Catalogue no. 73

97. Vase, ca. 1925

Copper, lacquer, eggshell
15.2 × 7.5 diam. (6 × 2¹⁵/₁₆)
Gift of Sydney and Frances Lewis, 85.258

See also:
Eugene Printz and Jean Dunand, *Bookcase*
checklist no. 305/catalogue no. 85

Pierre Legrain and Jean Dunand, *Cabinet*
checklist no. 222/catalogue no. 89

François-Louis Schmied and Jean Dunand, *Book,*
Ruth et Booz checklist no. 349/catalogue no. 94

Harvey Ellis
See: Gustav Stickley/Craftsman Workshops
checklist nos. 380-387

George Grant Elmslie
American (1871-1952)

98. Two Balusters, ca. 1899-1904

Cast iron
100.3 × 25.4 × 2.5 each (39½ × 10 × 1)
Gift of the Art Institute of Chicago, 73.69.1/2

99. Window, ca. 1916
Made for a residence on Seymour Street,
Minneapolis, Minnesota

Leaded glass, oak
125.1 × 26.7 (49¼ × 10½)
Museum Purchase, The Sydney and Frances
Lewis Art Nouveau Fund, 80.4

Camille Fauré
French (1872-1956)

100. Vase, ca. 1925

Enamel on copper
20.3 × 13.3 diam. (8 × 5¼)
Gift of Sydney and Frances Lewis, 85.59

101. Vase, ca. 1925

Enamel on copper
15.9 × 11.4 diam. (6¼ × 4½)
Gift of Sydney and Frances Lewis, 85.61

102. Vase, ca. 1925

Enamel on copper
11.4 × 13.1 diam. (4½ × 5⅜)
Gift of Sydney and Frances Lewis, 85.58

103. Vase, ca. 1925

Enamel on copper
12.7 × 12 diam. (5 × 4¾)
Gift of Sydney and Frances Lewis, 85.60
Catalogue no. 74

Alexander Fisher
English (1864-1936)

104. *The Graiae*, 1898

Enamel, silver
15.9 × 19 × .95 (6¼ × 7½ × ⅜)
Gift of Sydney and Frances Lewis, 85.57

Paul Follot
French (1877-1941)

105. Pair of Andirons, ca. 1900

Gilt bronze
22.5 × 38.1 × 30.5 each (8⅞ × 15 × 12)
Gift of Sydney and Frances Lewis, 85.269.1/2

Jean Louis Forain
French (1852-1931)

106. Poster, *Premier Salon des Humoristes, Paris*, 1904

Lithograph
106 × 78.1 (41¾ × 30¾)
Museum Purchase, The Sydney and Frances
Lewis Art Nouveau Fund, 73.16

Georges Fouquet
French (1862-1957)

107. Brooch, 1904

Gold, enamel, opal, unidentified ivory-colored
stones, engraved glass, diamonds, pearls
9.5 × 19.6 × 1.27 (3¾ × 7¾ × ½)
Gift of Sydney and Frances Lewis, 85.242
Catalogue no. 49

108. Comb, ca. 1900

18-carat gold, tortoiseshell, mother-of-pearl,
freshwater pearls
14.9 × 9.8 × 1.3 (5⅞ × 3⅞ × ½)
Gift of Sydney and Frances Lewis, 85.240

109. Necklace, 1924

Rock crystal, diamond, white gold, platinum
38.1 × 24.1 × 3.2 (15 × 9½ × 1¼)
Gift of Sydney and Frances Lewis, 85.241

110. Pendant, ca. 1900
Gold, enamel, diamonds, pearls
6.51 × 3.65 × .48 (2⁹⁄₁₆ × 1⁷⁄₁₆ × ³⁄₁₆)
Gift of Sydney and Frances Lewis, 85.238

111. Ring, ca. 1900

Plique-à-jour enamel, yellow gold, diamond,
enamel
2.54 × 2.22 diam. (1 × ⅞)
Gift of Sydney and Frances Lewis, 85.239

See also:
Alphonse Mucha and Georges Fouquet, *Adornment
for the Bodice*, checklist no. 276/catalogue no. 18

Jean Fouquet
French (1899-?)

112. Bracelet, ca. 1928-9

White gold, diamonds, jade
2.7 × 20.3 × .9 (1¹⁄₁₆ × 8 × ⅜)
Gift of Sydney and Frances Lewis, 85.237
Catalogue no. 87

113. Pendant, ca. 1925

Silver, enamel
8.73 × 4.13 × .48 (3⁷⁄₁₆ × 1⅝ × ³⁄₁₆)
Gift of Sydney and Frances Lewis, 85.236

Jean-Michel Frank
French (1895-1941)

114. Pair of Armchairs, ca. 1927

Sharkskin over wood, upholstery
67.3 × 67.9 × 73.6 (26½ × 26¾ × 29) 67.3 × 68.9
× 73.6 (26½ × 27⅛ × 29)
Gift of Sydney and Frances Lewis, 85.106.1/2
Catalogue no. 84

115. Table, ca. 1927

Sharkskin over wood
50.8 × 60.3 diam. (20 × 23¾)
Gift of Sydney and Frances Lewis, 85.107
Catalogue no. 84

Fulper Pottery Company
American (Flemington, New Jersey; active 1858-1929)

116. Handled Jar, 1910-1912/14

Ceramic
12.1 × 15.2 diam. (4¾ × 6)
Gift of Mrs. Peter Knowles, Richmond, Va.,
84.11

117. Mushroom Lamp, ca. 1910

Pottery, glass
45.7 × 33. diam. (18 × 13)
Gift of Sydney and Frances Lewis, 85.150 a/b
Catalogue no. 58

Eugène Gaillard
French (1862-1933)

118. Armchair, ca. 1900

Walnut, leather
95.2 × 61. × 74.9 (37½ × 24 × 29½)
Gift of Sydney and Frances Lewis, 85.109.1

119. Chair, ca. 1900

Walnut, leather
94. × 41.9 × 45.7 (37 × 16½ × 18)
Gift of Sydney and Frances Lewis, 85.109.2

120. Lectern, ca. 1900

Macassar ebony, brass
142.6 to 169.9 (adjustable) × 52.1 × 52.1 (56⅛
to 66⅞ × 20½ × 20½)
Gift of the Sydney and Frances Lewis
Foundation, 85.108

121. Nesting Tables, ca. 1900

Pear, walnut
71. × 69.8 × 69.8 (28 × 27½ × 27½)
Gift of Sydney and Frances Lewis, 85.110 a/e

122. Tea Table with Removable Tray, ca. 1902

Mahogany, brass
Tray: 1.9 × 41.5 × 41.5 (¾ × 16⅜ × 16⅜)
Table: 109.8 × 43.2 × 43.2 (43¼ × 17 × 17)
Gift of Sydney and Frances Lewis, 85.111 a/b
Catalogue no. 36

Emile Gallé
French (1846-1904)

123. Bowl, ca. 1900

Marquetry glass
9.9 × 10.8 diam. (3⅞ × 4¼)
Museum Purchase, The Sydney and Frances
Lewis Art Nouveau Fund, 73.12

124. Box with Lid, 1890-1900

Acid-etched cameo glass
5.7 × 10.1 (2¼ × 4)
Gift of Mr. and Mrs. Saul Viener, Richmond,
Va., 80.26 a/b

125. Chandelier, ca. 1900

Bronze, blown glass
45.7 × 75. × 75. (18 × 29½ × 29½)
Gift of Sydney and Frances Lewis, 85.148 a/d

126. Dragonfly Etagère, ca. 1900

Burl elm, maple, exotic woods, mirrored glass
135.8 × 83.8 × 43.8 (53½ × 33 × 17¼)
Museum Purchase, The Sydney and Frances
Lewis Art Nouveau Fund, 73.60
Catalogue no. 19

127. Ladle, ca. 1900

Marquetry, acid-etched, engraved, internally
decorated glass
14.6 × 25.4 × 10.2 (5¾ × 10 × 4)
Museum Purchase, The Sydney and Frances
Lewis Art Nouveau Fund, 75.6
Catalogue no. 24

128. Liqueur Set, ca. 1900

Acid-etched cameo glass
Decanters (2) each: 20.6 × 9.5 diam. (8⅛ × 3¾)
Liqueur glasses (10) each: 5.4 × 4.1 diam. (2⅛
× 1⅝)
Gift of Sydney and Frances Lewis, 85.203.1a/b,
.2 a/b, .3/12

129. Sideboard, 1903

Walnut, oak, chestnut, various fruitwoods, gilt
iron, glass
271.7 × 210.8 × 69.9 (107 × 83 × 27½)
Museum Purchase, The Sydney and Frances
Lewis Art Nouveau Fund, 77.4
Catalogue no. 39

130. Table, ca. 1900

Wood, inlay, bronze, mother-of-pearl
57.4 × 119.4 × 74.3 (62 × 47 × 29¼)
Gift of Sydney and Frances Lewis, 85.339

131. Vase, ca. 1900

Acid-etched cameo glass
7.9 × 6 diam. (3⅛ × 2⅜)
Gift of Sydney and Frances Lewis, 85.202

132. Vase, ca. 1900

Acid-etched cameo glass
18.4 × 6.7 diam. (7¼ × 2⅝)
Gift of Sydney and Frances Lewis, 85.201

133. Vase, ca. 1900

Ceramic
58.4 × 40.6 diam. (23 × 16)
Gift of the Sydney and Frances Lewis
Foundation, 85.51

134. Vitrine, ca. 1900

Teak, burl ash, maple, walnut, oak, glass, gilt
bronze
189.2 × 82.9 × 54.6 (74½ × 32⅝ × 21½)
Gift of Sydney and Frances Lewis, 85.85

Emile Gallé
French (1846-1904)
and
Ernst Cardeilhac
French (active from 1860)

135. Vase, ca. 1900

Silver, engraved, acid-etched glass
23.8 × 18 × 12.7 (9⅜ × 7⅛ × 5)
Gift of Sydney and Frances Lewis, 85.200

Simon Gate
Swedish (1883-1945)
for
Orrefors Glassworks
Swedish (Smaland; founded 1898)

136. Graal Bowl, 1917

Acid-etched, cased, blown glass
24 × 30.5 diam (9½ × 12)
Museum Purchase, The Glasgow Fund, 85.33

Antonio Gaudí y Cornet
Spanish (1852-1926)

137. Etagère, ca. 1900

Mahogany
130 × 30 × 30 (51½ × 19¾ × 19¾)
Gift of the Sydney and Frances Lewis
Foundation, 85.147

Gerdago
Spanish ? (dates unknown)

138. *Dancer*, ca. 1925

  Cold-painted bronze, ivory, onyx
  30.8 × 16.5 × 9.2 (12⅛ × 6½ × 3⅝)
  Gift of Sydney and Frances Lewis, 85.338

Alberto Giacometti
Swiss (1901-1966)
and
Diego Giacometti
Swiss (born 1902)

139. Standing Lamp (Woman's Head), ca. 1930

  Bronze
  154.9 × 22.2 diam. base (61 × 8¾)
  Gift of Sydney and Frances Lewis, 85.174

Mary Gilmour
Scottish (active 1893-1942)

140. Desk Set, ca. 1900

  Brass
  Inkwell: 8.2 × 9.5 × 9.5 (3¼ × 3¾ × 3¾)
  Tray: 1.2 × 22.8 × 8.9 (½ × 9 × 3¾)
  Letter opener: 3.8 × 19.6 (1½ × 7¾)
  Gift of Dr. and Mrs. Simon Russi, Alexandria,
  Va., in Memory of Their Parents, 80.64.1/3

Gorham Company
American (Providence, Rhode Island; founded 1818)

141. Pocket Watch, ca. 1935

  Silver, enamel, Longines clockworks
  5.7 × 4.1 × 1.1 (2¼ × 1⅝ × ⁷⁄₁₆)
  Gift of Mr. Furman Hebb, New York, 84.67

Gouda Zuid Holland Pottery Company
Dutch (Arnhem, Netherlands; 20th century)

142. Bowl, ca. 1900

  Ceramic
  19.7 × 27.3 diam. (7¾ × 10¾)
  Gift of Sydney and Frances Lewis, 85.41

Goujon
French (dates unknown)

143. Clock, ca. 1900

  Bronze
  48.9 × 30.5 × 20.3 (19¼ × 12 × 8)
  Gift of Sydney and Frances Lewis, 85.220

Jean Goulden
French (1878-1947)

144. Clock, 1929

  Silvered bronze, enamel, marble
  49.5 × 20.3 × 19. (19½ × 8 × 7½)
  Gift of Sydney and Frances Lewis, 85.219
  Catalogue no. 91

145. Lamp, ca. 1925

  Silvered bronze, enamel
  34 × 12.7 × 8.6 (13⅜ × 5 × 3⅜)
  Gift of Sydney and Frances Lewis, 85.168

P. E. Goureay
French (dates unknown)

146. *Figure of Max Dearly as a Jockey*, ca. 1925

  Gilt bronze, ivory
  21.3 × 12.7 × 7.9 (8⅜ × 5 × 3⅛)
  Gift of Sydney and Frances Lewis, 85.317

Eileen Gray
French (born Ireland; 1879-1976)

147. "Canoe" Sofa, ca. 1919-20

  Lacquered wood, silver leaf
  72.1 × 270 × 64.9 (28⅜ × 106⁵⁄₁₆ × 25⁹⁄₁₆)
  Gift of Sydney and Frances Lewis, 85.112
  Catalogue no. 63

148. Lamp, 1923

  Lacquered wood, painted parchment shade
  185.4 × 52 diam. (73 × 20½)
  Gift of Sydney and Frances Lewis, 85.169 a/c
  Catalogue no. 65

149. Screen, 1923

  Lacquered wood, aluminum
  181.9 × 178.6 × 1.9 (71⅝ × 70¼ × ¾)
  Gift of Sydney and Frances Lewis, 85.115

150. Table, 1922

  Painted oak, sycamore
  61 × 64.8 × 55.3 (24 × 25½ × 21¾)
  Gift of Sydney and Frances Lewis, 85.114

151. Table, 1927

  Chromed metal, aluminum
  99.6 × 61.75 × 50.5 (39³⁄₁₆ × 24⁵⁄₁₆ × 19⅞)
  Gift of Sydney and Frances Lewis, 85.113

Charles Sumner Greene
American (1868-1957)
and
Henry Mather Greene
American (1870-1954)

152. Living Room Table, ca. 1909

  Honduras mahogany, ebony, silver
  74 × 137.2 × 91.5 (29⅛ × 54 × 36)
  Gift of the Sydney and Frances Lewis
  Foundation, 85.63
  Catalogue no. 54

E. Gregor
French (dates unknown)

153. Vase, 1902

  Bronzed white metal
  44.1 × 22.2 × 16.5 (17⅜ × 8¾ × 6½)
  Gift of Sydney and Frances Lewis, 85.270

André Groult
French (1884-1967)

154. Chair, 1925

 Sharkskin over wood; upholstery
 80 × 49.5 × 52 (31½ × 19½ × 20½)
 Gift of Sydney and Frances Lewis, 85.116
 Catalogue no. 72

155. Sideboard, ca. 1925

 Ebony, sharkskin, ivory
 100 × 64.8 × 153.7 (39⅜ × 25½ × 60½)
 Gift of Sydney and Frances Lewis, 85.117

Jacques Gruber
French (1870-1936)

156. Desk and Chair, ca. 1898

 Mahogany, leather, gilt bronze
 Desk: 94.5 × 144.1 × 83.8 (37½ × 56¾ × 33)
 Chair: 79.3 × 77.5 × 63.5 (31¼ × 30½ × 25)
 Gift of Sydney and Frances Lewis, 85.86.1/2
 Catalogue no. 11

157. Lily Pad Window, ca. 1900

 Stained glass, lead
 151 × 133.3 (59½ × 52½)
 Museum Purchase, The Sydney and Frances
 Lewis Art Nouveau Fund, 75.26
 Catalogue No. 23

Jules-Alexandre Grün
French (1868-1934)

158. *La Cigale, Les Petits Croisés*, 1900

 Lithograph
 124.4 × 87.6 (49 × 34½)
 Museum Purchase, The Glasgow Fund, 72.9.4

Albert Guillaume
French (1873-1942)

159. *Ambassadeurs Duclerc*, ca. 1900

 Lithograph
 130.2 × 99 (51¼ × 39)
 Museum Purchase, The Glasgow Fund, 72.9.6

Hector Guimard
French (1867-1942)

160. Cabinet, ca. 1899

 Pear, ash, bronze, mirrored glass, glass
 297.2 × 237.5 × 49.5 (117 × 93½ × 19½)
 Museum Purchase, The Sydney and Frances
 Lewis Art Nouveau Fund, 72.12
 Catalogue no. 15

161. Fireplace Front, ca. 1900

 Cast iron
 90.2 × 80 × 10.1 (35½ × 31½ × 4)
 Museum Purchase, The Sydney and Frances
 Lewis Art Nouveau Fund, 73.10

162. Jardinière, ca. 1907

 Painted cast iron
 144.8 × 55.9 × 40.6 (57 × 22 × 16)
 Museum Purchase, The Sydney and Frances
 Lewis Art Nouveau Fund, 72.11 a/b

163. Office Salon, 1909

 Pearwood, mahogany, bronze, upholstery,
 glass, leather
 Armchair: 88.9 × 66.6 × 52.1 (35 × 26¼ × 20½)
 Chairs (2) each: 83.8 × 43.8 × 52
 (33 × 17¼ × 20½)
 Desk: 96.5 × 191.4 × 70.5 (38 × 75⅜ × 27¾)
 Files (2) each: 191.1 × 78.1 × 37.8
 (75¼ × 30¾ × 14⅞)
 Gift of Sydney and Frances Lewis, 85.87.1/6
 Catalogue no. 55

164. Parasol Handle, ca. 1900-10

 Fruitwood
 7.6 × 9.9 × 1.7 (3 × 3⅞ × ¹¹⁄₁₆)
 Museum Purchase, The Sydney and Frances
 Lewis Art Nouveau Fund, 73.9

165. Picture Frame, 1904

 Bronze
 31.8 × 25.4 × 19 (12½ × 10 × 7½)
 Museum Purchase, The Sydney and Frances
 Lewis Art Nouveau Fund, 73.61

166. Window, 1896-97
 Stained glass, lead
 201.6 × 102.2 (79⅜ × 40¼)
 Museum Purchase, The Sydney and Frances
 Lewis Art Nouveau Fund, 77.6.1/6

J. D. Guirande
French (dates unknown)

167. *Bacchante*, ca. 1925

 Silver, gilt bronze, marble
 55.2 × 25.4 × 8.6 (21¾ × 10 × 3⅜)
 Gift of Sydney and Frances Lewis, 85.318

Gustave Gurschner
Austrian (1873-   )

168. Nautilus Lamp, 1899

 Bronze, nautilus shell
 44.4 × 18.9 × 19. (17½ × 7⅜ × 7½)
 Museum Purchase, The Sydney and Frances
 Lewis Art Nouveau Fund, 72.19
 Catalogue no. 13

169. Pin Tray, ca. 1900

 Bronze, diamond
 8.9 × 14. × 22.2 (3½ × 5½ × 8¾)
 Gift of Sydney and Frances Lewis, 85.260

170. Vase, ca. 1906

Bronze
23.5 × 11.1 diam. (9¼ × 4⅜)
Museum Purchase, The Sydney and Frances
Lewis Art Nouveau Fund, 78.143

Gustave Gurschner
for
Johannes Loetz Witwe
Austrian (Klöstermühle; 1836-1939)

171. Lamp, 1900

Blown glass, bronze
45.6 × 20.3 diam. (18 × 8)
Gift of Sydney and Frances Lewis, 85.165

Katsu Hama-naka
Japanese (dates unknown)

172. Pair of Panels, ca. 1925

Lacquer over wood
181.5 × 36.5 each (71½ × 14⅜)
Gift of Sydney and Frances Lewis, 85.142.1/2

R. Heyner
French (?) (dates unknown)

173. Paper Knife, ca. 1900

Bronze
30.5 × 6 × .95 (12 × 2⅜ × ⅜)
SLD 286

Josef Hoffmann
Austrian (1870-1956)

174. Chair, 1903-06

Beechwood, leather
98.4 × 44.4 × 43.1 (38¾ × 17½ × 17)
Museum Purchase, The Sydney and Frances
Lewis Art Nouveau Fund, 72.18
Catalogue no. 43

175. Chandelier, ca. 1905

Chrome, glass
45.7 × 33. × 33. (18 × 13 × 13)
Gift of Sydney and Frances Lewis, 85.521

176. Footed Dish with Cover, 1902

Hammered silver, turquoise
16.2 × 7. diam. (6⅜ × 2¾)
Museum Purchase, The Sydney and Frances
Lewis Art Nouveau Fund, 72.20 a/b
Catalogue no. 33

177. Men's Jewelry Set, ca. 1900

18-carat gold, silk
Watch fob: 1.6 × 12.7 × .3 (⅝ × 5 × ⅛)
Cuff Links (2): 1.6 × 1.9 × .8 (⅝ × ¾ × 5/16)
Stickpin: 1.6 × 7.6 × .6 (⅝ × 3 × ¼)
Studs (3): .6 × .8 on 1.7 diam. base (¼ × 5/16 on
11/16 base)
Gift of Sydney and Frances Lewis, 85.225.1/7

178. Pair of Boxes, ca. 1920

Silver
7.7 × 10.5 diam. each (3 × 4¼)
Gift of Sydney and Frances Lewis, 85.290.1a/b,
.2a/b

179. Place Setting, 1904

Sterling silver
Dessert Knife: 17.7 × 1.5 × .3 (7 × ⅝ × ⅛)
Fish Knife: 17.9 × 1.5 × .3 (7³/32 × 19/32 × ⅛)
Fish Fork: 19.2 × 1.4 × .3 (7⁹/16 × ⁹/16 × ⅛)
Dessert Fork: 18.1 × 1.5 × .3 (7⅛ × ⅝ × ⅛)
Coffee Spoon: 13. × 1.3 × .2 (5⅛ × ½ × 3/32)
Egg Spoon: 12.2 × 1.3 × .2 (4¹³/16 × ½ × 3/32)
Gift of the Sydney and Frances Lewis
Foundation, 85.289.1/6
Catalogue no. 46

William H. Hutton and Company
English (Birmingham; 1800-1923)

180. Picture Frame, ca. 1902-3

Silver, enamel, abalone shell, wood
27 × 22.5 × 5.1 (10⅝ × 8⅞ × 2)
Museum Purchase, The Sydney and Frances
Lewis Art Nouveau Fund, 76.10

Henri Gabriel Ibels
French (1867-1936)

181. Advertisement, *Horloge - J. Mévisto*, ca. 1900

Lithograph
186 × 62.8 (73¼ × 24¾)
Museum Purchase, The Arthur and Margaret
Glasgow Fund, 72.9.5

Leon Idenbaum
Belgian ? (dates unknown)

182. Pair of Panels, ca. 1925

Carved and painted oak
27.3 × 146.3 × 1.9 (10¾ × 57⅝ × ¾)
26.3 × 146 × 1.9 (10⅜ × 57½ × ¾)
Gift of Sydney and Frances Lewis, 85.118.1/2

Sadie Irvine
American (1887-1970)
for
Newcomb Pottery
American (New Orleans; active 1895-1930)

183. Vase, 1910-15

Ceramic
42.5 × 20.3 diam. (16¾ × 8)
Museum Purchase, The Mary Morton Parsons
Collection of American Decorative Arts Fund,
84.46

Georg Jensen
Danish (1866-1935)

184. Belt Buckle, ca. 1904

Silver, opals
4.4 × 8.3 × 1.3 (1¾ × 3¼ × ½)
Museum Purchase, The Sydney and Frances
Lewis Art Nouveau Fund, 72.38
Catalogue no. 41

A. Edward Jones
English (1879-1954)

185. Bowl, 1904

Silver, earthenware
8.3 × 20.3 diam. (3¼ × 8)
Gift of Sydney and Frances Lewis, 85.293

René Joubert
French (died 1931)
and
Philippe Petit
French (died 1945)

186. Carpet, *Bakou*, 1927

Wool
486.9 × 325.1 (172 × 128)
SLD 298

187. Lady's Writing-Desk, ca. 1924

Palisander, ivory
119.4 × 80 × 41.9 (47 × 31½ × 16½)
Gift of Sydney and Frances Lewis, 85.119
Catalogue no. 67

Léon Jouhaud
French (born 1874)

188. Panel, *Sortie de l'Atelier*, ca. 1910

Enamel on copper
18.7 × 10.6 × .6 (7⅜ × 4³/₁₆ × ¼)
Gift of Mrs. T. Catesby Jones for the T. Catesby
Jones Collection 47.11.9

J. P. Kayser-Sohn
German (1874-1956)

189. Inkwell, ca. 1904

Pewter
8.5 × 32.4 × 7 (3⅜ × 12¾ × 2¾)
Museum Purchase, The Sydney and Frances
Lewis Art Nouveau Fund, 73.18

190. Wine Cooler, ca. 1899

Pewter
23.8 × 27.3 × 27.3 (9⅜ × 10¾ × 10¾)
Gift of Sydney and Frances Lewis, 85.282

Alexander Kelety
Hungarian (dates unknown)

191. *Affection*, ca. 1925-30

Silvered and cold-painted bronze, ivory,
marble
34.9 × 18.4 × 12.7 (13¾ × 7¼ × 5)
Gift of Sydney and Frances Lewis, 85.328
Catalogue no. 77

William B. Kerr & Co.
American (Newark, New Jersey; founded 1885)

192. Buckle, ca. 1900

Sterling silver
4.7 × 14.6 × 1.2 (1⅞ × 5¾ × ⁷/₁₆)
Gift of Sydney and Frances Lewis, 85.284

Archibald Knox
English (1864-1933)
for
Liberty and Company
English (London; founded 1875|

193. Vase, 1902

Sterling silver, enamel
25.4 × 17.8 diam. (10 × 7)
Gift of Sydney and Frances Lewis, 85.292

Attributed to Archibald Knox
English (1864-1933)
for
Liberty and Company
English (London; founded 1875)

194. Mirror, 1902

Silver, enamel, wood, mirrored glass
47.6 × 22.5 × 1.2 (18¾ × 8⅞ × ½)
Gift of Sydney and Frances Lewis, 85.177
Catalogue no. 35

Charles Korschann
French (born 1872)

195. Lamp with Inkwell, ca. 1900

Gilt bronze
45.7 × 44.1 × 31.7 (18 × 17⅜ × 12½)
Gift of Sydney and Frances Lewis, 85.170
Catalogue no. 21

196. Vase, ca. 1900

Gilt bronze
15.2 × 9.5 × 10.1 (6 × 3¾ × 4)
Gift of Sydney and Frances Lewis, 85.271

197. Vase, ca. 1900

Gilt bronze
13.6 × 7.9 × 3.1 (5⅜ × 3¼ × 1¾)
Gift of Sydney and Frances Lewis, 85.272

René Lalique
French (1860-1945)

198. Bowl, *Volubolis*, ca. 1925

Molded glass
5.7 × 21.5 diam. (2 × 8½)
Gift of Mrs. Thomas F. Martin, Ashland, Va.,
79.33

199. Brooch, 1902-05

Gold, opals, oriental pearl, enamel
10.2 × 6.3 × 1.27 (4 × 2½ × ½)
Museum Purchase, The Sydney and Frances
Lewis Art Nouveau Fund, 73.46.1
Catalogue no. 38

200. Brooch, ca. 1900-02

Silver, enamel
5.7 × 4.1 × .74 (2¼ × 1⅝ × 5/16)
Gift of Sydney and Frances Lewis, 85.250

201. Brooch, ca. 1896-98
Gold, enamel, engraved gems
4.9 × 5.1 × 2.54 (15/16 × 2 × 1)
Gift of Sydney and Frances Lewis, 85.251

202. Brooch/Pendant, ca. 1897-98

Gold, enamel, glass, pearl
7.93 × 4.76 × 1.11 (3⅛ × 1⅞ × 7/16)
Gift of Sydney and Frances Lewis, 85.246

203. Buckle, ca. 1900

Enamel
13.8 × 9.5 × 1.1 (57/16 × 3¾ × 7/16)
Gift of Sydney and Frances Lewis, 85.249 a/b

204. Chandelier, ca. 1900

Molded glass
68.6 × 58.4 diam. (27 × 23)
SLD 304

205. Collar, ca. 1900

Gold, enamel, glass, pearls
5.7 × 30.5 × .3 (23/16 × 12 × ⅛)
Gift of Sydney and Frances Lewis, 85.243

206. Collar, ca. 1900
Pearls, gold, enamel, diamonds, glass
5.4 × 33 × .63 (2⅛ × 13 × ¼)
Gift of Sydney and Frances Lewis, 85.245

207. Diadem, ca. 1900

Horn, diamonds, gold, tortoiseshell
8.9 × 18.7 × 15.2 (3½ × 7⅜ × 6)
Gift of Sydney and Frances Lewis, 85.244

208. Hand Mirror, ca. 1900

Enamelled bronze, pâte-de-verre, ivory,
mirrored glass
34.8 × 18 × 4.5 (13¾ × 711/16 × 1⅞)
Gift of Sydney and Frances Lewis, 85.273

209. *Medusa*, ca. 1900

Bronze
17.4 × 11.8 × 8.2 (6⅞ × 4⅝ × 3¼)
Gift of Sydney and Frances Lewis, 85.319

210. Necklace, ca. 1894-96

Gold, enamel, pearls, opals
19.4 × 19.4 × .95 (7⅝ × 7⅝ × ⅜)
Gift of Sydney and Frances Lewis, 85.248

211. Panel, 1929

Molded and acid-etched glass, sycamore
Central panels (3) each: 45. × 14.5 (17¾ × 511/16)
Top and bottom panels (6) each: 11. × 14.5
(4⅜ × 511/16)
Frame: 93.3 × 79.4 (36¾ × 31¼)
Gift of Sydney and Frances Lewis, 85.350
Catalogue no. 90

212. Ring, ca. 1902-04

Opal, enamel, gold
(1½ × ¾ × 1)
Gift of Sydney and Frances Lewis, 85.247

René Lalique
French (1860-1945)
and
Lamarre
French (dates unknown)
and
Charles Louchet
French (dates unknown)

213. Vase, 1898

Pottery, gilt-bronze, enamel
57.1 × 26.6 × 21. (22½ × 10½ × 8½)
Gift of Sydney and Frances Lewis, 85.49
Catalogue no. 9

Raoul François Larche
French (1860-1912)

214. Lamp, *Loïe Fuller*, ca. 1896

Gilt bronze
44.5 × 16.5 × 13.4 (17½ × 6½ × 5¼)
Museum Purchase, The Sydney and Frances
Lewis Art Nouveau Fund, 79.72
Catalogue no. 3

215. Lamp, *Loïe Fuller*, ca. 1900

Gilt bronze
45.7 × 20.2 × 25.4 (18 × 8 × 10)
Museum Purchase, The Sydney and Frances
Lewis Art Nouveau Fund, 72.5.1

Marie Laurençin
French (1883-1956)

216. Carpet, 1925

Wool
325 × 350 (131 × 150)
Gift of Sydney and Frances Lewis, 85.340
Catalogue no. 98

Pierre Legrain
French (1889-1929)

217. Armchair, ca. 1926-29

Leather, wood
86.4 × 90.2 × 91.4 (34 × 35½ × 36)
Gift of Sydney and Frances Lewis, 85.124

218. Pair of Armchairs, ca. 1926-29

Leather, wood
80 × 77.5 × 73. each (31½ × 30½ × 29)
SLD 324-5

219. Pair of Chairs, ca. 1926-29

Leather, sycamore, chrome
70.5 × 42 × 52 (27¾ × 16½ × 20½)
Gift of Sydney and Frances Lewis, 85.120.1/2

220. Stool, ca. 1923

Lacquer, sharkskin over wood
53.4 × 53.4 × 30.5 (21 × 21 × 12)
Gift of Sydney and Frances Lewis, 85.123

221. Table, 1929

Marble, chrome, glass, electrical lighting
fixture
76.2 × 81.3 diam. (30 × 32)
Gift of Sydney and Frances Lewis, 85.122

Pierre Legrain
French (1889-1929)
and
Jean Dunand
French (1877-1942)

222. Cabinet, 1926-29

Lacquer, wood, pewter, bronze
86 × 74 × 33.7 (33⅞ × 29⅛ × 13¼)
Gift of Sydney and Frances Lewis, 85.121
Catalogue no. 89

Agathon Léonard (pseudonym of Van Weydeveldt)
French (1841-1903)

223. *La Cothurne*, ca. 1900

Gilt bronze
53.3 × 26.7 × 17.8 (21 × 10½ × 7)
Museum Purchase, The Sydney and Frances
Lewis Art Nouveau Fund, 72.5.3

224. *Dancing Girl with Tambourine*, ca. 1900

Gilt bronze
57.1 × 29.2 × 17.2 (22½ × 11½ × 6¾)
Museum Purchase, The Sydney and Frances
Lewis Art Nouveau Fund, 72.5.2

A. Levy
French (dates unknown)

225. *Art Nouveau Interior*, 1909

Gouache, ink on paper
78.7 × 52.1 (31 × 20½)
Museum Purchase, The Sydney and Frances
Lewis Art Nouveau Fund, 73.50

Liberty and Company
English (London; founded 1875)

226. Carpet, ca. 1903

Wool
381 × 94 (150 × 37)
SLD 328

227. Set of Six Buttons, 1904

Sterling silver, enamel
1.9 diam. × 1.1 (¾ × 7/16)
Gift of Mr. Furman Hebb, New York, 84.58 a/f

Samuel Lipchytz
French (dates unknown)

228. *Jeune femme au miroir*, ca. 1925

Patinated bronze, ivory, marble base
39.4 × 24.1 × 9.5 (15½ × 9½ × 3¾)
Gift of Sydney and Frances Lewis, 85.321

229. *Tête de femme*, ca. 1925

Ivory, wood
15.8 × 4.8 × 4.4 (6¼ × 1⅞ × 1¾)
Gift of Sydney and Frances Lewis, 85.320

Johannes Loetz Witwe
Austrian (Klostermühle; glassworks active 1836-1939)

230. Vase, ca. 1900

Blown glass, applied metal
12.7 × 11.4 diam. (5 × 4½)
Gift of Mrs. J.F.M. Stewart, Upperville, Va.
74.15.16
Catalogue no. 28

231. Vase, ca. 1900

Blown glass
24.8 × 11.4 diam. (9¾ × 4½)
Gift of Mrs. David C. Morton, Richmond, Va.
72.2

232. Vase, ca. 1900

Blown glass
8.2 × 11.4 diam. (3¼ × 4½)
Gift of Sydney and Frances Lewis, 85.100

233. Vase, ca. 1900

Blown glass
9.8 × 6 diam. (3⅞ × 2⅜)
Gift of Mrs. Peter Knowles, Richmond, Va., 84.7

Lopez
French ? (dates unknown)

234. Tray, ca. 1900

Bronze
10.2 × 33. × 22.5 (4 × 13 × 8⅞)
Gift of Sydney and Frances Lewis, 85.274

Josef Lorenzl
Austrian (dates unknown)

235. Figure, ca. 1925

Bronze, ivory, onyx
22.8 × 5.4 × 7 (9 × 2⅛ × 2¾)
Gift of Sydney and Frances Lewis, 85.300

236. Statue of a Girl, ca. 1925

Bronze, ivory, onyx
19.2 × 4.1 × 7.1 (7¾ × 1⅝ × 2¹³⁄₁₆)
Gift of Sydney and Frances Lewis, 85.301

Jean Lurçat
French (1892-1966)

237. Carpet, ca. 1920-25

Wool
206 × 129 (81 × 50¾)
Gift of Sydney and Frances Lewis, 85.342

Margaret Macdonald
Scottish (1865-1933)

238. Panels, *The Four Queens*, 1909

Paint and gesso on wood panel
58.1 × 40 each (22⅞ × 15¾)
Gift of Sydney and Frances Lewis, 85.143.1/4
Catalogue no.56

Charles Rennie Mackintosh
Scottish (1868-1928)

239. Armchair, 1904

Stained wood, glass, upholstery
119.3 × 61.5 × 63.5 (47 × 24¼ × 25)
Gift of Sydney and Frances Lewis, 85.145
Catalogue no. 44

240. Chair, ca. 1897

Oak, rush
136.5 × 47.6 × 45.1 (53¾ × 18 × 17¾)
Museum Purchase, The Sydney and Frances
Lewis Art Nouveau Fund, 79.29

241. Chair, 1904

Oak, rush
73. × 67.3 × 58.4 (28¾ × 26½ × 23)
Gift of Sydney and Frances Lewis, 85.144

242. Fireplace Front, 1904

Wrought iron
70 × 152.5 × 12.2 (27½ × 60 × 5)
Gift of Sydney and Frances Lewis, 85.278

243. Mantel Clock, 1917

Ebonized wood, ivory, green Erinoid
23.7 × 13 × 11.3 (9¹¹⁄₃₂ × 5⅛ × 4⁷⁄₁₆)
Gift of Sydney and Frances Lewis, 85.222
Catalogue no. 61

244. Pair of Decorative Panels, 1905

Leaded glass, zinc, mirrored glass
55.2 × 14.1 (21¾ × 5¾)
Gift of Sydney and Frances Lewis, 85.351.1/2

245. Tea Table, 1904

Ebonized wood
61 × 94 × 50.8 (24 × 37 × 20)
Gift of Sydney and Frances Lewis, 85.146

Louis Majorelle
French (1859-1926)

246. Bedroom Suite, before 1909

Cuban mahogany, rosewood, various inlaid
woods, gilt bronze, upholstery
Bed: 200.1 × 204.5 × 228.6 (79 × 80½ × 90)
Night Stands (2) each: 119.3 × 55.8 × 44.5
(47 × 22 × 17½)
Armoire: 223.5 × 243.8 × 78.7 (88 × 96 × 31)
Armchairs (2) each: 113. × 66.6 × 64.1 (44½ ×
26¼ × 25¼)
Side chairs (2) each: 100.3 × 41.2 × 47 (39½ ×
16¼ × 18½)
Gift of Sydney and Frances Lewis, 85.90.1/8
Catalogue no. 57

247. Buffet, ca. 1898

Oak, ebony, maple, chestnut, palisander, other
woods
144.8 × 132 × 52 (57 × 52 × 20½)
Museum Purchase, The Sydney and Frances
Lewis Art Nouveau Fund, 73.46.2
Catalogue no. 10

248. Chandelier, ca. 1900

Bronze, blown glass
88.8 × 63.5 diam. (35 × 25)
Museum Purchase, The Sydney and Frances
Lewis Art Nouveau Fund, 72.31.3 a/d

249. Desk, ca. 1904

Mahogany, bronze
75 × 172 × 80 (29½ × 67¾ × 31½)
SLD 351

250. Desk and Chair, ca. 1900

Mahogany, gilt bronze
Chair: 83.8 × 76.1 × 63.5 (33 × 30 × 25) 72.31½
Desk: 99.1 × 132.1 × 78.7 (39 × 52 × 31)
Museum Purchase, The Sydney and Frances
Lewis Art Nouveau Fund, 72.31.1/2

251. Table, ca. 1900

Mahogany, various inlaid woods
73 × 66 × 44 (28¾ × 26 × 17¼)
Gift of Sydney and Frances Lewis, 85.88

Attributed to Louis Majorelle
French (1859-1926)

252. Chairs (11), ca. 1900

Oak, leather
Each chair: 108.3 × 51.8 × 52.7 (42⅝ × 20¼ ×
20¾)
Gift of Sydney and Frances Lewis, 85.89.1, SLD
353-362

Louis Marcoussis
French (1883-1941)

253. Carpet, ca. 1926

Wool
252 × 140 (99 × 55)
Gift of Sydney and Frances Lewis, 85.343
Catalogue no. 80

Marcus & Company
American (New York, founded 1892)

254. Box, ca. 1900
Sterling silver, copper, brass
8.3 × 24.4 × 14.2 (3¼ × 9⅝ × 5⅝)
Gift of Sydney and Frances Lewis, 85.285 a/b

Martin Brothers
English (1877-1915)

255. Spoon-Warmer, 1895
Stoneware
14.6 × 26 × 14.6 (5¾ × 10¼ × 5¾)
Gift of Sydney and Frances Lewis, 85.48

Lucia K. Mathews
American (1870-1955)
for
The Furniture Shop
American (San Francisco; 1906-1920)

256. Jar, ca. 1906

Painted and gilded wood
31.7 × 25.4 diam. (12½ × 10)
Gift of the Sydney and Frances Lewis Foundation, 85.299 a/b
Catalogue no. 53

M. Melchoir
French (dates unknown)
and
Emile Gallé
French (1846-1904)

257. Fire Screen, ca. 1900

Maple, tooled leather, glass
99 × 67.3 × 34.3 (39 × 26½ × 13½)
Gift of Sydney and Frances Lewis, 85.91

Clément Mère
French (1870- ?)

258. Armchair, ca. 1925

Macassar ebony, ivory, repoussé leather
72.4 × 63.5 × 55.9 (28½ × 25 × 22)
Gift of Sydney and Frances Lewis, 85.125
Catalogue no. 71

259. Room Divider, ca. 1925

Rosewood, tooled leather, St. Anne marble
89. × 84. × 45. (35½ × 33 × 17½)
SLD 369

Gustave Miklos
Hungarian (1888-1967)

260. Sculpture, ca. 1926

Rock crystal, silver, enamel, silver gilt
33.7 × 25.4 × 10.1 (13¼ × 10 × 4)
Gift of Sydney and Frances Lewis, 85.329
Catalogue no. 82

Koloman Moser
Austrian (1868-1918)

261. Chair, 1904

Rosewood, maple, mother-of-pearl
94.9 × 55.8 × 52.3 (37⅜ × 22 × 20⅝)
Gift of Sydney and Frances Lewis, 85.80
Catalogue no. 45

262. Cupboard, 1903

Painted wood, mirrored glass
187 × 50.7 × 59 (73⅝ × $19\frac{15}{16}$ × 23¼)
Gift of Sydney and Frances Lewis, 85.81

263. Pair of Vases, ca. 1904

Blown glass
19 × 6.7 × 6.7 (7½ × 2⅝ × 2⅝)
Museum Purchase, The Sydney and Frances Lewis Art Nouveau Fund, 72.44.1/2

Koloman Moser
Austrian (1868-1918)
and
Jutta Sika
Austrian (1877-1964)

264. Breakfast Set, 1902

Porcelain
Teapot: 19.7 × 9. diam. (7¾ × $3\frac{9}{16}$)
Creamer: 8.4 × 7.6 diam. ($3\frac{5}{16}$ × 3)
Sugar Bowls (2) each: 11.1 × 10.6 diam. (4⅜ × $4\frac{3}{16}$)
Plates (12) each: 3. × 19. diam. ($1\frac{3}{16}$ × 7½)
Coffee Pot: 16.5 × 13.2 diam. (6½ × $5\frac{3}{16}$)
Egg Cups (11) each: 4.7 × 4.6 diam. (1⅞ × $1\frac{13}{16}$)
Tea Cups (11) each: 5.9 × 10.6 × 8.3 ($2\frac{5}{16}$ × $4\frac{3}{16}$ × 3¼)
Saucers (12) each: 2.1 × 16. diam. ($\frac{13}{16}$ × $6\frac{5}{16}$)
Gift of Sydney and Frances Lewis, 85.40.1/39

Alphonse Mucha
Czechoslovakian (1860-1939)

265. Advertisement, *Imprimerie Cassan Fils*, 1897
Lithograph
171.4 × 64.8 (67½ × 25½)
Museum Purchase, The Arthur and Margaret Glasgow Fund, 72.9.7

266. Book, *Documents Décoratifs*, 1902
Lithography and letterpress
14.2 × 33.7 × 3.8 (18 × 13¼ × 1½)
Gift of Sydney and Frances Lewis, 85.38

267. Illustration (Plate 49) from *Documents Décoratifs*, 1902
Lithograph
29.5 × 21.0 (11⅝ × 8¼)
Museum Purchase, Council Graphic Arts Fund, 72.23.1

268. Illustration (Plate 59) from *Documents Décoratifs*, 1902
Lithograph
32.4 × 22.5 (12¾ × 8⅞)
Museum Purchase, Council Graphic Arts Fund, 72.23.3

269. Illustration (Plate 61) from *Documents Décoratifs*, 1902
Lithograph
32.7 × 22.2 (12⅞ × 8¾)
Museum Purchase, Council Graphic Arts Fund, 72.23.2

270. Illustration from *Rama* by Paul Verola, 1898
Lithograph
17.1 × 13.0 (6¾ × 5⅛)
Museum Purchase, Council Graphic Arts Fund, 72.23.4

271. "Iris" from the series *La Femme Animée en Fleur*, 1898
Lithograph on silk
104.1 × 43.2 (41 × 17)
Museum Purchase, The Sydney and Frances Lewis Art Nouveau Fund, 73.11.3/4

272. "Lys" from the series *La Femme Animée en Fleur*, 1898
Lithograph on silk
104.1 × 43.2 (41 × 17)
Museum Purchase, The Sydney and Frances Lewis Art Nouveau Fund, 73.11.2/4

273. "Oeillet" from the series *La Femme Animée en Fleur*, 1898
Lithograph on silk
104.1 × 43.2 (41 × 17)
Museum Purchase, The Sydney and Frances Lewis Art Nouveau Fund, 73.11.4/4

274. "Rose" from the series *La Femme Animée en Fleur*, 1898
Lithograph on silk
104.1 × 43.2 (41 × 17)
Museum Purchase, The Sydney and Frances Lewis Art Nouveau Fund, 73.11.1/4

275. *Nature*, ca. 1900
Gilt bronze, silver, marble
69.2 × 27.9 × 30.5 (27¼ × 11 × 12)
Museum Purchase, The Sydney and Frances Lewis Art Nouveau Fund, 72.13
Catalogue no. 14

Alphonse Mucha
Czechoslovakian (1860-1939)
and
Georges Fouquet
French (1862-1957)

276. Adornment for the Bodice, ca. 1900
Gold, enamel, emeralds, baroque pearl, watercolor, metallic paint
17. × 8.6 × .7 (6¹¹⁄₁₆ × 3⅜ × ⁹⁄₃₂)
Gift of Sydney and Frances Lewis, 85.253
Catalogue no. 18

Edvin Ohrstrom
Swedish (1906-?)
for
Orrefors Glassworks
Swedish (Orrefors, Småland; founded 1898)

277. Vase, after 1936
Blown glass
10.1 × 7 diam. (4 × 2¾)
Gift of Sydney and Frances Lewis, 85.212

Joseph Maria Olbrich
Austrian (1867-1908)

278. Pair of Candlesticks, ca. 1910
Pewter
36.7 × 17.1 × 11.4 each (14½ × 6¾ × 4½)
Museum Purchase, The Sydney and Frances Lewis Art Nouveau Fund, 72.32.1/2

279. Clock, before 1900
Mahogany, lacquer, silver leaf, clockworks
52.7 × 25.7 × 15 (20¾ × 10⅛ × 5⅞)
Gift of Sydney and Frances Lewis, 85.216

280. Clock, 1902
Ivory, maple, mother-of-pearl, clockworks
39 × 21.7 × 15.9 (15⅜ × 8⁹⁄₁₆ × 6¼)
Gift of the Sydney and Frances Lewis Foundation, 85.215

281. Coffee and Tea Service, ca. 1904
Pewter, teak
Coffee Pot: 19.1 × 11.4 × 17.1 (7¾ × 4½ × 6¾)
Sugar: 13. × 11.1 × 11.1 (5⅛ × 4⅜ × 4⅜)
Teapot: 23.5 × 10.1 × 20.8 (9¼ × 4 × 8)
Tray: 4.1 × 57.8 × 37.7 (1⅝ × 22¾ × 14⅞)
Gift of Sydney and Frances Lewis, 85.280.1/4
Catalogue no. 48

282. Decanter and Five Cups, 1901

Pewter
Decanter: 33.7 × 9.9 × 11.1 (13¼ × 3⅞ × 4⅜)
Cups (5) each: 9.5 × 5.1 diam. (3¾ × 2)
Gift of Sydney and Frances Lewis, 85.279.1/6

Roland Paris
Austrian (born 1894)

283. *The Winged Dancer*, ca. 1925

Ivory, bronze, marble
36.9 × 19.7 × 8.9 (14½ × 7¾ × 3½)
Gift of Sydney and Frances Lewis, 85.302

Dagobert Peche
Austrian (1887-1923)

284. *Wiener Werkstätte*, ca. 1920

Lithograph
95.2 × 62.9 (37½ × 23¾)
Gift of Mrs. Jean Brown, Tyringham, Massachusetts, 73.71.2

Peleska
Austrian ? (dates unknown)

285. Statuette of a Girl, ca. 1925

Painted bronze, ivory
19 × 9.2 × 5.7 (7½ × 3⅝ × 2¼)
Gift of Sydney and Frances Lewis, 85.322

Edward Penfield
American (1866-1925)

286. Cover, *Harper's November*, ca. 1900

Lithograph
44.9 × 33.9 (17¹¹⁄₁₆ × 13⅜)
Museum Purchase, The Adolph D. and Wilkins C. Williams Fund, 74.10

Jean Perzel
German (1892-?)

287. Pair of Lamps, ca. 1928

Frosted glass, chrome
Each lamp: 43.8 × 17.8 × 17.8 (17¼ × 7 × 7)
Gift of Sydney and Frances Lewis, 85.171.1/2

Paul Philippe
Polish (dates unknown)

288. Statue, *Dancer with Turban*, before 1929

Ivory, cold-painted bronze, onyx
67 × 34.2 × 17.8 (26⅜ × 13½ × 7)
Gift of Sydney and Frances Lewis, 85.330

François Alphonse Piquemal
French ? (dates unknown)

289. Card Holder, ca. 1900

Pewter
30.2 × 20.9 × 19.4 (11⅞ × 8¼ × 7⅝)
Gift of Sydney and Frances Lewis, 85.323

Plateelbakkerij Zuid-Holland
Dutch (Gouda; founded 1898)

290. Vase, ca. 1905-10
Porcelain
38 × 19.5 × 19.5 (15 × 7½ × 7½)
Gift of Sydney and Frances Lewis, 85.42

François Pompon
French (1855-1933)

291. *L'Ours Blanc* (The White Bear), ca. 1926

Marble
25.5 × 44.8 × 10.8 (10 × 18 × 4¼)
Gift of Sydney and Frances Lewis, 85.324

292. *Le Perdrix* (Partridge), 1923

Bronze
25.4 × 21.2 × 10.2 (10 × 8⅜ × 4)
Gift of the Estate of T. Catesby Jones, Petersburg, Va., 47.10.89

Johann Ferdinand Preiss
German (1882-1943)

293. *Bat Dancer*, 1925-30

Cold-painted bronze, ivory, onyx, marble
22.9 × 28.6 × 8.3 (9 × 11¼ × 3¼)
Gift of Sydney and Frances Lewis, 85.312

294. *Bather on Geometric Mound*, 1925-30

Cold-painted bronze and ivory; onyx and marble base
17.1 × 18.7 × 6.7 (6¾ × 7⅜ × 2⅝)
Gift of Sydney and Frances Lewis, 85.309

295. *Bather on Rock*, 1925-30

Ivory, cold-painted bronze, marble
25.7 × 18.2 × 13.1 (10⅛ × 7⅜ × 5⅜)
Gift of Sydney and Frances Lewis, 85.313

296. *Breasting the Tape*, 1925-30

Cold-painted bronze, ivory, onyx
26.7 × 12.7 × 27.9 (10½ × 5 × 11)
Gift of Sydney and Frances Lewis, 85.311
Catalogue no. 97

297. *Ecstasy*, 1925-30

Ivory, marble
21. × 8.6 × 4.5 (8¼ × 3⅜ × 1¾)
Gift of Sydney and Frances Lewis, 85.308

298. *Fisher Boy*, 1925-30

Ivory, onyx
19.3 × 4.8 × 4.8 (7⅝ × 1⅞ × 1⅞)
Gift of Sydney and Frances Lewis, 85.307

299. *Girl in a Ballet Dress*, 1925-30
Gilt bronze, ivory, marble
18.4 × 10.2 × 5.7 (7¼ × 4 × 2¼)
Gift of Sydney and Frances Lewis, 85.306

300. *Girl with Rabbits*, 1925-30
Ivory, onyx
13.7 × 7.3 × 7.3 (5⅜ × 2⅞ × 2⅞)
Gift of Sydney and Frances Lewis, 85.303

301. *Nude*, 1925-30
Ivory, marble
13. × 12.1 × 6.4 (5⅛ × 4¾ × 2½)
Gift of Sydney and Frances Lewis, 83.305

302. *Tennis Player*, 1925-30
Bronze, ivory, onyx
27.6 × 17.8 × 12.7 (10⅞ × 7 × 5)
Gift of Sydney and Frances Lewis, 85.310

303. *Thoughts*, 1925-30
Ivory, marble
11.5 × 12.1 × 6.5 (4½ × 4¾ × 2⁹⁄₁₆)
Gift of Sydney and Frances Lewis, 85.304

Eugène Printz
French (1889-1948)

304. Carpet, 1927
Wool 170.2 × 91.5 (67 × 36)
Gift of Sydney and Frances Lewis, 85.344

Eugène Printz
French (1889-1948)
and
Jean Dunand
French (1877-1942)

305. Bookcase, ca. 1927-28
Palmwood, sycamore, copper, silver
144.7 × 308.9 × 50.2 (57 × 121⅝ × 19¾)
Gift of Sydney and Frances Lewis, 85.126
Catalogue no. 85

Jean Puiforcat
French (1897-1945)

306. Box, ca. 1925
Silver, marble
15.2 × 31.8 × 20.3 (6 × 12½ × 8)
Gift of Sydney and Frances Lewis, 85.296 a/b

307. Covered Box, ca. 1925
Sterling silver, silver gilt, rose quartz
15.2 × 25.4 diam. (6 × 10)
Gift of Sydney and Frances Lewis, 85.298 a/b

308. Tea Set, 1937
Rosewood, sterling silver
Coffee Pot: 13.1 × 17.8 × 10.1 (5⅜ × 7 × 4)
Cream: 7.6 × 12. × 7.9 (3 × 4¾ × 3⅛)
Sugar: 7.6 × 11.4 × 7.9 (3 × 4½ × 3⅛)
Teapot: 13.1 × 17.8 × 10.1 (5⅜ × 7 × 4)
Tray: 3.8 × 86.4 × 22.9 (1½ × 34 × 19)
Gift of Sydney and Frances Lewis, 85.295.1/5
Catalogue no. 100

309. Vase, ca. 1927-8
Sterling silver, plate glass
37.5 × 18.5 diam. (14¾ × 7¼)
Gift of Sydney and Frances Lewis, 85.297

Waldemar Raemisch
German (1888-1955)

310. Pair of Table Lamps, 1923
Brass
69.2 × 16.5 × 20.3 each (27¼ × 6½ × 8)
Gift of Sydney and Frances Lewis, 85.172.1/2
Catalogue no. 66

Paul Ranson
French (1869-1900)
and
France Ranson
French (dates unknown)

311. Folding Tripartite Screen, ca. 1892
Mahogany, silk embroidery, stenciled dyes
154.3 × 207. × 6 (60¾ × 8½ × 2⅜)
Gift of Sydney and Frances Lewis, 85.92
Catalogue no. 1

Albert-Armand Rateau
French (1882-1938)

312. Ashtray, ca. 1925
Patinated bronze, brass
9 × 20 diam. (3½ × 7⅞)
Gift of Sydney and Frances Lewis, 85.275

Attributed to Albert-Armand Rateau
French (1882-1938)

313. Table, ca. 1925
Lacquer over wood, alabaster
70.5 × 50.8 × 30.5 (27¾ × 50.8 × 12)
Gift of Sydney and Frances Lewis, 85.127

Reed & Barton
American (Taunton, Massachusetts; established 1840)

314. Salad Set, *Love Disarmed*, 1905
Sterling silver
Fork: 27.3 × 7.3 × 3.8 (10¾ × 2⅞ × 1½)
Spoon: 27.3 × 7.6 × 3.8 (10⅜ × 3 × 1½)
Gift of Sydney and Frances Lewis, 85.286.1/2

Ruth Reeves
American (1892-1966)

315. Bed, ca. 1928

Lacquered steel
34.3 × 189.2 × 78.7 (13½ × 74½ × 31)
Gift of the Sydney and Frances Lewis
Foundation, 85.65

316. Pedestal, ca. 1928

Lacquered steel
114.3 × 21. × 21. (45 × 8½ × 8½)
Gift of the Sydney and Frances Lewis
Foundation, 85.64

Richard Riemerschmid
German (1868-1957)

317. Chair, ca. 1898

Oak, leather
80.6 × 55.2 × 57.1 (31¾ × 21¾ × 22½)
Gift of Sydney and Frances Lewis, 85.140
Catalogue no. 12

Gerrit Rietveld
Dutch (1888-1964)

318. Chair, 1917

Painted wood
87.5 × 60.3 × 82.5 (34⁷/₁₆ × 23¾ × 32½)
Gift of Sydney and Frances Lewis, 85.83
Catalogue no. 62

G. Rigot
French (dates unknown)

319. *Standing Woman*, ca. 1925

Ivory, marble
35.6 × 9.2 × 7.7 (14 × 3⅝ × 3)
Gift of Sydney and Frances Lewis, 85.325

Jozef Rippl-Rónai
Hungarian (1861-1927)
for
Zsolnay Ceramic Works
Hungarian (Pécs; founded 1862)

320. Vase, ca. 1900

Ceramic
15.2 × 10.7 diam. (6 × 4¼)
Museum Purchase, The Sydney and Frances
Lewis Art Nouveau Fund, 78.144
Catalogue no. 29

Robj
French (dates unknown)

321. Lamp, ca. 1925-33

Blown glass, bronze
12.7 × 10.1 diam. (5 × 4)
SLD 421

Pierre Roche
French (1855-1922)

322. Book, *Loïe Fuller* by Roger Marx, 1904

Gypsographs (engraving on plaster, printed
with water-base inks on damp paper), printed
by Presses de Maire;
Text, "Auriole Italique," designed by G.
Peignot; printed by Ch. Herrissey.
26 × 20 × 1.3 (10¼ × 7⅞ × ½)
Museum Purchase, The Sydney and Frances
Lewis Art Nouveau Fund, 78.99

Charles Rohlfs
American (1853-1936)

323. Desk, 1898-1901

White oak, iron, brass
142.2 × 64.7 × 60.3 (56 × 25½ × 23¾)
Gift of Sydney and Frances Lewis, 85.66
Catalogue no. 16

324. Library Table, 1900

Oak
74.3 × 87.3 × 87.3 (29¼ × 34⅜ × 34⅜)
Gift of Sydney and Frances Lewis, 85.67

325. Rocker, 1901

Oak, leather
84.5 × 59.6 × 61. (33¼ × 23½ × 24)
Gift of Sydney and Frances Lewis, 85.68

Clément Rousseau
French (1872-?)

326. Chair, ca. 1925

Rosewood, sharkskin, upholstery
92.7 × 43.2 × 52.1 (36½ × 17 × 20½)
Gift of Sydney and Frances Lewis, 85.129
Catalogue no. 70

327. Chair, ca. 1925

Rosewood, mother-of-pearl, sharkskin,
upholstery
92.7 × 43.2 × 52.1 (36½ × 17 × 20½)
Gift of Sydney and Frances Lewis, 85.128
Catalogue no. 70

The Roycroft Shops
American (East Aurora, New York; 1893-1938)

328. Double-Door Bookcase, 1905-10

Oak, painted copper
167. × 140.3 × 40 (65¾ × 55¼ × 15¾)
Gift of Sydney and Frances Lewis, 85.69
Catalogue no. 50

329. Magazine Pedestal, 1902

Oak
162. × 45.5 × 45.5 (63¹³/₁₆ × 17¹⁵/₁₆ × 17¹⁵/₁₆)
Museum Purchase, The Mary Morton Parsons
Collection of American Decorative Arts Fund,
78.128

330. Table Lamp, ca. 1910

Copper, mica
36.2 × 30.5 diam. (14¼ × 12)
Museum Purchase, The Adolph D. and Wilkins
C. Williams Fund, 79.30

Rozenburg Pottery Company
Dutch (The Hague; 1885-1917)

331. Covered Jar, ca. 1900

Porcelain
36.2 × 11.8 × 11.8 (14¼ × 4⅝ × 4⅝)
Gift of Sydney and Frances Lewis, 85.43 a/b

332. Vase, ca. 1900

Porcelain
10.8 × 5.4 × 6.4 (4¼ × 2⅛ × 2½)
Gift of Sydney and Frances Lewis, 85.44

Emile-Jacques Ruhlmann
French (1879-1933)

333. Armchairs (2), ca. 1931

Macassar ebony, upholstery
93.4 × 65.4 × 90.2 each (36¾ × 25¾ × 35½)
SLD 431-2

334. "Sun" Bed, 1930

Macassar ebony, oak
195.6 × 212.1 × 217.8 (77 × 83½ × 85¾)
Gift of Sydney and Frances Lewis, 85.130
Catalogue no. 95

335. Carpet, ca. 1928

Wool
331.5 diam. (130½)
Gift of Sydney and Frances Lewis, 85.345

336. Corner Cabinet, 1916

Lacquered rosewood, ivory, rare woods
128.3 × 85.1 × 60.3 (50½ × 33½ × 23¾)
Gift of Sydney and Frances Lewis, 85.135
Catalogue no. 60

337. Coffee Table, 1929

Amboyna wood, ivory, brass
85.4 × 74.9 × 45.7 in tilt position (33⅝ × 29½ × 18)
Gift of Sydney and Frances Lewis, 85.134

338. Desk, 1925-27

Macassar ebony, snakeskin, ivory, silvered bronze
72.4 × 134.6 × 72.4 (28½ × 53 × 28½)
Gift of Sydney and Frances Lewis, 85.136
Catalogue no. 69

339. Desk-Table, 1921

Macassar ebony, ivory, brass
73 × 110.8 × 69.8 (28¾ × 43⁵⁄₁₆ × 19⅝)
Gift of Sydney and Frances Lewis, 85.132

340. Settee and Two Chairs, ca. 1931

Macassar ebony, upholstery, bronze
Settee: 95.6 × 152.4 × 91.4 (38 × 60 × 36)
Chairs (2) each: 94.6 × 65.4 × 90.5 (37¼ × 25¾ × 35⅝)
Gift of Sydney and Frances Lewis, 85.133

341. Table, ca. 1925

Macassar ebony
69.8 × 65.1 × 40.3 (27½ × 25⅝ × 15⅞)
Gift of Sydney and Frances Lewis, 85.131

342. Table Mirror, 1919

Macassar ebony, mirrored glass, ivory, bronze
35.6 × 34.3 × 12.7 (14 × 13½ × 5)
Gift of Sydney and Frances Lewis, 85.178

343. Tall-Case Clock, ca. 1922

Mahogany, glass, bronze; clockworks by
Rousseau à Paris
196.5 × 67.3 × 36.8 (77½ × 26½ × 14½)
Gift of Sydney and Frances Lewis, 85.221

Maurius-Ernest Sabino
French (dates unknown)

344. Lamp, ca. 1930

Molded glass, bronze, marble
22.2 × 46.3 × 12.7 (8¾ × 18¼ × 5)
SLD 442

Gérard Sandoz
French (born 1902)

345. Brooch, 1928

Gold, onyx, enamel, diamonds
6.5 × 5.4 × 1.6 (2⁹⁄₁₆ × 2⅛ × ⅝)
Gift of Sydney and Frances Lewis, 85.254
Catalogue no. 86

346. Pendant, ca. 1928/30

Gold, aventurine, onyx
10.6 × 5.6 × .9 (4³⁄₁₆ × 2³⁄₁₆ × ⅜)
Gift of Sydney and Frances Lewis, 85.255

347. Pendant, ca. 1928

Gold, onyx, enamel, jade
11.4 × 4.76 × 1.43 excluding cord (4½ × 1⅞ × ⁹⁄₁₆)
Gift of Sydney and Frances Lewis, 85.256

Ad. Schellenberg
German (dates unknown)

348. Pair of Wine Cruets, ca. 1900

Sterling silver, glass
30.5 × 11.5 diam. each (12 × 4½)
SLD 862

François-Louis Schmied
French (1873-1941)
and
Jean Dunand
French (1877-1942)

349. Book, *Ruth et Booz*, 1930

Cover (Dunand): leather, enamel
Binding and wood engravings (Schmied)
36.9 × 31.1 × 6.4 (14½ × 12¼ × 2½)
Gift of Sydney and Frances Lewis, 85.39 a/b
Catalogue no. 94

Schneider Glassworks
French (Epinay-sur-Seine; founded 1913)

350. Vase, ca. 1920

Acid-etched cameo glass
31.1 × 20.9 diam. (12¼ × 8¼)
Gift of Mr. Sidney Trattner, Richmond Va.,
80.47

Théophile-Alexandre Steinlen
French (1859-1923)

351. *L'Eté - Chat sur une Balustrade*, 1909

Lithograph
50.1 × 62.8 (19¾ × 24¾)
Museum Purchase, The Sydney and Frances
Lewis Art Nouveau Fund, 73.19

Steuben Glass Works
American (Corning, New York; founded 1903)

352. Cluthera Vase, ca. 1920

Blown glass
25.4 × 17.8 × 8.5 (10 × 7 × 3⅜)
Gift of Mrs. Peter Knowles, Richmond, Virginia,
84.8

353. Vase, ca. 1920

Blown and applied glass
19.7 × 17.8 diam. (7¾ × 7)
Gift of Sydney and Frances Lewis, 85.181

354. Vase, ca. 1915

Blown glass
20.6 × 10.5 × 9.8 (8⅛ × 4¼ × 3⅞)
Gift of Sydney and Frances Lewis, 85.180

Gustav Stickley
American (1857-1952)
for
Craftsman Workshops
American (Syracuse, New York; 1900-1915)

355. Cellarette, ca. 1907-08

White oak, copper
102.2 × 40.0 × 56.6 (40¼ × 15¾ × 21½)
SLD 736

356. Chair, ca. 1905-09

White oak, leather
104.2 × 76.8 × 91.4 (41 × 30¼ × 36)
SLD 759

357. Chandelier, ca. 1902

Oak, copper, glass, iron, wrought iron
114.3 × 58.4 × 58.4 (45 × 23 × 23)
Gift of Sydney and Frances Lewis, 85.149

358. Chest of Drawers, ca. 1910

White oak
128.3 × 91.4 × 50.8 (50½ × 36 × 20)
SLD 802

359. Chest of Drawers, ca. 1909

White oak, copper
101.7 × 49.5 × 94. (40 × 19½ × 37)
SLD 735

360. China Cabinet, ca. 1910

White oak, glass, copper
152.4 × 91.4 × 38.1 (60 × 36 × 15)
SLD 803

361. Costumer, ca. 1909-12

White oak, copper
118.1 × 55.9 × 182.9 (46½ × 22 × 72)
SLD 745

362. Footstool, 1907-12

White oak, leather
31.1 × 31.1 × 11.8 (12¼ × 12¼ × 4⅝)
SLD 832

363. Library Table, ca. 1905-09

White oak
72.4 × 75. × 121.9 (28½ × 29½ × 48)
SLD 761

364. Library Table, ca. 1907-08

White oak
76.2 × 90.1 diam. (30 × 35½)
SLD 760

365. Library Table, ca. 1909

White oak, copper
76.2 × 137.1 × 81.2 (30 × 54 × 32)
SLD 786

366. Mantel Clock, ca. 1912-16

White oak, copper, Seth Thomas clockworks
35.6 × 22.8 × 12.7 (14 × 9 × 5)
Gift of Sydney and Frances Lewis, 85.214

367. Pair of Chairs, ca. 1912-16

White oak, leather, brass
95. × 47. × 43. each (37½ × 18½ × 17)
Museum Purchase, The Adolph D. and Wilkins
C. Williams Fund, 77.29.2/3

368. Rocking Chair, 1906-12

White oak, leather
95.2 × 69.2 × 72.7 (37½ × 27¼ × 28⅝)
SLD 461

369. Armchair Rocker, ca. 1904-12
White oak, leather
102.2 × 73.7 × 91.4 (40¼ × 29 × 36)
SLD 785

370. Server/Sideboard, 1912-16
White oak, copper
99. × 111.9 × 50.8 (39 × 44 × 20)
SLD 743

371. Settee, ca. 1910
White oak, leather
76.2 × 142.2 × 54.6 (30 × 56 × 22½)
SLD 787

372. Settle, ca. 1905
White oak, leather
124.5 × 120.6 × 59.7 (49 × 47½ × 23½)
Gift of Sydney and Frances Lewis, 85.354

373. Sideboard, ca. 1905-12
White oak, iron
99 × 167.7 × 59 (39 × 66 × 23¼)
SLD 737

374. Sideboard, ca. 1905-16
White oak, copper
125 × 142 × 55.5 (49¼ × 55¹⁵/₁₆ × 21¾)
Museum Purchase, The Williams Fund, 77.29.1

375. Sideboard, ca. 1905
White oak, iron
106.7 × 136.5 × 56.5 (42 × 53¾ × 22¼)
SLD 853

376. Table, ca. 1909-12
White oak
68.6 × 76.2 diam. (27 × 30)
SLD 746

377. Table, 1909
White oak
76.2 × 38.1 × 96.6 (30 × 15 × 38)
SLD 850

378. Tabourette, ca. 1904-08
White oak
44.4 × 40. diam. (17½ × 15¾)
SLD 789

379. Tall-Case Clock, ca. 1903
Oak, copper, brass, clockworks
178.4 × 54 × 33 (70¼ × 21½ × 13)
Gift of Sydney and Frances Lewis, 85.213

Gustav Stickley/Craftsman Workshops
American (Syracuse, New York; 1900-1916)
and
Harvey Ellis
American (1852-1904)

380. Bookcase, ca. 1903-04
White oak, leaded glass, copper
147.3 × 152.4 × 33 (58 × 60 × 13)
Gift of Sydney and Frances Lewis, 85.71

381. Chair, ca. 1903-04
White oak, copper, pewter, inlaid woods
71.7 × 66 × 70.5 (28¼ × 26 × 27¾)
Gift of Sydney and Frances Lewis, 85.72

382. Chair, 1903-04
White oak, copper, pewter, inlaid woods
107.9 × 43.6 × 47 (42½ × 17 × 18½)
Gift of Sydney and Frances Lewis, 85.73

383. Chest with Mirror, ca. 1906
White oak, mirrored glass, copper
167 × 121.9 × 5.9 (65¾ × 48 × 22)
SLD 712

384. Dresser, 1906
Maple, maple veneer, pewter, exotic woods
109.2 × 106.6 × 50.8 (43 × 42 × 20)
SLD 805

385. Fall-Front Desk, ca. 1903-04
White oak, copper, pewter, exotic woods
116.8 × 106.6 × 29.2 (46 × 42 × 11½)
Gift of Sydney and Frances Lewis, 85.70

386. Side Chair, ca. 1904-06
White oak, inlay
101.6 × 41.9 × 35.6 (40 × 16½ × 14)
SLD 806

387. Vanity with Mirror and Chair, ca. 1904-06
White oak, mirrored glass, inlaid woods
Vanity: 142.2 × 91.4 × 45.7 (56 × 36 × 18)
Chair: 81.3 × 40.6 × 35.6 (32 × 16 × 14)
SLD 807-8

J. George Stickley
American (1871-1921)
and
Leopold Stickley
American (1869-1957)
for
L. & J. G. Stickley
American (Fayetteville, New York; founded 1902)

388. Armchair, 1918-22
White oak
94.6 × 67.3 × 52.1 (37¼ × 26½ × 20½)
SLD 458

389. Bookcase, ca. 1910
White oak, glass, copper
138.4 × 121.9 × 38.1 (54¼ × 48 × 15)
SLD 459

390. Chairs (3), 1918-22

White oak
89.5 × 45.1 × 95.1 each (35¼ × 17¾ × 17¾)
SLD 453-7

391. Lamp Table, ca. 1912-17

White oak
73.6 × 61 diam. (29 × 24)
SLD 699

392. Sideboard, 1918-22

White oak, copper
116.8 × 142.3 × 55.9 (46 × 56 × 22)
SLD 460

393. Table, 1918-22

White oak
73.7 × 121.9 diam. (29 × 48)
SLD 452

394. Table, 1912-17

White oak
45.7 × 40.7 × 40.7 (18 × 16 × 16)
SLD 713

395. Table, 1912-17

White oak
43.2 × 38.1 × 38.1 (17 × 15 × 15)
SLD 714

396. Table, 1912-17

White oak
43.2 × 38.1 × 38.1 (17 × 15 × 15)
SLD 715

Stickley and Brandt Chair Company
American (Binghamton, New York; 1889-1919)

397. Chair, ca. 1910-12

White oak, leather
88.9 × 55.9 × 58.4 (35 × 22 × 23)
SLD 744

Louis Süe
French (1875 - 1968)
and
André Mare
French (1887-1932)

398. Cabinet, 1927

Ebony, mother-of-pearl, silver
156.6 × 89.8 × 40 (61⅞ × 35⅜ × 15¾)
Gift of the Sydney and Frances Lewis
Foundation, 85.137
Catalogue no. 83

Raymond Templier
French (1891-1968)

399. Bracelet with Brooch, ca. 1925-30

Silver, platinum, gold, onyx, diamonds
53 × 58 × 64 (2⅛ × 2¼ × 2½)
Gift of the Sydney and Frances Lewis
Foundation, 85.257 a/b
Catalogue no. 76

400. Purse, ca. 1925

Sueded leather, silver, enamel, cotton cording
20.3 × 12.7 × 2.5 (8 × 5 × 1)
Gift of Sydney and Frances Lewis, 85.252

Peter Tereszczuk
Austrian (dates unknown)

401. Bowl, ca. 1910

Bronze
6.3 × 13.9 × 10.4 (2½ × 5½ × 4⅛)
Gift of Sydney and Frances Lewis, 85.261

402. Figure, ca. 1910

Bronze, ivory
18.4 × 7.6 × 12.7 (7¼ × 3 × 5)
Gift of Sydney and Frances Lewis, 85.326

Gebrüder Thonet (Thonet Brothers)
Vienna (founded 1853)

403. Pair of Armchairs, ca. 1904

Beechwood, leather
100.3 × 58.4 × 59.7 each (39½ × 23 × 23½)
SLD 468-9

404. Suite of Furniture, ca. 1850

Laminated beechwood, upholstery, caning
Sofa: 99.1 × 121.9 × 50.2 (39 × 48 × 19¾)
Table: 76.8 × 80 diam. (30¼ × 31½)
Chairs (2) each: 93.9 × 60.9 × 61.6
(37 × 24 × 24¼)
SLD 470-3

Tiffany & Co.
American (New York; established 1834)

405. Cigarette Box, ca. 1930

Sterling silver, diamonds, jade, tsuba (Japanese
sword-guard)
149.9 × 8.9 × 4.8 (5⅞ × 3½ × 1⅞)
Gift of Mr. Furman Hebb, New York, 84.51

406. Coffee Pot and Cream Jug, ca. 1875-91

Hammered silver
Coffee Pot: 17.8 × 7.3 × 12.7 (7 × 2⅞ × 5)
Cream Jug: 10.1 × 6.0 × 8.2 (4 × 2⅜ × 3¼)
Gift of Sydney and Frances Lewis, 85.283.1/2

Louis C. Tiffany
American (1848-1933)
for
Louis C. Tiffany and Co. Associated Artists
(1879-1885); **Tiffany Glass Co.** (1885-1892); **Tiffany
Glass and Decorating Co.** (1892-1900); **Tiffany
Studios** (1900-1938)

Architectural Features

407. Lunette, ca. 1900

    Made for Mannheimer Residence, St. Paul,
    Minnesota
    Leaded glass, oak
    91.5 × 132.1 including frame (36 × 52)
    SLD 482

408. Pair of Doors, ca. 1900
    Made for Mannheimer Residence, St. Paul,
    Minnesota

    Leaded glass, oak
    243.9 × 132.1 (96 × 52) over all; 176.2 × 41.3
    (69⅜ × 16¼) each panel
    SLD 481

409. Sample Slab, ca. 1900

    Mosaic, glass, concrete
    73.8 × 45.9 × 2.8 (29¹/₁₆ × 18¹/₁₆ × 1⅛)
    Museum Purchase, The Sydney and Frances
    Lewis Art Nouveau Fund, 75.7

410. Window Design, ca. 1892-1900

    Watercolor on paper
    10.1 × 10.1 (4 × 4)
    Museum Purchase, The Adolph D. and Wilkins
    C. Williams Fund, 74.7

411. Magnolia and Apple Blossom Window, ca.
    1900
    Made for Dimock Residence, Elizabeth,
    New Jersey

    Leaded glass, oak
    294.6 × 375.9 (116 × 148)
    Museum Purchase, The Sydney and Frances
    Lewis Art Nouveau Fund, 73.47.1/9

Boxes

412. Box, ca. 1900

    Enamel on copper
    5.4 × 12.1 (2⅛ × 4¾)
    Museum Purchase, The Sydney and Frances
    Lewis Art Nouveau Fund, 81.201 a/b

413. Scarab Box, after 1900

    Ash, glass, bronze
    10.8 × 10.8 (4¼ × 4¼)
    Museum Purchase, The Sydney and Frances
    Lewis Art Nouveau Fund, 77.49

Candlesticks

414. Candlestick, ca. 1900

    Blown glass, bronze
    47. × 13.6 diam. (18½ × 5⅜)
    Gift of Sydney and Frances Lewis, 85.199

415. Candlestick, ca. 1900

    Blown glass, bronze
    31.1 × 13. diam. (12¼ × 5⅛)
    Gift of Sydney and Frances Lewis, 85.198

416. Candlestick, ca. 1900

    Blown glass
    17.8 × 11.1 diam. (7 × 4⅜)
    Gift of Helen K. Mackintosh in Honor of Her
    Parents, the Reverend and Mrs. D. C.
    Mackintosh, 81.213

417. Cypriote Candlestick, ca. 1900

    Blown glass, bronze
    35.5 × 12. diam. (14 × 4¾)
    Gift of Sydney and Frances Lewis, 85.195

418. Pair of Candlesticks, ca. 1900

    Blown glass, bronze
    20.3 × 10.4 diam. (8 × 4¼)
    20.3 × 9.5 diam. (8 × 3¾)
    Gift of Sydney and Frances Lewis, 85.191.½

419. Pair of Candlesticks, ca. 1900

    Blown glass, bronze
    37.8 × 17.7 diam. (14⅞ × 7)
    37.6 × 17.9 diam. (14¹³/₁₆ × 7¹/₁₆)
    Gift of Sydney and Frances Lewis, 85.197.1/2

Desk Set

420. Abalone Desk Set, ca. 1906-1918

    Gilt bronze, abalone
    Blotter Ends: 48.8 × 5.7 1. (19¼ × 2¼ × ⅜)
    Bookends: 14. × 13.6 × 13.6 (5½ × 5 × 5⅜)
    Inkstand: 7.9 × 9.2 × 9.2 (3⅛ × 3⅝ × 3⅝)
    Letter Clip: 6. × 6.3 × 2.8 (2⅜ × 2½ × 1⅛)
    Paper Knife: 25.1 × 2.2 × .6 (9⅞ × ⅞ × ¼)
    Paper Rack: 14. × 24.1 × 6.9 (5½ × 9½ × 2¾)
    Pen Tray: 1.9 × 21.9 × 6.3 (¾ × 8⅝ × 2½)
    Calendar: 14.5 × 16.5 (5¾ × 6½)
    Photograph Frame: 30.8 × 24.1 (12⅛ × 9½)
    Reading Glass: 22.5 × 10.8 × 1.9 (8⅞ × 4¼ × ¾)
    Stamp Box: 3.2 × 9.8 × 5.4 (1¼ × 3⅞ × 2⅛)
    Gift of Mrs. A. Stuart Bolling, Jr., Suffolk, Va.;
    Miss Mary Stuart Bolling, Richmond, Va., and
    Mrs. Peter Knowles, Richmond, Va., 84.45.1/11

Glassware

421. Bowl, ca. 1910

    Engraved blown glass
    9.2 × 24.7 diam. (3⅝ × 9¾)
    Gift of Mrs. Peter Knowles, Richmond, Va.,
    84.12

422. Bowl and Stand, ca. 1900

    Blown glass
    Bowl: 7.5 × 12.0 diam. (2¹⁵/₁₆ × 4¾)
    Stand: 2.8 × 15.2 diam. (1⅛ × 6)
    SLD 474-5

423. Champagne Flute, ca. 1900

    Blown glass
    13.3 × 10.2 diam. (5¼ × 4)
    SLD 478

424. Compote, ca. 1892-93
Blown glass
14.6 × 15.3 diam. (5¾ × 6)
Gift of Helen K. Mackintosh in Honor of Her Parents, the Reverend and Mrs. D. C. Mackintosh, 81.212

425. Compote, ca. 1900
Blown glass
12.5 × 14.6 diam. ($4\frac{15}{16}$ × 5¾)
Museum Purchase, The Sydney and Frances Lewis Art Nouveau Fund, 81.198

426. Compote, 1909
Blown glass
13.9 × 17.8 diam. (5½ × 7)
Gift of Mr. and Mrs. B. Warwick Davenport, Richmond, Va., 76.7

427. Decanter and Liqueur Glasses, 1897
Blown glass
Decanter: 27.9 × 12.7 diam. (11 × 5)
Glasses (12) each: 5.1 × 3.8 diam. (2 × 1½)
Gift of the Family of Mr. and Mrs. Lewis C. Williams, Richmond, Va., 76.14.1/13

428. Finger Bowl and Stand, ca. 1900
Blown glass
Bowl: 7. × 12.5 diam. (2¾ × $4\frac{15}{16}$)
Stand: 1.6 × 15.9 diam. (⅝ × 6¼)
Gift of Sydney and Frances Lewis, 85.189 a/b

429. Fluted Bowl, ca. 1900
Blown glass
8. × 18.1 diam. (3⅛ × 7⅜)
Gift of Helen K. Mackintosh in Honor of Her Parents, the Reverend and Mrs. D. C. Mackintosh, 81.210

430. Fluted Bowl, ca. 1900
Blown glass
8.3 × 24.8 diam. (3¼ × 9¾)
Gift of Helen K. Mackintosh in Honor of Her Parents, the Reverend and Mrs. D. C. Mackintosh, 81.214

431. Footed Bowl, ca. 1900
Blown glass
8.9 × 11.6 diam. (3½ × $4\frac{9}{16}$)
SLD 575

432. Goblet, 1900
Blown glass
12.6 × 7.6 diam. ($4\frac{15}{16}$ × 3)
Gift of Helen K. Mackintosh in Honor of Her Parents, the Reverend and Mrs. D. C. Mackintosh, 81.211

433. Goblets (4), ca. 1900-38
Blown glass
1) 11.4 × 8.2 diam. (4¼ × 3¼)
2) 9.2 × 6.1 diam. (3⅝ × 2⅝)
3) 11.1 × 7. diam. (4⅜ × 2¾)
4) 11.1 × 7. diam. (4⅜ × 2¾)
SLD 485-8

434. Liqueur Glasses (9), ca. 1900
Blown glass
12. × 4.5 diam. each (4¾ × 1¾)
SLD 548-57

435. Nut Dishes (4), 1904
Blown glass
1.6 × 8 diam. each (⅝ × 3⅛)
Gift of Helen K. Mackintosh in Honor of Her Parents, the Reverend and Mrs. D. C. Mackintosh, 81.205.1

436. Pair of Salts, ca. 1900
Blown glass
4.5 × 5.1 diam. (1¾ × 2)
4.3 × 5.1 diam. ($1\frac{11}{16}$ × 2)
SLD 476-7

437. Plate, ca. 1900
Blown glass
3.5 × 23.5 diam. (1⅜ × 9¼)
Gift of Helen K. Mackintosh in Honor of Her Parents, the Reverend and Mrs. D. C. Mackintosh, 81.206

438. Punch Bowl with Ladles, 1900
Blown glass, silver gilt
Bowl: 36.2 × 60.9 diam. (14¼ × 24)
Ladles (3) each: 6.3 × 8.9 × 25.4 (2½ × 3½ × 10)
Museum Purchase, The Sydney and Frances Lewis Art Nouveau Fund, 74.16 a/d

439. Rosewater Sprinkler, 1908
Blown glass
35.1 × 12.7 diam. ($13\frac{15}{16}$ × 5)
Gift of Sydney and Frances Lewis, 85.182

440. Saucer, ca. 1900
Blown glass
2.5 × 15.3 diam. (1 × 6)
Gift of Helen K. Mackintosh in Honor of Her Parents, the Reverend and Mrs. D. C. Mackintosh, 81.209

441. Sherbets (7), ca. 1896-1905
Blown glass
1) 7.3 × 11.1 diam. (2⅞ × 4⅜)
2) 8.8 × 8.2 diam. (3½ × 3¼)
3) 8.8 × 8.1 diam. (3½ × $3\frac{3}{16}$)
4) 9.2 × 8.8 diam. (3⅝ × 3½)
5) 8.7 × 8.4 diam. ($3\frac{7}{16}$ × $3\frac{5}{16}$)
6) 8.8 × 8.4 diam. (3½ × $3\frac{5}{16}$)
7) 9.2 × 8.4 diam. (3 ⅝ × $3\frac{5}{16}$)
SLD 560-66

442. Sherbet, ca. 1900

Blown glass
8.9 × 8.5 diam. (3½ × 3⅜)
SLD 559

443. Shot Glass, ca. 1900

Blown glass
5.7 × 4.5 diam. (2¼ × 1¾)
SLD 567

444. Tile, ca. 1900

Moulded glass
10.1 × 10.1 (4 × 4)
Gift of Mrs. John A. Pope, Washington, D.C.
73.39

445. Wine Goblets (6), 1900-38

Blown glass
1) 12.0 × 6.4 diam. (4¹¹⁄₁₆ × 2½)
2) 11.6 × 6.2 diam. (4 × 2⁷⁄₁₆)
3) 12.1 × 6.2 diam. (4¾ × 2⁷⁄₁₆)
4) 12.1 × 6.2 diam. (4¾ × 2⁷⁄₁₆)
5) 12.2 × 6.0 diam. (4¹³⁄₁₆ × 2⅜)
6) 12.6 × 6.2 diam. (4¹⁵⁄₁₆ × 2⁷⁄₁₆)
SLD 577-82

Inkwells

446. Inkwell, ca. 1900

Gilt bronze, blown glass
10.2 × 11.4 diam. (4 × 4½)
Museum Purchase, The Sydney and Frances
Lewis Art Nouveau Fund, 73.17

447. Inkwell, ca. 1906-12

Bronze, oyster shell
8.9 × 19. × 19. (3½ × 7½ × 7½)
Gift of Sydney and Frances Lewis, 85.84

Lamps

448. Arrowroot Lamp, ca. 1900

Leaded glass, bronze
66. × 50.8 diam. (26 × 20)
SLD 494

449. Autumn Leaves Lamp, ca. 1906

Leaded glass, bronze
80. × 27.3 diam. (31½ × 10¾)
Gift of Sydney and Frances Lewis, 85.156 a/b
Catalogue no. 26

450. Azalea Lamp, ca. 1900

Leaded glass, bronze
74.9 × 50.8 diam. (29½ × 20)
SLD 496

451. Bamboo Floor Lamp, ca. 1900

Leaded glass, bronze
170.2 × 61. diam. (67 × 24)
SLD 130

452. Begonia Lamp, ca. 1900

Leaded glass, bronze
41.9 × 33. diam. (16½ × 13)
Gift of Sydney and Frances Lewis, 85.159 a/b

453. Bridge Lamp, ca. 1900

Blown glass, bronze
147.3 × 30.5 diam. (58½ × 12)
SLD 499

454. Candelabrum Floor Lamp, 1899-1920

Blown glass, bronze
156.8 × 68. × 38.1 diam. (61¾ × 26¾ × 15)
SLD 500

455. Cherry-Tree Pony Lamp, ca. 1900

Leaded glass, bronze
41.9 × 26. diam. (16½ × 10¼)
SLD 492

456. Clematis-on-Trellis Chandelier, ca. 1900

Leaded glass
31.8 × 67.3 × 67.3 (12½ × 26½ × 26½)
SLD 495

457. Clematis-Blossom Lamp, ca. 1909

Leaded glass, bronze
62.3 × 12.7 × 45.7 diam. (24½ × 5 × 18)
SLD 701

458. Cobweb Lamp, ca. 1906

Glass mosaic tiles, leaded glass, bronze
74.9 × 50.8 diam. (29½ × 20)
Gift of Sydney and Frances Lewis, 85.164 a/b
Catalogue no. 51

459. Colonial Lamp, ca. 1900

Leaded glass, bronze
55.2 × 40.6 diam. (21¾ × 16)
SLD 502

460. Daffodil Lamp, 1900

Leaded glass, bronze, mosaic-glass tiles
44.5 × 40.7 diam. (17½ × 16)
SLD 504

461. Daffodil and Lily-Pad Lamp, ca. 1900

Leaded glass, bronze
60.3 × 40.6 diam. (22¾ × 16)
SLD 503

462. Dogwood Lamp, ca. 1900

Leaded glass, bronze
78.7 × 55.8 diam. (31 × 22)
SLD 506

463. Dragonfly Lamp, ca. 1900

Leaded glass, bronze
71.1 × 55.8 diam. (28 × 22)
Gift of Sydney and Frances Lewis, 85.160 a/c

464. Dragonfly/Hanging-Head Lamp, ca. 1900

Leaded glass, bronze
81.3 × 55.8 diam. (32½ × 22)
SLD 508

465. Fabrique Linenfold Lamp, ca. 1920

Leaded glass, gilt bronze
61 × 50.8 diam. (24 × 20)
SLD 509

466. Fish Lamp, ca. 1906

Leaded glass, bronze, copper, mosaic-glass tiles
45.7 × 40.6 diam. (18 × 16)
Gift of Sydney and Frances Lewis, 85.153 a/b

467. Flowering Water-Lily Lamp, ca. 1900

Leaded glass, bronze
69.2 × 50.8 diam. (27¼ × 20)
SLD 777

468. Flowering Water-Lily Lamp, ca. 1900

Leaded glass, bronze
55.9 × 52.1 diam. (22 × 20½)
SLD 512

469. Fruit Lamp, ca. 1900

Leaded glass, bronze
114.3 × 61. diam. (45 × 24)
Gift of Sydney and Frances Lewis, 85.154 a/c

470. Geometric Lamp, ca. 1900

Leaded glass, bronze
77.5 × 57.2 diam. (30½ × 22½)
SLD 490

471. Gould Peacock Lamp, before 1914

Blown glass, enamel on copper
102.9 × 33. diam. (40½ × 13)
Gift of the Sydney and Frances Lewis Foundation, 85.152 a/b
Catalogue no. 59

472. Green-Leaf Cherry Tree Lamp, ca. 1900

Leaded glass, bronze
76.2 × 63.5 diam. (30 × 25)
SLD 491

473. Hydrangea Chandelier, ca. 1900

Leaded glass, bronze
35.7 × 63.5 diam. (15¼ × 25)
Gift of Sydney and Frances Lewis, 85.355

474. Hydrangea Floor Lamp, ca. 1900

Leaded glass, bronze
203.2 × 63.5 diam. (80 × 25)
SLD 613

475. Hydrangea Lamp, ca. 1900

Leaded glass, bronze
66. × 40.6 diam. (26 × 16)
SLD 675

476. Laburnum Floor Lamp, ca. 1900

Leaded glass, bronze
203.2 × 61. diam. (80 × 24)
Gift of Sydney and Frances Lewis, 85.161 a/c

477. Laburnum Lamp, ca. 1900

Leaded glass, bronze
68.6 × 55.9 diam. (27 × 22)
SLD 756

478. Lily Lamp (three-light), ca. 1900

Blown glass, bronze
22.2 × 26.6 × 24.1 (8¾ × 10½ × 9½)
SLD 516

479. Lily Lamp (eighteen-light), 1900

Blown glass, bronze
52.7 × 40.6 diam. (20¾ × 16)
SLD 517

480. Lily-Pad Lamp, ca. 1900

Leaded glass, bronze
66. × 50.8 diam. (26 × 20)
SLD 519

481. Maple-Leaf Floor Lamp, ca. 1900

Leaded glass, bronze
163.2 × 55.9 diam. (64¼ × 22)
Gift of Mr. and Mrs. Arthur S. Brinkley, 72.15

482. Nasturtium Lamp, ca. 1900

Leaded glass, bronze
64.1 × 48.2 diam. (25¼ × 19)
SLD 522

483. Nautilus Lamp, ca. 1900

Leaded glass, bronze
34.3 × 20.3 × 13.3 (13½ × 8 × 5¼)
SLD 523

484. Oriental Poppy Lamp, ca. 1900

Leaded glass, bronze
67.3 × 45.5 diam. (26½ × 18)
SLD 656

485. Peacock Lamp, ca. 1900

Leaded glass, bronze, enamel
68.5 × 47. diam. (27 × 18½)
SLD 524

486. Pebble Lamp, ca. 1900

Leaded glass, blown glass, gilt bronze
50.8 × 38.1 diam. (20 × 15)
Gift of Sydney and Frances Lewis, 85.163 a/c

487. Peony Lamp on Turtleback Base, ca. 1900

Leaded glass, blown glass, mosaic-glass tiles, bronze
83.8 × 55.9 diam. (33 × 22)
Gift of Sydney and Frances Lewis, 85.155 a/c

488. Pond Lily Lamp, ca. 1906

leaded glass, bronze
67.3 × 48.2 diam. (26½ × 19)
Gift of Sydney and Frances Lewis, 85.162 a/b

489. Poppy Lamp, ca. 1900

Leaded glass, bronze
66. × 50.8 diam. (26 × 20)
SLD 529

490. Scarab Lamp, ca. 1900

Blown glass, bronze
27.9 × 15.8 × 13.3 (11 × 6¼ × 5¼)
SLD 530

491. Spider Lamp, ca. 1900

Leaded glass, bronze
45.7 × 35.6 diam. (18 × 15)
SLD 610

492. Spider Lampshade, ca. 1900

Leaded glass, bronze
45.7 × 35.6 diam. (6 × 15)
SLD 531

493. Spring Peony Lamp, ca. 1900

Leaded glass, bronze
63.5 × 45.7 diam. (25 × 18)
Gift of Mrs. David C. Morton, Richmond, Va.,
67.46.2 a/c

494. Spring Peony Lamp, ca. 1900

Leaded glass, bronze
66. × 45.7 diam. (26 × 18)
SLD 526

495. Squash Lamp, ca. 1906

Leaded glass, blown glass, bronze
80. × 73.6 diam. (31½ × 29)
Gift of the Sydney and Frances Lewis
Foundation, 85.151a/h
Catalogue no. 52

496. Standard Floor Lamp, ca. 1900

Leaded glass, bronze
196.8 × 62.5 diam. (77½ × 24⅝)
SLD 535

497. Trumpet-Vine Lamp, ca. 1900

Leaded glass, bronze
69.8 × 48.2 diam. (27½ × 19)
Gift of Sydney and Frances Lewis, 85.158 a/b

498. Tulip Lamp, ca. 1900

Leaded glass, bronze
44. × 35.5 diam. (17¼ × 14)
SLD 537

499. Tulip Lamp, ca. 1900-38

Leaded glass, bronze
64.7 × 46.3 diam. (25½ × 18¼)
SLD 538

500. Turtleback Lamp, ca. 1900

Blown glass, bronze
36.8 × 25.4 × 16.2 (14½ × 10 × 6⅜)
SLD 539

501. Turtleback Chandelier, ca. 1900

Leaded glass, blown glass, bronze
82.5 × 50.8 diam. (32½ × 20)
SLD 540

502. Turtleback Chandelier, ca. 1900

Leaded glass, blown glass, bronze
92.7 × 35.5 diam. (36½ × 14)
SLD 721

503. Turtleback Lamp, ca. 1900

Leaded glass, bronze
59.7 × 40.6 diam. (23½ × 16)
SLD 541

504. Turtleback Lamp, ca. 1900

Leaded glass, blown glass, bronze
69.8 × 52.1 diam. (27½ × 20½)
SLD 542

505. Wisteria Lamp, ca. 1900

Leaded glass, bronze
68.6 × 47. diam. (27 × 18½)
Gift of Sydney and Frances Lewis, 85.157 a/b

506. Wisteria Pony Lamp, ca. 1900

Leaded glass, bronze
41.9 × 27.3 diam. (16½ × 10¾)
SLD 544

507. Yellow Rose-Bush Chandelier, ca. 1900

Leaded glass, bronze
22.8 × 62.8 diam. (9 × 24¾)
SLD 689

Miscellaneous Small Accessories

508. Letter Rack, ca. 1900

Enamel on copper
19.7 × 22.2 × 6.4 (7¾ × 8¾ × 2½)
Museum Purchase, The Sydney and Frances
Lewis Art Nouveau Fund, 73.59

509. Mirror, ca. 1900

Enamel, bronze, mirrored glass
46. × 45. × 18.4 (18⅛ × 17¾ × 7¼)
Gift of Sydney and Frances Lewis, 85.179

510. Necklace, ca. 1900

Enamel, Mexican opals, gold, pearl
22.2 × 10.8 × 1.11 (8¾ × 4¼ × 7/16)
Gift of Sydney and Frances Lewis, 85.224

Vases

511. Vase, ca. 1900

Blown glass
10.2 × 11.4 × 10.2 (4 × 4½ × 4)
Gift of Sydney and Frances Lewis, 85.188

512. Vase, ca. 1900

Bronzed earthenware
13.3 × 6.4 diam. (5¼ × 2½)
Museum Purchase, The Sydney and Frances
Lewis Art Nouveau Fund, 81.197

513. Vase, ca. 1900

Blown glass
5.7 × 3.8 diam. (2¼ × 1½)
SLD 573

514. Vase, 1902

Blown glass
9.5 × 7.5 diam. (3¾ × 2¹⁵⁄₁₆)
Gift of Helen K. Mackintosh in Honor of Her
Parents, the Reverend and Mrs. D. C.
Mackintosh, 81.208

515. Vase, 1902

Blown glass
17.8 × 10.1 diam. (7 × 4)
Gift of Mr. A. Smith Bowman, Sunset Hills, Va.,
80.12

516. Vase, 1904

Blown glass
14. × 8.6 diam. (5½ × 3⅜)
Gift of Helen K. Mackintosh in Honor of Her
Parents, the Reverend and Mrs. D. C.
Mackintosh, 81.207

517. Vase, 1897

Blown glass
7.6 × 5. diam. (3 × 2)
Gift of Mrs. Peter Knowles, Richmond, Va.,
84.13

518. Intaglio-Carved Vase, ca. 1900

Blown and engraved glass
23.5 × 14.6 diam. (9¼ × 5¾)
Gift of Sydney and Frances Lewis, 85.183

519. Aquamarine Vase, ca. 1900

Blown glass
11.1 × 7. × 7. (4⅜ × 2¾ × 2¾)
Gift of Sydney and Frances Lewis, 85.193

520. Aquamarine Vase, ca. 1911

Blown glass
22.2 × 10.2 diam. (¾ × 4¼)
Gift of Sydney and Frances Lewis, 85.185

521. Cypriote Vase, ca. 1900

Blown glass
11. × 12.9 diam. (4⁵⁄₁₆ × 5¹⁄₁₆)
Museum Purchase, The Sydney and Frances
Lewis Art Nouveau Fund, 81.196

522. Cypriote Vase, ca. 1900

Blown glass
17.5 × 18.4 diam. (6⅞ × 7¼)
Gift of Dr. Robert and Mrs. Gladys Koch,
Stamford, Connecticut, 82.12

523. Flower-Form Vase, 1903

Blown glass
28.5 × 12.8 diam. (11¼ × 5¹⁄₁₆)
Gift of Sydney and Frances Lewis, 85.194

524. Jack-in-the-Pulpit Vase, 1905

Blown glass
43.8 × 25.7 × 13.3 (17¼ × 10⅛ × 5¼)
Gift of Sydney and Frances Lewis, 85.196

525. Lava Vase, ca. 1900

Blown glass
13.7 × 17.7 diam. (5⅜ × 7)
Museum Purchase, The Sydney and Frances
Lewis Art Nouveau Fund, 81.195
Catalogue no. 27

526. Melon-Shaped Vase, ca. 1900

Blown glass
10.3 × 14.8 diam. (4¹⁄₁₆ × 5¹³⁄₁₆)
Museum Purchase, The Sydney and Frances
Lewis Art Nouveau Fund, 81.200

527. Paperweight Vase, 1904

Blown glass
15.9 × 8.2 diam. (6¼ × 3¼)
Gift of Sydney and Frances Lewis, 85.186

528. Paperweight Vase, 1904

Blown glass
4.4 × 6.2 diam. (1¾ × 2⅝)
Gift of Sydney and Frances Lewis, 85.192

529. Paperweight Vase, 1908

Blown glass
12.7 × 11.4 diam. (5 × 4½)
Gift of Sydney and Frances Lewis, 85.187

530. Peacock/Jack-in-the-Pulpit Vase, 1906

Blown glass
24.1 × 22.5 × 12.7 (9½ × 8¹⁵⁄₁₆ × 5)
Gift of Sydney and Frances Lewis, 85.190

531. Reactive Vase, 1918

Blown glass
14.6 × 8.2 diam. (5¾ × 3¼)
Gift of Sydney and Frances Lewis, 85.184

532. Tell el-Amarna Vase, ca. 1900

Blown glass
25.1 × 11.7 diam. (9⅞ × 4⅝)
Museum Purchase, The Sydney and Frances
Lewis Art Nouveau Fund, 81.199

533. Tell el-Amarna Vase with Separate Foot, ca. 1900

Blown glass
34.9 × 24.5 diam. (13¾ × 9⅝)
Museum Purchase, The Sydney and Frances
Lewis Art Nouveau Fund, 81.202 a/b

Henri de Toulouse-Lautrec
French (1864-1901)

534. Poster, *La Revue Blanche*, 1895

Lithograph
127.6 × 91.4 (50¼ × 36)
Museum Purchase, The Sydney and Frances
Lewis Art Nouveau Fund, 72.7

Pierre Turin
French (1891-?)

535. Medallion, *Exposition Internationale des Arts décoratifs et industriels modernes*, Paris, 1925

Bronze
6 × 6 × .31 (2⅜ × 2⅜ × 5/16)
Gift of Sydney and Frances Lewis, 85.276

Unger Brothers
American (Newark, New Jersey; 1891-ca. 1910)

536. Lorgnette, ca. 1900

Silver gilt, glass
12.1 × 3.2 × 1.9 (4¾ × 1¼ × ¾)
Gift of Sydney and Frances Lewis, 85.287

537. Purse, ca. 1900

Silver-gilt mesh
11.1 × 6.9 × 2.2 (4⅜ × 2¾ × ⅞)
Gift of Sydney and Frances Lewis, 85.288

Albert R. Valentien
American (1862-1925)
for
Rookwood Pottery
American (Cincinatti, Ohio; 1880-1967)

538. Lady's-Slipper Vase, 1901

Ceramic
43.1 × 17.1 diam. (17 × 6¾)
Museum Purchase, The Sydney and Frances
Lewis Art Nouveau Fund, 72.43.1

Henry van de Velde
Belgian (1863-1957)

539. Cuff Buttons, ca. 1900

Gold
2 diam. × .3 each (13/16 × ⅛)
Gift of Sydney and Frances Lewis, 85.226.1/2

540. Side Chair, 1896-98

Padouk wood, rush
94. × 44.1 × 41.7 (37 × 17⅜ × 16)
Gift of Sydney and Frances Lewis, 85.82
Catalogue no. 4

Henry van de Velde
Belgian (1863-1957)
and
Theodor Müller
Belgian (dates unknown)

541. Jardinière and Four Candlesticks, ca. 1900

Silver
Jardinière: 14.5 × 44.4 × 4.1 (5¾ × 17½ × 9½)
Candlesticks (4) each: 39.3 × 22.8 × 13.9 (15½ × 9 × 5½)
Museum Purchase, The Sydney and Frances
Lewis Art Nouveau Fund , 72.14.1/5

Charles F. Annesley Voysey
English (1857-1941)

542. Mantel Clock, 1896

Painted wood, brass
50. × 27. × 17 (19 11/16 × 10⅝ × 7)
Gift of Sydney and Frances Lewis, 85.217
Catalogue no. 2

Otto Wagner
Austrian (1841-1918)

543. Armchair, 1902-04

Bent beechwood, plywood, aluminum
77.5 × 55.6 × 55.9 (30½ × 21⅞ × 22)
Museum Purchase, The Sydney and Frances
Lewis Art Nouveau Fund, 84.82
Catalogue no. 37

Alf Wallander
Swedish (1862-1914)
for
Rörstrand
Swedish (Stockholm; established 1726)

544. Candlestick, ca. 1897

Porcelain
23.5 × 10.1 × 10.1 (9¼ × 4 × 4)
Gift of Sydney and Frances Lewis, 85.55

545. Soup Tureen, ca. 1897

Porcelain
20.3 × 36.8 × 21.6 (8 × 14½ × 8½)
Gift of Sydney and Frances Lewis, 85.56 a/b
Catalogue no. 6

Alméric V. Walter
French (1859-1942)
and
Henri Bergé
French (died 1930)

546.   Ashtray, 1900

   Pâte de verre
   10.2 × 20.3 × 15.2 (4 × 8 × 6)
   Gift of Sydney and Frances Lewis, 85.210

547.   Covered Box, ca. 1900

   Pâte de verre
   13.6 × 11.2 diam. (5⅜ × 4⅝)
   Gift of Sydney and Frances Lewis, 85.211 a/b

Wiener Werkstätte
Austrian (Vienna, 1903-1928)

548.   Book, *Die Wiener Werkstätte 1903-1928: Modernes Kunstgewerbe und sein Weg*, 1929

   Cover: papier mâché
   22.8 × 21.9 × 2.54 (9 × 8⅝ × 1)
   Gift of Sydney and Frances Lewis, 85.36 a/b

Weller Pottery Company
American (Zanesville, Ohio; active 1873-1948)

549.   Vase, ca. 1920-30

   Ceramic
   15.2 × 10.1 diam. (6 × 4)
   Gift of Mrs. Peter Knowles, Richmond, Va.,
   84.14

Werner
German (dates unknown)

550.   Lamp, ca. 1900
   Stained glass, bronze
   48.9 × 34.9 × 24.1 (19¼ × 13¾ × 9½)
   SLD 604

Fernand Windels
German (dates unknown)

551.   Carpet, 1928

   Wool
   170.2 × 256.5 (67 × 101)
   Gift of Sydney and Frances Lewis, 85.346

Philippe Wolfers
Belgian (1858-1929)
for the firm of
Emile Müller
French (Ivry; established 1854)

552.   "Orchidées" Cachepot, ca. 1900

   Stoneware
   36.8 × 48.2 × 47 (14½ × 19 × 18½)
   Museum Purchase, The Sydney and Frances
   Lewis Art Nouveau Fund, 81.27
   Catalogue no. 5

Frank Lloyd Wright
American (1867-1959)

553.   Armchair, ca. 1904-06
   Made for Larkin Building, Buffalo, New York

   Painted steel, leather
   95.2 × 62.7 × 53.6 (37½ × 24¹¹⁄₁₆ × 21⅛)
   Gift of the Sydney and Frances Lewis
   Foundation, 85.75

554.   Chair, ca. 1915-22
   Made for Imperial Hotel, Tokyo, Japan

   Oak, upholstery
   95.9 × 39.4 × 45 (37¾ × 15½ × 17¾)
   Gift of Sydney and Frances Lewis, 85.77

555.   Desk with Attached Chair, ca. 1904-06
   Made for Larkin Building, Buffalo, New York

   Painted steel, leather
   109.2 × 123.1 × 61 (43 × 48½ × 24)
   Gift of the Sydney and Frances Lewis
   Foundation, 85.76

556.   Dining-Room Chair, 1906
   Made for P.A. Beachy House, Oak Park, Illinois

   Oak, upholstery
   116.8 × 36.5 × 45.7 (46 × 14⅜ × 18)
   Gift of Sydney and Frances Lewis, 85.78

557.   Pair of Windows, 1912
   Made for Avery Coonley Playhouse, Riverside,
   Illinois

   Stained and leaded glass
   77.8 × 32.1 × .32 each (30⅝ × 12⅝ × ⅜)
   Gift of Sydney and Frances Lewis, 85.348.1/2

558.   Side Chair, 1904
   Made for Frank Lloyd Wright Residence,
   Oak Park, Illinois

   Oak, leather
   102.2 × 38.1 × 47.6 (40¼ × 15 × 18¾)
   Gift of the Sydney and Frances Lewis
   Foundation, 85.74
   Catalogue no. 47

559.   Tree-of-Life Window, 1903-05
   Made for Darwin Martin Residence, Buffalo,
   New York

   Stained and leaded glass, oak
   120.5 × 81.3 (47⅞ × 32)
   104.8 × 66.7 (without frame) (41¼ × 26¼)
   Gift of the Sydney and Frances Lewis
   Foundation, 85.347
   Catalogue no. 42

560.   Window, 1904
   Made for Darwin Martin Residence, Buffalo,
   New York

   Stained and leaded glass, oak
   105.4 × 57.1 × 3.2 (42½ × 22½ × 1¼)
   97.8 × 48.5 (without frame) 38½ × 19⅛)
   SLD 742

Württembergische Metallwärenfabrik
German (Geislingen; founded 1853)

561. Coffee Service, ca. 1900

Silverplate over Britannia ware
Coffee pot: 19.6 × 19.6 × 11.4 (7¾ × 7¾ × 4½)
Sugar: 11.4 × 13.9 × 9.2 (4 ½ × 5 ½ × 3 ⅝)
Creamer: 8.9 × 10.8 × 8.5 (3½ × 4¼ × 3⅜)
Gift of an Anonymous Donor in Memory of
Mrs. Marie Edgeworth MacDonald, 79.9.1/3

Attributed to Suzanne Alice Zaborowska
French (dates unknown)

562. Fan, ca. 1900

Abalone shell, sequins, watercolor on silk
24.1 × 47 (9½ × 18½)
Museum Purchase, The Sydney and Frances
Lewis Art Nouveau Fund, 75.31

Zsolnay Ceramic Works
Hungarian (Pécs; founded 1862)

563. Vase, ca. 1900

Ceramic
13.9 × 24.1 diam. (5½ × 9½)
Museum Purchase, The Sydney and Frances
Lewis Art Nouveau Fund, 72.43.2

564. *Mother and Child*, ca. 1900

Pottery
22.9 × 8.8 × 8.5 (8¾ × 3½ × 3⅜)
Gift of Sydney and Frances Lewis, 85.52

ARTIST UNKNOWN

American, 20th century

565. Brooch, ca. 1930

Gold, garnets
6.4 × 6.4 (2½ × 2½)
SLD 118

566. Pair of Footlight Covers, 1927

Bronze
34.3 × 27.9 × 1.90 (13½ × 11 × ¾)
SLD 143-4

567. Serving Tray, ca. 1905

Hammered copper
52. diam. (20½)
SLD 831

568. Watch Fob, ca. 1910

Gold
8.3 × 2.5 × 1. (3¼ × 1 × ⅜)
Gift of Mr. Furman Hebb, New York, 84.59

Austrian, 20th Century

569. Cigarette Case, ca. 1910

Silver, pearls, glass
8. × 8. × 1.9 (3⅛ × 3⅛ × ¾)
Gift of Mr. Furman Hebb, New York, 83.160

Danish, 20th century

570. Jewel Chest, ca. 1900

Silver, enamel, wood
13.9 × 28.5 × 15.9 (5¼ × 11¼ × 6¼)
Gift of the Estate of Lillian Thomas Pratt,
Fredericksburg, Va., 47.20.425

English, 20th century

571. Cigarette Case, ca. 1930

Silver, copper
8. × 8.9 × 1.1 (3⅛ × 3½ × ⅜)
Gift of Mr. Furman Hebb, New York, 83.161

572. Cigarette Case, ca. 1931

Silver, jade
8. × 8. × 1.5 (3⅛ × 3⅛ × ⅝)
Gift of Mr. Furman Hebb, New York, 83.159

573. Evening Bag, ca. 1925-30

Yellow gold, green gold, platinum, diamonds
15.2 × 15. × 1.42 (6 × 5⅞ × 9/16)
Gift of Mr. Furman Hebb, New York, 84.50

574. Mirror, ca. 1900

Copper, oak, mirrored glass
62.8 × 78.2 × 2.9 (24¾ × 31 × 1⅛)
SLD 772

575. Mirror, ca. 1910

Copper, mirrored glass
55.8 × 55.8 (22 × 22)
SLD 147

576. Pendant, ca. 1900

Silver, enamel
10.3 × 7.3 × .95 (excluding chain)
(4 1/16 × 2⅞ × ⅜)
Gift of Sydney and Frances Lewis, 85.227

577. Purse, 1901

Silver, leather
17.5 × 27.3 (excluding chain) (6⅞ × 10¾)
Gift of Sydney and Frances Lewis, 85.291

578. Tea Service, 1925-30

Pewter, jadeite
13.3 × 25.4 × 23.5 (5¼ × 10 × 9¼)
Gift of Sydney and Frances Lewis, 85.281.1/4

European, 20th Century

579. Cigarette Case, ca. 1885

Silver
16.8 × 9.8 × .95 (6⅝ × 3⅞ × ⅜)
Gift of Mr. Robert Goesling, Richmond,
Virginia, 85.35

French, 20th century

580. Pair of Ashtrays, ca. 1925

Bronze
8.9 × 37.5 × 6.7 (3½ × 14¾ × 2⅝)
Gift of Sydney and Frances Lewis, 85.263.1/2

581. Black Peacock Pendant, ca. 1900

166-carat black fire opal, 18-carat gold, plique-
à-jour enamel, baroque pearl
12.4 × 7.9 × 1.9 (4⅞ × 3⅛ × ¾)
Gift of Sydney and Frances Lewis, 85.228
Catalogue no. 22

582. Brooch/Pendant, ca. 1925

Tiger's-eye, diamond, enamel
6.8 × 6.5 × 1.5 (2¹¹⁄₁₆ × 2⁹⁄₁₆ × ⅝)
Gift of Sydney and Frances Lewis, 85.229

583. Cane Handle, ca. 1906

Silver
10.1 × 10.8 × 1.5 (4 × 4¼ × ⅝)
Gift of Mr. Furman Hebb, New York, 84.53

584. Cane Handle, Miniature, ca. 1900

Silver
7.9 × 6. × 1.8 (3⅛ × 2⅜ × ½)
Gift of Mr. Furman Hebb, New York, 84.55

585. Carpet, ca. 1925

Wool
284.5 × 177.8 (112 × 70)
SLD 660

586. Carpet, ca. 1925

Wool
284.5 × 249. (112 × 98)
SLD 794

587. Carpet, ca. 1925

Wool
267. × 267. (105 × 105)
SLD 793

588. Carpet, ca. 1930

Wool
304.8 × 312.4 (120 × 123)
SLD 39

589. Fire Screen, ca. 1930

Brass
74.9 × 75.6 × 9.8 (29½ × 29¾ × 3⅞)
Gift of Sydney and Frances Lewis, 85.259

590. Fox and Grapes Mirror, ca. 1930

Silvered bronze, mirrored glass
101.6 × 64.8 × 3.8 (40 × 25½ × 1½)
Gift of Sydney and Frances Lewis, 85.352

591. Pair of Door Handles, ca. 1900

Bronze
12.1 × 3.2 × 14. (4¾ × 1¼ × 5½)
12.1 × 3.2 × 5.7 (4¾ × 1¼ × 2¼)
Gift of Mr. Furman Hebb, New York, 84.61.1/2

592. Pair of End Tables, ca. 1925

Macassar ebony, silvered bronze
73.2 × 38.1 × 28. each (29 × 15 × 11)
SLD 74-75

593. Pendant with Bust of Woman, ca. 1900

Sterling silver
3.8 × 3.5 (1½ × 1⅜)
Gift of Mr. Furman Hebb, New York, 83.155

594. Vase, ca. 1920

Ceramic
12.1 × 8.9 diam. (4¾ × 3½)
Gift of Mrs. Peter Knowles, Richmond, Va.,
84.15

595. Watch Fob, ca. 1900

Gold
2.5 × 2.5 × 1.8 (1 × 1 × ½)
Gift of Mr. Furman Hebb, New York, 84.60

German or Austrian, 20th century

596. Belt Buckle, ca. 1925

Alpaca metal, glass
6. × 10.2 × 1.1 (2⅜ × 4 × ⁷⁄₁₆)
Gift of Mr. Furman Hebb, New York, 84.63 a/b

597. Cane Handle, ca. 1900-10

Silver
6.9 × 10.8 × 1.9 (2¾ × 4¼ × ¾)
Gift of Mr. Furman Hebb, New York, 84.54

598. Wallet, 1900-10

Silver, leather, ruby
11.7 × 6.6 × 1.6 (4⅝ × 2⅝ × ⅝)
Gift of Mr. Furman Hebb, New York, 84.56

599. Wallet, ca. 1900-10

Silver, leather
12.7 × 8.9 × 1. (5 × 3½ × ⅜)
Gift of Mr. Furman Hebb, New York, 84.57

Selected Bibliography

Adler, Rose. *Reliures présenté par Rose Adler*. Paris: Editions d'Art Charles Moreau, no date.

Amaya, Mario. *Art Nouveau*. London: Studio Vista Limited, 1966.

———.*Tiffany Glass*. New York: Walker and Co., 1967.

Anscombe, Isabelle and Gere, Charlotte. *Arts & Crafts in Britain and America*. New York: Rizzoli International Publications, Inc., 1978.

Applegate, Judith. *Art Deco*. New York: Finch College Museum of Art, 1970.

Arwas, Victor. *Art Deco*. London: Academy Editions, 1976.

———. *Art Deco*. New York: Harry N. Abrams, Inc., 1980.

———. *Glass: Art Nouveau to Art Deco*. New York: Rizzoli International Publications, Inc., 1977.

———. *The Liberty Style*. New York: Rizzoli International Publications, Inc., 1979.

Barilli, Renato. *Art Nouveau*. London: The Hamlyn Publishing Group Limited, 1969.

Baroni, Daniele. *Gerrit Thomas Rietveld Furniture*. London: Academy Editions, 1978.

Bascou, Marc; Brabcova, Jana; Kotalic, Jiří; and Lacambre, Genevieve. *Alfons Mucha: 1860-1939*. Darmstadt: Mathildenhöhe, 1980.

Battersby, Martin. *Art Nouveau*. London and New York: Paul Hamlyn, 1969.

———. *The Decorative Thirties*. New York: Walker and Company, 1971.

———. *The Decorative Twenties*. New York: Walker and Company, 1969.

———. *The World of Art Nouveau*. New York: Funk & Wagnalls, 1969.

Bayard, Emile. *L'Art Appliqué Français d'Aujourd'hui*. Paris: Ernest Grund, no date.

Bayer, Patricia. "Emile-Jacques Ruhlmann, Master of French Art Deco." *Portfolio* 3 (1981): 68-71.

———. "Jean Dunand: Premier Craftsman of the Art Deco Style." *Art & Antiques* 5 (1982): 56-63.

Billcliffe, Roger. *Charles Rennie Mackintosh: The Complete Furniture Drawings & Interior Designs*. New York: Taplinger, Poach and Company, 1979.

——— and Vergo, Peter. "Charles Rennie Mackintosh and the Austrian Art Revival." *The Burlington Magazine* 119 (1977): 739-44.

Bing, S. "Art Nouveau." *The Architectural Record* 12 (August 1902): 279-85.

———. *Artistic America. Tiffany Glass and Art Nouveau*. Cambridge, Massachusetts, and London: The M.I.T. Press, 1970.

———. "L'Art Nouveau." Translated from the French by Irene Sargent. *The Craftsman* 5 (1903): 1-15.

Blount, Berniece and Henry. *French Cameo Glass*. Des Moines, Iowa: privately printed, 1968.

Borsi, Franko, and Godoli, Ezio. *Paris 1900*. New York: Rizzoli International Publications, Inc., 1978.

Bott, Gerhard. *Kunsthandwerk um 1900*. Darmstadt, West Germany: Eduard Roether Verlag, 1965.

Brandon-Jones, John; Heseltine, Joanna; Simpson, Duncan; Aslin, Elizabeth; Morris, Barbara; and Bury, Shirley. C.F.A. *Voysey: Architect and Designer 1857-1941*. London: Lund Humphries Publishers Ltd., 1978.

Brandt, Frederick R. *Art Nouveau*. Richmond: The Virginia Museum of Fine Arts, 1971.

———. "In the Spirit of the Times: Art Deco Furniture." *The Antiques Journal* 35 (1980): 16-9, 42-4.

———. "Serpentine Seating: Art Nouveau Chairs." *The Antiques Journal* 34 (1979): 18-21, 46-7.

Brunhammer, Yvonne. "Hector Guimard or the Obsession with Line." *Arts in Virginia* 20 (1979): 39-47.

———. *Jean Dunand/Jean Goulden*. Paris: Galerie du Luxembourg, 1973.

———. *Le Style 1925*. Paris: Baschet et Cie, 1975.

———. *1925*. Paris: Les Presses de la Connaissance, 1976.

————. *The Nineteen Twenties Style*. London: The Hamlyn Publishing Group Limited, 1969.

———— and Merklen, Colette. *L'Oeuvre de Rupert Carabin*. Paris: Galerie du Luxembourg, 1974.

Brunhammer, Yvonne; Beyer, Victor; Weill, Alain; Watelet, Jacques-Gregoire; Culot, Maurice; Loyer, François; Blondel, Alain; and Plantin, Yves. *Art Nouveau Belgium France*. Houston: Rice University, 1976.

Buffet-Challie, Laurence. *The Art Nouveau Style*. London: Academy Editions, 1982.

Burckhardt, Lucius, ed. *The Werkbund: History and Ideology 1907-1933*. Woodbury, New York: Barron's Educational Series, Inc., 1977.

Camard, Florence. *Ruhlmann*. Paris: Editions du Regard, 1983.

Castle, Wendell, and Hunter-Stiebel, Penelope. *The Fine Art of the Furniture Maker*. Rochester: Memorial Art Gallery of the University of Rochester, 1981.

Cather, David M. *Furniture of the American Arts and Crafts Movement*. New York: New American Library, 1981.

Champigneulle, Bernard. *Art Nouveau*. Woodbury, New York: Barron's Educational Series, Inc., 1976.

Chappey, Marcel, ed. *Le XXème Salon des Artistes Décorateurs, 1930*. Paris: Vincent Frael et Cie, 1930.

Chassé, Charles. *The Nabis and Their Period*. New York: Frederick A. Praeger, 1969.

Cinquantenaire de L'Exposition de 1925. Paris: Musée des Arts Décoratifs, 1976.

Clark, Robert Judson, ed. *The Arts and Crafts Movement in America 1876-1916*. Princeton, New Jersey: Princeton University Press, 1972.

Clouzot, Henri. *Ferronnerie Moderne*. Paris: Editions d'Art Charles Moreau, no date.

de Gary, Marie-Noel; Mathey, François; Gere, Charlotte; Bascou, Marc; Brunhammer, Yvonne; and Deslandres, Yvonne. *Les Fouquet*. Paris: Musée des Arts Décoratifs, 1983.

Deroubaix, Brigitte Loye. *Eileen Gray, Architecture, Design 1879-1976*. Paris: Ministère de l'Urbanisme et du Logement, 1983.

Dewey, Tom, II. *Art Nouveau, Art Deco and Modernism: A Guide to the Styles, 1890-1940*. Jackson, Mississippi: Mississippi Museum of Art, 1983.

Dufrène, Maurice, ed. *Intérieurs Français au Salon des Artistes Décorateurs en 1926*. Paris: Editions d'Art Charles Moreau, 1926.

Duncan, Alastair. *Art Deco Furniture*. New York: Holt, Rinehart and Winston, 1984.

————. *Art Nouveau and Art Deco Lighting*. London: Thames and Hudson Ltd., 1978.

————. *Art Nouveau Furniture*. New York: Clarkson N. Potter, Inc., 1982.

————. *Art Nouveau Sculpture*. New York: Rizzoli International Publications, Inc., 1978.

Eidelberg, Martin. E. *Colonna*. Dayton, Ohio: The Dayton Art Institute, 1983.

————. "Edward Colonna's 'Essay on Broom-Corn'." *The Connoisseur* 176 (February, 1971): 123-30.

————. "The Life and Work of E. Colonna." *The Decorative Arts Newsletter* 7, Nos. 1,2,3 (1981).

————. "Tiffany Favrile Pottery, A New Study of a Few Known Facts." *The Connoisseur* 169 (September 1968): 57-61.

Eisler, Max. *Österreichische Werkkultur*. Vienna: Anton Schroll, 1916.

Encyclopédie des Arts Décoratifs et Industriels Modernes au XXème Siècle. 12 volumes. New York: Garland Publishing Incorporated. 1977.

Feldstin, William Jr., and Duncan, Alistair. *The Lamps of Tiffany Studios*. New York: Harry N. Abrams, Inc., 1983.

Fenz, Werner. *Kolomon Moser: Graphik, Kunstgewerbe, Malerei*. Salzburg and Vienna: Residenz Verlag, 1984.

Follot, Paul. *Intérieurs Français aus Salon des Artistes Décorateurs, 1927*. Paris: Editions d'Art Charles Moreau, 1927.

Fouquet, Jean. *Bijoux et Orfèvrerie*. Paris: Editions d'Art Charles Moreau, no date.

Frankl, Paul. *Form and Reform*. New York: Harper and Brothers, no date.

————. *New Dimensions: The Decorative Arts of Today in Words and Pictures*. New York: Payson & Clarke Ltd., 1928.

Frantz, Henri. "Emile Gallé and the Decorative Artists of Nancy." *The Studio* 28 (1903): 108-17.

Freeman, John Crosby. *The Forgotten Rebel: Gustav Stickley and His Craftsman Mission Furniture*. Watkins Glen, New York: Century House, 1966.

Garner, Philippe. *Emile Gallé*. New York: Rizzoli International Publications, Inc., 1976.

———. "Emile Gallé: His Art and His Industry." *Arts in Virginia* 20 (1979): 31-7.

———. "The Bronzes of Alphonse Mucha." *Art at Auction* 1971-2. New York: The Viking Press, 1972: 432-7.

———. *Twentieth-Century Furniture*. New York: Van Nostrand Reinhold Company, 1980.

———. ed. *The Encyclopedia of Decorative Arts: 1890-1940*. New York: Van Nostrand Reinhold Company, 1978.

Gilman, Roger. "The Paris Exposition: A Glimpse Into the Future." *The Art Bulletin* 8 (1925): 33-42.

Grady, James. "Hector Guimard: An Overlooked Master of Art Nouveau." *Apollo* 89 (April 1969): 284-95.

Grady, James. "Nature and the Art Nouveau." *Art Bulletin* 37 (September 1955): 187-94.

Graham, F. Lanier. *Hector Guimard*. New York: The Museum of Modern Art, 1970.

Grover, Ray and Lee. *Art Glass Nouveau*. Rutland, Vermont: Charles E. Tuttle Company, 1967.

———. *Carved and Decorated European Art Glass*. Rutland, Vermont: Charles E. Tuttle Company, 1970.

Gysling-Billeter, Erika. *Objekte des Jugendstils*. Zürich: Museum Bellerive Zürich, 1975.

Hamilton, Charles F. *Roycroft Collectibles*. New York: A.S. Barnes & Company, Inc., 1980.

Hamlin, A.D.F. "L'Art Nouveau, Its Origin and Development." *The Craftsman* 3 (December 1902): 129-143.

Hanks, David A. *The Decorative Designs of Frank Lloyd Wright*. New York: E.P. Dutton, 1979.

Harris, Margaret Haile. *Loïe Fuller: Magician of Light*. Richmond: The Virginia Museum of Fine Arts, 1979.

Herbst, René. *Jean Puiforcat: Orfèvre Sculpteur*. Paris: Flammarion, 1951.

Hillier, Bevis. *Art Deco of the 20s and 30s*. London: Studio Vista Limited, 1968.

———. *The World of Art Deco*. New York: E.P. Dutton, 1971.

Holme, Charles, ed. *The Art-Revival in Austria*. London: The Studio, 1906.

Howarth, Thomas. *Charles Rennie Mackintosh and the Modern Movement*. London: Routledge Kegan Paul, 1952.

Hubbard, Elbert. *This Then is a William Morris Book Being A Little Journey By Elbert Hubbard, & Some Letters, Heretofore Unpublished, Written to His Friend & Fellow Worker, Robert Thomson, All Throwing a Side-Light, More or Less, On the Man and His Times*. East Aurora, New York: The Roycrofters, 1907.

Hunter, Penelope. "Art Deco and The Metropolitan Museum of Art." *The Connoisseur* 179 (April 1972): 273-281.

Jacques, G.M. "Le Meuble Français et l'Exposition." *L'Art Décoratif* (April-September 1900): 142-9.

Jaffe, Hans L.C. *De Stijl: 1917-1931 Visions of Utopia*. New York: Abbeville Press, 1982.

Johnson, J. Stewart. *Eileen Gray: Designer 1879-1976*. London: Debrett's Peerage Ltd., 1979.

Jones, Harvey L. *Mathews: Masterpieces of the California Decorative Style*. Oakland, California: The Oakland Museum, 1972.

Joubin, André. "La Studio de Jacques Doucet." *L'Illustration* (May 3, 1930): 17-20.

Julian, Philippe. *The Triumph of Art Nouveau: Paris Exhibition 1900*. New York: Larousse & Co., Inc., 1974.

Kempton, Richard. *Art Nouveau: An Annotated Bibliography*. Los Angeles: Hennessey & Ingalls, Inc., 1977.

Kjellberg, Pierre. *Art Deco: Les Maîtres du Mobilier*. Paris: Les Editions de l'Amateur, 1981.

Koch, Alexander. *Schmuck und Edelmetallarbeiten*. Darmstadt: Alexander Koch, 1905.

Koch, Robert. "Art Nouveau Bing." *Gazette des Beaux-Arts* 53 (March 1959): 179-90.

———. *Louis Comfort Tiffany*. New York: The Museum of Contemporary Crafts, 1958.

————. *Louis C. Tiffany, Rebel in Glass*. New York: Crown Publishers, Inc., 1964.

————. *Louis C. Tiffany's Glass-Bronzes-Lamps*. New York: Crown Publishers, Inc., 1971.

————. "The Tiffany Exhibition Punch Bowl." *Arts in Virginia* 16 (Winter/Spring 1976): 32-39.

Komanecky, Michael, and Butera, Virginia Fabbri. *The Folding Image: Screens by Western Artists of the Nineteenth and Twentieth Centuries*. New Haven: Yale University Art Gallery, 1984.

Lesieutre, Alain. *The Spirit and Splendour of Art Deco*. New York: Paddington Press Ltd., 1973.

Madsen, Stephan Tschudi. *Sources of Art Nouveau*. New York: Wittenborn and Company, 1956.

Maenz, Paul, *Art Deco: 1920-1940*. Cologne: M. Du Mont Schauberg, 1974.

Mannoni, Edith. *Meubles et Ensembles Style 1900*. Paris: Editions Charles Massin, 1968.

Mebane, John. *The Complete Book of Collecting Art Nouveau*. New York: Coward-McCann, Inc., 1970.

Meyer, C. James. "René Lalique: Sea Horse Brooch." *Metalsmith* 2 (Winter 1981/82): 26-7.

Moffitt, Charlotte. "The Rohlfs Furniture." *House Beautiful* 7 (1899): 81-5.

Mourey, Gabriel. "L'Exposition Georges de Feure." *Art et Décoration* (1903): 162-4.

Mourey, Gabriel. "Round the Exhibition I. The House of the 'Art Nouveau Bing'." *International Studio* 12 (1900): 164-81.

Mucha, Jiři. *Alphonse Mucha: The Master of Art Nouveau*. Prague: Knihtisk Artia, 1966.

Naylor, Gillian. *The Arts and Crafts Movement*. London: Studio Vista, 1971.

Neustadt, Egon. *The Lamps of Tiffany*. New York: The Fairfield Press, 1971.

Objects 1900 and Today. New York: The Museum of Modern Art, 1933.

O'Neal, William B. "Three Art Nouveau Glass Makers." *Journal of Glass Studies* 2 (1960): 124-7.

Ostergard, Derek E. *Mackintosh to Mollino: Fifty Years of Chair Design*. New York: Barry Friedman Ltd., 1984.

Percy, Christopher Vane. *The Glass of Lalique: A Collector's Guide*. New York: Charles Scribner's, 1977.

Pevsner, Nikolaus. *Pioneers of Modern Design from William Morris to Walter Gropius*. New York: The Museum of Modern Art, 1949.

Pulos, Arthur J. *American Design Ethic*. Cambridge, Massachusetts: The M.I.T. Press, 1983.

Read, Helen Appleton. "The Exposition in Paris, Part I." *International Studio* 82 (1925): 93-7.

————. "The Exposition in Paris, Part II." *International Studio* 82 (1925): 160-5.

Revi, Albert Christian. *American Art Nouveau Glass*. Camden, New Jersey: Thomas Nelson and Sons, 1968.

Rheims, Maurice. *The Flowering of Art Nouveau*. New York: Harry N. Abrams, Inc., 1966.

————. *L'Objet 1900*. Paris: Arts et Métiers Graphiques, 1964.

Ruskin, John. *The Two Paths: Being Lectures on Art and Its Application to Decoration and Manufacture*. New York: John Wiley & Sons, 1885.

Russell, Frank, ed. *A Century of Chair Design*. New York: Rizzoli International Publications, Inc., 1980.

[E.P.S.] "Some Recent Designs By Mr. Voysey." *The Studio* 7 (1896): 209-18.

Sargent, Irene. "A Minor French Salon." *The Craftsman* (April-September 1903): 450-9.

Scarlett, Frank and Townley, Marjorie. *Arts Décoratifs 1925: A Personal Recollection of the Paris Exhibition*. London: Academy Editions, 1975.

Schmutzler, Robert. *Art Nouveau*. New York: Harry N. Abrams, Inc. 1964.

————. "The English Origins of Art Nouveau." *Architectural Review* 117 (February, 1955): 108-17.

Schopfer, Jean. "L'Art Nouveau: An Argument and Defence." Translated by Irene Sargent. *The Craftsman* 4 (1903): 229-38.

Schweiger, Werner J. *Wiener Werkstätte: Kunst und Handwerk* 1903-1932. Vienna: Christian Brandstätter, 1982.

Selz, Peter and Constantine, Mildred, eds. *Art Nouveau: Art and Design at the Turn of the Century.* New York: The Museum of Modern Art, 1959.

Simpson, Duncan. *C.F.A. Voysey: An Architect of Individuality.* New York: The Whitney Library of Design, 1981.

Stickley, Gustav. *Catalogue of Craftsman Furniture.* Eastwood, New York: Craftsman Workshops, 1909. Reprint. Watkins Glen, New York: The American Life Foundation, 1978.

Tilbrook, A.J. *The Designs of Archibald Knox for Liberty & Co.* London: Ornament Press Ltd., 1976.

Verneuil, M.P. "The Applied Arts in the Paris Salons of 1904." Translated by Irene Sargent. *The Craftsman* 2 (April-September; 1904): 431-45.

Warmus, William. *Emile Gallé: Dreams Into Glass,* 1984. Corning, New York: The Corning Museum of Glass, 1984.

Warren, Geoffrey. *All Color Book of Art Nouveau.* London: Octopus Books, 1972.

Weisberg, Gabriel P. "George de Feure's Mysterious Women: A Study of Symbolist Sources in the Writings of Charles Baudelaire and Georges Rodenbach." *Gazette des Beaux-Arts* 84 (October 1974); 223-30.

————. "Georges von Sluijters 'De Feure': An Identity Unmasked." *Gazette des Beaux-Arts* 84 (October 1974): 231-2.

————. "L'Art Nouveau Bing." *Arts in Virginia* 20 (1979): 3-15.

Die Wiener Werkstätte: Modernes Kunsthandwerk von 1903-1932. Vienna: Österreichisches Museum für Angewandte Kunst, 1967.

White, Gleeson. "Some Glasgow Designers and Their Work." *The Studio* 11 (1897): 86-100.

Wilk, Christopher. *Thonet: 150 Years of Furniture.* Woodbury, New York: Barron's Educational Series, Inc., 1980.

Index of Artists

This list includes only names of artists and decorative arts firms cited in the essays and the catalogue section of this book. For additional references see the checklist, which is arranged alphabetically by name of artist.

OTHER CATALOGUES OF THE COLLECTIONS OF THE VIRGINIA
MUSEUM OF FINE ARTS:

Fabergé: A Catalog of the Lillian Thomas Pratt Collection of Russian Imperial Jewels
(1960; rev. 1976)

European Art in the Virginia Museum (1966)

Ancient Art in the Virginia Museum (1973)

Treasures in the Virginia Museum (1974)

The Sydney and Frances Lewis Contemporary Art Fund Collection (1980)

*Eighteenth-Century Meissen Porcelain from the Margaret M. and Arthur J. Mourot
Collection in the Virginia Museum* (1983)

*Oriental Rugs: The Collection of Dr. and Mrs. Robert A. Fisher in the Virginia
Museum of Fine Arts* (1984)

*French Paintings: The Collection of Mr. and Mrs. Paul Mellon in the Virginia
Museum of Fine Arts* (1985)

*British Sporting Paintings: The Paul Mellon Collection in Virginia Museum of Fine
Arts* (1985)

*Late Twentieth-Century Art: Selections from The Sydney and Frances Lewis
Collection in the Virginia Museum of Fine Arts* (1985)

This book was composed in Novarese by Typographics, Richmond, Virginia, and is printed on Warren Lustro Enamel Dull by Carter Printing Co., Richmond, Virginia.